Testing Children

Contributors

Marcia Collins-Moore, Ph.D.

Jan L. Culbertson, Ph.D.

Jean C. Elbert, Ph.D.

Robert G. Harrington, Ph.D.

J. Ray Hays, Ph.D., J.D.

Marc S. Herman, Ph.D.

Stanley H. Kohn, J.D.

Robert D. Lyman, Ph.D.

Lee M. Marcus, Ph.D.

Ruth Ann Mertens, Ph.D.

Mary Mira, Ph.D.

J. Gregory Olley, Ph.D.

Kathleen N. Osborn, Ph.D.

Michael C. Roberts, Ph.D.

Donald J. Routh, Ph.D.

Dennis P. Swiercinsky, Ph.D.

S. Joseph Weaver, Ph.D.

Karen L. Westphal, Ph.D.

Diane J. Willis, Ph.D.

Testing Children

A REFERENCE GUIDE FOR EFFECTIVE
CLINICAL AND PSYCHOEDUCATIONAL
ASSESSMENTS

S. Joseph Weaver, Ph.D.
General Editor

Foreword by Alan S. Kaufman, Ph.D.

TEST CORPORATION OF AMERICA
KANSAS CITY

To Randee Jae Shenkel

LIBRARY OF CONGRESS CATALOGING IN PUBLICATION DATA
Main entry under title:

Testing children.

    Includes bibliographies and index.
    1. Psychological tests for children. 2. Handicapped children—Testing. I. Weaver, S. Joseph (Sampson Joseph), 1926-
BF722.T47 1984   616.89′075   84-8882
ISBN 0-9611286-2-3

Printed in the United States of America

Contents

III. LEGAL CONSIDERATIONS

Foreword

ALAN S. KAUFMAN, PH.D

When I wrote *Intelligent Testing with the WISC-R* in the late 1970's, a number of professionals encouraged me to change the title, facetiously noting that "intelligent" was a totally inappropriate adjective for describing "testing." In 1983, when the K-ABC came out, some professionals asked, without facetiousness, "Why would anyone in this day and age waste time developing a new intelligence test?"

Indeed, I too had seen a good deal of stupid testing and case report writing, which was the main impetus in trying to set up a paradigm for intelligent testing—an approach that elevates the clinician above the test battery, and that places a far greater premium on *why* the child obtained a particular profile rather than on his or her precise levels of performance. Similarly, Nadeen and I were well aware of the anti-testing sentiments that pervaded public and professional opinion when we first began constructing the K-ABC in March, 1978. One can hardly ignore the impact of legislation and condemnation, coupled with pleas for a moratorium on intelligence testing or the total replacement of standardized tests with criterion referenced tests and informal assessment techniques. Yet total abandonment of intelligence tests never struck us as an appropriate solution to the many practical problems that beset the use of tests for clinical and educational purposes. Neither did we feel that the existing measures for assessing intelligence, developed 100 years ago in Paris and refined during World War I and the age when radio was king, had to be accepted as the only criteria for quantifying a person's mental ability. So we developed the K-ABC for many of the same reasons I wrote *Intelligent Testing*—in the hopes that some of the difficulties in the assessment of children's intelligence could be overcome by capitalizing on the strengths of standardized intelligence tests instead of damning them for their weaknesses, and with the belief that the field of assessment would change to keep pace with the rapid changes occurring within the microcosms of psychology and education, and within the broader spectrum of society as a whole.

Dr. Weaver's book reflects these hopes and beliefs. When reading through the chapters written by experts in their respective fields I felt a sense of optimism about the future of assessment, and a sense of elation in witnessing intelligent testing in action. Far from reducing children to a series of test scores, virtually every chapter treats assessment as a dynamic process that focuses on a human understanding of the child's test performance. Paramount in each author's view are pleas to the reader to be aware of changes in our society and in research findings; to be sensitive to the complexities and nuances of various handicapping conditions, environmental circumstances, and legal issues; to break stereotypes that may exist about handicapped children by being informed about updated research results and being receptive to the clinical observations of those with first-hand knowledge and experience; and to understand subtle differences between key concepts (e.g., blindness, legal blindness, visual impairment, and visual handicap) to enable clinicians to be more intelligent assessors of special populations.

All of these pleas by the authors of the diverse chapters basically serve a single mandate: to encourage psychologists and other clinical examiners to recognize the expanding nature of their job functions if they are truly to serve children, and to acquire the wide-ranging knowledge and skills requisite for competence when entering new arenas and exploring new horizons. The implication is that to succeed in the 1980's and 1990's psychologists cannot be isolated from other disciplines or other professionals; yet, to a large extent, I believe that isolation has caused many of the criticisms of testing and assessment that have beset the fields of psychology and education, and is at the root of so much of the discontent with standardized tests.

The type of isolation I am speaking of takes many forms, and seems much less prevalent than it was a decade ago. Initially, I was most troubled by isolation in interpretation of a single test, with the Wechsler scales serving as a good illustration. Rather than attending mostly to the global Verbal and Performance scales (an approach that has considerable factor-analytic support), many clinicians treated the tests as containing nothing but a collection of 10 or 11 or 12 separate skill areas. A low score in Picture Completion was immediately seen as a deficiency in "distinguishing essential from nonessential details;" never mind that the examinee performed very well on other subtests that required the identical skill, such as Picture Arrangement. Isolation, not integration, became for many the keynote of Wechsler interpretation.

Even more disturbing was the separation that I saw so frequently in interpreting the results of different tests. Case reports would be organized systematically with sections devoted to "behavioral observations," "intelligence," "achievement," "visual-motor integration," "personality," "psycholinginstic ability," and so forth. Each section would focus on a single topic or instrument, and never would the twain meet from section to section. A child would be proclaimed as having poor visual-motor integration based on Bender-Gestalt performance, with no attention paid to above average performance on WPPSI Block Design; poor auditory reception on the ITPA would be declared, ignoring above average success on many WISC-R verbal items with long, complex, verbal stimuli; "bizarre" reponses to some pictures on the Thematic Apperception Test would be interpreted as evidence of emotional disturbance, a conclusion reached without considering the severe visual perceptual difficulties discussed in an earlier section of the case report; inadequate short-term memory would be inferred from low Digit Span even though this poor performance was attributed to anxiety and extreme distractibility in the section on behaviors.

But the level of isolation displayed in case reports merely mirrored the widespread isolation occurring on a larger scale within the field as a whole. School psychologists, psychoeducational diagnosticians, remedial reading teachers, learning disabilities specialists, speech and language pathologists, and other professionals in special education and psychology tended to be worlds apart. Prior to the mandate in the mid-70's for multidisciplinary assessment, communication among these specialists was limited, as was knowledge of each other's domain. There was much redundancy in the tests administered by different professionals to the same child, and virtually no integration of the clinical and empirical data. Translation of the test results from one professional to another, such as from school psychologist to teacher, was often filled with miscommunications or impracticalities, and the child's parents were often kept in isolation from everyone.

The separateness of professionals and parents has diminished greatly with the passage and implementation of PL 94-142, and interdisciplinary teams have become the rule rather than the exception. Mutual understanding and effective communication have become more prevalent, and integration has, in many cases, begun to replace isolation. Nevertheless, there is still much room for growth. Some professionals still understand little outside of their own domains, particularly when dealing with low incidence handicaps. Redundant testing still occurs, and the data obtained by different professionals are often not integrated at a sophisticated level. Furthermore, territoriality has become fraught with vehemence. Exactly *who* is allowed to give a WISC-R, a K-ABC, or a Woodcock-Johnson? If a test battery gets the reputation of being for special educators, you can be sure school psychologists will steer clear of it, and vice versa.

I feel that Dr. Weaver's book will accelerate integration among various disciplines, and will enable even the most experienced clinical assessor to become a more intelligent tester. Each chapter is deliberately brief, but not basic; the contents reflect insightful treatments of varied topics, and should be studied and savored. Anyone who takes the time to read each chapter will automatically become a well informed clinician with the tools needed for conducting integrated and intelligent assessments—for mastering, as Weaver puts it in the Introduction, the art and science of interpretation and integration of findings.

Numerous practical suggestions are offered which should make clinicians more aware of the special needs of handicapped populations, and of the subtle ways in which low scores may be obtained by some children because of the examiner's ignorance of their particular problems. Thus, Lyman and Roberts implore clinicians to expand their knowledge of diseases, particularly psychosomatic disorders, and to be alert for any report of regression or deterioration in intellectual abilities that may signify the onset of a major medical or psychological problem. Willis, Culbertson, and Mertens note that special supportive chairs may be needed when assessing children with cerebral palsy since special positioning can affect their scores; it is known that certain body orientations elicit primitive reflex movements, thereby impairing purposeful motoric behavior. Mira advises examiners that they *should* talk to hearing impaired children to help assess their responsiveness to language and their expressions that accompany language, but *not* when simultaneously presenting gestures. Collins-Moore and Osborn offer information that affects examiners' interpretations of clinical *behaviors* rather than test scores: some low vision children may not maintain direct eye contact during communication *not* because of a social or emotional problem, but because a visual field defect may require the use of peripheral vision to get the best view. What we are constantly reminded in each chapter is that the intelligent assessment of handicapped children requires more than just good clinical sense or generalized testing experience; it demands specialized knowledge of the children's handicaps, coupled with sensitivity, and the ingenuity to secure valid results. According to Olley and Marcus, this need for flexible assessment strategies and tests may hold the key for obtaining meaningful data on autistic youngsters.

Internalizing the practical suggestions that abound in this book will curb the types of isolation I spoke of earlier. Also encouraging an integrated approach to assessment are the emphases by most chapter authors on understanding the impact of changes in our knowledge of handicapping conditions, and of changes in society, on the roles played by clinicians. Willis, Culbertson, and Mertens point out that medical technological advances have led to the doubling of the incidence of genetic disorders in the past ten years; examiners need to be able to meet the assessment needs of this expanding proportion of children with physical and health related disorders. Collins-Moore and Osborn inform us that 50-70% of visually handicapped children have other handicaps as well, further complicating assessment of this group, and remind examiners (as Mira does regarding hearing impaired children) that children with a particular impairment are a heterogeneous population and cannot be responded to in simplistic or stereotyped ways. However, Olley and Marcus point out that about 80% of autistic children are also mentally retarded, and that the disorder is almost always lifelong; despite occasional popular misconceptions, the youngsters are simply not potentially bright children who merely need to break out of their shells.

Nowhere are the changes in our society more evident than in the chapters on child neglect (Mira) and legal aspects of testing (Hays). Clinicians need to understand changes in statutes dealing with rights of children, rights of parents, and due process for children, and they need to be well versed in "informed consent" and the distinction between confidentiality and privilege. Mastery of these laws and concepts is essential as examiners strive for competency in their new roles as witness, maintainer of ethical and objective standards, and key professional in the disposition of cases of child neglect. These complex roles expand the job functions of school psychologists and other clinical evaluators well beyond that of test giver, and reflect involvement in social arenas that were unimaginable a generation ago.

In reading each chapter of this book I am left with the feeling that assessors need to learn a good deal about a wide variety of topics; lists such as Swiercinsky's of neuropsychological symptoms and central nervous system disorders are invaluable. I am also left, simultaneously, with the awareness of how sophisticated each tangential field is, and how important it is for assessments to be conducted by a team of competent professionals in a multitude of disciplines who have both an understanding of, and a healthy respect for, each other's domain. One interesting illustration of the essential need for multidisciplinary teams is offered by Elbert and Willis regarding the assessment of children with cleft palates, where a psychologist and speech and language pathologist may need to be joined by a general physician, audiologist, otorhinolaryngologist, dentist, plastic surgeon, and oral surgeon!

California School of Professional Psychology
San Diego, California
June, 1984

Preface

The goals and limitations of the present book should be noted here to place the discussion within a proper context. The purpose of the book was originally to offer a relatively brief manual on the essentials of psychological assessments for the general classes of problems in children and youth that present themselves to psychologists in general practice. There are very few psychological training programs that train clinicians to specialize in children (Tuma, 1982). Experts in child clinical psychology have lamented the failings of adult-oriented training programs in preparing practitioners to work with children and youth. Since adult programs make up the overwhelming majority of psychology programs in existence, many psychologists who subsequently take positions in general practice find themselves faced with assessments for which they have had minimal training.

One fact compelling many psychologists to carry out evaluations on children is the nature of their employment. Most psychologists are employed in public institutions, rather than in private practice (Rosenfeld, Shimberg, & Thornton, 1984; Vandenbos, Stapp, & Kilburg, 1981). Psychologists in such positions are committed to a general practice by the generic nature of 1) their training, 2) the population that the institution or agency is committed to serve, and 3) the unrelenting demand for psychological services for all people in the face of inadequate numbers of providers. Reality dictates that psychologists in community mental health and welfare agencies, schools, and federal, state, and municipal hospitals will be strongly pressed to perform first level psychological evaluations of children and youths.

Another factor bearing on the need for special help in the particular competencies required for psychological assessment is the relative decline in training in the late 1960s and 1970s of exactly those skills. Surveys and reports (Levitt, 1973; Shemberg & Keeley, 1974; Shemberg & Leventhal, 1981) have persistently documented over the last ten years the considerable dissatisfaction of directors of internships with academic preparation in assessment and clinical skills. A precursor to the decline in assessment skills was the development of negative attitudes toward psychological testing in general by various sectors of society. Even within psychology, vociferous demands called for the elimination of testing. One result of these societal trends determined that many psychology students passed through training programs with relatively cursory education and supervised practice in psychological testing. Some students also acquired negative attitudes and values regarding clinical assessment skills. The scientific basis and value of testing have been re-established (National Academy of Sciences, 1982), and the unfounded nature of some of the loudest complaints have been pointed out by reviews of authoritative research (Sattler, 1982), but the legacy of these times lingers.

The motivation to prepare a basic manual of guidelines for psychological assessments of children and youth came also from another reason related to the previous discussion. Many psychologists graduating from programs that omitted adequate assessment courses and practica were later dismayed to discover that they could not meet state licensure requirements (which typically demand a certain number of documented assessment training hours). Some of these psychologists, therefore, sought positions within state or federal institutions, since psychologists in such agencies are exempt from state licensing requirements. The exemption usually turns out to be no blessing when the psychologist discovers the often overwhelming number of assessments demanded in the institutional setting. Thus, many psychologists did not discover the need for further assessment knowledge until after they began their careers.

For these reasons, a handbook covering the essentials of psychological evaluations for populations that demand a great deal of services should serve a real need. To meet the need it ought to be practical and reasonably brief, and the information should be presented in a straightforward and basic manner. In any single delimited area such a handbook might appear too superficial or too simplistic to a knowledgeable diagnostician or specialist in the area. The generalist, however, might find in such a guide exactly what is most useful when faced with an immediate demand for an adequate first level assessment or screening.

Since practicality was to be the byword for this handbook, the organization of chapter topics was to follow the arrangement in the *Diagnostic and Statistical Manual of Mental Disorders, 3rd Edition* (DSM-III). It soon became apparent that strict adherence to the table of contents in DSM-III could not be maintained. In order to deal adequately with some major classes of problems facing psychologists who work with children and youth, it became necessary to follow recent developments in the field. Advances in psychological assessment of children have accumulated knowledge in certain areas that did not conform exactly to the organization of the diagnostic categories in DSM-III. Topics such as psychosomatic disorders, physical or health-related disorders, child abuse and neglect, neuropsychology, and legal aspects of psychological assessments did not follow the rubrics neatly, yet the topics were too important to be omitted. Furthermore, some topics, such as the assessment of the hearing impaired or visually handicapped, fall outside of the main axis of DSM-III but must be dealt with from time to time by a general practitioner who sees children. A manual or handbook ought to offer some guidelines on evaluating these populations. The solution indicated including the DSM-III categories that do present themselves to general practitioners and expanding or adding to those major categories where necessary. Despite these changes, coverage of the DSM-III categories for children and adolescents was achieved.

Another goal here was to advocate a comprehensive approach to assessment as opposed to a psychometric one. Psychologists are encouraged to look at all the significant aspects of a child and his or her world, not just test scores. The depressing effects of physical illnesses and traumatic events on intellectual and educational performance has been well documented. Yet many psychological reports persist in focusing exclusively on sub-test score patterns that "suggest" this or that "cognitive deficit." A child is called "learning disabled" because of a gap between intellect and reading performance, with no or scant weight attached to a history of poor health, a family living chaotically on the edge of poverty, or the evidence of anger and despair written on the child's face. To achieve this goal, a simple mnemonic P-I-E-E-S, standing for Physical, Intellectual, Emotional, Educational, and Social factors, was suggested as a guide for discussions. Further, the authors of the first chapters were urged to write relatively brief pieces that would state plainly what they might say in a supervisory session with a junior colleague, assistant, or trainee. Some authors were able to do this effectively and their chapters provide a rare view of the practical details of what a senior psychologist says to supervisees when in the midst of carrying out an assessment. The first major division of the book presents such examples. It also presents a foreshadowing of some difficulties that arose later in the book when such a model intersects with the difficulties of explaining how to evaluate very unusual populations, e.g., the visually handicapped, the speech and language impaired, the hearing impaired. Several authors of those chapters argued very persuasively that certain background material was absolutely essential. Could an evaluation of anxiety or depression be worth its salt unless the commonly accepted but somewhat complicated definitions were understood? Could a visually impaired person be assessed accurately by someone who did not understand the differences between visual handicap, legal blindness, blindness, and impairment? These arguments, which are well demonstrated in the chapters themselves, were compelling. One result was that the somewhat mechanical mnemonic (P-I-E-E-S) had to give way to the more important consideration of explicating the major concepts, issues, methodologies, "caveats," and practical recommendations deemed essential for that special population. Consequently, some chapters demonstrate a considerable variety in their usage of the mnemonic; nevertheless, they argue in their own way for that balanced consideration of the many facets of a client's life. They demonstrate the need for psychologists to become knowledgeable at some basic level about other allied fields of expertise, such as medicine, neurology, education, physical and occupational therapy, speech and language therapy, nursing, audiology, nutrition, and social work.

Practitioners should further their knowledge and skills in particular areas if they find regular demand for those skills. One excellent fundamental and comprehensive text that could be used as a foundation is Jerome Sattler's *Assessment of Children's Intelligence and Special Abilities* (1982). An especially informative text on interpreting the children's Wechsler is Alan Kaufman's *Intelligent Testing with the WISC-R* (1979). A psychodynamically oriented approach is illustrated brilliantly in the *Interpretation of Psychological Tests* (1968) by Joel Allison, Sidney Blatt, and Carl Zimet. Two books that serve as manuals or handbooks for different populations than those described in the present book are James Choca's *Manual for Clinical Psychology Practicums* (1980), and Gordon Ulrey and Sally Rogers' *Psychological Assessment of Handicapped Infants and Young Children* (1982). Finally, a select bibliography of more sophisticated references tailored to the population and/or problem under discussion is given at the end of each chapter.

A final goal of the book was to give the busy practitioner a select description of the tests that one can utilize in assessing the populations involved. At first, the expectation was that a relatively short list of tests would evolve. As chapter manuscripts arrived, however, the number of tests swelled greatly. Knowledge is increasing rapidly in each of the special categories and with it comes new tests and procedures. The Appendix of tests may turn out to be one of the book's most useful features. Without seeking out a library the practitioner who notes a reference to a test can turn to the Appendix and discover the essential information needed to decide whether or not it meets the unique demands of one's practice. For each cited test that it was possible to do so, the Appendix describes the knowledge, skills, or abilities measured by the test, its content and structural composition, time required, scores produced, cost, and publisher, and also serves as an index to the contributor's recommendations.

Acknowledgements

My first acknowledgement must go to my wife, Randee Jae Shenkel, who encouraged me to undertake this book and who patiently supported me emotionally and professionally throughout the course of the project. Without her there would have been no book. She also deserves the credit for eliminating sexist language and for some of the better editing.

Richard Sweetland, the president of the Test Corporation of America, originally conceived the idea of melding a compendium of tests used in a specialized field with a text on assessment of exceptional children and youth. He was also strongly supportive of me and the book at times when difficulties and delays were discouraging. Daniel Keyser also deserves recognition for freely lending his knowledge and advice.

As project coordinator and copy editor Jane Guthrie has been a great resource and indefatigable worker. It is doubtful the book would have ever been finished without her expertise. Terry Faulkner, managing editor, discreetly oversaw the project and simultaneously kept everyone happy and humming.

The chapter authors hold a warm spot in my heart. Although I felt I was fairly knowledgeable in the area of child assessment, I was surprised and chagrined on reading their manuscripts to discover how much more they knew. The breadth and depth of their scholarship, clinical experience, and wisdom is the strength of the book.

Finally, Sandy Hoffman deserves my special gratitude for her ability and willingness to clean up my grammar and punctuation, make sense of my self-taught typing, and turn out impeccable manuscripts overnight.

S.J.W.

REFERENCES

Allison, J., Blatt, S., & Zimet, C.N. (1982). *The interpretation of psychological tests.* New York: Harper & Row.

Choca, J. (1980). *Manual for clinical psychology practicums.* New York: Brunner/Mazel, Inc.

Kaufman, A.S. (1979). *Intelligent testing with the WISC-R.* New York: John Wiley & Sons.

Levitt, E.E. (1973). Internship versus campus: 1964 and 1971. *Professional Psychology, 4,* 129-132.

National Academy of Sciences. (1982). *Ability tests: Uses, consequences and controversies.* Washington, DC: National Academy Press.

Rosenfeld, M., Shimberg, B., & Thornton, R. (1984). *Job analysis of licensed psychologists in the United States and Canada.* Princeton, NJ: Educational Testing Service.

Sattler, J.M. (1982). *Assessment of children's intelligence and special abilities* (2nd ed.). Boston: Allyn & Bacon, Inc.

Shemberg, K.M., & Keeley, S.M. (1974). Training practices and satisfaction with preinternship preparation. *Professional Psychology, 5,* 98-105.

Tuma, J.M. (1982). Training in pediatric psychology. In J.M. Tuma (Ed.), *Handbook for the practice of pediatric psychology.* New York: John Wiley & Sons.

Ulrey, G., & Rogers, S. (1982). *Psychological assessment of handicapped infants and young children.* New York: Thieme-Stratton, Inc.

Vandenbos, G.R., Stapp, J., & Kilburg, R.R. (1981). Health service providers in psychology: Results of the 1978 APA Human Resources Survey. *American Psychologist, 36,* 1395-1418.

1

Introduction to the Psychological Assessment Process

S. JOSEPH WEAVER, PH.D.

The purposes of the present chapter are to first describe the basic aspects of a well-done general psychological assessment of children and youth, and then to familiarize the reader with the book's format. The term "assessment" is used rather than the simpler word "testing" because a comprehensive, integrated appraisal of the individual's problems was desired. If one thinks just of "testing," the evaluation process is apt to be dominated by the "tests." In such an event, the psychologist might start the initial conceptualizations of the case by focusing on familiar or available instruments. Such considerations are relevant, but they should not dominate or constrict thinking about the case at such an early stage. Instead, the psychologist should utilize an approach that encourages thinking broadly about the problems. Such an approach helps to pick up unusual yet possibly important factors in an individual case, and at the same time encourages narrowing down the range of possibilities, so that expensive and time-consuming diagnostic efforts yield the maximum amount of information in a minimum amount of time.

One practical method of discussing an assessment that is comprehensive yet appropriately selective lies in a combined use of 1) a model of the teaching process used by supervisors in formal psychology training practica and internships; and 2) a simple mnemonic schemata, P-I-E-E-S, integrated throughout the process. For the purposes of this book, the steps in the teaching process have been labeled: *Prediagnostic Staffing, Administration of Tests and Procedures, Interpretation and Integration of Findings,* and *Communication of Results.* In the P-I-E-E-S mnemonic each initial signifies an area of functioning: P = Physical, I = Intellectual, E = Emotional, E = Educational, and S = Social.

The four major steps in the supervision of a psychological assessment, i.e., the prediagnostic staffing, the administration of tests and procedures, the interpretation and integration of findings, and the communication of results, can be used to structure the flow of an analysis of assessment to insure that one gives adequate consideration to each component. The steps may be compressed in actual clinical practice by an experienced clinician. Such a veteran may mentally carry out the first

1

two steps immediately after getting the referral. The last two steps would probably be similarly condensed in the written report. For the purpose of instruction, however, this book uses the expanded format. This format allows detailed discussion of the questions, issues, and actual content of each section.

One concrete way of conveying the thinking, exploring, and decision-making entailed in a diagnostic psychological assessment involves going step-by-step through each of the major sections of the process. Examples are given of the questions, suggestions, clinical hypotheses, interpretations of findings, and conclusions that a senior supervising psychologist might make in meetings with a junior colleague. Throughout the early and middle stages of this process, it is proper to draw clinical hypotheses on the basis of very little evidence.

PREDIAGNOSTIC STAFFING

After a referral is received, an intake worker usually makes an effort to obtain additional information via a brief telephone interview with the parent or referring professional. A more extended telephone interview might be carried out by a junior colleague assigned to the case. In some agencies, a complete social interview may precede any psychological evaluation. In others, and in most private practices, an initial interview is scheduled with the parent and child or possibly the entire family, depending on the nature of the case and the psychologist's theoretical orientation. Records may be collected from family physicians, schools, and other professionals or institutions that have previously worked with the client. In a hospital, the search for additional information might involve only a reading of the hospital chart and a talk with the referring physician, nurses, and other personnel involved in the case.

A meeting then takes place between the supervising psychologist and the junior colleague, during which the historical information, questionnaire responses, and/or information from interviews are studied and dimensions of the case that seem important are discussed. Clinical hypotheses are ventured, corrected, modified, rejected, and accepted for the time being. Reviews of syndromes and assessment technologies may be checked and readings may be suggested. Eventually, some strategies for assessment and specific instrumentation are chosen. For our purposes, this meeting has been labeled *a prediagnostic staffing*.

Organization of content by P-I-E-E-S schemata

The content of each stage of the assessment process can be structured overall in a relatively simple manner to insure consideration of the significant areas of functioning. For many years, psychological reports were routinely divided into three major categories: intellectual, emotional, and social functioning. Supervisors of training programs involving children, however, found they had to consider two other categories: physical (or developmental) and educational functioning. For sociological and historical reasons related to their client populations, child psychologists much more than adult psychologists had to deal with problems that involved physical conditions, including those of a chronic and/or handicapping nature. The child's development in the many areas that fell into the physical realm provided an indispensible source of information for understanding the problems presented. For example, the presence of a sensory or motor deficit or delay impacts significantly on virtually all areas of a child's psychological functioning and must always be considered even if it cannot be measured by some psychological test. Similarly, education assumes such an important role in a child's life that one must always investigate functioning in that area. Indeed, problems surfacing in the educational sphere comprise one of if not *the* major reasons for referrals to child psychologists. The addition of these two important content areas (physical and educational functioning) to the traditional ones (intellectual, emotional, and social functioning) make up the P-I-E-E-S mnemonic. The use of such an outline should encourage a more holistic approach to structuring the assessment process and its content.

Since the functioning (whether deviant or normal) in each of these areas in turn impacts on that of virtually all the other categories, the same mnemonic, P-I-E-E-S, can be nested as a subheading within each area to insure that one takes into account the influence of interactions among the categories. For example, an immaturity in fine motor development (Physical) might exacerbate a condition of mental retardation (Intellectual) in a primary-grade child, so that learning to read is delayed much more severely than would have been predicted from either the mental retardation alone or the fine motor delay alone. The recognition and interpretation of even more complex interactions are also facilitated through the use of such a mental outline. For example, in the case of the retarded child (Intellectual) with a fine motor deficit (Physical), the slower development of reading skills may come to a complete halt if the teaching method in the classroom (Educational) relies heavily on a fine motor skill such as copying.

The use of a P-I-E-E-S mnemonic does not obviate utilization of other outlines. One can still discuss defenses, characteristic habit patterns, social facades, etc. This simply serves as an easily remembered standard organizing system to help the clinician carry out a comprehensive investigation with some emphasis on the roles of interactions among significant components.

P-I-E-E-S and the prediagnostic staffing stage

The psychologist can use the P-I-E-E-S system to organize historical information and data from previous evaluations. In a great many agencies for children and youth, such information is available in the form of school records, hospital charts, agency questionnaires, and occasionally previous psychological evaluation reports. Such material can be voluminous and the mass of data poses problems for anyone attempting to abstract the psychologically significant information. One practical way of attacking the problem involves taking a sheet of note paper and writing the initials P-I-E-E-S widely spaced down the left margin. Then, while perusing the material, one can list possibly significant information under the appropriate initial as one comes across it. The resulting summary list should help the psychologist in several ways during the various stages of assessment. First, the process itself helps fix in one's mind the important dimensions and developmental progressions of the case. Second, marked improvement, deterioration, or failure to develop in any category should be easier to discover. Third, deviance in any one of the major categories automatically raises a major diagnostic question that one must take into account in the overall evaluation. This will be discussed in the section on *Administration of Tests and Procedures*. Fourth, the outlined worksheet practically dictates the section of the psychological report usually entitled "Background of the Problem" or "Developmental History."

All practitioners do not enjoy the advantages of voluminous intake information prior to their first contact with a client. Nevertheless, they must collect analogous information in some manner—probably through interviews. Whether or not they make a list of notes using the P-I-E-E-S categories, they must survey much the same parameters of the client's life. It seems sensible therefore to do this in a fashion that facilitates psychological conceptualizations at several stages during the assessment.

ADMINISTRATION OF TESTS AND PROCEDURES

Closer to the time of the first clinical interview or testing session, a second meeting is held that focuses on the incorporation of any additional information into final and more detailed plans for the administration of specific tests and procedures. Changes in the tests, adjustments in the procedures tailored to the idiosyncratic personal features of the examinee, and a variety of other test-taking considerations all provide grist for this mill. Samples of such considerations follow.

The receipt of significant information may alter materially the psychologist's understanding of the major reason for referral. The specific question, "Is this child retarded?" may have been posed, but a subsequent report of a previous psychological evaluation may be received from the child's school that clearly demonstrates normal intelligence. The focus of the evaluation would instantly shift in such an instance not only to the child's current intellectual functioning, but also to the possible reasons for any change in functioning. The reasons for the change could be quite varied, such as a tumor or the onset of a psychosis.

Receipt of new information may lead the psychologist to call for consultation from other professionals. In the example given, where some significant deterioration of intellectual functioning was suspected, the new data might implicate an organic diagnosis. Referral to a neurologist would be mandatory in such a case and, presumably, the neurologist and psychologist would combine their findings in order to present a more comprehensive assessment to the clients.

Adjustments may become necessary to suit unforeseen events. For example, a private practitioner or a psychologist in a child development center occasionally obtains some surprising information just before the assessment of a case involving a question of proper educational placement. The information may reveal that the school system has just carried out an evaluation using the standard tests the practitioner was planning to employ. One must then substitute comparable but different tests or devise some other strategy. If the child routinely uses compensatory devices such as eyeglasses or hearing aids, the examiner must be sure they are worn during the assessment. Similarly, any unusual circumstance such as the taking of medication or the sudden onset of illness symptoms must be monitored and proper action taken.

The psychologist may discover the need for some adjustments during the study of records or preliminary interviews. Documented physical handicaps dictate the choice of some instruments and/or the rejection of others. Failure to search for such idiosyncracies can prove embarrassing and spoil tests. Suppose a review of medical reports reveals that a young child has a remarkably small bladder, requiring very frequent urination. That knowledge could prevent an examiner from making the usual interpretation of simple anxiety when the child makes frequent requests to go to the lavatory. When it is known that a child suffers from marked anxiety and low self-esteem, this can alert the examiner to offer preventive reassurance. Considerable anxiety is sometimes generated by repeated failures on a string of items at the end of some tests, such as the Wechsler scales or the Stanford-Binet, where it is necessary for several consecutive failures to occur. At other times, the psychologist will deliberately follow a procedure even though pertinent historical data indicate that some noticeable deficit in performance could ensue. For example, a child referred for refusing to complete written schoolwork, over-active or disobedient behavior in the classroom, and marked clumsiness and poor fine-motor ability might also demonstrate acceptable verbal achievement. The psychologist might expect considerable resistance or disruptive behavior to surface on the performance tests on the Wechsler scales; nevertheless, the verbal and performance tests might be deliberately administered in proper alternating sequence, partially to ascertain if the oppositional behavior that is a major referral problem appears and disappears with the appropriate content. In other words, this strategy provides an opportunity to observe if the behavior occurs almost exclusively during the frustratingly difficult (for that child) visual motor tests but not on the relatively easy verbal tests.

Some special preparations for motivational or emotional factors may be discerned and arrangements planned in the meeting just prior to testing. One might counter reports of previous failure to obtain valid test results because of refusal to attempt tests or blatant lack of effort with some use of motivational aids such as achievement ladders, token rewards, or even concrete rewards.

The list of factors relevant to the administrative meeting are as lengthy and varied as the individual characteristics of the children, their problems, and the social circumstances that surround them. Each chapter in this book details those significant factors that are characteristic of the problems in question. The psychologist needs to be aware of the issues and search for possible clues in order to handle difficulties properly.

The selection of specific psychological tests or procedures to use in the assessment follows naturally from the formation of significant diagnostic questions raised by study of the historical information at hand (as modified by the initial interview), as well as by the complaint that brought the client to one's office. In some cases, the issues are plain from the moment one hears the complaint stated by the referring person. The question, "Is this child retarded?" clearly indicates a major diagnostic question that one must address. In this case, procedures should include a good standardized individual test of intelligence and a good measure of adaptive behavior. Study of the case material may uncover the presence of additional diagnostic questions that indicate the necessity to include additional tests and/or procedures in the assessment. For example, in the previously mentioned question of mental retardation, the psychologist may have also noted signs of emotional disturbance and indicated this as an important question. As it would then be necessary to choose some methods of assessing that problem, one might consider and possibly select some anxiety scales, projective tests, or objective personality measures. Considerations that dictate the choice of specific tests are discussed in detail in subsequent chapters devoted to specific problem populations. The use of the P-I-E-E-S schemata to guide a general approach for the selection of tests is discussed later in this chapter.

Modifications to such choices may also be made in some cases during the testing itself or following the tests' administrations. The psychologist may alter a choice of instruments based on insufficient or vague information when the child's actual performance dictates another test. For example, the planned administration of a Wechsler Preschool and Primary Scale of Intelligence (WPPSI) to a young child suspected of mental retardation may be interrupted when the psychologist finds that the child cannot score high enough to pass the most elementary items. Rather than simply report the child "fell below the norms," one might quickly switch to a Stanford-Binet test and find a reasonably accurate mental age. Similarly, a detailed study of the case results during the interpretative staffing may bring unsuspected findings to light that call for further testing or other investigations.

P-I-E-E-S, diagnostic questions, and selection of tests

Prior to the final selection of specific tests and procedures, a psychologist must first determine the major diagnostic questions posed by the patient's problems. These questions may be the same as those stated by the patient or the referring agent or additional ones that surfaced during study of the prediagnostic material or an initial interview. One can find a simple technique to insure comprehensive consideration of all the questions probably involved in an extension of the P-I-E-E-S worksheet. A column labeled "Diagnostic Questions" can be entered on the worksheet to the right of the column of probably significant historical information.

The psychologist can then review all the items in a category and determine the necessity of investigating a major diagnostic question related to any P-I-E-E-S category in the *psychological* evaluation.

The term *psychological* is emphasized because not all diagnostic questions are psychological and thus may be answered by other disciplines. The psychologist does have an obligation however to note any crucial problem areas, even those that might fall outside of one's own special professional competence to diagnose and treat. Such problems must be resolved—perhaps by study of previous reports from other disciplines or by referral to the appropriate professional. Perhaps the clearest examples arise in cases where significant physical problems, such as visual impairments, auditory impairments, symptoms of well-known medical diseases or conditions, and even chronic illnesses and crippling conditions, are discerned in the prediagnostic materials along with no evidence of proper diagnosis and treatment of the problems. Since virtually all of these problems fall in the physical sphere, they can be noted opposite the Physical category under the column entitled "Diagnostic Questions." There they will serve as a reminder to the psychologist to resolve them in some way, even though they may not require the administration of any specifically psychological tests or procedures.

There is a major psychological diagnostic question that does belong alongside the "Physical" rubric and should be investigated by psychological tests and procedures: it is the question of brain damage. If one's study of the possibly significant information listed with the "Physical" heading does raise this question, "Brain Damage" should be written in the "Diagnostic Question" column. This reminds the psychologist to include specific psychological tests and procedures designed to offer evidence supporting or negating the presence of brain damage in the evaluation. The particular instruments chosen will depend on the specific diagnostic question and the specific problem. Subsequent chapters concerned with specific problem populations discuss the indications for selection of such tests.

At the first level of general psychological evaluation, almost all referral questions can be related to the five P-I-E-E-S categories. Usually, the psychologist is being asked in general to ascertain whether or not psychological evidence exists for or against brain damage (Physical category), mental retardation (Intellectual), emotional disturbance (Emotional), learning disability (Educational), and social disorder (Social). If one broadly conceptualizes these five diagnostic questions, they encompass the overwhelming proportion of all referrals to psychologists who work in community mental health centers, school systems, primary health agencies, and private offices. There are, of course, more unusual and subtle reasons for referrals, such as suitability for psychotherapy, potential for suicide, implications for compliance with medical regimens, etc. For these more specific and sophisticated referral questions, the P-I-E-E-S worksheet system may not suffice.

The addition of a third column labeled "Tests and Procedures" may complete the usefulness of the worksheet. The psychologist can note whether a major diagnostic question was entered beside a category, study the summary list of significant information, and then decide on the particular tests and procedures to employ. These can be listed in the third column. Usually, sensory motor tests are listed in the row labeled Physical, intellectual measures in the Intellectual row, etc. A test listed in one row may assess functioning in two or more categories. For example, the Wechsler Intelligence Scale for Children-Revised may be used to provide data on diagnostic questions of brain damage, mental retardation, and emotional disturbance. The listing of the tests and procedures also ought to stimulate consideration of the sequencing of the tests and the times involved during administration. The final result produces a rough worksheet documenting the psychologist's study of pertinent history and environment, determination of diagnostic questions, and consideration of factors influencing test selection.

INTERPRETATION AND INTEGRATION OF FINDINGS

The process of interpretation and integration of findings is a complex one, involving perhaps as much art as science. The goal of this section is to present a basic method of approaching the problem that general clinicians could use across all types of assessments. The process should encourage the consideration of all significant aspects of the client's problems, yet focus attention on the major causative and contributive factors. Similarly, the discernment of interactions between two or more factors should be stimulated to avoid uncritical acceptance of simplistic explanations. Inconsistencies in the data or outright contradictory evidence should be visible so that one can modify or reject hypotheses based on insufficient evidence. In the end, the individual interpretations of historical information, clinical observations, reports from significant others, test scores, etc., should all be drawn together into an integrated picture. It should "make sense" to a knowledgeable critic, and if it does not, the evaluation has not succeeded and further steps must be considered.

Once again, one can find a model for such a process in the procedures worked out over many years by supervisors in formal psychology training programs. Following the testing and other data collection, the intern collates all test scores and other information and brings them to a meeting with the supervisor. The junior colleague usually presents them already organized in a first draft of a written report. In some instances, the raw protocols and/or intermediately summarized information are physically presented; that is, the intern may spread out on a large table all of the interview notes, test protocols, scores, observation sheets, etc. In cases of group supervision, the intern is sometimes asked to present a written summary sheet(s) of the notes or data, or to summarize the material orally while using a chalkboard.

An imaginary picture of an intern spreading out on a large table all the papers containing various information on the case may provide a useful illustration of the melding of the P-I-E-E-S device with the supervisory model. Imagine the intern beginning at the upper left corner of the table with a paper (perhaps the first page of a questionnaire filled out by the parent) listing all of the identifying information. Next to it across the top of the table another paper is placed, detailing the pregnancy history. A third paper details the birth and/or its complications. A sheet follows with all the facts on childhood diseases, allergies, etc. The fifth item in the row lists the developmental milestones of sitting, walking, feeding, toileting, etc. A paper or two may be added describing the emotional problems, performances in preschools, and relationships with family and other children. Nevertheless, the bulk of the information in the row pertains to physical or developmental history and functioning.

The intern then begins laying down a second row of papers under the first. The first item shows the front of the record booklet for the Wechsler Intelligence Scale for Children-Revised with all of the scores and the graph. The next shows the Kaufman Assessment Battery for Children's front page. The third displays the drawings and scoring from the Bender Visual Motor Gestalt Test. The fourth does the same for the Draw-A-Person test. The fifth is a summary of previous group intellectual achievement measures administered in school. The sixth provides a summary of the results of a previous psychological evaluation by a school psychologist several years ago. The information in this row reports the intellectual functioning of the child.

The intern then lays out a third row of papers. These depict pertinent histories of the child's emotional behavior, including previous evaluations; treatments prescribed and the response to them; a Bellak-style summary of the Children's Apperception Test; the profile graph for the Personality Inventory for Children; clinical observations from interviews and test behavior; parental interview notes; and reports on emotional behavior from teachers.

A fourth row similarly presents data, from previous educational evaluations; cumulative record data; educational test scores from such tests as the Wide Range Achievement Tests, the Peabody Individual Achievement Tests, Spache's Diagnostic Reading Scales, Revised, and the Woodcock Johnson Psycho-Educational Battery; teacher rating scales and other observations; etc. This row illuminates the child's educational functioning.

A fifth row is devoted to parental reports, by questionnaire and interview of family and social functioning; a Family Relations Test graph; data from observations of the parents and child carrying out a joint Kinetic Family Drawing and playing a structured parent-child game; etc. This row presents the child's social functioning.

Row by row the intern verbally reviews the important aspects of each paper, in turn emphasizing those that bear on some hypothesis. Initially, ideas or hypotheses may be presented that have little evidence to support them. As the presentation moves along, however, additional supporting evidence may come to light or the hypotheses may be discarded as contradictory data or a paucity of confirmatory evidence is revealed. Eventually, some relatively strongly based findings become evident. Some conclusions of only moderate or faint strength may evolve, and some hypotheses are definitely discarded.

The intern proceeds in similar fashion across each row. Throughout the process, the supervisor questions interpretations, suggests alternate ones, and points out evidence confirming or contradicting various hypotheses. Occasionally, information from one row cross-validates a hypothesis or finding from another row; on the other hand, data in one row may critically invalidate an earlier conclusion. The process continues until the intern and supervisor arrive together at a set of findings supported by evidence from a variety of sources, i.e., histories; institutional records; interviews; intelligence test batteries; projective tests; achievement tests; teacher questionnaires and rating scales; parent inventories; clinical observations; self-reports; etc. Some findings can be stated confidently and in definite terms, others may possess a lower degree of certainty, and some may have to be qualified considerably. Eventually, the two agree on a set of interpretations, conclusions, inferences, recommendations, and possibly predictions that they are willing to state publicly.

This compilation of results should result from repeated cross-validation across several different sources of information and through disparate modes of functioning. The totality should present a coherent picture of the individual's functioning in different and important aspects of life. This does not mean there should be no incongruities, no absences, or even no contradictions in the data. The major conclusions however should be supported strongly enough to stand, and if they do not, then that in itself provides the major conclusion and it should be so stated.

COMMUNICATION OF RESULTS

The communication of the results of a psychological evaluation can take many forms. It can be written or oral. It can be presented to a neurosurgeon or to a migrant worker. It can be presented in several sessions, each lasting more than an hour over a period of several weeks, or in less than five minutes during a ward staffing. It can be done with one parent, or with a complex multidisciplinary team including professionals from ten disciplines, parents, school professionals, administrators, state legislators, and attorneys.

The major goals of such communications are equally varied. One goal may be to offer definitive objective information for a placement or a treatment decision that could profoundly alter a child's life. Another may be to convince some parents of the need to carry out a recommendation. A third may reflect the desire to influence other professionals (who had previously espoused opinions seemingly contradictory to one's own) to discern a subtle discrimination between your results and theirs, so that some resolution of views may occur. A fourth may require the psychologist spontaneously to create graphic or pictorial materials to convey the essence of some concept. The vagaries of the communication process itself may require the psychologist to call upon personal special training and skills in the interpersonal communication of feelings and ideas, in order to handle emotions and social dynamics that threaten to overwhelm the process.

Although oral reports are common and important, in practice they typically form either distillations or expansions of some written documentation of the evaluation. Even when the major or most critical communication of the results takes an oral form, it is wise to document the essentials for a variety of reasons. One can quickly forget important facts, lines of reasoning, rationales for recommendations, and so on. One may receive requests for findings and recommendations from many of the subsequent helping professionals and agencies involved with the case. Critical placements and treatments for the child may depend on the psychologist's interpretations and recommendations. Even legal determinations may hinge on these records. Finally, the ethical standards of the profession specifically call for good written documentation of one's professional work.

Effective written documentation of work can be quickly and relatively easily adapted to a wide variety of oral presentations and/or consultations. Indeed, the standard practice in most institutions requires a psychologist to prepare some written report and to talk from it in staff conferences or parent interpretations. The psychologist should analyze the social and psychological dynamics of the meeting beforehand and then adapt material in the report to fit.

General Guidelines

Eric Berne, the father of Transactional Analysis, advised psychotherapists to pause before entering the therapy room and say to themselves, "Primum no nocere" ("First no harm"). This self-reminder to place first in the scheme of things the warning to avoid doing harm might well be adopted by psychologists beginning reports of their findings. Reports of psychological evaluations can carry great weight in decisions that significantly affect the entire lives of individuals. Whether or not children are classified as mildly mentally retarded and placed in segregated classrooms (where they are apt to remain for most of their schooling) essentially depends on the psychologist's findings. Similar statements might be made about whole populations of children, such as the emotionally disturbed and the learning disabled. Although PL 94-142 does mandate an interdisciplinary team decision, the psychologist's support or opposition to any judgment of the team is crucial. It is doubtful that a team's decision to classify a child in one of these categories could be successfully maintained if the psychologist's opinion was contrary. The same position could be well taken in regard to other populations, such as juvenile delinquents, victims of child abuse and neglect, or children involved in custody cases. Jerome Sattler (1982) felt so strongly about this issue that he devoted a substantial part of the first chapter in his text on the assessment of children to a case history that illustrates poignantly the tragic power of words in psychological reports. Therefore, let the first and primary guideline for all communications of psychological findings be "Primum non nocere."

More detailed general guidelines are also available. Perhaps the best involve those basic assumptions underlying psychological testing in general. The psychologist who keeps those premises in mind when constructing reports or delivering interpretations should not go far astray. The two most prominent authorities in the field have each suggested lists of such basic premises and guidelines. Sattler (1982) listed the following guidelines that he considered important:

1) Tests are samples of behavior.
2) Tests do not reveal traits or capacities directly.
3) Tests purporting to measure a particular ability or skill should have adequate reliability and validity.
4) Test results should be interpreted in light of the child's cultural background, primary language, and handicapping conditions.
5) Test scores and other test performances may be affected by temporary states of fatigue, anxiety, or stress; by basic disturbances in personality; or by brain damage.
6) Tests purporting to measure the same ability may provide different scores for that ability.
7) Tests results should be interpreted in relationship to other behaviors and to case history information; test results should never be interpreted in isolation.
8) Test results are dependent on the child's cooperation and motivation.

Alan Kaufman (1979) begins his discussions on an approach to WISC-R interpretation with the following premises:

1) *The WISC-R subtests measure what the individual has learned.* From this vantage point, the intelligence test is really a kind of achievement test; not of the same type as reading or science, but a measure of past accomplishments that is predictive of success in traditional school subjects.
2) *The WISC-R subtests are samples of behavior and are not exhaustive.* As samples of behavior, one must be cautious about generalizing the results to other behaviors or to performance under different circumstances.
3) *The WISC-R assesses mental functioning under fixed experimental conditions.* The standardized procedures for administration and scoring help insure objectivity in evaluating a child, but they sacrifice the in-depth understanding of a youngster's cognitive processing.

Kaufman and Sattler state these guidelines positively on the whole; however, the flavor of warnings can be noted in the cautionary phrases and in the outright "do not's" and "should not's" sprinkled throughout the lists. One could even reword the lists in order to emphasize the cautionary aspects. In his further discussion of guidelines, Kaufman does issue a series of precautionary statements. They warn the psychologist that the WISC-R alone should never be used to diagnose or place children; that precise cut-off points for IQ scores would result in misdiagnosis and mistreatment; that the discovery of a child's relative strengths is more useful than classification in the mentally retarded range; that hypotheses derived from test scores, the case history, and observations, rather than the scores themselves, are the heart of interpretations; that those hypothoses that were confirmed should dictate the recommendations; that much experience with physically handicapped youngsters is necessary before an examiner can distinguish whether the reason such a child failed on a test was the physical disability or a lack of mental ability; and that the examiner of Black, Spanish-speaking, and other bi-lingual children must accord a primary place to cultural and linguistic factors in all interpretations.

The psychologist who heeds all of these fundamental premises and guidelines for psychological assessment should present a professionally competent report of his findings.

Improving Communication Dynamics

Unfortunately, the construction of a professionally competent psychological report does not by itself guarantee the *effective* communication of important findings and recommendations. In any communication process there is a sender, a receiver, and usually an interaction. This is most obvious in a parent or staff conference, although it also holds true for two-person communications such as those between the psychologist and a physician. To communicate the findings and recommendations effectively the psychologist must take into account the variety of characteristics of the receiver(s) and the situation. The parent or staff persons hold their own impressions of the child, expect or fear certain findings and hope for others. Some results will be easy to accept and act upon, and others will arouse powerful negative emotions. The psychologist must analyze the recipients of the findings in order to anticipate their probable reactions, especially involving very rigidly held beliefs or defenses that may block understanding and/or acceptance. Finally, some approaches to communicating the results must be devised that will handle possible resistance and maximize the probabilities of positive action on the recommendations.

Rue L. Cromwell designed a sequence of communicative behaviors for just such a purpose in his chapter in Baumeister's *Mental Retardation* (1967). Cromwell advised the psychologist to begin the feedback conference by summarizing the goals and hopes held in common and then moving to present those results that match the ones already held by the recipient. From that presumably comfortable basis, the psychologist should begin to present findings that alternate between acceptable and threatening. The parent or staff member should be asked to respond to the negative conclusions and the psychologist should react non-directively in order to encourage the other person to express fears, misunderstandings, and even outright rejections. It is better that they be voiced at this time, when misperceptions of fact can be corrected and unprofitable attitudes countered, than hidden behind a passive facade and later rejected or ignored. Cromwell further states that when difficulties with an interpretation are voiced, the psychologist can many times show the recipients how the two points of view are not totally incompatible. If rejection continues, the material is probably too threatening to be accepted at that time. One should then seek to uncover in detail the reasons for the rejection and determine whether other ways of presenting the material exist that do not evoke rejection. If specific labels or personal constructs are at the root of the problem, they may be translated into more acceptable terms. Furthermore, the psychologist may suggest some actions to the recipient for gaining a better understanding of the findings and recommendations. Educational readings, meetings with other parents, and attendance at parents' organizations are all techniques that have value. The use of an extended feedback system also proves useful when reaching such impasses. The psychologist can ask the parent to return in a week or so to explore further the implications of the examination's results. The latter is a positive way of offering to continue to help both the child and the parents handle their problems, and it often yields surprisingly successful outcomes. In this way, Cromwell points out, the parent is treated as the psychologist's partner in the problem-solving process. Such an approach has much to commend it.

REFERENCES

Cromwell, R.L., (1967). Personality evaluation. In A.A. Baumeister (Ed.) *Mental Retardation: Appraisal, education, and rehabilitation* (pp. 66-85). Chicago: Aldine.
Kaufman, A.S. (1979). *Intelligent testing with the WISC-R.* New York: John Wiley & Sons.
Sattler, J.M. (1982). *Assessment of children's intelligence and special abilities* (2nd ed.). Boston: Allyn and Bacon.

2

Appraisal of Children with Learning and Behavior Problems

DONALD K. ROUTH, PH.D.

This chapter is concerned with the appraisal of school-age children and youth and focuses on three overlapping but distinct syndromes: specific learning disabilities (LD), attention deficit disorder with hyperactivity (ADD), and aggressive conduct disorder (CD). Specific learning disabilities include deficits in basic academic skills such as reading, spelling, and arithmetic, that are important to identify in order that the child receive appropriate remedial help. Attention deficit disorder with hyperactivity may be important to diagnose because there are treatments including medications and behavioral procedures in the classroom that aid in its management. Conduct disorder is important to identify because of its negative implications for the child's long-term prognosis.

PRE-DIAGNOSTIC INFORMATION GATHERING

When learning or behavioral problems are the chief concern, the referral of the child may come from the teacher, from the parent, or from some community agency such as the juvenile court. Sometimes, of course, the parent asks for a psychologist's help as a result of a recent school conference or because of concern over a youth's misbehavior in the community. In any case, a first step in evaluating the problem might involve an interview with the child's parents and with the child personally. The interview usually begins with an elaboration of the presenting complaint and includes a description of the current family situation, a developmental history, and a review of the child's experiences and behavior at home, at school, and in the community.

No particular format for such an intake interview is recommended; instead, it is preferable to keep the format flexible and responsive to the parents' or child's immediate concerns. One of the main purposes of such an interview is in fact to build rapport with both the parents and child, and to let them know that the clinic will do its best to help them. There are, of course, various standardized interview procedures which can be used in diagnostic work, and they do have the advantage of

15

covering thoroughly both the present situation and the child's history (there are usually problems the parents or the child will not think to mention unless they are asked, and these tend to be overlooked in unstandardized interviews). However, its lack of flexibility makes such a standardized interview unsatisfactory for use in the initial intake process.

Physical

One does not usually find gross evidence of brain damage in a child with learning disability, attention deficit disorder, or conduct disorder. Nevertheless, it is certainly true that brain damage (congentital or acquired) increases the risk of academic and behavior problems. The initial interview with the parents should thus seek to elicit information about any complications of pregnancy or delivery, or any medical or neurological abnormality present either now or in the child's early development. Often the interview will turn up only some information of questionable significance to the issue of neurological impairment, for example that the child was born prematurely or had a bad bump on the head as a toddler. In the interview with a youth, a brief mental status exam can be included that, for example, incorporates assessment of orientation in time, place, and person, and memory for recent events. The best way of following up such information is to communicate with the family physician or perhaps, when indicated, to suggest that the child or youth also be taken for a medical examination. The parents will need to sign a release of information allowing the medical information to be shared with the psychologist.

Intellectual

If the child were moderately or severely mentally retarded, this would have become evident long before school age, such as in delayed development of self-help and communication skills. Thus, a child being evaluated for academic and behavioral problems is probably functioning at least in the range of mild or educable mental retardation. The parents of many mildly retarded children (who themselves may have limited education) do not see anything wrong with the rate of their child's mental development even when the developmental milestones they recall seem to represent to the interviewer a significant delay. Therefore, it may be more appropriate for the interviewer to pay attention to the actual description of the child's development rather than to the parents' evaluation of it.

Emotional

The clinician should ask the parents to comment on any history of disobedience or noncompliance with their requests, temper tantrums, aggressive or destructive behavior, stealing, etc. They should be asked to describe any such problems in concrete detail, both in terms of the circumstances which elicited misbehavior and the ways they tried to deal with it. A useful mnemonic device for the interviewer in questioning the parents of younger children in this area is *ABC,* where *A* stands for "antecedents," *B* for "behaviors," and *C* for "consequences" of the child's conduct.

Educational

The parents should be asked about the child's educational history, when he or she entered school, and whether the child was ever retained in a grade. The teacher provides, of course, the best source of information about the child's current educational situation.

Social

The clinician can infer the degree to which the family is socially disadvantaged from the parents' appearance and manner in the interview and from information about their educational level and occupational status. Another kind of social information that is important regards the extent to which the child's or youth's misbehavior may have become evident to the community at large. For example, it is of interest to know whether the child has a history of being disciplined, suspended, or expelled from school, and also about any brush with the law.

ADMINISTRATION OF TESTS AND PROCEDURES

Physical

Psychologists who work in an adult psychiatric setting are accustomed to using tests such as the Bender Visual Motor Gestalt Test or the Benton Revised Visual Retention Test as neurological screening devices. Indeed, in an adult psychiatric population, such screening tests will pick out approximately 75% of those with neurological problems.

Similar tests involving drawing or visual memory (for example, the Bender, the copy version of the Benton, the Developmental Test of Visual-Motor Integration, or the Memory-for-Designs Test) are often used with children, but the rationale must be entirely different. In school-age children (but not in adults), such drawing tasks represent relatively sensitive indices of general intellectual status but are not too sensitive as screening devices for neurological impairment. The experienced psychological examiner will recall, for example, that on the Stanford-Binet Intelligence Scale, the 3-year-old is asked to draw a circle, the 5-year-old a square, and the 7-year-old a diamond. For children, drawing is an intellectually demanding task and not just a psychomotor one.

Unfortunately, at the present time no brief psychological tests seem to exist which can serve as neurological screening procedures for school-age children being evaluated for academic and behavior problems. For adolescents, screening tests such as the Bender begin to have some value as specific neuropsycholgical assessment procedures.

Intellectual

Any child being evaluated for deficiencies in academic performance should receive a standardized individual intelligence test in order to distinguish the problem of *specific* learning disabilities from that of general mental retardation. The oldest established test used for this purpose is the Stanford-Binet, but a disadvantage of this test lies in that it gives only a single score, the overall IQ score. Most psychologists today would prefer a test that distinguishes between verbal and non-verbal aspects of the child's intellectual functionings, such as the Wechsler Intelligence Test for Children-Revised (WISC-R) or the Kaufman Assessment Battery for Children (K-ABC). One reason an intellectual profile is preferable to a single IQ score is that it permits one to identify the child who has problems in the general area of language, which may underlie the academic skill deficits. Although present remedial programs are more likely to be directed at the child's specific academic skills, in the future it may be possible to refer the child for more general help in the language area if psychological tests suggest that this would be helpful. Thus, such a child would get help with learning the meaning of vocabulary words and not just with how to read or spell them.

Emotional

Traditionally psychologists have relied mainly on the parents' statements to help them appraise the child's emotional and behavioral problems, supplemented to a certain extent by observations of the child's behavior in the playroom and during psychological testing. However, this approach is no longer satisfactory. If research on attention deficit disorder has done nothing else, it has sensitized us to the utility of teacher ratings, not only in evaluating a child's behavior initially but also in monitoring the child's progress and response to treatment. Today the evaluation of a school-age child is not complete without obtaining standardized behavioral ratings from at least one teacher and preferably more than one. If the teachers disagree, it may be because they have idiosyncratic views of the child or because the behavior varies from one class or time of day to another; if they agree, the psychologist has more confidence that the child's school behavior is indeed a matter of concern. For this purpose the Conners Teacher Rating Scale is recommended. This scale is in the public domain and not conveniently available from commercial test publishers. Thus, one can make photocopies of the Conners Scale from Barkley's (1981) book, *Hyperactive Children,* for teachers to fill out and use the age norms provided by Barkley in evaluating the results. The teachers' ratings may be translated into standard scores for the child's age on the Conduct Problems, Hyperactivity, and Inattention-Passivity subscales, and also on the Hyperactivity Index.

Educational

The clinician should obtain information from the school regarding the child's grades in academic subjects and deportment. Also, if school records contain the results of standardized group achievement tests such as the Iowa Tests of Basic Skills, it would be useful for the psychologist to know them. Parents will need to sign a release form if the clinic is not part of the school system.

One should give the child individually administered achievement tests at least in the areas of reading, spelling, and arithmetic. Among the tests most commonly used in psychology clinics for this purpose are the Wide Range Achievement Test (WRAT) and the Peabody Individual Achievement Test (PIAT). The WRAT reading subtest consists essentially of a list of words for the child to read aloud, and can be considered as providing at least a crude estimate of ability to decode both familiar and unfamiliar written words to speech. Thus, the WRAT reading subtest should be supplemented by one which measures reading comprehension (such as one of the PIAT subtests). The WRAT also includes an oral spelling test and a test of the child's skills in arithmetic.

These individual achievement tests are worthwhile essentially as educational screening devices. If they suggest that the child has specific difficulty in reading, spelling, or arithmetic, considerably more evaluation by an educational consultant is necessary before useful prescriptive recommendations can be made to the child's teacher. The teacher, for example, needs to know the proper instructional level for the child in terms of the particular basal reading program, or the appropriate set of remedial materials to use. There should be a more detailed analysis of the child's sight-word vocabulary, using a list that represents better than the WRAT the most common sight-words that might be encountered. One should examine word-attack skills more closely by having the child read or spell phonetically regular nonsense words. Comprehension should be examined by having the child read passages of some length and answer questions about them, and so on. Some psychologists are knowledgable enough to carry out this kind of educational diagnostic appraisal, but many are not. Psychologists who lack this kind of educational expertise should realize the limitations of commonly used individual achievement tests. For example, contrary to popular opinion, a child's reading grade-level on the WRAT does *not* indicate the level of reading materials the child can actually handle in the classroom.

Social

The clinician can obtain some information about the child's social relationships by questioning the parents and also by examining the teacher ratings already mentioned. However, it is often useful to supplement this by obtaining peer sociometric data. This may seem like a lot of trouble to go through, but can be of unique value. A well-known study by Cowen, Pederson, Babigian, Izzo, and Trost (1973) found that the best way to predict the long-term outcome of third-grade children (as indexed by their listing on a community psychiatric register eleven to thirteen years later) was by the number of negative roles assigned them by peers in "A Class Play," a peer sociometric measure devised by Bower (1969). A child's peers seem to possess valuable information about the child's social relationships not easily accessible through parents, teachers, or formal psychological tests.

In practice, one may photocopy "A Class Play" from Bower's book and have it filled out by each child in the class. Naturally, they are not told that this has anything to do with the child being examined. This procedure asks each child to pretend that he or she is the director of a play and to assign classmates' names to different roles in the play. The scoring involves simply counting the number of negative roles (such as "a mean, cruel boss") assigned by peers to each child in the class, and then ranking the children in the class in terms of assigned negative roles. In past clinical work, it is amazing how many times this procedure has disclosed that the child being examined is the most rejected one in the class, or perhaps the second-most-rejected. These findings are interpreted confirmation of the presence of a conduct disorder in the child and of the need for intervention to focus on the child's social skills.

INTERPRETATION AND INTEGRATION OF FINDINGS

Physical

If the history obtained from the parents and inferences from psychological test data concerning possible neurological impairment are confirmed by the physician's examination, the next step may really be up to the physician. Obviously, treatable neurological problems such as an operable tumor or a seizure disorder in need of anticonvulsant medication should be dealt with by a medical person, with the psychologist playing a supportive role. If on the other hand the neurological lesion is static, there may be few implications for psychosocial management. If the child has a behavioral or academic problem, the psychologist's recommendations are often the same regardless of the presence or absence of a neurological basis to the difficulty. The presence of brain damage should not be taken to imply that the child cannot benefit from educational remediation or cannot learn to bring behavior under control.

Intellectual

A major problem arises in integrating findings about the child's intellectual status when intelligence test scores and academic achievement data suggest mental retardation, but the parents are unaware of any problem in the child's development. This situation is even more difficult when the family comes from an ethnic minority background. The courts have tried to deal with this situation in diverse ways, for example by forbidding the use of IQ tests by the schools. Test publishers have responded by restandardizing their instruments to include minority children, by making tests available in different languages (e.g., Spanish), and by providing separate norms by SES level and ethnic status (as in the System of Multicultural Pluralistic Assessment measures). As useful as all these approaches may be, they do not solve the concrete problem of what placement to recommend for a minority child or one who is doing poorly in school but well in the parents' eyes. The best solution would seem to involve the parents in the decision-making process, informing them as well as possible about both the child's academic level in different skill areas and the placement alternatives available. If the local special education program (including self-contained EMR classes, resource teachers, etc.) is really a superior one, the parents might conclude the discussion by requesting some such services for their child. If however knowledgable informants regard the local special education program as a side-tract or a dead end, with poorly equipped classrooms or teachers perceived as rejects, the parents might rightly prefer that their child stay in the regular classroom and not be singled out for different treatment.

Emotional and Social

In integrating information from the parents' interview, teacher's ratings, and peer sociometrics, plus any other available information (such as direct behavioral observations of the child in one context or another), it is best to use the criteria of the *Diagnostic and Statistical Manual* of the American Psychiatric Association (DSM-III, 1980) as a guide. The diagnostic criteria for attention deficit disorder or the different varieties of conduct disorder are still very controversial, but DSM-III is more operational than its forerunners and at least can provide a basis for communication between clinicians with diverse views.

Educational

The main information to be integrated in educational diagnosis comes from school records (e.g., grades), group and individual achievement tests, and intelligence testing. A specific learning disability is diagnosed mainly on the basis of an educationally significant discrepancy between the child's performance in a particular academic area and overall level of intellectual development. Issues of definition of the different types of LD remain controversial, so once more the best advice may to be to use DSM-III diagnostic criteria where they seem to be applicable. Psychologists working within a particular school system will have to pay attention as well to the legal guidelines defining special educational categories within a particular jurisdiction.

COMMUNICATION OF RESULTS

Physical

If the parents are to be given information that is new to them about their child's neurological impairment, this should probably be done by the physician. The psychologist can, at most, suggest that psychological screening results indicate the need for a neurological examination, or elaborate on the behavioral and educational implications of a neurological diagnosis already given by a physician.

Intellectual

As stated, if a child is moderately, severely, or profoundly mentally retarded, the parents will know long before school age and will not need to be convinced by the psychologist. Usually, middle-class parents of a mildly retarded child have long been aware of the child's deficient performance in academically relevant areas and can be given a straightforward interpretation of the child's mild mental retardation.

However, parents either themselves poorly educated or who come from a disadvantaged background may not find the diagnosis of mild or educable mental retardation palatable. Indeed children from such a background rarely seem to accept this diagnosis as a self-label, but see themselves in conflict with the school system's collective opinion of them. The best strategy in interpreting test results to such parents and children may be to focus on the concrete academic difficulties of the child and what remedial possibilities exist in the school system. After all, the parents and the psychologist cannot be expected to resolve, in one conversation, philosophical difficulties about which the courts and the best psychometric talent have not been able to agree.

Emotional

If the diagnosis is attention deficit disorder with hyperactivity, the psychologist should perhaps inform the parents that some physicians treat this with medication. They should also be informed that purely behavioral treatment strategies exist. If the child is taken to a physician who decides on a trial of medication, the psychologist may perform an important service by acting as liaison to the school to see that the effects of the medication are properly monitored via repeated teacher ratings. Unfortunately, a breakdown often occurs in physician-school communication during this kind of treatment.

Educational

Just as the presence of a neurological problem or a question regarding medication requires close coordination with physicians, educational recommendations need to be dealt with in collaboration with school personnel (teachers, special educational consultants, school psychologists, etc.) With the advent of recent federal legislation, school systems now have a more elaborate process by which placement decisions are made and Individual Educational Programs (IEPs) written. The psychologist working outside the school system needs to be aware of this process and should channel any educational placement or programming recommendations through the staff team. Often the psychologist can perform a real service by helping the parents learn to negotiate this complicated system to their child's ultimate benefit.

Social

The child or youth with aggressive or antisocial behavior tends to have a guarded prognosis. In the famous study by Robins (1966) described in her book,

Deviant Children Grown Up, it was found that the children and youth referred to a child guidance center with a complaint of antisocial behavior had a 28% chance of meeting rigorous criteria for antisocial personality disorder (i.e., sociopathy) in adulthood, significantly higher than control subjects. At this point treatment strategies for dealing with aggressive and antisocial behavior in children are undergoing active research. Although treatments have not yet been identified which researchers agree to have long-term efficacy, there is hope that such treatments eventually will be found. In the meantime, clinicians should know what they are up against regarding populations of children at highest risk for adult difficulties. In talking with the parents of such high-risk children, There is thus good reason for an expression of concern, and for the psychologist, physician, school, and parents to work actively in trying to "beat the odds" in the case of the individual child.

REFERENCES

American Psychiatric Association. (1980). *Diagnostic and statistical manual of mental disorders.* (3rd ed.). Washington, D.C.: Author.
Barkley, R.A. (1981). *Hyperactive children.* New York: Guilford.
Bower, E.M. (1969). *Early identification of emotionally handicapped children in school.* Springfield, IL: C.C. Thomas.
Cowen, E.L., Pederson, A., Babigian, H., Izzo, L.D., & Trost, M.A. (1973). Long-term follow-up of early detected vulnerable children. *Journal of Consulting and Clinical Psychology, 41,* 438-446.
Robins, L.N. (1966). *Deviant children grown up.* Baltimore: Williams and Wilkins.

3

Evaluation of Neuropsychological Impairment

DENNIS P. SWIERCINSKY, PH.D.

The neuropsychological evaluation of children and youth has unfortunately received considerably less research attention than has the neuropsychological evaluation of adults. Availability of well-defined empirical associations between neuropsychological instruments and confirmed structural brain impairment in children is lacking. This is primarily due to the fact that the child's brain continues to mature until at least the middle teen years. The variable rate of maturation and the complex interrelationship of environmental and educational factors, along with genetic and congenital factors, make evaluation of neurofunctional development difficult, let alone evaluation of acquired organic brain impairment.

This chapter prepares the clinician to conduct a sensitive and adequate initial neuropsychological assessment. Due to the specialized nature of neuropsychological knowledge, difficult or questionable diagnostic cases must be referred to the specialist. This is particularly true when a life-threatening or treatable central nervous system lesion process is suspected but not confirmed by independent neurological examination. Where interest focuses on the assessment of neurofunctions to understand the behavioral consequences of a known lesion process or to define rehabilitation or education goals, the directions provided herein should suffice for the clinician experienced in working with children.

The brevity of the material presented assumes that the clinician has at least some knowledge of the neuropsychological literature relative to children. For clinicians wishing to broaden their knowledge beyond the scope of this chapter, reference is made to four recent publications. Filskov & Boll (1981) is recommended as a first source to become acquainted with the broad field of neuropsychology, especially the chapter on "Neuropsychology of Brain Damage in Children" by Boll & Barth. Pincus & Tucker (1978) provide appreciation of the link between neurology and psychiatry in their classic volume *Behavioral Neurology*. Two additional volumes, which offer considerably expanded information in both the selection of test instruments and the application of neuropsychological knowledge in schools, are Lezak (1983) and Hynd & Oberzut (1981).

24

PRE-DIAGNOSTIC STAFFING AND SCREENING

Human Behavior and its Biological Substrate

As every clinician recognizes, there is a complex interaction between the psychodynamic, developmental, and biological factors that underlie human behavior. In recent years the significance of the biological substrate has been made abundantly clear through the emerging field of neuropsychology. Similarly, the emergence of sophisticated rehabilitation techniques and chemical treatment programs have demanded the most careful assessment of clinically significant abnormal behavior as these relate to biological bases.

The single most significant difference between understanding the neurofunctional characteristics of children and that of adults is that in adult neuropsychology the focus appears to be on evaluation of impaired past functioning, where general intelligence is essentially preserved. In the child with a central nervous system disorder, intelligence is usually impaired with implications for potential future learning, and this comprises the focus of impairment. Recognition of this singular significant difference clearly emphasizes the importance of the pliability of the young brain and the impact that any organic lesion has for whole-brain functioning. Where a lesion in an adult may not diminish intelligence, it most likely would in a child.

Aside from this generalized characteristic of the effect of organic impairment on children, the clinician must not simplify the task by giving a single test for or making a unitary diagnosis of "organic" impairment. The central nervous system is much too complex to settle for a simplistic diagnosis, which is useful only in the most primary of steps in the process of understanding complex brain-behavior relationships and their implications for child development and education. Beyond the recognition gained through neuropsychological tests that an organic impairment may exist, a definition of the wide range of neurofunctional categories is necessary for practical utility of the evaluation.

Defining Symptoms

Table 1 lists many of the behavioral signs or changes that may suggest neuropsychological impairment. In many cases a single symptom may be insufficient to cause alarm, but when several of these symptoms appear in the behavior or history of the youth, one must suspect neurological impairment. Many of the signs, particularly those having to do with impaired levels of consciousness, demand concurrent neurological intervention. The clinician obtaining a history or making observations of a youngster should be particularly alert to every one of the signs listed in Table 1 and should have an appreciation of the neurological correlations. Virtually all of these signs, especially if they represent a deviation from a previous level of functioning, suggest change in central nervous system functioning.

TABLE 1

Pre-diagnostic Signs or Behavioral
Changes Indicating Neuropsychological Impairment

These signs and symptoms frequently indicate central nervous system problems. Any of these symptoms that represents a change from a previous normal behavior should alert the clinician that brain functioning may be abnormal. Neurological signs usually appear in logical clusters that reflect neuroanatomical foci.

ATTENTIONAL DEFICITS
erratic inattention
distractable
inability to maintain normal
  concentration
frequent perplexity
delerium
drowsiness

MOTOR SIGNS
clumsy or unbalanced gait
cautious motor behavior
idiomotor apraxia
ideational apraxia
constructional apraxia
dressing apraxia

SENSORY SIGNS
diplopia
tinnitis
anaesthesia over a defined body area
loss of peripheral field of vision

MEMORY
forgetfulness of recent events
time distortion
forced recall
confusion (perhaps with
  confabulation)

JUDGMENT
impulsivity
illogical social judgment

PERCEPTIONS
hallucinations
strange feelings or experiences
  (esp. olfactory, gustatory)
spatial distortions, disorientation
occasional hypnogogic state
inability to recognize familiar faces
loss of depth perception
amusia

SLEEP
increased, decreased amount
restlessness
arousal difficulty

TEMPER AND MOOD
low frustration tolerance
behavior unpredictability
extreme mood lability
lethargy
hyperexcitability
hostility and extreme defensiveness

SPEECH
slow verbalization
pressured speech
anomia
word finding difficulty
agnosia
slurring
disarticulation
incoherence
neologisms
abnormal fluency
any changes in quality or quantity
other aphasic signs

THOUGHT PROCESSES
perseverations
fragmentations
circumstantiality
tangentiality
loose associations
blocking of ideas
flight of ideas
confabulations
thoughts of unreality
delusions
depersonalization
concretism

The first step in conducting a neuropsychological examination typically consists of obtaining a complete history and behavioral observation. The history should be obtained from the child, the parents, school personnel, and medical and psychiatric treaters. Before testing begins, the clinician should have a comprehensive description of the child's typical behavior with note of recent behavioral changes or other deviations from normal development.

A complete history also includes details about current symptoms and treatment; medications; family background and characteristics; the nature of the family support system; chronological history leading to the present attention to professional intervention; birth and developmental history; educational history; medical and neurological history; and detailed behavioral observations and impressions. These sources will provide the basis for formulating tentative diagnoses and evaluation strategy. The clinician must always juggle the interrelationship between biological conditions and the psychological/emotional reactions to them.

Formulation of Assessment and Diagnostic Strategy

Based upon the impressions gained from the initial interview and history collection, the clinician must first make the decision whether to proceed unassisted by neurological or pediatric professionals. If the child is referred from such professionals, of course, this issue becomes irrelevant. However, if the child was referred by the family or by school personnel and has not had any neurological assessment, the clinician should initiate a complete neurological examination, particularly if significant recent behavioral changes are noted in the areas of attentional deficits, motor or sensory signs, sleep disturbances, or speech abnormalities. The clinician must rely on personal judgment about whether to obtain neurological data in cases of other behavioral abnormalities or diagnostic questions.

Depending on the pattern of signs and symptoms observed in the interview and history, the clinician should formulate an assessment strategy based on the nature of the diagnostic issues in question. If the child is referred for examination due to minimal brain dysfunction or learning disability, and neither the precise diagnosis is in question nor is a focal or medically treatable condition suspected, the focus will be on the management of the child at home or the application of educational remediation techniques. If the referral arises from behavioral abnormalities or recent changes in functioning, the clinician is faced with a differential evaluation of functional or dynamic issues versus organic dysfunction. In the latter case, the clinician relies more heavily on those tests that provide empirical indices of organic dysfunction, and must collect clinical and psychometric data that provide a comprehensive understanding of neurofunctional characteristics and are appropriate given the knowledge of normal brain functioning and development.

ADMINISTRATION OF TESTS AND PROCEDURES

The reference book *Tests* (1983) lists many procedures specifically designed to assess organic impairment in children and youth. Since most clinicians are likely unfamiliar with the majority of these tests, only those that most clinicians are familiar with or those that provide the most comprehensive information about neurofunctioning will be described here. Table 2 lists the recommended psychological tests applicable and interpretable for neuropsychological diagnosis. Four tests form the core of all evaluations: the Quick Neurological Screening Test, the Single and Double Simultaneous Stimulation Test, the Wechsler Intelligence Scales (either the child or adult form), and the Wide Range Achievement Test. Clinicians may substitute other more familiar tests, particularly achievement tests, but the core set described here provides a comprehensive base for completing an assessment. Additional tests may be employed to clarify specific areas of functioning. A full battery of neuropsychological tests often proves very useful but requires special training and experience in the use of these tests.

TABLE 2

Recommended Psychological Tests
Applicable and Interpretable for Neuropsychodiagnosis

Core Battery

Quick Neurological Screening Test
Single and Double Simultaneous Stimulation Test
Wechsler Intelligence Scale (WISC-R or WAIS-R)
Wide Range Achievement Test
Tactual Performance Test (from the Reitan Evaluation of
     Hemispheric Abilities and Brain Improvement Training)*
Symbol Digit Modalities Test*
Elizur Test of Psycho-Organicity: Children & Adults*

Extended Battery

Luria-Nebraska Neuropsychological Battery
Illinois Test of Psycholinguistic Abilities
Bender Visual-Motor Gestalt Test
Reitan Evaluation of Hemispheric Abilities and Brain
     Improvement Training

*Optional tests

Physical

Neurological Screening. The Quick Neurological Screening Test (QNST) provides the clinician with an assessment strategy for observing physically normal versus abnormal neuromotor and sensorimotor system development. The test is applicable for virtually all age ranges and allows ample opportunity not only to derive a quantitative assessment with cutoff scores described in the manual, but affords the opportunity for considerable impressionistic observation of process and attentional skill as well. If the child evidences significant impairment on the QNST a referral to a neurologist is imperative. The manual provides an extensive description of neuropathological signs revealed by the test.

Sensory-Motor Evaluation. The Single and Double Simultaneous Stimulation Test provides a sensitive measure for examining the possibility of lateralized organic brain impairment. Although exclusively lateralized hemispheric impairment is relatively rare in children, this sensitive test can prove invaluable in revealing a life-threatening lesion. Since clearly lateralized or focal lesions tend to be more life threatening, in that they represent tumor or cerebral vascular lesions, a thorough examination of these possibilities is crucial.

Intellectual Evaluation

The Wechsler Intelligence Scale for Children-Revised or the Wechsler Adult Intelligence Scale-Revised provide a wealth of comprehensive information regarding functioning in a variety of brain-behavior functional areas. True for both adults and children, research indicates that the two most sensitive Wechsler subtests for any nature of organic impairment are the Block Design and Digit Symbol or Coding subtests. If these are particularly impaired in comparison with the remainder of the profile, organic impairment is almost certainly indicated.

The Wechsler Scales also provide an opportunity to assess a wide range of intellectual functioning, including logical reasoning; abstract thinking; perceptual-motor coordination; both immediate and delayed memory processing; arithmetic reasoning; language production; language comprehension; visual-spatial processing; anticipatory responding; and other cognitive characteristics, all potentially influenced by neurological disease or impairment.

Emotional

The list of diagnostic signs in Table 1 suggests several emotional functioning characteristics that potentially herald a neurological condition. Emotional confusion, inappropriateness, impulsivity, distortion, lethargy, lability, and extremes are all seen, particularly with recent onset or acute brain syndromes. Of course, these rarely exist in the absence of physical, intellectual, or educational abnormalities when there is organic brain dysfunction. As an isolated set of symptoms, functional causes are more likely. The clinician can assess these areas by using conventional childhood emotional-personality evaluation procedures.

Educational Achievement Levels

The Wide Range Achievement Test is recommended as the test of choice for academic assessment because of its brief administration time and the excellent normative data available for wide age ranges. Particularly in the assessment of learning disabilities and minimal brain dysfunction, as well as the assessment of recent intellectual changes, it is imperative to compare percentile rankings of the standard reading, writing, and arithmetic achievement levels with general intellectual quotient percentiles. Under normal conditions the percentile equivalent of the full IQ score will approximately equal the grade rating percentile for reading and spelling. Large discrepancies most surely indicate abnormal brain functioning.

Social

Similar in intent and scope to the evaluation of emotional characteristics, the child's social adjustment, especially recent changes, must be examined. Frustration, mood changes that affect peer relationships, ability to interact appropriately all are considered concurrently with physical, intellectual, emotional, and educational functioning.

Using a Neuropsychological Battery

Several additional tests and extended batteries are indicated in Table 2. In common neuropsychological assessment batteries, the foregoing tests are often considered a part of those batteries and thus the clinician who already uses these instruments has relatively few additional assessment procedures to learn. The value of the extended battery, particularly the Luria-Nebraska Neuropsychological Battery and the Reitan evaluations, is that ample research has been conducted on these batteries and empirical correlations with neurostructural lesions or neurological conditions have been well defined. Clinicians are encouraged to use these batteries as their training permits. Brain damage, of almost any cause and nature, impairs functioning in all realms. A battery of tests and clinical procedures that contributes data to these areas is thorough and provides the database from which the clinician can make a more accurate assessment.

COMMON CENTRAL NERVOUS SYSTEM DISORDERS

One of the problems inherent in the literature comparing child neuropsychology with adult neuropsychology is a generally significant difference in diagnostic baserates. Children tend to have more generalized brain damage conditions, such as learning disabilities, minimal brain dysfunction, whole brain physical trauma, primary systemic diseases and infections. Adults who are studied in neuropsychology frequently have well defined and focal lesions, stemming from strokes, aneurysms, tumors, and penetrating traumatic injuries. Thus, the absence of focal neurological signs in a child does not at all mean that a significant brain dysfunction does not exist.

Table 3 lists most of the common possible central nervous system disorders of children and youth. The clinician should be familiar with virtually every one of these conditions and have at least a cursory understanding of the possible behavioral consequences and process of each of the diseases or conditions. The most difficult to formulate neurologically are, of course, minimal brain dysfunction and specific learning disability. Traumatic brain injury can involve shearing stress lesions throughout the brain that interrupt the normal course of neuroanatomical development and proliferation of association fibers. This means that accessing previous knowledge will be difficult as well as building on new knowledge.

A child with a congenital brain injury may start out with impaired neuroanatomical substrates and experience progressively minimal opportunity for accumulating intellectual growth. This is particularly true if brain cells have been killed, as in the course of anoxia or hydrocephalus.

Idiopathic convulsive disorders remain a constant mystery in neurology. But significance, as long as all life threatening neurological processes have been ruled out, must focus on neurofunctional characteristics that may be impaired in association with the convulsive disorder and recommended appropriate educational and remediation action.

Infectious diseases, particularly encephalitis, meningitis, and primary systemic disorders (such as rheumatic fever or pneumonia), can cause permanent damage to brain tissue and impede further intellectual development. Similarly, a variety of metabolic, toxic, and systemic conditions can have primary or secondary effect on central nervous system development.

The clinician must recognize the relatively rare, but also possible, childhood neoplasms and vascular abnormalities. They will most likely present some focal sensory and motor signs, but in the absence of signs will still result in general intellectual impairment because of the lack of well focalized neurofunctional development in the younger child. The significance of focal signs becomes more prominent with the advancing age of the child, as brain development becomes less pliable.

INTERPRETATION AND INTEGRATION OF FINDINGS

Cognitive Patterns

The process of neuropsychological assessment essentially requires three steps: 1) the gathering of initial history and interview impressions as described in the prediagnostic staffing section; 2) the accumulation of empirical and associated

TABLE 3

Common Possible Central Nervous Disorders of Children and Youth

Minimal brain dysfunction

Specific learning disability

Traumatic brain injury
concussion
shearing stress lesions
contusion
traumatic hemorrhage,
    hematoma

Congenital brain injury
hydrocephalus
cerebral palsy
spina bifida
temporary anoxia
prematurity
physical trauma

Neoplasm
glioma
secondary neoplasm (metastatic)

Vascular abnormality
spontaneous hemorrhage
    (aneurysms, vascular
    malformations)
cerebral ischemia (numerous
    causes)

Convulsive disorder
centrecephalic epilepsy
absence seizure
petit mal seizure
focal epilepsy

Infectious disease
encephalitis
meningitis
rheumatic fever
pneumonia

Metabolic and toxic disorders
diabetes
alcoholic deterioration
chemical abnormality
endocrine disease
carbon monoxide poisoning
anemia, nutritional deficits
biochemical exposures

Other and systemic conditions
blood disease
respiratory compromise
anoxic episodes
electrical, chemical shock
muscular dystrophy

impressionistic data from formal tests and batteries; and 3) the summarization of the previous two steps into a description of comprehensive cognitive patterns. At this point the clinician should be able to describe in fair detail the wide range of neurofunctional skills that evidence strengths, normality, or impairment among all data sources.

Table 4 lists the general cognitive skill areas revealed in neuropsychological examination and the specific assessment procedures recommended above that are associated with each subcategory. Of course, there is considerable opportunity for overlap, particularly in the accumulation of impressionistic data, and the assessment procedures listed are the key ones rather than the only ones for discerning level of functioning in the cognitive skill areas. It is recommended that the clinician develop a relative functioning scale to aid in generating an actual profile and thus facilitating inter-area comparisons.

Some relatively well documented empirical and impressionistic signs must be considered in addition to the course of investigation provided by clinical impression.

The Quick Neurological Screening Test provides numerous cutoff points for assessing empirical evidence of brain impairment. These will not be discussed further here, for the reader can refer to the QNST manual.

The significance of a verbal versus performance IQ split, particularly as revealed on the Wechsler scales, is a very strong sign of organic impairment. Research has proven this true for both children and adults, with one major exception in interpretation. A verbal-performance split in adults suggests a localized hemispheric impairment, with the right hemisphere typically represented by performance subtests and the left by verbal subtests. In the less well focalized development of the young brain, however, a verbal-performance split usually means more generalized brain damage. However, the strength of this research-based finding goes back to the issue of base rates in the types of diagnostic problems typically studied.

Very little consistent research has been produced revealing patterns on the Wechsler Intelligence Scale for Children-Revised that correlate with known central nervous system pathology. Whenever there is any relatively wide-ranging pattern among the subtests, however, this suggests that intellectual potentials are not evenly distributed and it must be due to some organic limitation or acquired deficit.

One finding relatively consistent with children and adults is the rather universal one of impaired visual-spatial perceptual skills. In other words, verbal skills (except in the areas where specific language areas of the brain are impaired) will retain higher functioning levels than the ability to discern complex spatial relationships or to manipulate objects in space. Again, this likely reflects a cultural bias in that education is typically verbally oriented rather than spatially oriented. Any generalized organic impairment will thus be revealed first in the weakest neurofunctional system.

Another sign to look for among the data is inconsistency in accomplishing tasks. Wide dispersion of item responses on the Wechsler Scale, for example, can indicate either that learning has not been evenly attained or that accomplishing memory associations is difficult.

TABLE 4

Discerning Neurofunctional Skills

Cognitive Skills Areas	Assessment*
Attention	
concentration (attention maintenance)	QNST, W-D, W-I, W-DS
discriminatory responding (selective)	QNST, SDSS, W-PC
Orientation	
person	QNST
spatial	QNST
Memory	
auditory-verbal short-term	QNST, W-D, W-A
visual-figural short-term	W-PC, W-DS
passive, incidental learning	W-DS, TPT (memory), SDMT
general long-term, remote	W-I, W-V
Receptive Language	
word recognition	WRAT-R
reading comprehension	WRAT-R, W-A (child)
auditory comprehension	W-A, W-C, W-D
Expressive Language	
writing skill	QNST
conversational fluency	W-V, W-I, W-C
spelling skill	WRAT-S
word knowledge	W-V, W-I, W-S
Mathematics	
calculation skill	WRAT-A
practical problem solving	W-A
visuospatial perception	
figure-ground differentiation	W-PC
spatial visualization	W-BD, W-OA, W-PC, MZ
Abstract and Organizational Reasoning	
verbal abstract thought	W-S
visual-spatial abstract thought	W-BD
general organizational thinking	W-C
Problem Solving and Reasoning	
mental flexibility	W-C, W-PA
verbal practical judgment	W-C
sequential planning	W-PA
social judgment	W-C, W-PA
insight	W-C
Sensory-Motor Skills	
tactile	SDSS
visual	QNST
auditory	QNST
coordination	QNST

*QNST=Quick Neurological Screening Test; SDSS=Single and Double Simultaneous Stimulation Test; W=Wechsler Intelligence Scale (Children or Adults), followed by subtest symbol: I=Information, C=Comprehension, A=Arithmetic, S=Similarities, D=Digit Span, V=-Vocabulary, PC=Picture Completion, PA=Picture Arrangement, BD=Block Design, OA=-Object Assembly, DS=Digit Symbol (Coding), MZ=Mazes; WRAT=Wide Range Achievement Test, followed by subtest symbol: R=Reading, A=Arithmetic, S=Spelling; TPT-=Tactual Performance Test; SDMT=Symbol Digit Modalities Test.

The other classical signs mentioned earlier such as lateralized motor or sensory impairments, those described and evaluated by the Quick Neurological Screening Test, will usually be found in association with some areas of cognitive deficit.

Syndromes

The clinician must formulate at this point two areas of syndromes. First, a neurological diagnosis is based upon a syndrome of signs and test results that "hangs together" neurologically. One would not expect to find a vocabulary scaled score of 6 or 7 on the Wechsler Scale and a spelling score in the 60th percentile on the Wide Range Achievement Test. This kind of inconsistency clearly makes no neurological or educational sense. Similarly, in a normally right handed child, a superior performance IQ score would not be expected in view of several left side sensory and motor impairments that cannot be linked to any peripheral damage. These examples are extreme, of course, but illustrate the need for the clinician to look for consistent patterns that suggest a logical neurological explanation.

The second area of syndrome formulation lies in neurofunctional skills, more or less irrelevant to the issue of structural neurological impairment syndromes. Here the issue is defining neurofunctional strengths and weaknesses and cognitive patterns that can be related to educational or rehabilitation applications.

The general cognitive skill areas described in Table 4 can provide the outline for describing the major skill areas that the clinician would want to provide educational or rehabilitation professionals.

Diagnostic Decisions

As has been suggested throughout this chapter, the clinician completing a neuropsychological evaluation of a child has a responsibility in diagnosing the presence of an organic lesion that may require treatment by a medical or neurological professional. Whenever any strong empirical sign of organic impairment is present, a referral for neurological examination becomes imperative. Otherwise, diagnoses will usually reflect static, non-progressive, or congenital lesions as opposed to an active or progressive life-threatening lesion. The diagnoses of static lesions usually result in the need to focus on neurofunctional characteristics and to consider the neurological diagnosis as a secondary issue.

COMMUNICATING RESULTS

The Stigma of "Brain Damage"

Once the neuropsychological assessment is completed, the profiles drawn, and the narrative report written, the task remains to communicate the results to parents, school personnel, or other professionals. In virtually all cases, restraint must be exercised in providing any label that will stigmatize the child's future. Similarly, the use of the term "organic" should be avoided. Communicating results to a medical or neurological professional, of course, can include any and all of the neurological diagnoses identified as possibilities based on the psychological tests. This information will help such professionals but may cause undue anxiety and likely misinterpretation for many parents or school personnel.

Focus on Practical Neurofunctions

The nature of any psychological examination, and particularly a neuropsychological one, creates enormous anxiety for both parents and client. Conveying results to parents in a sensitive and straightforward manner is as important as the task of actual data collection. Therefore, providing a written outline in the vernacular of the parents, as well as providing a feedback session that allows them to ask questions about the findings, can be extremely therapeutic.

REFERENCES

Filskov, S. B., & Boll, T. J. (Eds.). (1981). *Handbook of clinical neuropsychology.* New York: John Wiley & Sons.

Hynd, F. W., & Oberzut, J. E. (Eds.). (1981). *Neuropsychological assessment and the school-aged child.* New York: Grune & Stratton.

Lezak, M. D. (1983). *Neuropsychological assessment.* (2nd ed.). New York: Oxford University Press.

Pincus, J. H., & Tucker, G. J. (1978). *Behavioral neurology.* (2nd ed.). New York: Oxford University Press.

Sweetland, R. C., & Keyser, D. J. (Eds.). (1983). *Tests: A comprehensive reference for assessments in psychology, education and business.* Kansas City, MO: Test Corporation of America.

4

Assessment of Children with Psychosomatic Disorders

ROBERT D. LYMAN, PH.D., MICHAEL C. ROBERTS, PH.D.

In recent years there has been increased recognition of the importance of the relationship between physical and psychological illnesses and health in children. In 1977 Wright recommended that the term psychosomatic should include physical problems caused by emotional disturbance as previously accepted, and it should also be expanded to include physical problems caused by difficulties in learning, development, and personality, as well as the psychological effects of physical illness. Using this expanded definition, well over 100 major psychosomatic disorders have been identified that affect a large percentage of children seen in both mental and physical health-care settings. The problems seen under Wright's psychosomatic tripartite rubric include: 1) physical symptoms produced by psychological problems or stress, such as psychogenic asthma, vomiting, recurrent pain, anorexia nervosa, and ulcerative colitis; 2) physical problems caused or maintained by faulty learning history or developmental anomalies, such as encopresis, enuresis, psychogenic seizures, self-mutilation, or tracheotomy addiction; and 3) psychological problems associated with or following medical disorders, such as incompetent compliance with various medical regimens (i.e. diabetic), psychological maladjustment to such chronic diseases as hemophilia, kidney disease, leukemia, and following lead poisoning, burns, or encephalitis. For a detailed discussion of these and other psychosomatic disorders, the reader might consult relevant texts by Wright, Schaefer, & Solomons (1979) and Walker & Roberts (1983).

This chapter will attempt to alert clinicians to the importance of comprehensive assessment in psychosomatic disorders influencing children's health and will describe assessment procedures useful in delineating relevant factors in specific disorders. We should note that "psychosomatic" is often used by lay people to mean "the problem is all in the head." *Hypochondriac* has been used synonomously with *psychosomatic*. If relied on, these naive distortions are traps for the clinician since they dismiss the importance of psychological causation and sequelae. More precise thinking and use of terminology related to specific disorders will lead to more profitable interventions.

PRE-DIAGNOSTIC SCREENING

Children suffering from psychosomatic disorders frequently are seen by medical practitioners who either ignore the role of psychological factors in the origin or maintenance of the disorders, or fail to consider the psychological effect of an illness. It is rare that these children are initially seen in mental health settings. In many cases, only after negative diagnostic results or unsuccessful medical treatment is a mental health practitioner consulted. Upon receipt of a referral, the mental health practitioner should first ascertain what medical diagnostic and/or treatment procedures have been implemented. In the unlikely event that medical consultation has not been sought, it is imperative that the psychologist involve a physician in the diagnosis and treatment of any case with possible physical cause or medical implications. Following this step, the clinician must try to obtain from the patient or family a complete history of the present problem and any preceding episodes. The clinician needs a comprehensive understanding of the symptoms of problems as well as their antecedents and consequences. Often parents have learned medical jargon and diagnoses through their usually numerous physician interactions, and we suggest that the astute clinician go far beyond these in the assessment phase. One might ask the parents and child a question such as, "Describe the last time the problem occured—what happened before, during, and after?" In the interview, the clinician should also focus on the presence of overt anxiety or depression in the child, the developmental history, any exacerbating and ameliorating stimulus events, and possible reinforcement mechanisms maintaining the disorder. It is also important to obtain information regarding family interactions; for this purpose, joint interviews with the child, parents, and siblings are often useful.

We strongly recommmend that the clinician read the pertinent medical and psychological literature, for help both in understanding the problem and in determining recommended assessments and interventions for each psychosomatic disorder. The immense variety of disorders in the psychosomatic category prevents a presentation of one set approach to all problems. Some problems share common characteristics and may be assessed similarly. The approaches to psychogenic pain wherever manifested (head, stomach, joints) will be similar; assessments of the emotional adjustment to chronic illnesses will also be alike. However, the assessment of a child with encopresis or bruxism is significantly different from that of a child recovering from meningitis, and from that of a child starting treatment for diabetes. The first typically requires less intellectual assessment and more physical, behavioral, social, and emotional evaluation; the second, more intellectual and educational evaluation for sequelae related to this disease affecting the brain; the third, more social and emotional assessment to aid in teaching and monitoring the diabetic regimen.

Specific areas of diagnostic concern are delineated in this chapter.

Physical

It is essential that children with psychosomatic disorders have a comprehensive initial medical evaluation and that they be medically monitored throughout assessment and treatment. Many disorders that appear to be psychosomatic in origin can have purely physical causes. In addition, some psychosomatic disorders with psychological origin can have life-threatening medical complications. For instance, anorexia nervosa is fatal for 15% of its victims, who die of complications of malnutrition.

In addition to obtaining medical consultation, the mental health practitioner needs to obtain a detailed medical history of the child and other members of the family, particularly focusing on illnesses similar to the current disorder. Research has shown that modeling of parents' or others' "sickness" is a frequent causal factor in childrens' psychosomatic disorders (e.g., headache or stomachache). Even excessive family conversation on the topic of bowel habits has been found to be responsible for encopretic and enuretic conditions.

The mental health practitioner should also address the issue of the parents' response to the child's illness, with the goal of determining whether over-attention may be a factor in maintaining a psychosomatic condition. Observation of family interactions may provide more information on this point that overt questioning.

Finally, the clinician should question the parents regarding general prenatal, perinatal, and childhood health history. Childhood medical problems or subtle neurological deficits can produce a variety of psychosomatic symptoms (e.g., Hirschprung's disease and spinal injury for encopretic symptoms).

Intellectual

A child's intellectual level can be a significant factor in the assessment of psychosomatic disorders for a number of reasons. First, mental retardation places a child at risk for a number of psychosomatic disorders resulting from faulty learning and/or actual physical impairment. These include feeding problems, enuresis, encopresis, and seizure disorders. Secondly, a child's intellectual level greatly affects the response to physical illness and the ability and willingness to comply with a medical regimen, with mental retardation greatly increasing the problems for both medical and psychological treatment. For example, the ongoing regimens for diabetes, kidney disease, and hemophilia may be too complex for a retarded person to master. Finally, the mental health intervention chosen depends greatly on the child's intellectual level. Some more verbal and participatory treatment techniques require at least average intelligence. Psychotherapy for anorexia nervosa and counseling the child adjusting to the chronic illness of muscular dystrophy or sickle cell anemia are two examples.

Parents should be interviewed concerning the child's early developmental history and later school performance. The clinician should be particularly alert to reports of significant delays in reaching developmental milestones such as walking and talking; however, it is important to note that parents' memories of such events are often inaccurate or influenced by expectations or wishes. More objective information, which might be obtained from pediatrician's records or preschool teachers, is frequently more useful. The psychologist should also question teachers in later grades regarding their assessment of the child's intellectual capabilities and academic performance. Of particular significance is any report of regression or deterioration in intellectual abilities which might signify the onset of a major medical or psychological problem.

Emotional

Research has shown that children's emotional states, particularly anxiety and depression, prove highly significant in psychosomatic disorders, both in precipitating symptoms and as a result of a physical illness. The parents and child should be interviewed at length to ascertain the presence of high levels of either anxiety or depression. Indicators of excessive anxiety include numerous fears, sleep problems including nightmares or night terrors, obsessive-compulsive behaviors and rumination about possible negative events. Extreme difficulty in separating from the mother can be a sign of anxiety in some children and may be an early sign of such problems as school phobia. Frequent somatic complaints without physical basis are also common indicators of anxiety in children and exist in the premorbid histories of such psychosomatic disorders as anorexia nervosa.

The clinician should also question parents and child concerning the presence of symptoms of childhood depression. Recent research suggests that most depression in children has symptomatology roughly parallel to that of the adult disorder. Blunted or predominantly negative affect, tearfulness, sleep problems, loss of appetite, inactivity, social withdrawal, preoccupation with death, and statements of suicidal intent present significant indicators of childhood depression. In infants, the presence of a depressive analogue has been suggested as a causal factor in non-organic failure-to-thrive, usually following parental neglect or separation of the child from the parents. Lassitude, inactivity, poor feeding, and apparent negative affect have been described in children as young as several months. Unless adults provide physical affection and contact, a significant percentage of these infants die. Severe mental depression frequently causes the parental neglect in such cases, and thus parental emotional states should also be assessed by the clinician.

A child's teacher is in a uniquely good position to assess emtional/psychological functioning. The teacher spends time with the child for a number of hours each day, in a variety of different situations, and usually has internalized a well-developed set of norms for usual behavior of children that age.

Educational

The psychologist should question both parents and teachers about the child's educational progress. Frequent absences from school may indicate the presence of medical or psychosomatic problems or a pattern of parental reinforcement for hypochondriacal complaints. A child's educational progress may also serve as an index of general psychological functioning. Significant levels of anxiety and depression may manifest themselves in poor test performance, panic attacks, failure to complete homework assignments, and inability to speak before the class.

Social

Information concerning a child's social interactions with siblings, peers, or others in the community can relate to a determination of psychosomatic illness. A consistent pattern suggestive of anxiety or depression, attention-seeking behavior, or psychologically caused physical problems can first become apparent in a child's social relationships. The degree of social support available to the child and the likelihood that this social network can be utilized to support treatment efforts are also relevant to prognostic predictions and choice of treatment interventions. For instance, treatment for emotionally triggered asthma attacks will probably not succeed if a child's entire social network reinforces the occurence of such attacks through attention and excusing the child from obligations. Similarly, treatment regimens frequently require the family's participation (e.g., in cystic fibrosis and cerebral palsy). As accompaniments to the medical problem, these may be considered psychosomatic problems. The social supports can make or break both the medical and the psychological treatment.

It is also significant if a child acts far differently in the context of family relationships than with others. If, for instance, the previously mentioned asthma attacks occur only in the presence if the mother or father, then this may strongly indicate that something unique in those relationships precipitates the asthmatic condition.

Administration of Tests and Procedures

Due to the diverse nature of childhood psychosomatic disorders, no single test or even single battery of tests exists that is comprehensive enough to assess adequately all possible conditions. Instead, the clinician must rely on information gathered in the literature search and during prediagnostic screening to tailor the assessment procedures to the specific disorder and the presumed causal mechanisms involved in a particular case. For instance, assessment procedures can vary drastically in a case of anxiety-induced asthma, a case of enuresis related to mental retardation, or a case of non-compliance with diabetic medical treatment reinforced by parental attention.

The following sections will list possible testing procedures appropriate for psychosomatic children; however, selection for use in a particular case depends upon the clinician's assessment of the relevant variable in that case.

Physical

Another chapter in this volume discusses a number of tests useful in assessing neurological functioning in children. Such instruments as the Bender Visual-Motor Gestalt Test and the Wechsler Intelligence Scale for Children-Revised are likely to be familiar and available to the majority of clinicians. Other tests, such as the Quick Neurological Screening Test and the Reitan-Indiana Neuropsychological Test Battery for Children, may require that the clinician seek specialized training or refer the case to a colleague experienced in the administration and interpretation of these tests. A number of test instruments have also been developed which assess specific parameters of a child's psychosomatic illness, including the Headache Checklist, the Asthma Symptom Checklist, the Children's Respiratory Illness Opinion Survey, and the Seizure Disorder Survey Schedule. These types of checklists and tests have been developed, for the most part, within the context of specific research projects or clinical practices, and are neither available commercially nor adequately normed and validated. They can, however, prove useful in providing the clinician with a standardized assessment of the child's symptomatology and the attitude toward the illness.

Evaluation of the physical symptoms is paramount in psychosomatic disorders where the symptoms present the major problem facing the clinician. Regardless of the presenting problem, it is imperative that the clinician do more than get a diagnostic label. The psychologist must ask specific questions about the particular symptoms manifested—what are the symptoms? When, how often, where, and with whom do they occur? This behavioral assessment will aid the clinician in understanding the psychosomatic disorder. In the absence of a psychometric scale, the clinician can devise a personally useful instrument by attending to the questions noted here and by reviewing relevant literature for salient features. Wright, et al.'s *Encyclopedia of Pediatric Psychology* is a gold mine of such information.

Intellectual

The Wechsler Intelligence Scale for Children-Revised and the Stanford-Binet Intelligence Scale remain the most widely used tests of intelligence in clinical practice. The Kaufman Assessment Battery for Children is a newer test that is being used increasingly. Very often, in the assessment of children with psychosomatic disorders, only a rough estimate of intellectual capability is needed. In such cases, tests like the Slosson Intelligence Test or Peabody Picture Vocabulary Test-Revised, which require only 20 to 30 minutes to administer, may prove adequate. In cases of clear mental retardation, the clinician may be less interested in a specific IQ score than in an assessment of the child's ability to adapt to the environment. In these cases, such scales as the AAMD Adaptive Behavior Scale, School Edition; the Adaptive Behavior Inventory for Children; or the Vineland Social Maturity Scale may prove more useful than intelligence tests.

Assessment of infants' cognitive functioning may be relevant in cases of nonorganic failure-to-thrive or rumination disorder of infancy. The Denver Developmental Screening Test provides a brief assessment of infant development in the areas of social, motor, and language functioning, while the Bayley Scales of Infant Development and the Neonatal Behavioral Assessment Scale by Brazelton provide a more comprehensive evaluation.

Emotional

As discussed earlier, anxiety and depression are the two most relevant emotional states in children's psychosomatic disorders. The most widely used specific measure of children's anxiety is the State-Trait Anxiety Inventory for Children, although several other scales, such as the Child Anxiety Scale, also exist. Specific tests of childhood depression include the Children's Depression Scale and the Children's Depression Inventory. All of the above are self-report measures. The psychologist can also use a number of other tests to assess simultaneously both anxiety and depression. These include such projective tests as the Thematic Apperception Test and Children's Apperception Test, which rely on the clinician's judgment to determine levels of anxiety and depression based on the child's responses to picture stimuli. A more objective test assessing both anxiety and depression is the Personality Inventory for Children (PIC), which uses parent responses to 600 true-false questions to generate a personality profile. In addition to the separate subscales for anxiety and depression, the PIC also contains scales indexing overall adjustment, family relations, intellectual ability, hyperactivity, psychosis, and withdrawl.

Behavior checklists also prove useful to the diagnosis of attention deficit disorders in children, a condition that is considered by some a psychosomatic disorder. The Conners Teacher Rating Scale and the Conners Parent Symptom Questionnaire are the most widely used for this purpose, although the Personality Inventory for Children includes a hyperactivity scale.

The psychologist can assess the issue of children malingering and consciously faking physical ailments through use of the validity scales of the Personality Inventory for Children and the lie scale of the Junior Eysenck Personality Inventory. Other assessment instruments can aid in evaluating the psychological adjustment to chronic illness. For example, high scores on the Hypochondriasis Scale of the Minnesota Multiphasic Personality Inventory typify a poor prognosis for diabetes management in adolescents. Similarly, clinicians have used self-concept measures (e.g., Coopersmith Self-Esteem Inventories) to assess adjustment to chronic illness.

Educational

Most children have received comprehensive group achievement tests in their schools. The results from these tests can be compared to school grades and intelligence test results. Large discrepencies may indicate specific conflicts in the school environment, poor teaching, inappropriate class placement, or a lack of academic effort on the child's part. Depression may serve to reduce school grades by its interference with sustained work. Anxiety may increase during standardized testing, lowering achievement test scores. All of these patterns of discrepency may provide useful information in cases of psychosomatic disorder. The most commonly administered group achievement tests are the California Achievement Tests, the Iowa Tests of Basic Skills, and the Iowa Tests of Educational Development.

In addition to scores on group achievement tests, the clinician should obtain scores on individual achivement tests. The Wide Range Achievement Test (WRAT) and the Peabody Individual Achievement Test are both brief screening instruments that provide limited information concerning academic achievement. Neither test assesses narrative writing skills, and the Reading subtest on the WRAT assesses only phonetic ability or word calling, not reading comprehension. However, the information gained from these tests can comprise a useful adjuct to intelligence test results, school grades, and group achievement test results. Behavioral observations during the completion of these tests can also provide valuable information about the child's attitude toward school work. Related educational assessments may also include assessment of the child's specific knowledge about medical illness and treatment, when such information is correlated with psychological adjustment. For example, the psychologist might test the extent of the diabetic's knowledge of the disease and ability to assume treatment responsibility.

Social

Teacher and parent checklists and behavior rating scales can be helpful in assessing a child's social interactions. In addition to the checklists already mentioned, the Walker Problem Behavior Identification Checklist: Revised 1983, The Devereux Child Behavior Rating Scale, and the Child Behavior Rating Scale have been used to assess children's social functioning. The patterns of social disability that appear most relevant to children's psychosomatic disorders are those of extreme dependency and social isolation. One should also attend to a child's general style of social interactions and ways of getting attention and controlling others.

Some practitioners have found that a variety of sociometric techniques aid in obtaining social interaction data. These techniques include such things as peer nomination procedures in which, for example, each child in a group is asked whom they would most and least like to sit with (or study with, etc.) and the data is then summarized for the whole group. Similarly, peer ratings or behavioral observations of positive and negative social interactions complied by teachers or others can provide valuable information concerning a child's social status and pattern of interaction. Some disorders have more social ramifications than others and need more assessments in this area. For example, the "stinky" encopretic child may be overtly rejected by peers, while another child's bruxism (or teeth-gnashing) may not be evident. The diabetic adolescent, despite special diet, may be seen by the peer group as less differences than the child with asthmatic or chronic pain symptoms that prevent participation in normal physical activities. The clinician should attend to these differences in assessing the social area.

INTERPRETATION AND INTEGRATION OF FINDINGS

For the mental health practitioner involved in assessing a possible psychosomatic disorder, the major conclusions demanded are whether psychological factors are involved in causing the disorder or whether the child is experiencing major psychological effects of a physically caused disorder. One must consider all information obtained from the physical, intellectual, emotional, educational, and social assessments in drawing these conclusions. In the case of some disorders (i.e., anorexia nervosa, conversion reactions, hypertension, self-mutilation), there is likely to be little doubt that emotional factors are significant in causing the illness, and the true value of the clinician's assessment lies in pinpointing exactly which emotional factors are important. In other cases (e.g., chronic pain, eating disorders, encopresis, asthma), there may be reason to question whether the disorder is psychogenic in origin at all, so the practitioner needs to research the professional literature carefully to ascertain which psychological factors have been found important by others and how to assess their effects.

In cases of physical disorders with major psychological sequelae (e.g., burns, diabetes, meningitis, hemophilia), again the clinician needs to combine information from all areas of assessment with data gleaned from a comprehensive review of the research literature. In these cases, the psychologist will frequently find that the long-term psychological effects of illness are as significant as the physical effects, and that psychological factors are vitally important in progress and recovery. In addition to the general references noted earlier of Wright, et al. (1979) and Walker & Roberts (1983), we have found useful information on this topic in Tuma (1982) and Magrab (1978).

Physical

Besides providing information concerning the neurological integrity of the child and specific parameters of the child's illness, assessment in the physical area may offer the only objective measure by which to index improvement in the child's condition in relationship to specific symptoms. It is vitally important to consider in the assessment those stimuli which exacerbate or ameliorate the child's condition and to develop a complete picture of the antecedent and consequent events at every stage or episode of the illness. This information may prove important even in cases where the cause of the illness is totally physical.

Intellectual

In most cases, only gross categorizations of intellectual ability are required in the assessment of children's psychosomatic disorders. If intellectual ability is found to be within the normal range and to correlate highly with educational achievement, then this factor ceases to have much further significance in the assessment of the case. Practitioners need to be aware of the social and racial biases of most standardized intelligence tests and to adjust their interpretations correspondingly. Findings of significant retardation may require consultation with experts in this field regarding training techniques and prognosis.

Emotional

The psychologist must analyze information regarding a child's emotional state in conjunction with data concerning parameters of illness, social interactions, and possible reinforcement mechanisms. The resulting information may prove valuable in two regards: first, an extreme state of anxiety or depression may be the cause of the psychosomatic disorder, and second, emotional state may provide an indication of the psychological effects of physical illness. As mentioned earlier, psychological testing may provide the only objective measure of a child's progress; therefore, serial testing may be nesessary. It is much less important that psychological testing lead to a standard psychiatric diagnosis than that this assessment help the clinician to understand the role of emotional factors in the child's illness. On occasion it may be necessary also to assess the emotional status of siblings or parents in order to truly understand the factors involved in the the illness.

Educational

Frequently the greatest significance of assessment information obtained from the school lies in any discrepancies with other information. The child who does not achieve academically despite a normal IQ score, for instance, may have adjustment problems specific to the school environment. Also, information from school records may provide a check on the accuracy of parent reports. The overprotective mother, for example, may report that her child misses little school due to asthma attacks, while school attendance records clearly indicate that this is a major problem. School officials are fortunate in that they spend long periods of time with children over an extended duration; therefore, even their off-hand or seemingly irrelevant observations should receive careful consideration.

Social

In integrating social assessment information, the practitioner should take care not to neglect any significant aspect of the child's life. Circumscribed problems can easily be missed if the psychologist confines the assessment to one area of activity. Asthma attacks, for example, may only occur during athletics, or enuresis may only pose a problem when sleeping at friends' houses. Failure to obtain information from these sources will result in a misinterpretation of the problem. In many cases, direct observation is preferable to relying on either secondhand reports or sociometric measures, and should be implemented whenever possible.

COMMUNICATION OF RESULTS

Physical

In no other childhood psychological disorder is it as important that the mental health practitioner work closely with the child's physician. In most cases of psychosomatic disorders, one should first discuss the assessment information concerning neurological functions, medical history, or physical symptoms with the physician, and then communicate the information jointly to the parents. It is essential that the physician and mental health professional be consistent both in attributing the illness to physical or psychological factors and in recommending treatment. If parents are confused or forced to choose between mutually exclusive treatment approaches, then a successful treatment outcome becomes unlikely. One must bear in mind that the psychologist is not competing with the physician for the right to treat the patient and that primary medical responsibility for the case resides with the physician, although sometimes the mental health practitioner will direct the major intervention.

Intellectual

Communicating intelligence-test results to parents must involve some education of the parents about what these results mean. Parents are usually unaware of the subjective nature of the IQ score and often attach almost mystical significance to this single number. The focus of feedback should be kept away from specific scores and instead should concentrate on patterns of strength and weaknesses and on any specific educational, vocational, or treatment plans suggested by the test results. The psychologist should also avoid the labeling of IQ ranges (mildly retarded, etc.) if possible. The relationship of intellectual functioning to the psychosomatic disorder and any treatment implications should be described.

Emotional

In communicating test results of the emotional area, one should also avoid focusing on diagnostic labels, but concentrate instead on the child's pattern of emotional responses and specific treatment needs. Particularly if test results are communicated to the schools, the use of psychiatric diagnosis may stigmatize the child and interfere with future adjustment. It is important that test results be communicated to parents in an objective, non-accusatory way. If parents perceive blame for their child's emotional problems, they are unlikely to be willing partners in the treatment effort. Since emotional components play a role in the psychosomatic symptoms, this relationship should be pointed out with sensitivity toward the parents' own emotional state. All too frequently, clinicians engage in theoretical digressions not necessarily facilitative to the therapeutic process. Stimulating discussions about etiological factors should not be carried on among colleagues with the parent present unless necessary. In most cases of encopresis, for example, one may not need to understand etiology completely to make an accurate diagnosis and to implement appropriate treatment. Sometimes the clinician better serves the case by describing only the findings and the recommended intervention, and leaving out the less important theorizing about etiology that may confuse or even "blame" the parents.

Educational

It is important to communicate information regarding a child's educational achievement and needs to both parents and school officials. Children spend so much time in school that effective treatment is impossible without the cooperation of the teacher and other school personnel. Equally important, the psychologist should advise both school and parents of inappropriate educational placements or other school factors which may be exacerbating a child's conditon. For instance, anxiety over excessively high academic demands may prove a factor in such conditions as asthma or ulcerative colitis. It is also essential to advise parents of both their rights under federal and state laws to appropriate educational placement for a child with special needs and their right to participate in the planning of their child's educational program. Children with psychosomatic conditions are covered under these laws and special arrangements may be considered (e.g., for the hemophiliac, leukemic, or lead-poisoned child who requires special education).

Social

It is necessary to emphasize for parents the importance of a child's social interactions in the causation and maintenance of a psychosomatic disorder. Treatment may require major changes in many of these interactions or monitoring of a child's social functioning in a variety of contexts. Of particular significance are social interactions within the family. The psychologist may consider it advisable at times to communicate assessment findings to siblings, grandparents, or other extended family members in order to terminate maladaptive family patterns of reinforcement and to encourage consistency. For example, the clinician may determine that intervention requires withdrawing reinforcement for school absences because of somatic complaints; increasing the demands for appropriate physical activity from an overprotective parent of a chronically ill child; or decreasing demands for perfection and reducing stress for an asthmatic child. These changes in social interactions are not readily accepted by well-meaning parents, grandparents, or siblings, and careful communication of the assessment findings will enhance acceptance. Parents may also request that the clinician communicate findings regarding social interactions to school officials, athletic coaches, church personnel, or a variety of others involved with the child. Such communications should recognize the family's right to confidentiality and should involve no more elaboration than necessary.

A final note concerning communication of results involves the child personally. Almost every child above the age of infancy should receive honest, age-appropriate feedback about his or her own test results. In the final analysis it is the child who must work to resolve the illness, with the help of family and treatment personnel, and that effort can be greatly aided by an honest sharing of assessment findings.

REFERENCES

Magrab, P.R. (Ed.) (1978). *Psychological management of pediatric problems.* (Vols. I & II). Baltimore: University Park Press.
Tuma, J.M. (Ed.) (1982). *Handbook for the practice of pediatric psychology.* New York: Wiley-Interscience.
Walker, C.E., & Roberts, M.C. (Eds.) (1983). *Handbook of clinical child psychology.* New York: Wiley-Interscience.
Wright, L. (1977). Conceptualizing and defining psychosomatic disorders. *American Psychologist, 32,* 625-628.
Wright, L., Schaefer, A.B., & Solomons, G. (1979). *Encyclopedia of pediatric psychology.* Baltimore: University Park Press.

5

Assessment of Mentally Retarded Children

S. JOSEPH WEAVER, PH.D.

Mental retardation has been fairly clearly defined as a diagnostic category, and there is relatively good agreement among professionals of many disciplines and theoretical persuasions regarding the definition and the procedures and tests necessary to establish the diagnosis. Certain psychological tests administered by a psychologist are generally required for such a diagnosis. Furthermore, general consensus exists on the definitions of subclassifications or levels of retardation and the similarly essential role of psychological assessment in such instances. This chapter is primarily concerned with making a general diagnosis of retardation and determining subclassifications or levels of retardation, and does *not* focus on the many possible etiologies of mental retardation. However, some understanding of the familial versus organic distinction is sufficiently general and important enough to be required of all psychological diagnosticians and therefore demands discussion. There are also several major legal requirements (PL 94-142) and differential diagnostic issues that either pervade the area or are at least frequent enough to merit consideration even at the level of a general psychological evaluation. Readers wishing a comprehensive text should look to Robinson & Robinson (1976), which is generally considered an authoritative psychological treatment of the area.

General Considerations

Definitions

The American Association on Mental Deficiency (AAMD) has published the following definition generally accepted by all disciplines:

> Mental retardation refers to significantly subaverage general intellectual functioning existing concurrently with deficits in adaptive behavior and manifested during the developmental period. (Grossman, 1983)

In 1980 the American Psychiatric Association published an almost identical definition in the third edition of *Diagnostic and Statistical Manual of Mental Disorders* (DSM-III). Four key phrases in these definitions need explanation. "Intellectual functioning" is operationally defined as performance on standardized

50

individual intelligence tests, e.g., Wechsler scales, Stanford-Binet. "Significantly subaverage" means a score of two or more standard deviations below the mean of the standardized test used. The standard individual intelligence tests usually have a mean of 100 and a standard deviation of 15. Therefore, a score must fall below 70 in order to meet the standard of minus two standard deviations. It is assumed in this discussion that psychodiagnosticians are familiar with the probable error involved in IQ scores, as well as the variations in standard deviations, and take these into account in interpretation and classification. "Adaptive behavior" refers to how well the individual meets the standards of personal independence and social responsibility ordinarily expected of persons in one's age and cultural group. "Developmental period" is that time between the individual's birth and age eighteen.

Table 1 shows the appropriate ranges in IQ scores, educational classifications, and approximate percent of cases in the population for each of the four major levels of retardation (see Table 1). It should be noted that according to these figures almost 90% of all cases of mental retardation fall into the category of mild (or educable) mental retardation. This fact is of great importance for any psychologist doing primary level evaluations and it is the basis of discussion under the topic of familial retardation.

The four levels of retardation—mild, moderate, severe, and profound—are determined by performances on both intelligence tests and measures of adaptive behavior. Table 1 demonstrates the ranges in IQ scores that characterize each classification. The AAMD system requires that the individual fall into the retarded range on *both* intelligence and adaptive behavior to be classified as mentally retarded. One cannot emphasize too strongly that an individual who falls *above* the top of the mildly retarded range in *either* intellectual or social functioning (e.g.,

TABLE 1

Levels of Mental Retardation

DSM-III CODE	LEVEL	EDUCATIONAL TERM	IQ RANGE FOR LEVEL	ESTIMATED PREVALENCE
317.0	Mild	Educable	50-55 to approx. 70	2.7%
318.0	Moderate	Trainable	35-40 to 50-55	0.2%
318.1	Severe	Trainable	20-25 to 35-40	0.1%
318.2	Profound	Custodial	Below 20 or 25	0.05%

adaptive behavior) should not be labeled as mentally retarded. Some of the major controversies about the use of intelligence tests and misclassifications of individuals have come about as a result of the failure of psychologists in schools and clinics to take the social functioning of the referred individuals into account before labeling them "retarded."

A point to note about the AAMD definition is that it is concerned only with present behavior. Thus, an individual may have functioned at a retarded level some time in the past yet not be classified as such now if present adaptive behavior or intelligence warrants such a change. Similarly, an individual may function at a retarded level in one setting such as school, and at a normal level in others such as home and community. In these cases, the clinician must come to a general conclusion based on clinical judgment. In the example given, the conclusion of "not retarded socially" should undoubtedly prevail.

The distinctions between the AAMD and DSM-III systems are probably moot since the reliabilities of the differential diagnoses in question are debatable. One difference between the two definitions is that the AAMD definition does *not* differentiate mental retardation from other childhood disorders such as brain damage, autism, or childhood schizophrenia, while DSM-III does. Another difference between the classifications is that the AAMD system requires concomitant levels of adaptive behavior at all four levels of retardation and only successively lower IQ scores are needed in the DSM-III definitions. Table 2 delineates the types of social functioning associated with the four retardation levels at each of three major ages.

The actual assessment of adaptive behavior should be carried out through the use of the best standardized individualized test or scale available. Unfortunately, currently available scales such as the AAMD Adaptive Behavior Scale or the Vineland Social Maturity Scale suffer from flaws. The first is based primarily on institutionalized populations, while the second does not meet acceptable standards regarding the size or representativeness of its sample. Nevertheless, such scales should be employed since they do provide a standardized and relatively objective factual basis for the required clinical judgment regarding social functioning. Fortunately, a revision of the Vineland (called the Vineland Adaptive Behavior Scales) will be available in 1984 that appears to meet technical standards for normative populations, reliability, and validity. It also offers an interesting bonus in that scores on it can be directly compared with scores on the Kaufman Assessment Battery for Children (K-ABC), since overlaps between the national standardization samples were employed.

The Education for All Handicapped Children Act

The Education for All Handicapped Children Act, familiarly known as PL 94-142, states as its goal:

TABLE 2

Levels of Adaptive Behavior in Mental Retardation

DEGREE	DEVELOPMENTAL CHARACTERISTICS		
	Preschool Age *0-5 years*	*School Age* *6-21 years*	*Adult* *over 21*
MILD	Rarely diagnosed	Usually learns academic and pre-vocational skills. Needs special education. Can reach 6th grade level by late teens.	Usually lives and works in general society. May not be identified as retarded. Usually needs advice and support under stress.
MODERATE	Probably talks. Moderate delays in motor development. Can learn to care for basic needs. Requires moderate supervision.	Probably learns functional academic skills to 4th grade level in special education. May be independent in familiar environments.	Usually performs semi- or unskilled work in sheltered workshops. Requires direction and support for stress.
SEVERE	Poor motor development, minimal speech, self-help training frequently unprofitable. May have physical handicaps.	May talk or learn to care for personal needs.	May contribute to self-support under supervision in working and living.
PROFOUND	Overall functioning is minimal, even in sensory-motor areas. Frequently needs nursing care. Often has secondary physical handicaps.	Some motor development may be present. May be taught basic self-care skills. Needs complete care.	May have minimal speech and motor development. May care for basic needs. Needs nursing care.

. . . to assure all handicapped children have . . . a free appropriate public education which emphasizes special education and related services designed to meet their unique needs . . . . (20 U.S.C. Sec. 1401, 1975).

The major point for psychodiagnosticians to note is that *all* children and youth between the ages of three and twenty-one are entitled to a free public education and related services.

The definition of mental retardation in the act is identical to the AAMD's, but adds the clause, "which adversely affects a child's educational performance." This clause does not appear to make any substantial change in practice, with the exception that a child who demonstrated normal educational performance would presumably not come under the provisions of the act.

Psychosocial Disadvantage and Familial Retardation

A brief discussion of the importance of psychosocial disadvantage and familial retardation may be of great use to the general practitioner. Approximately 90% of all individuals suffering from mental retardation fall into the mildly retarded or educable category (IQ scores between 50 and 70). A very high percentage of this group would be diagnosed as *familial* rather than *organic*. These individuals are relatively normal people in both physical and mental functioning who fall on measures of intellectual and social functioning at the lowest end of normal curves (less than two standard deviations). Despite their lowered functioning, one can identify no organic reason (infection and intoxication, trauma or physical insult, metabolic or nutritional deficiency, gross brain disease, prenatal influence, chromosomal anomalies, or other conditions originating in the perinatal period) as the cause of their retardation. Several psychosocial factors, which may cumulatively account for lowered functioning, are prevalent and one family member is similarly retarded. A quotation from Grossman (1983) may best describe the condition:

> The specific etiology of mental retardation classified as *psychosocial disadvantage* is still somewhat obscure. Unlike many forms of biological defect in which a single causative agent can be identified, this form of retardation appears to involve several sets of interactive factors, none sufficient in themselves to account for the intellectual and behavioral deficits manifested. The involved individuals come from environments that are psychologically, socially, and economically impoverished. Housing and hygiene are poor, nutrition and medical care inadequate, and infectious diseases common. One or more of the parents and other children in the family evidence mentally subaverage performance.

The major point here for the psychologist entails not expecting to find physical anomalies in such cases in order to diagnose mental retardation.

PRE-DIAGNOSTIC STAFFING

Referrals come from a variety of sources, including parents, teachers, welfare and community workers, physicians, etc. Frequently, the parent makes the appointment at the request of one of the other sources. A secretary usually gathers some basic identifying information and a statement of the reason(s) for referral. Afterward, different agencies and professionals follow different paths.

In private practices or agencies where significant efforts are made to collect fees, financial considerations dictate attention to costs. The psychologist in private practice may find that clients and third-party payers will not pay for observations of the child in the classroom, while the school psychologist who visits the child's school weekly may easily do so as part of the regular work schedule. Some private practitioners and clinics mail out pre-appointment questionnaires, which cover birth, health, developmental, and presenting complaint histories. Sometimes, brief historical forms are completed in the waiting room. Occasionally, a short formal instrument such as the Walker Behavior Problem Checklist is routinely administered. In cases where the presenting complaint involved a learning or other school problem, teacher rating forms may be mailed to the home or school. School records, previous evaluation reports, and even the reports of school staffings such as Individual Educational Plans (IEPs) are also requested at this time.

Many professionals, on the other hand, prefer to interview the parents and child first before requesting such information. Both methods have merit and the choice may depend upon situational variables. In a large medical center where the parents and child might have traveled hundreds of miles for an appointment, the prior collection of information may save much time and money. In a small school district, institution, or a circumscribed local practice, the psychologist may find it more expeditious to see the clients first.

Physical

The psychologist needs to be alert to any clues of abnormal physical findings when a diagnosis of mental retardation is suspected. Significant difficulties during the pregnancy and delivery, any injury or condition requiring medical treatment, medications, or simply the parents' or others' perception of some apparent abnormality in sensory or motor development should be noted for exploration later. In cases of positive findings the clinician should ask for a report from the child's physician. Referrals to other disciplines should probably be deferred until one has had a chance to see the child and question the parents. Perfectly adequate evaluations of various problems may have been carried out previously though not yet reported to the psychologist.

Intellectual

Since the child is presumably of at least school age, it becomes very unlikely that the case is a first referral for a question of moderate, severe, or profound retardation. Such children very early exhibit marked failures of normal development, such as failure to talk, and are almost invariably diagnosed as retarded in infancy or at preschool age. Next to the question of retardation itself, perhaps the most frequent reason for these referrals is to determine the correct level as mild or moderate. Such a determination may have great implications for treatment or placement as well as for the child's whole future. The prospects for educable or mildly retarded children offer a relatively normal life, including regular even if unskilled work, marriage, and children. For moderately retarded or trainable youngsters, the prospect is generally for an abnormal, semi-dependent life that does not include regular work, marriage, or children. Even though less frequently encountered, such a diagnostic determination should be approached and carried through with professional care. When doubt exists, one should err on the side of the angels.

If the child's records are accessible, the psychologist should look for previous intellectual scores. Sometimes multiple scores are available and one can construct a simple graph showing changes in IQ scores over time. It is informative to correlate other events in life with such IQ score changes and, hopefully, to draw some worthwhile hypotheses from them. Apparently marked discrepancies in IQ scores can occasionally be explained on the basis of physical illness, interpersonal trauma, or environmental circumstances. In this regard, the usual discounting of group intelligence scores (and achievement measures also) should not hold completely. While low scores can be discounted, high scores deserve greater credibility. The fact that a child could achieve a high level of intellectual functioning even on a group test evidences higher intelligence, despite the well-known shortcomings of group tests for individual assessment.

Emotional

The clinician should also note any descriptions of unusual or significant behavior. Descriptions such as "untestable" or "performing in a totally uninterested fashion" should alert the psychologist to prepare special methods for establishing rapport or motivating the child. Confusing, irrational, and contradictory scores on different tests or battery subtests signal for the diagnostician that some method of resolving the differences must be incorporated in assessment plans.

During the initial referral, parents will often use phrases such as "temper tantrums," "destructive behavior towards toys," "lives in a world of his own," "short attention span," "can't finish anything he starts," "sloppy work," etc. These should indicate to the clinician that some emotional component may be present or, possibly, even predominate.

Educational

The referral phone call may reveal that the request for assessment has been fueled by school difficulties or failure. Although referring personnel may couch the request in terms of a check on learning problems or lack of progress in school, the underlying question may regard mental retardation. The term "learning disabilities" is much more palatable than "retardation" and may also be used by the parent. If the psychologist can obtain school records and test scores, these may document the child's significant failure to perform in school. Note that such test scores (usually group in nature) and grades do not positively prove that the child does not have the intellectual abilities to succeed in school. Grades are notoriously unreliable and group scores may not be valid with the type of child seen in clinics.

Social

At this stage of the assessment, the parents may offer little discussion of social disorder unless behavior problems are as much the reason for a referral as mental retardation. For instance, a mother filling out a pre-appointment questionnaire might reveal an alcoholic husband, but she would more likely withhold such socially sensitive information until a personal interview. Indeed, extremely significant social information such as a suicidal intention is frequently not mentioned until later in the assessment process, perhaps in part because the parents or child have not felt enough trust to reveal such emotional material until then. Also, interviews are more confidential than questionnaires. Referral information from schools appears to offer particularly deficient material on the social functioning of the family. Considerable observations may be presented on how Johnny or Sally get along with classmates, follow directions in class, or play at recess; however, family relations are rarely commented on in school reports. Once again, such information may come to light in the more confidential atmosphere of a teacher interview. The clinician should note the socioeconomic status of the family, neighborhood, and school. The occupations and residence of the family usually offer gross clues, but these need to be checked later with observed language, behavior, and corroborating information given by the parents themselves. The placement of a family in a certain class may not prove nearly as significant as the discovery of a mismatch. For example, one of the most difficult situations to remediate is that of a child with normal but very low average intellect, i.e., borderline or dull normal, in an upwardly striving, achievement-oriented, middle-class family, who lives in a well-off suburb where the typical child falls into the bright normal range in intellectual ability and academic achievement. Such a child looks retarded in the school setting.

ADMINISTRATION OF TESTS AND PROCEDURES

Physical

Since a certain percentage of children suspected of mental retardation will suffer from physical handicaps, the examiner must plan to minimize their impact. If remedial appliances such as glasses or hearing aids are prescribed for the child, they should be worn during the assessment. Children with crippling orthopedic problems may warrant special seating arrangements. Consultation with occupational therapists or physical therapists would be desirable in such situations. One should give careful attention to physical factors such as fatigue in children with chronic illnesses or under medication. A request to the family physician for the cessation of medication during testing is appropriate and necessary in many cases where it is known the drugs interfere with mental and emotional functioning. Some perceptual motor tests such as the Bender Visual Motor Gestalt Test or the Benton Revised Visual Retention Test are recommended, but not as indicators of brain damage; although ordinarily touted as such years ago, these perceptual motor or copying tests have not shown sufficient validity for use in this way. They are, on the other hand, good indicators of the developmental maturity level of fine motor or eye-hand coordination. Some tests of the draw-a-person variety have very good reliability and validity as nonverbal intelligence measures. Also, if performance is markedly defective or bizarre and other clinical signs emerge that lead one to suspect brain damage, this may stimulate a referral to a neurologist or neuropsychologist.

Intellectual

A good standardized intelligence test comprises one essential part of any assessment for mental retardation. The Wechsler Preschool and Primary Scale of Intelligence (WPPSI), the Wechsler Intelligence Scale for Children-Revised (WISC-R), and the Wechsler Adult Intelligence Scale-Revised (WAIS-R) afford the best instruments at present, although the Kaufman Assessment Battery for Children (K-ABC) is rapidly carving a niche for itself. Each of these is a battery of many tests, and they offer the one great advantage of allowing separate measures of verbal and nonverbal functioning. Furthermore, cautious and conservative interpretation of subtest performances may provide many valuable insights or support for hypotheses concerning details of intellectual functioning. Alan Kaufman's text, *Intelligent Testing with the WISC-R* (1979), depicts general approaches, do's and don'ts, formulae, and illustrations that virtually blueprint the way to interpret such profiles. The importance of getting a valid test performance cannot be emphasized too much. When feeling for any reason that such has not been achieved, the examiner must declare the results spoiled and administer another test at another time.

Emotional

Careful interviewing of the parents and child should attempt to establish a relatively factual picture of the important emotional characteristics of both child and family. One should take care to avoid an uncritical acceptance of vague phrases like "aggressive behavior," which could mean anything from impetuous uttering of verbal complaints to bashing the head of an unsuspecting playmate. The circumstances that stimulated such behavior should be delineated as well as the consequences to the child—especially the response of the parents. The first advice to the interviewer is to suspend any disbelief or criticism of the parent's or child's storytelling. Secondly, one should project empathetic acceptance of the teller's version of events. Virtually all individuals are loath to reveal sensitive personal stories to strange individuals. They usually offer some small snippet of the whole story and observe the listener for signs of a sympathetic reception. The listener who lapses in this respect may never hear the remaining details of a critical incident, perhaps more essential to understanding the person than all the test scores.

The Personality Inventory for Children (PIC) provides a battery of reliable personality scores that have sufficient validity to encourage their use in individual assessment. Constructed in the tradition of the Minnesota Multiphasic Personality Inventory (MMPI), the PIC battery provides a similar profile of the child on a variety of scales, i.e., family relations, somatic concern, depression, delinquency, anxiety, psychosis, hyperactivity, and withdrawal. Caution regarding the validity of parental perception of the problem is necessary since parents complete the test, not the child. Fortunately, the battery does have MMPI-like validity scales (i.e., Lie-Scale, F-Scale), which give measures of the parents' tendencies to give socially acceptable or distorted views of the child. This has the extra advantage of providing an abbreviated but nevertheless objective standardized assessment of the parents. The PIC's other advantages are that it can be scored and graphed quickly by a secretary and interpreted very rapidly by a psychologist when the results are uncomplicated.

The Family Relations Test, on the other hand, gives the child's perception of relationships with the family. Responses show the positive and negative feelings the child experiences both toward and from family members. Although some very limited normative data are available in research studies (Kaufman, Weaver, & Weaver, 1971) it is best to consider this a structured interview of the child. With surprising frequency, this test generates interesting hypotheses that are later confirmed. The doll-play nature of the task seems to involve elementary-grade school children to the extent that they often reveal much more than they would in direct questioning. For example, intense sibling rivalry is common with children who have significant reading disabilities.

Brief behavioral observation of the parents and child engaged in a task has proven a remarkably rich source of information for emotional interactions as well as the parent's child-raising styles. Several versions of these procedures exist, most of which are available in the public literature. Some manuals of these procedures are also available (see Mira & Cairns, 1979; Green, Forehand, & McMahon, 1979). Those most frequently used focus on the child's compliance to parental requests for cooperative play with a toy or other materials. The parent's typical responses (directions, requests, questions, commands, etc.) are counted along with the child's cooperative efforts or noncompliance. Since the parents are well aware they are being evaluated, unusually negative parental behavior takes on special credibility and significance. Also, a child who demonstrates very high noncompliance can usually be safely described as oppositional. Reliability is usually acceptable and the results enjoy a clear face validity.

A variation of these observational procedures is the kinetic family drawing task, in which the entire family is asked to draw the family engaged in some activity. Still another version asks the family members to play at performing some regular family activity such as setting the table. Generally, no objective data are recorded but the clinician observes and notes recurrent or striking patterns of behavior. The father, for example, may remain a nonparticipant or two of the children may vie strenuously for attention and a preponderance of parental approval. Doll play and a diagnostic play therapy session are unstructured observational techniques that the examiner may wish to implement as well.

Unfortunately, time and cost considerations usually force the practitioner to choose only one or two of the previously described procedures. Generally, parent and child interviewing should take precedence over the others. One can almost always employ the Personality Inventory for Children since it takes very little professional time. The choice of one of the other tests or procedures must be dictated by the nature of the problems and other idiosyncratic case considerations. For example, despite the sizable time required, the instances in which the Rorschach Psychodiagnostic Test or the Children's Apperception Test might be fruitfully employed are those cases where one suspects obsessive preoccupations, recurring depressive themes (i.e., death or suicide), and thought disorder.

The use of projective tests is not recommended in general. Although they may prove worth the time when used by a well-trained and quite experienced practitioner, very few psychologists can claim such qualifications honestly. Research has overall not supported the claims for the reliability and validitiy of projective tests. It may be true as the advocates of projectives assert that this is due to psychology departments assigning new faculty members of lowest rank and least experience to teach projective testing. Or, possibly the interpretation of the Rorschach, Thematic Apperception Test (TAT), and Children's Apperception Test (CAT) consists more of an art than a science and not enough psychologists are artists of that genre. Regardless of the reason, the use of such tests by general practitioners with little training and supervised experience cannot be recommended.

One valuable source of data on personality style and emotional behavior frequently and inappropriately given short shrift concerns the emotional and stylistic behavior demonstrated by the parents and child during other aspects of the assessment. Excellent checklists of such behavior are given in Sattler (1982) and the astute clinician should make notes when a particular trait or response pattern becomes clear. For example, the Wechsler Scales all require an examinee to face frustration and failure, since the only way to terminate most subtests is by failing a set number of consecutive items. Anxiety, dependency, and poor self-esteem are often demonstrated clearly on those tests. The tasks on intellectual tests also elicit tendencies toward impulsiveness, avoidant behavior, and manipulativeness. A penetrating description on the use of intellectual tests to observe emotional behavior can be found in Blatt & Allison (1968).

Educational

Some information on real-world achievement should comprise part of the assessment. School records, teacher reports and ratings, grades, achievement test scores, and even reports of psychological evaluations in the schools are usually available upon request and parental release. Sometimes, such records cover many years and one can graph the rate of progress. One can sometimes correlate marked changes, such as an unusual spurt ahead or a flattening out, with significant events such as a major illness or family disruption. At times, the referral question may be quite delimited (e.g., is Johnny retarded?), and educational achievement tests may be required for such a diagnosis if PL 94-142 is in effect. Since education entails an important part of a child's life, it behooves the clinician at least to survey the educational information to see that nothing widely discrepant with the diagnosis is present. In many cases where the school has already collected adequate scores, formal achievement testing may not be required. The clinician however may still wish to administer an individualized educational measure, and the Wide Range Achievement Test (WRAT) and the Peabody Individual Achievement Test (PIAT) are two commonly used instruments. The relative ease of administration may provide one of the reasons for their popularity. Few psychologists outside of the schools are trained in educational diagnosis. The general psychologist's educational assessment might be thought of as a cross between a screening and a very basic educational evaluation. If findings indicate significant educational deficits or any discrepancies from the other data on the child, the clinician should make a referral to an educational diagnostician.

Some tests having commendable technical standards are the Woodcock-Johnson Psycho-Educational Battery, Achievement Section; the Woodcock Reading Mastery Tests; and the achievement section of the Kaufman Assessment Battery for Children (K-ABC). These tests should attract the psychologist relatively untutored in educational diagnostics, since the excellence of their standardization renders them capable of mastery by the examiner trained in psycholgical testing.

Social

In this area one should first attempt to develop a general picture of the child's social life. Naturally, family life is of paramount importance and its major characteristics should be developed first. Perhaps the most efficient way to assess this involves the study of pertinent questionnaires and by parent (or family) interviews. One can often grossly and most rapidly delineate the members of the family, their ages, roles, and emotional relationships by clinical interviewing. If the questionnaires cover brief histories of birth, health, development, and presenting problems, a quick perusal of those data may reveal unusual or significant information, even omissions, that raise questions worth exploring in more detail during an interview. The examiner should seek information on social functioning in the neighborhood and school. Teacher reports and/or ratings are often available and sometimes present a different picture than that reported by the parents.

A test of adaptive behavior is essential for a diagnosis of mental retardation in order to meet the standard AAMD and DSM-III definitions. With an institutionalized individual, the AAMD Adaptive Behavior Scales (ABS) probably offers the best choice since it was standardized on an institutionalized population. The AAMD Adaptive Behavior Scale, School Edition (ABS-SE) is another version normed on a public school population in California. Questionable validity has been found for distinguishing the slow learners from the mildly retarded group, and since this covers exactly the diagnostic question for which the overwhelming number of evaluations are necessary, it limits the usefulness of this instrument. The Adaptive Behavior Inventory for Children (ABIC) is part of the System of Multicultural Pluralistic Assessment (SOMPA), which was originally devised as a response to the difficulties of obtaining an adequate social assessment of minority children. Unfortunately, the technical qualities of the scale have not proven sufficient to recommend its nationwide usage.

The Vineland Social Maturity Scale is dated and suffers from similar problems of technical inadequacy by today's standards. Fortunately, a completely new revision called the Vineland Adaptive Behavior Scales will be available in 1984. Standardization on a representative national sample, and apparently adequate reliability, offer the promise of a technically adequate measure of social functioning. If the validity data come up to the normative standards employed, this test will probably become the instrument of choice. An interesting advantage also includes direct comparability with scores on the K-ABC, a measure of cognitive ability. Overlaps between the normative samples for these two instruments provide the basis of this comparability.

At times the denial of mentally retarded functioning by one parent can be offset by a more accurate perception by the other. If such a situation seems to arise, the more perceptive parent can be asked to fill out the PIC or to act as the informant for the Vineland. The incongruity of the parental reports may then be used to persuade the denying parent to suspend automatic rejection of the possibility of retardation.

INTERPRETATION AND INTEGRATION OF FINDINGS

Physical

If any positive findings of a physical nature have arisen in the assessment process, the psychologist usually refers to a professional competent in the area in question. One should first, of course, have checked with the parents and the records to determine whether the physical problem noted has already been handled adequately. Occasionally, new data warrant asking the previously involved professional to review the case. Suggestions of neurological impairment indicate a referral to a neurologist. Difficulties in speech and language are relatively frequent in questions of mental retardation and may cloud the diagnosis; the opinion of a speech pathologist is thus necessary. Similarly, suggestions of a hearing loss, such as misinterpretations of words and questions on the intellectual tasks, should lead to an audiological referral. One may have to defer a diagnostic statement until the findings of such professionals can be integrated.

The diagnostic dilemma involved in cases of sensory or motor impairment concerns whether the "second" impairment is primary. For example, a pre-existing hearing impairment may result in such reduced learning opportunities that the child earns scores on measures of intelligence that fall into the retarded category. In such a case, the primary handicap is audiological and that diagnosis would take precedence. Similarly, positive findings from neurologists and speech pathologists indicating the presence of a neurological or speech disorder would require that their physical diagnoses assume the position of "primary disorder."

The major findings of a physical nature that a psychologist is apt to uncover might best be called delays of development in sensory-motor functioning. Whether the clinician should think of these as "physical" depends on whether one wishes to place findings concerning lags in physical development under that rubric. Psychologists do note from time to time a marked difference in the level of functioning between perceptual motor or performance test scores and scores on verbal tests. These differences may be first noted in markedly low scores on some visual motor test such as the Draw-A-Person test and reinforced by significantly poorer scores on the Performance IQ scale on the Wechsler. Provided one uses appropriate statistical significance levels, brain damage can be suspected from such evidence; however, the term "delay in development" is more appropriate for the psychologist to use until a neurologist has confirmed through examination and medical data the presence of brain damage.

Intellectual

The decision the psychologist has to make in the intellectual area regards whether or not the IQ score accurately portrays the general intellectual functioning of the individual. The preeminence of the IQ score is determined by its specification in the officially adopted definitions of mental retardation. If all the other observations, histories, and data confirm that score, the psychologist can do little except classify the intellectual functioning of the individual in question within the level of retardation indicated. On the other hand, if the psychologist prefers to discard the test performance or to support another level of intellectual retardation, that choice must be supported by countervailing facts and argument sufficient to justify overriding the IQ score.

Reasons exist for not accepting the overall IQ score as the definitive determinant of an individual's intellectual classification. The psychologist may have repeatedly observed blatant rejection or refusal to attempt items in the test, so that the resulting score can be definitely labeled as an under-representation of the individual's abilities. Sometimes a pattern is observed that suggests higher capabilities, although they are not displayed consistently enough during testing for the child's performance to meet scoring standards. Extremely high scores on some subtests may be balanced with virtual zeros on others, rendering the overall score a meaningless average. Bizarre associations or marked disruption of thought process may signal mental illnesses such as psychosis or brain damage. Sensory or motor handicaps may render standard IQ scores meaningless, i.e., one could not expect a deaf person to score very highly on a verbally administered test. Many of the other chapters in this book explicitly deal with the necessity for bypassing conventional IQ scores and standardized administration procedures in order to obtain a more accurate understanding of intelligence in such individuals.

Kaufman (1979) has written a text on interpreting intelligence scores on the WISC-R that devotes a sizable amount of space to advocating a strategy that tries to "declare the Full Scale IQ ineffectual as an explanation of the child's mental functioning." Highly significant differences between the Verbal and Performance IQ scores would be one of the first signals that the overall IQ score was not an accurate representation of the individual's mental functioning. Kaufman lists several possible reasons for such a differential in verbal and performance functioning, i.e., different verbal and performance intelligence; fluid versus crystallized intelligence; psycholinguistic deficiency; bilingualism; Black dialect; motor coordination deficit; time pressure (implicating anxiety and impulsivity); and socioeconomic influences.

The psychologist must realize from this discussion that it is possible to discount a specific IQ score; however, one must marshall sufficient facts to support a cogent argument for taking such a stand. The discounting of the IQ score may lead to diagnoses other than mental retardation.

Emotional

Sensitive interviewing and observation of the emotional behavior of parents and child should serve as the touchstone against which other sources of information are checked. One should, however, be aware of the situational specificity of many behaviors. The child who seems quiet and shy during the first hour of evaluation in the clinic may present a whirlwind of motion on the playground. The changes in emotional responses to the evaluation over time (i.e., from a tense, guarded, minimally verbal style to a more relaxed, friendly, talkative pattern) should tell the psychologist much.

To balance the subjective observations, one should attach considerable weight to the objective data collected on such measures as the Personality Inventory for Children (PIC) and rating scales from teachers. When statistically significant results are noted, the clinician should make every effort to understand their meaning in the overall picture. Hopefully, they may simply corroborate hypotheses already formed on less scientific observations. While some disparate results can be tolerated, the goal is a coherent description of the child and the child's world that integrates the information from many sources. The parents may perceive their child as a "normal" youngster when all the test data and everyone else's evaluation shows functioning at a significantly below normal level. Such an apparent disparity can be explained if one has also observed the parents excusing every sub-par performance of the child and demonstrating angry, hostile, and defensive emotions to the mildest suggestions that the poor performances may indicate relatively lowered capabilities. Such a parental response would not invalidate a diagnostic determination of the child carefully constructed from all the other data sources; it would indicate the need for sensitive interpretation of the findings and the necessity for planning to take into account the parents' possible rejection of the results.

The interpretation of data obtained during the observation of structured parent-child tasks is generally straightforward. A total lack of praise or nonverbal approvals speaks for itself. Similarly, an overwhelming preponderance of commands, directions, criticisms, corrections, and disparaging remarks points toward an interpersonal climate between parent and child that can only have deleterious effects on the child's personality and self-esteem.

A more difficult interpretation may arise when the child is already so sensitized to parental disapproval that even the slightest sign of disapproval will trigger an instant decrement in performance. An obvious example of this process occurred once with an apparently intelligent child who was failing in school. During the assessment, he appeared to be looking in vain to his mother for approval of his quite successful efforts on the WISC; she sat in the corner of the examining room staring at the ceiling. The examiner finally asked her to present the Block Designs cards to him again. The boy had already performed the task at the bright normal level with the examiner. The mother flipped up the first card and immediately resumed her stare at the ceiling. The child correctly put the blocks together in a few seconds and proudly called her attention to the result. After a startled glance at the blocks, she said, "You cheated!" in an angry tone. The exact sequence was repeated on the second card with the same accusatory response by the mother. The child's face fell into despair and his body slumped in dejection. He finished the task, but this time earned a score that fell into the borderline retardation range. Needless to say, the major interpretation of this evaluation focused upon the impact of the parental rejection and denigration on the child's self-esteem and motivation to achieve.

Educational

In a case involving mental retardation, the most important determination a general psychologist may be called upon to make in the educational sphere involves whether the child's academic functioning has been adversely affected. This can be ascertained by studying the school's records of grades and achievement tests as well as by administering individualized achievement tests. Common sense interpretations of the data will prevail in virtually all cases. Individualized achievement test scores significantly below those of the child's age-mates demonstrate the adverse effect. Psychologists not trained in educational diagnosis should take care to base their conclusions in this area on well standardized and normed tests.

Social

Interpretation of the adaptive behavior scale findings requires knowledge of test weaknesses, sensitivity to possible distortions in the reporting of the informant, and cautious clinical judgment. The adaptive behavior scales currently available all require a trained interviewer for a good reason: the scoring of the items demands a judgment on the interviewer's part. Furthermore, the interviewer may note certain types of answers that will influence the later interpretation. For example, a mother interviewed on the Vineland may repeatedly state that she cannot answer a question because her child never has to carry out the activity. She may argue that she is sure he *could* use a knife to cut meat but she always cuts it for him. Aside from the fact that the interviewer is expected to be knowledgeable enough to score such answers as "no opportunity" rather than "pass," the interpreter should pick up on the pattern of overprotection and its probably deleterious effects on training the child toward self-care and independence. Such clinical judgment might also influence a psychologist to interpret an overall low score as reflecting a lack of proper training rather than some inherent mental defect, and make recommendations (e.g., parent training) aimed at remediating that problem.

A problem sometimes arises when a psychologist in private practice or in an agency other than the schools is asked for a "second opinion" regarding a child's classification as mentally retarded. The psychologist may administer an adaptive behavior scale with the mother as informant and conclude the child is not retarded socially and should not be classified overall as mentally retarded. The school authorities may then claim that the parents' information given in the adaptive behavior interview was distorted (i.e., reflecting their tendency to deny retarded behavior in their child). In such a case, it would behoove the psychologist to check on the validity of the parental reports. If possible, one should secure ratings or even anecdotal reports from other persons (e.g., teachers, babysitters).

COMMUNICATION OF RESULTS

Physical

Virtually all findings of a physical nature secured by a psychologist either reflect delays in perceptual motor development or fall into the neuropsychological sphere. One should avoid the use of terms such as "brain damage" or "organic impairment" with parents or non-medical personnel in psychological reports. Parents themselves are frequently quick to note physical clumsiness. Some accept it easily and do not worry about it; others may seize upon any physical label as the only cause of lowered functioning. In the 1970s, the phrases "visual motor deficits," "perceptual motor handicaps," etc., were faddishly used by parents and professionals alike to explain lowered functioning, especially in the area of learning disabilities. In the area of mental retardation, the psychologist must be careful not to diagnose such developmental lags without taking the level of overall mental functioning into account. One would expect a mentally retarded youth to function on visual motor tasks at a much lower level than chronological age-mates.

Intellectual

Reporting intelligence test results and a classification of mental retardation present two of the psychologist's major and most difficult communication tasks. The specification of intelligence tests and adaptive behavior determinations in the accepted definitions of mental retardation have determined this central role. In cases of profound, severe, and moderate retardation, the diagnosis has usually been done at infant and preschool ages, frequently by physicians. Mild mental retardation offers one of the most difficult interpretations to parents when they hear it for the first time. The child usually has no obvious physical defects. Although parents may have observed the child as "slow" to develop, they may have rationalized the "backwardness" in various ways and expect the child to "grow out of it." Several strategies may assist in the delivery of such difficult information.

One strategy involves asking the parents at what age they think their child now functions. A surprising number of them will place the level fairly accurately with such phrases as "at about the 3-year level," or "about like his younger brother who is four." One can then contrast this with the chronological age, point out the gap, and explain that such a gap is what defines mild mental retardation.

Using another strategy, the clinician summarizes or highlights specific items or areas of functioning in adaptive behavior, emphasizing that the parents reported that the child did not do this or that. One can even compliment the parents on the astuteness of their observations regarding their details of the child's behavior. The gap between what a child normally does socially at a certain age and what their child is doing can be demonstrated and mild mental retardation explained in terms of failure to perform these behaviors. At this point, the reporting of social or adaptive behavior and intellectual functioning overlap. The parents' main interest in intellectual functioning usually regards whether or not it classifies their child as mentally retarded. Of necessity, adaptive behavior must enter such a discussion.

In another strategy the psychologist asks the parents to describe their understanding of mental retardation. Frequently, they hold a picture that corresponds to the moderately, severely, and profoundly retarded. An immediate correction of that misapprehension is in order, together with a brief explanation of mild retardation. One should tell the parents that mildly retarded youngsters generally live at home, go to public schools, enjoy the normal activities of all children, learn to read and write, get jobs, marry, and have children; they simply do not learn academically as well as most children and similarly their general social development lags.

The general rule provides that the psychologist has a professional obligation to report the reality of the findings. One should carry out this reporting, however, with sensitivity to feelings and in language understandable to a lay person. Omission of the word "retardation" is *not* acceptable. The euphemism "slow" is inaccurate as well as enabling parents to believe almost anything they want.

With minority and/or bilingual children, the clinician has a special obligation to make sure that one has taken all the discriminatory conditions into account. The issue of whether or not the apparent social retardation is real, and not an artifact of reporting procedures, is well worth exploring with the parents during the interpretation.

Finally, the psychologist should always stay aware of the probabilistic nature of test results and communicate this. One should describe children whose scores fall close to the dividing lines between classifications as *either* at the top of one classification *or* at the bottom of another.

Emotional

Interpretations of emotional disorder in a child evoke emotional responses in parents. Many times the responses are positive, signifying relief and acceptance. The parents may have struggled with the problem for years without any understanding and they are relieved to obtain an "answer." More frequently, their reaction is negative and rejecting. Even with a positive reaction, the chances are not high of the parent obtaining appropriate treatment at an affordable price. The costs of individual psychotherapy, let alone any private institutional care, lie well beyond the budgets of average people. The psychologist should become knowledgeable about available mental health resources and continue to advise the family until they find a treatment program. This may entail many calls to social agencies as well as continuing interpretations to the family. Such a "follow-up" will also reveal those families who, handling an unwelcome diagnosis by passive avoidance, simply fail ever to make the arrangements for family counseling or psychotherapy, even when the psychologist directs them to a nearby, very low cost mental health center.

One strategy that may render the diagnosis of emotional disorder more acceptable to parents is to present in some detail the results of parent ratings in tests such as the Personality Inventory for Children. The emphasis here focuses on how cleverly the parent has noted the aberrant behavior of the child. Parents find it difficult to defend against their own observations and frequently will acquiesce to sensitively worded summaries of their test responses.

In another strategy the clinician presents the observational data gathered during structured parent-child tasks. Once again, parents find it difficult to deny or rationalize away a record of their own behavior that documents, for example, 100 directive, negative, or controlling verbalizations, and no examples of praise or approval during a twenty-minute play period with their child.

Using a third strategy, the clinician documents the child's perception of interpersonal relationships by some means (e.g., a videotape-recorded interview or the Family Relations Test results) and emphasizes that the child's view of emotional relationships is the child's reality, even if it does not represent the "way things really are." For example, the child may have described almost no emotional relationship at all with the father—who coincidentally has worked at an out-of-town job for many years.

Finally, another way to handle developing parental resistance to a finding of emotional disturbance is to ask for a psychiatric consultation, in the hopes that the psychiatrist's findings will buttress those of the psychologist and dispel the family's doubts.

Educational

The findings from individualized educational achievement tests are usually reported in terms of grade, age, and standard scores, as well as percentile ranks. Teachers, parents, and administrators find grade equivalents and percentile ranks most easy to understand. Psychologists ought to be aware of the probable error involved in group administered tests since it may be quite large and extend over more than two grade levels. One interpretation that the psychologist may need to communicate involves the interaction between the lowered level of mental functioning and the child's discouragement and lack of motivation to achieve. After continual failure in academic tasks such as reading, the child may understandably have developed patterns of avoidance and/or lack of effort. One should instruct the parents and teachers to praise and reward generously every effort the child makes on educational matters. The development of positive habits of approach to and persistance on educational tasks will have a great payoff in later life when such personality habits will probably act as the major determinant of success.

Social

Social findings are sometimes difficult to separate from emotional ones. Although one may seem to focus more on individual feelings and the other on interpersonal or environmental relationships, in practice the two often intertwine. Nevertheless, a particular facet of social and community life may stand out as a factor in the presenting problems. For example, the presence of diametrically opposed child-rearing practices in the mother and father indicate a conflict that can only confuse a child and promote behavior problems.

Careful study of answers on the adaptive behavior scale or responses during parent-child observations may reveal patterns of overprotection or overindulgence that can form a focus for discussion in the interpretation conference with the parents. A useful strategy throughout these conferences raises a significant or anomalous finding and asks the parents to help the professionals integrate it into their understanding of the child. The psychologist can employ this same device with other "social" findings as well, such as certain scores of withdrawal, delinquency, and family relations on the Personality Inventory for Children.

REFERENCES

American Psychiatric Association. (1980). *Diagnostic and statistical manual of mental disorders* (3rd ed.). Washington, DC: Author.

Blatt, S.J., & Allison, J. (1968). The intelligence test in personality assessment. In A.I. Rabin (Ed.), *Projective techniques in personality assessment.* (pp. 421-460). New York: Springer.

Green, K.D., Forehand, R., & McMahon, R.J. (1979). Parental manipulation of compliance and noncompliance in normal and deviant children. *Behavior Modification, 3,* 245-266.

Grossman, J.H. (Ed.). (1983). *Classification in mental retardation.* Washington, DC: American Association on Mental Deficiency.

Kaufman, A.S. (1979). *Intelligent testing with the WISC-R.* New York: Wiley-Interscience.

Kaufman, J.M., Weaver, S.J., & Weaver, A. (1972). Family Relations Test responses of retarded readers. *Journal of Personality Assessment, 36,* 353-360.

Mira, M., & Cairns, G. (1979). *Handbook of positive parenting.* Shawnee Mission, KS: Child Behavior and Development Consultants.

Robinson, N., & Robinson, H.B. (1976). *The mentally retarded child: A psychological approach* (2nd ed.). New York: McGraw-Hill.

Sattler, J.M. (1982). *Assessment of children's intelligence and special abilities* (2nd ed.). Boston: Allyn & Bacon, Inc.

6

Considerations in the Assessment of Children with Autism

J. GREGORY OLLEY, PH.D., LEE M. MARCUS, PH.D.

Autistic children and youth often present a difficult challenge to psychologists, educators and others who wish to obtain a practical and valid assessment. There is often confusion about which children should be classified autistic and what the accepted features are of the disorder. Further, the usual approaches to testing may yield little useful information about the child for teachers or parents.

Despite this history of misconceptions and the perception of these children as "untestable," useful assessment of children with autism can be readily obtained through a broad scope of testing strategies and thorough knowledge of the nature of autism.

First, although autism has only been recognized as a childhood disorder for a little over 40 years, views toward the nature of autism have changed during that time. Some of the past problems in assessment have been a result of out-of-date notions about the problem. Autism is no longer seen as an emotional disorder caused by cold or insensitive parents, but rather is currently viewed as a set of behavioral characteristics that may be caused by any of several (often unknown) biological factors.

In addition, autism can coexist with other disorders. It is accompanied in about 80% of cases by mental retardation. Thus, autistic children are no longer seen as potentially bright children who need simply to "break out of their shell"—they are children with severe cognitive limitations that result in problems with language and social relationships, and the disorder is almost always lifelong (Rutter, 1983).

DEFINITION

Part of the recent change in the definition of autism has served to broaden the category. Rather than the narrowly defined and very rare group described by Kanner in 1943, current definitions acknowledge the overlap with other groups and claim a higher incidence, ranging from 4 or 5 births per 10,000 for autism (National Society for Autistic Children, 1978) to 21 per 10,000 for related "impairments of social interaction" (Wing & Gould, 1979). Changes in points of view toward autism have been described in detail by Schopler (1983).

The definition of autism endorsed by The National Society for Children and Adults with Autism (National Society for Autistic Children, 1978) has four essential features "typically manifested prior to 30 months of age." They are "disturbances of (1) developmental rates and/or sequences, (2) responses to sensory stimuli, (3) speech, language, and cognitive capacities, and (4) capacities to relate to people, events, and objects" (p. 162). Associated features, such as "stereotypic and repetitive movements," may also be present.

Although autism shares some traits with other childhood disorders (e.g., childhood schizophrenia, sensory impairments, learning disabilities) and can coexist with some of them (most notably mental retardation and seizure disorders), it does have a recognizable pattern of characteristics. In the following sections of this chapter, practical considerations in the assessment of children who may have the characteristics of autism are discussed. These considerations begin with the prediagnostic staffing and continue through the formal testing, observation in natural settings, and the application of the resulting findings.

PREDIAGNOSTIC STAFFING

Prior to the formal and direct testing phase of assessment, it is useful to gather information in several areas. The child's parents may be the most helpful source of information at this time. In the Treatment and Education of Autism and related Communication Handicapped Children (TEACCH) program at the University of North Carolina, we ask parents to complete a history form and respond to seven open-ended questions. The completed history form provides standard demographic information, a chronology of developmental and medical factors, a checklist of possible autism symptoms, and information concerning any problems in the extended family.

The questionnaire asks:

1. Describe a typical day with your child.
2. What are your main problems and concerns about your child at this time?
3. What is most distressing to you about your child?
4. What is most gratifying to you about your child?
5. What effect has this child had on other aspects of your life? (Marriage, family relations, social relations, work, etc.)
6. With what aspects of your relationship with your child do you want help? What kind of help?
7. What do you expect from your participation in this program?

Parents are also asked to estimate their child's level of functioning and to express their ideas about what the future will be like for them and the child. This information not only helps the staff gain a preliminary understanding of the parents' experience and concerns, but also introduces the family to the practical, collaborative approach of the program (Schopler & Olley, 1982).

The clinician must also carefully examine reports of earlier assessment and treatment. In addition to the usual information about tests and scores, it is informative to find out how the problem has been described by others. In some instances, the problem is labeled autism; in others, the characteristics of autism are described but given another label. Whatever the case, it is important to know what the parents were told about their child. This information and the parents' self-report are useful to keep in mind during the assessment. The success of any assessment or treatment effort will depend to a great extent upon parental interest and involvement, so it is essential to gauge the information and attitudes that parents already have.

Two very practical pieces of information that the clinician can obtain prior to the formal assessment are the child's preferred way of communicating as well as likes and dislikes. About half of autistic children are mute, and the others have varying verbal abilities with nevertheless serious communication problems. A little preliminary information about how best to communicate with the child may make a crucial difference in the assessment. Information on likes and dislikes proves valuable for managing behavior during testing. Implementing rewards, high interest activities, or breaks from work are not common in testing most children, but for the autistic child such approaches can avoid disruptive behavior and yield profitable information for future teaching programs.

When examining records and parent reports, noticing the themes that frequently appear can be useful in preparing to see the child. Themes often noted or noted by several sources may offer clues to proper classification or present good indicators of the child's strengths or weaknesses, leading to preliminary hypotheses to be confirmed or denied later in the assessment.

ADMINISTRATION OF TESTS AND PROCEDURES

Assessment of autistic children is usually intended to help answer the following questions:

1. Does this child have the characteristics associated with autism? (classification)
2. What is the best educational placement for this child? (placement)
3. What should be the focus of this child's individualized education program? (treatment)
4. What programs should be carried out at home and in other community settings? (generalization)

The answers to these questions should come from several sources. Prior assessments, reports of earlier programs, and parent reports are significant, as previously mentioned. Formal testing is another important means of assessment, but when testing autistic children the clinician must observe certain cautions and limitations. For instance, like other severely handicapped children, those with autism generalize their skills very poorly. In addition, their best performance may be demonstrated in their familiar routine, and a change in this routine may lead to disruptive behavior and poor performance.

For these reasons, testing procedures usually applied to other children may be unsuccessful and misleading with autistic children. Reactions to an unfamiliar examiner, a strange location, and new demands are not likely to represent the child's best performance; therefore, some special considerations in choice of tests, method of administration, and confirmation of findings in other settings are necessary. In addition to test data, the clinician needs to assimilate information both from parent interviews and by observation of the child in other settings in order to gain a complete picture of the child's abilities.

Characteristics of Tests for Autistic Children

Most standardized tests have very rigid rules for administration or require certain prerequisite skills, making them inappropriate for use with autistic children. For instance, most tests involve verbal instructions and verbal replies, but language may represent the area of greatest handicap for this group. In addition, examiners may overestimate the autistic child's developmental level and thus administer a test beyond the child's abilities, resulting in behavior problems and unsuccessful performance. An appropriate test requires minimal verbal skills.

Flexibility in administration is an asset in a test for autistic children. It should be possible to give instructions in a variety of ways and to alter the administration to accommodate the individual child. Repeating instructions in a different way or prompting a response violates the rules of administration for most tests, but such steps can actually yield very useful information. If a child cannot complete a task with standard instructions but can with a demonstration or a gestural prompt, it is more useful to know that than simply to know that the item was failed. Variations in administration such as repeating an item, changing the sequence of items, or taking frequent breaks will usually produce better performance and less disruption or distractability. It will also, of course, invalidate the score for many tests, but the score is not necessarily the main purpose of assessment. A flexibly administered test gives information about what the child can and cannot do under certain circumstances, and that helps more in planning a program than a standardized score does.

Finally, a test for autistic children must be reinforcing for the child. The clinician learns little if the test does not hold the child's fleeting interest. This goal can be accomplished by choosing tests of interest to the child or by introducing reinforcing consequences into the test administration. An example of a test that holds the interest of many autistic children is the Merrill Palmer Scale (Stutsman, 1931). This test, of course, was not designed for children with autism, but it has few verbal demands, can be administered flexibly, and consists of primarily manipulative tasks that are interesting to many autistic children.

If the test materials and activities do not interest the child, it may be necessary to introduce reinforcing consequences for completing tasks. These may include food, favorite activities, praise, or just the chance to take a break. If the child responds well to any of these consequences or if a routine of work-then-break can be quickly established, this information is very useful for later teaching.

In short, many autistic children have been considered "untestable" in the past because they could not complete a test under the usual, rigid demands of testing and because the tests given were too advanced developmentally. If appropriate tests are chosen and good behavioral strategies carried out during the administration, useful information can be gained about all autistic children.

Classification of Autistic Children

The question of whether a child should have the classification of autism is a central issue in most assessments. This question is often asked for research or administrative reasons. Parents also often wish to have a clear answer in light of confusing and contradictory diagnoses that they may have received earlier. Although a legitimate question, one should not assume that the answer will have a large impact on individual treatment decisions. The classification of autism does aid planning in some general ways. It makes the nature of the child's cognitive deficit clearer than would be the case if the diagnosis were mental retardation only (Rutter, 1983), indicates that the child will need structure for optimal learning, and points out the need for lifelong planning. One specific step that can be taken on the basis of the classification alone is to direct the parents to the resources of The National Society for Children and Adults with Autism.

As the clinician gains more information about an individual child, further specific decisions can be made. Autistic children's needs are very heterogeneous. Thus, knowing that a child has this disorder does not tell us whether the child should be in a certain class or receive a certain type of treatment.

Several objective scales are now available for answering the diagnostic or classification question. These approaches have been reviewed in detail recently by Parks (1983). The method used in the TEACCH program is the Childhood Autism Rating Scale (Schopler, Reichler, DeVellis, & Daly, 1980), a reliable observational scale based upon observations during the formal assessment of the child.

Because the available psychological and developmental tests were not well suited for young children with autism, Schopler and Reichler (1979) developed the Psychoeducational Profile (PEP). Its format includes some important emphases that yield useful information about autism. The PEP does not emphasize verbal skills, and its administration is flexible in many ways. The choice of items allows observation of developmental skills appropriate for young children as well as pathological behaviors associated with autism.

The scoring of the PEP is also unique. In addition to pass and fail categories, an item can be scored *emerge* to indicate that although a passing level was not reached, the child could do part of the task or could do it if extra help were given. These emerging skills are logical starting places for teaching. In addition, the PEP does not emphasize a summary score but offers a profile of abilities in seven function areas and a developmental score.

Psychological Tests

As mentioned earlier, most standardized developmental or intelligence tests are inadequate for autistic children, but some are useful in the assessment of certain characteristics. Further, for administrative or research purposes, an approximation of an IQ score is often needed because this score is a strong predictor of adult outcome (Rutter, 1983). Baker (1983) and Marcus & Baker (in press) have summarized the advantages and disadvantages of those tests applicable to autistic children. This information appears in Table 1.

Since these tests may make difficult demands on autistic children, the management of behavior problems during testing is important. Marcus & Baker (in press) have suggested some strategies for managing the behavior of children with autism during testing. These suggestions appear in Table 2.

Assessment of Adolescents

Most of the research literature on autism and subsequently most of the literature on assessment emphasizes young children. However, autism is almost always a lifelong disability, and the needs and characteristics of children with autism change with the onset of adolescence. Whereas the assessment of young autistic children usually stresses developmental skills in an effort to determine basic cognitive strengths and weaknesses, assessment of older students has different goals.

As adolescence approaches, it is important to know the student's practical or functional skills in order to plan for vocational activities and other demands of the world outside of school. In order to fulfill this need, Mesibov, Schopler, & Schaffer (1984) have developed the Adolescent and Adult Psychoeducational Profile. This instrument retains some aspects of the Psychoeducational Profile that are designed for autistic students, but the content is designed for older clients.

Parent Interview

Another crucial aspect of formal assessment is the interview with the parents. This provides an opportunity to review information gathered earlier, to learn more about the child's strengths and weaknesses from the parents' points of view, to determine what teaching approaches the parents already use, and to clarify the parents' goals and priorities for their child.

The parent interview presents the opportunity to establish a constructive and mutually respectful parent-professional relationship on which to build future work. Even the parents of very young children may have already experienced being blamed for their child's disorder. In the parent interview, it is essential to let parents know that their point of view is respected, that they are not to blame for the problem, and that future programs will be built on a strong parent-professional partnership.

Observation in Classroom and Other Settings

Formal testing, interviews, and observation in the assessment setting can identify many characteristics in the areas of learning, behavior problems, communication, etc., but offer no assurance that this impression is representative of the child's performance in other settings and at other times. A strong individualized program cannot be established until one confirms the generality of these findings.

In the TEACCH program, the next step involves scheduling a series of return visits called *the extended diagnostic evaluation*. During this time new teaching methods and activities are tried, and both parent(s) and therapist work with the child and observe each other. This provides time to learn from each other and to continue the assessment process (Schopler & Olley, 1982).

Further observation in the clinic or classroom should focus on several practical issues. For instance, some of the characteristics of autism may be evident only at certain times or settings or with certain people, and some may vary in severity. Self-stimulation or self-injury, language skills, perceptual problems, social interest, activity level, and motivation for different tasks should be noted. In the classroom, does the child use all available language skills? Are the child's behaviors variable or consistent across structured work or playtimes, when moving about the building, during mealtimes, when meeting people, etc.? When carrying out a task, is the child in the right place and oriented properly? Does the student use objects appropriately? Are social initiations and responses appropriate? Do problem behaviors interfere with the task? When the environment or routine changes, does the child's level of performance deteriorate?

These observations are important in determining the best educational program. Is one to one instruction required, or does the student have enough independent work skills to function alone for some time? Can the child work in a group? How does the child perform with non-handicapped peers? Are the child's motor skills strong enough for all school activities?

Some children may pass or fail an item on a test but perform differently with a similar item at school or home. Is the difference consistent? Observation across environments (school, clinic, home, community, leisure), people (parent, teachers, stranger), and time (time of day, length of session, after weekends or holidays) is useful.

It is essential to observe not only the circumstances in which a child fails but also to note what the child does. How does the child cope with failure? Autistic children are quite variable in this regard, some will do nothing and wait for help, others may have a temper tantrum or become aggressive. Still others may self-stimulate or engage in ritualistic behaviors. Autistic children who have had the

TABLE 1

Summary of General Intelligence Tests

TEST	AGE RANGE	DESCRIPTION	AUTISTIC CHILDREN FOR WHOM TEST IS BEST SUITED	ADVANTAGES	DISADVANTAGES
Bayley Mental Scale of Infant Development	2 mo. to 30 mo.	Motor, language, and social skills assessed in tasks designed to measure small increments of ability.	Young or severely delayed children, particularly if attentional and behavioral skills are poor.	Breaks down social and language skills into small components. Tasks require only brief attention.	For children with poor language and social skills but good visual-motor skills, range of visual-motor tasks may be too low.
Merrill-Palmer Test of Mental Abilities	18 mo. to 6 yrs.	Wide range of visual-motor tasks, smaller number of language items.	Children whose conceptual and language deficits make higher tests inappropriate, but who have relatively good visual-motor skills.	Attractive materials. Language and non-language items fairly well separated.	Language skills not comprehensively assessed. Autistic children with good visual-motor skill may score misleadingly high. No derived IQ.
Leiter International Performance Scale	3 yrs. to 18 yrs.	Non-language test used with deaf children. Child demonstrates understanding of concepts by matching blocks to a pictorial key.	Children whose conceptual abilities greatly exceed their language or who have difficulty with tasks requiring social interaction.	Little interaction with examiner required. Repetitive routine of administration minimizes stress for many autistic children.	No language assessment. Very little assessment of interpersonal skills, score may not be accurate reflection of ability in "real life" situations.
Hiskey-Nebraska Test of Learning Aptitude	3 yrs. to 16 yrs.	Non-language test used with deaf children. Various subtests involve imitation and memory as well as matching.	Children whose conceptual abilities greatly exceed their language, and who can sustain attention to and interaction with examiner.	Tests wide range of concepts and interpersonal skills with no language demands. Can be given with or without verbal instructions.	No language assessment. Longer and more demanding than Leiter. No derived IQ.

Test	Age range	Description	Suitable for	Strengths	Limitations
McCarthy Scales of Children's Abilities	2½ yrs. to 8½ yrs.	Five subscales, partially overlapping, measure verbal, perceptual-performance, quantitative, motor, and memory skills.	Children whose language skills are not severely delayed and who have relatively good attentional and behavioral skills.	2½-8½ year range better suited to many children than Wechsler tests. Fewer tasks dependent on language. Attractive materials. Administration allows for repeated demonstration, encouragement.	Language and conceptual demands too difficult for many autistic children. Comparison of subtest scores difficult.
Wechsler Preschool and Primary Scale of Intelligence (WPPSI)	4 yrs. to 6½ yrs.	Verbal and Performance subscales. Emphasis on language skills. Several subtests assess formally acquired knowledge (e.g., Arithmetic, Information).	Higher-level autistic children, whose language skills are only mildly delayed, and who have good attentional and behavioral skills.	Well designed and well standardized. Several subtests assess skills emphasized in school. Alternation of Verbal and Performance subtests helps reduce language demands.	Language and conceptual demands too difficult for most autistic children. Receptive language important even on Performance subtest. Administration guidelines fairly rigid.
Wechsler Intelligence Scale for Children—Revised (WISC-R)	6 yrs. to 17 yrs.				
Kaufman Assessment Battery for Children (K-ABC)	2½ to 12 yrs.	Separates abilities from acquired knowledge; format requires simple motor responses or short verbal answers; measures variety of cognitive & achievement skills.	Similar to Wechsler group—need for further study as test becomes more widely used.	Well designed & standardized; age range wider than Wechsler or McCarthy; teaching items for each subtest allows for flexibility of administration; expressive language demands minimal; visually oriented format; easy to administer.	Does not allow for assessment of language peculiarities and problems picked up by Wechsler; neuro-psychology model (Sequential-Simultaneous dichotomy) of questionable value for autistic group; lack of research & clinical use with this population warrants cautious approach to interpretation.

TABLE 2

Strategies for Management of Autistic Handicaps during Testing

HANDICAPS	TEST SELECTION	TESTING STRUCTURE	TEST ADMINISTRATION	USE OF ALTERNATIVE COMMUN. SYSTEMS
A. Severe Communication deficits	use of tests with limited language demands & many nonverbal items		1. modification of verbal instructions; 2. alternation of verbal & nonverbal	1. gestures; 2. pictures; 3. visual cues such as token or "finished" box
B. Deficits in social judgment & relating to people	use of tests requiring minimal social interaction	clear routines & expectations not dependent on social cues	1. simple social interactions by examiner; 2. on low demands for response from child; 3. awareness of child's skills in relating	
C. Attention, organization, & perceptual problems	use of material interesting but not overly distracting to child	1. uncluttered room & work table; 2. visually distinct work & play areas	1. clear, simple presentation of materials; 2. short work periods followed by breaks; 3. careful pace & timing of testing to fit child's attention patterns	
D. Uneven pattern of development	use of more than one instrument if needed to cover range of child's skills		awareness of child's strengths & weaknesses & modification of instructions & reinforcers on difficult items	
E. Motivational deficits			1. flexible use of wide variety of reinforcers; 2. sensitivity to child's source of motivation; 3. modification of or testing limits of items to provide success experiences	
F. Other atypical behaviors (e.g., motor stereotypes)	avoidance of over-stimulating materials		1. flexibility in deciding when to interrupt behaviors; 2. distract child; or 3. allow behavior as a tension-relieving break	

Note: From "Assessment of Autistic Children" by L. M. Marcus & A. F. Baker in *Psychological Assessment of Special Children* (in press) R. J. Simeonsson (Ed.), 1984, Boston: Allyn & Bacon. © Copyright 1984 by Allyn & Bacon. Reprinted by permission.

benefit of good educational programs may respond to failure by attempting to correct the error or by trying a new strategy.

Part of the formal and informal assessment should include an indication of how long behavior problems last. Some children make a mistake and become upset for the rest of the day, others may have a brief tantrum but soon return to the task.

The need for observation of autistic children is a clear indication that assessment is an ongoing process. Assessment does not end with testing; rather, it continues throughout treatment and provides the data to evaluate treatment progress. The observation process also makes it clear that assessment is a team effort. Information from formal testing complements testing done by teachers in the classroom and observation from several sources. Frequently used classroom tests include the AAMD Adaptive Behavior Scale, School Edition (Nihira, et al., 1975), The Brigance Diagnostic Inventory of Early Development (Brigance, 1978), and the Vulpé Assessment Battery (Vulpé, 1977).

INTERPRETATION AND INTEGRATION OF FINDINGS

Although assessment is a continuing process, the formal testing phase of evaluation concludes with an integration of findings and communication of those findings and recommendations to parents. It may be useful to consider the following categories as an aid to integration of findings: physical, intellectual, emotional, educational (or employment), and social (including communication) issues.

Physical

The stereotype of the autistic child is that of a boy (80% are male) who is physically intact, yet autism may also occur concurrently with physical handicaps and/or various stigmata. The characteristics of autism may be found in children with visual or hearing impairments, motor handicaps, seizure disorders, and syndromes such as tuberous sclerosis and congenital rubella (Rutter, 1983). These additional handicaps may make the prognosis for the child even poorer and will certainly require a wider array of services.

Intellectual

Although most children with autism function at a mentally retarded level, the range of intellectual abilities is great. Level of intellectual functioning is one of the strongest early predictors of adult adjustment (Rutter, 1983); thus, planning for an autistic child with an IQ score below 50 should include some realization that the disorder will almost surely be severe and lifelong. This program does not imply a need for highly restrictive residential care, but does indicate that planning and supervision are very important.

A small number of autistic children (fewer than 10%) have exceptional abilities or talents in one area, although they are at least moderately retarded in all other areas. These talents are not well understood, but it is clear that they are not indicators of great intellectual potential (DeMyer, 1979). Such children may benefit from their talent (e.g., art or music), or it may simply provide them with an activity (e.g., isolated mathematical skills), but such individuals continue to be handicapped in other areas.

About 20% of autistic people function above an IQ score of 70. Their chances for independent or minimally supervised adult living and employment are good, but as a group their social skills are poor. Even at higher intellectual levels, those with autism appear socially odd and may have serious adjustment problems.

Emotional

The adjustment problems noted above should not be thought of as an emotional disturbance but rather as a consequence of the cognitive deficit associated with autism. Difficulties in understanding, reacting to, and expressing affect are common in autism. These problems are considered in the section to follow on social problems.

Educational

As noted earlier, a classification of autism should not automatically lead to any particular educational placement. Nearly all autistic children benefit from a highly structured program with clear expectations and consequences and a predictable routine. When planning for the individual, the assessment can be quite helpful in identifying the least restrictive type of class in which the child can succeed and determining appropriate teaching objectives.

Children with autism almost always require a strong emphasis on communication and social skills throughout their educational experience. Placements that offer good language and social models and opportunities for broad experience have a clear advantage over those in more restrictive settings.

The results of the Psychoeducational Profile give good indications of beginning teaching objectives for young children. For instance, if a child shows emerging skills in the *fine motor* area, it is important to design fine motor activities that are at a reasonable level of difficulty for the child and also use functional materials. Teaching the child to pick up small plastic chips and put them in a slot to receive a food reward would have little value, whereas buttoning buttons on the child's own clothing, putting coins in a vending machine, or picking up small pieces of popcorn and eating them are all functional tasks with natural consequences that can be taught in many settings. The Adolescent and Adult Psychoeducational Profile also yields useful educational information, however the emphasis is much more vocational.

Information regarding the extent of pathology and observations about the best ways to structure testing and teaching must be integrated with the developmental testing data in order to make recommendations. For instance, a child may have relatively high developmental skills but quite severe interfering behaviors and be unresponsive to readily available reinforcers. Such a child may require a very structured and more restrictive placement with emphasis on behavior management even though cognitively capable of higher level tasks.

Social/Communication

The social deficit from which autism draws its name is likely to be quite evident in testing and to affect performance in other areas. Lack of interest in others, lack of compliance, inappropriate play, and odd language are common. At an earlier time, these findings led to recommendations for psychotherapy to address an emotional problem but today these problems are approached by focusing on social and language skills in assessment and treatment from an early age.

In addition to intelligence, the development of functional speech before age 5 is a strong predictor of adult adjustment (Rutter, 1983). Although interest in others may be slight, it is critical to initiate communication and social skills training at an early age. Lack of such skills in adolescence will severely limit opportunities for work. In some cases, inappropriate social initiations may be seen inaccurately as aggression, sexual assault, or signs of severe mental illness.

COMMUNICATION OF RESULTS

Most of the issues in communicating the results of assessment regarding autistic children are similar to those faced with other populations. However, a few unique concerns exist.

Reports of testing may be read by many audiences with varying degrees of sophistication about autism, so it is important to use terms consistently and accurately and to write in a very clear style.

The report and the verbal presentation to parents should clearly state whether or not the disorder is autism. Autism occurs in degrees, and results of the Childhood Autism Rating Scale or other diagnostic measures can help in describing the degree of autism. If, however, the findings *do not* support a diagnosis of autism, one should avoid the use of ambiguous terms such as *autistic-like*. Other terms, such as *atypical child* and *symbiotic psychosis* have been used in a manner that overlaps with autism. Such terms should not be used as substitutes or euphemisms for autism (Schopler, 1983). In the same vein, the characteristics associated with autism also may be found in other handicapping conditions. To say that a child is *not autistic* but has *autistic characteristics* is very confusing and should be avoided.

The report of results should cover all of the areas noted above: physical, intellectual, emotional, educational/employment, and social/communication. Children and youth with autism as well as other disorders may require the services of several disciplines, and the nature of the multiple problems and recommended services should be clearly described.

By law, school placement is the responsibility of the school system, but written recommendations based on assessment are important contributions to that decision. Recommendations for beginning curriculum, teaching approaches, type of class, and related services should all be stated.

The assessment process for autistic children and youth draws upon principles of assessment applicable to many populations. However, some of the unique characteristics of autism demand nontraditional and flexible assessment strategies and tests; the result can provide information that is quite useful both in planning a treatment and education program and in developing opportunities for future work and community living.

REFERENCES

Baker, A.F. (1983). Psychological assessment of autistic children. *Clinical Psychology Review, 3*, 41-59.
DeMyer, M.K. (1979). *Parents and children in autism.* Washington, DC: Winston.
Kanner, L. (1943). Autistic disturbances of affective contact. *Nervous Child, 2*, 217-250.
Marcus, L.M., & Baker, A.F. (in press). Assessment of autistic children. In R.J. Simeonsson (Ed.), *Psychological assessment of special children.* Boston: Allyn and Bacon.
National Society for Autistic Children. (1978). National Society for Autistic Children definition of the syndrome of autism. *Journal of Autism and Childhood Schizophrenia, 8*, 162-169.
Parks, S.L. (1983). The assessment of autistic children: A selective review of available instruments. *Journal of Autism and Developmental Disorders, 13*, 255-267.
Rutter, M. (1983). Cognitive deficits in the pathogenesis of autism. *Journal of Child Psychology and Psychiatry, 24*, 513-531.
Schopler, E. (1983). New developments in the definition and diagnosis of autism. In B.B. Lahey & A.E. Kazdin (Eds.), *Advances in clinical child psychology* (Vol. 6, pp. 93-127). New York: Plenum.
Schopler, E., & Olley, J.G. (1982). Comprehensive educational services for autistic children: The TEACCH model. In C.R. Reynolds & T.R. Gutkin (Eds.), *The handbook of school psychology* (pp. 629-643). New York: Wiley.
Schopler, E., & Reichler, R.J. (1979). *Individualized assessment and treatment for autistic and developmentally disabled children: Vol. 1. Psychoeducational Profile.* Baltimore: University Park Press.
Stutsman, R. (1931). *Mental measurement of preschool children.* Yonkers-on-Hudson, NY: World Book.
Wing, L., & Gould, J. (1979). Severe impairments of social interaction and associated abnormalities in children: Epidemiology and classification. *Journal of Autism and Developmental Disorders, 9*, 11-29.

7

Assessment of
Learning Disabled Children

ROBERT G. HARRINGTON, PH.D.

The meaning of the term "learning disabilities" (LD) has been a source of much controversy since first popularized by Kirk (1963). Far from being the neutral term it was intended to be, many speculations have been made about what might be the cause of such learning problems. At one time or another each of the following hypotheses has been offered, including minimal brain damage; disorders of attention; visual-perceptual problems; auditory-processing deficits; developmental lags; sensory integration disorders; and hyperactivity and uncoordination. In fact, many children presently diagnosed as learning disabled might have been placed in programs for educating and treating mentally retarded or emotionally disturbed children in past years. This condition of confusion and flux has raised some rather complex diagnostic questions for the clinician. In order to address these issues the purpose of this chapter is threefold: 1) to describe the federal definition of learning disabilities and its implications for psychological assessment; 2) to present a rationale and specific strategies for screening learning disabled children during the preassessment phase; and 3) to specify formal and informal assessment procedures to be used in LD diagnosis and intervention planning. This chapter also exemplifies with a case vignette the psychoeducational assessment of a learning disabled child.

IMPLICATIONS OF PL 94-142 FOR PSYCHOLOGICAL ASSESSMENT
OF LD CHILDREN

Psychologists, teachers, researchers, and parents all seem to agree that some children have serious difficulty with schoolwork, but there is very little consensus among them about what should constitute a learning disability. Besides the definitional ambiguities, there are a variety of educational, legal, political, and economic reasons why the LD category has remained so elusive and heterogeneous. For example, some psychologists may be tempted to advocate an LD placement for practically any slow learner, especially when alternative programs are unavailable or additional program funds accompany such placements (Hewett & Forness, 1974).

85

Unlike the stigma of mental retardation, parents may exert undue pressure on diagnostic teams for placement of their children in LD programs (Schumaker, Deshler, Alley, & Warren, 1980). Parents may perceive the LD label as non-threatening and serving to shift the blame they feel at home back to the school. Finally, some regular classroom teachers may seek to place certain students in LD programs because these students are disruptive and hard-to-teach (Shepard & Smith, 1981). In this regard Coles (1978) has claimed that by labeling a child as learning disabled, children rather than schools have been blamed for educational failures. Beyond such personal investments in the LD label, overidentification of LD children may also be attributed to the fact that the criteria for identification of learning disabled children often changes from state to state. The result has been that a child may be diagnosed as learning disabled in one state, move to another state and not be eligible for learning disabilities services.

In 1975 the Education for All Handicapped Children Act or PL 94-142 became law (Federal Register, 1975). The significance of this law rests in that the federal government has recognized learning disabilities as a handicapping condition, has allocated funds for the education of these children, and has mandated that a free and appropriate public education must be provided to all learning disabled children. This law leaves practicing psychologists in the quandry of having both to diagnose a handicapping condition that researchers have so far failed to define adequately and to face the risks of misidentifying individual children.

Fortunately, at least a broad definition of learning disabilities exists that multidisciplinary teams must follow in order to comply with PL 94-142. A description and definition of specific developmental disorders such as Developmental Reading and Arithmetic Disorders is also offered in the *Diagnostic and Statistical Manual of Mental Disorders* (DSM-III) published by the American Psychiatric Association (1980). The DSM-III diagnostic criteria are similar to, albeit somewhat less detailed than, the federal guidelines. The diagnostic criteria for Developmental Reading Disorder (315.00) and Developmental Arithmetic Disorder (315.10) state that:

> Performance on standardized, individually administered tests of reading skill (or arithmetic achievement, in the case of Arithmetic Disorder) is significantly below expected level, given the individual's schooling, chronological age, and mental age (as determined by an individually administered IQ Test). In addition, in school, the child's performance on tasks requiring reading skills (or arithmetic skills) is significantly below his or her intellectual capacity.

Without a doubt the controversy has run high regarding whether Developmental Reading and Arithmetic Disorders should be classified as mental disorders. The fact is that many of these children show no other signs of child "psychopathology," and their identification and treatment takes place in the educational system, not the mental health system.

Since state and federal funds for LD educational programs are contingent on meeting the federal definition of learning disabilities, psychologists performing assessments for possible placements in the public schools must comply with the specific components of the federal definition. According to the federal definition of learning disabilities contained in PL 94-142 (Federal Register, 1977):

Specific learning disability means a disorder in one or more of the basic psychological processes involved in understanding or in using language, spoken or written, which may manifest itself in an imperfect ability to listen, think, read, write, spell, or to do mathematical calculations. The term includes such conditions as perceptual handicaps, brain injury, minimal brain dysfunction, dyslexia, and developmental aphasia. The term does not include children who have learning problems which are primarily the result of visual, hearing or motor handicaps, of mental retardation, of emotional disturbance, or of environmental, cultural, or economic disadvantage.

This definition is further operationalized as: 1) a severe discrepancy between achievement and intellectual ability in one or more of the following areas: oral expression; listening comprehension; written expression; basic reading skills; reading comprehension; mathematics calculations; and mathematics reasoning; and 2) achievement not commensurate with children's age and ability level in the previously mentioned areas when provided with learning experiences appropriate for their age and ability levels.

In general the federal definition of LD offers only limited guidance for the diagnostician because the criteria are vague, subjective, and open to interpretation. Furthermore, the definition appears to place almost a greater emphasis on exclusionary criteria than inclusionary, so that psychologists may feel they are classifying problematic children as LD if the *do not* meet the criteria for any other handicapping condition. The intent of PL 94-142 is not to restrict the LD diagnostic category to a single profile, because learning disability is quite heterogeneous in its composition. The extensive exclusionary criteria exist so that children with other types of learning handicaps will not be confused with LD children. In the following section a rationale for preassessment and specific screening strategies useful in satisfying the exclusionary criteria of the federal definition will be explained.

A RATIONALE AND SPECIFIC STRATEGIES FOR PREASSESSMENT SCREENING

Depending on how loosely one interprets the federal definition, the prevalence rate for learning disabilities in the U.S. population may range from 3-15% (Phye & Reschly, 1979). From four to eight times as many boys as girls can be expected to be identified (Marsh, Gearhart, & Gearhart, 1978). Furthermore, many studies have found a moderate correlation between learning disabilities and socioeconomic status (Johnson & Johnson, 1971). When the intelligence factor is controlled, however, socioeconomic status does not seem to be a factor. Such wide-ranging and indecisive statistics are due in part to the fact that included in these statistics are many children who may have some learning problems but are not necessarily LD. In a research study comparing LD and low-achieving pupils from the same schools on 49 variables, Ysseldyke, et al. (1982) found 82-100% overlap. When these two groups' test scores were examined in light of the federal definition of LD, 40% or more were considered misclassified.

Included among the misidentified LD cases are students with behavior problems; students from different cultural backgrounds; slow learners; the poorly taught; remedial education students; the mentally handicapped; environmentally or economically deprived students; children lacking consistent educational instruction; and students evidencing visual, hearing or motor handicaps (Poplin, 1981). Any one or any combination of these conditions may confound an LD diagnosis. Each situation is capable of precipitating a learning *problem* in a student but not necessarily a learning *disability*. For this reason children experiencing any one of these conditions must be excluded from consideration as LD. In order to include a child in the LD diagnostic category the learning disability and not some other disorder must be the *primary disability*.

For instance, if a third-grader is having serious learning problems because of changing schools six times since kindergarten, then the psychologist should not be surprised to find gaps in the child's learning and poor achievement. There are no discrepancies between the low level of achievement and what one might expect under the circumstances. The learning problems can be completely explained without invoking the LD construct. Similarly, if a fifth-grade girl continuously becomes involved in unprovoked fights in the classroom, resides in an impoverished and unstimulating home environment, and speaks English with difficulty as a second language, one could easily expect that this child would be behind her classmates in learning to read. As long as she progresses at a reasonable rate given the circumstances and nothing anomalous exists in how she learns to read, a learning disability should not be considered the primary disability; other, more primary explanations would cover this child's reading disabilities.

At first glance it may appear that the exclusionary criteria reject all possibility that hearing-impaired children, certain poor children, or motorically disabled children could also be learning disabled, but this is not true. The deciding factor is the extent to which the child is more learning impaired than would have been expected given the other disabling circumstances. If a severe discrepancy exists between the present level of achievement and what one would expect given the nature of the child's circumstances, then LD may be considered the "primary disability."

The purpose of preassessment procedures is to screen-out those cases that clearly fit the exclusionary criteria better than the LD criteria. By screening these cases before they are referred for comprehensive diagnostic assessment, time and cost efficiency may be increased, the regular teacher may be assisted with consultative services, and the child may be served in the most appropriate and least restrictive educational environment. If none of the exclusionary criteria apply then the child should be referred for a comprehensive evaluation to discover possible learning disabilities.

The first step a practitioner should take in the LD preassessment screening process is to define operationally the specific nature of the problem in collaboration with the referral agent. Statements such as, "Jean has trouble in math," or "Jim never completes his language arts assignments" provide little information about the specific observable behaviors of concern. No possible remedies can be formulated for such global statements, nor do they indicate previous attempts to remediate the problem in the regular classroom. Instead, the psychologist should assist referral agents in formulating comments such as, "I have tried the following three methods of teaching math facts and Jean is still having difficulty in remembering what she has learned."

Once the problem behavior has been adequately defined, the psychologist must systematically evaluate and exclude all the alternative hypotheses described in the federal definition's exclusionary criteria before considering the child for a comprehensive LD evaluation. At a minimum the preassessment screening of exclusionary criteria should include the following components:

1. Educational history, including present academic status
2. Social functioning/behavioral status
3. Environmental/cultural status
4. Motor functioning
5. Speech and language screening
6. Health/medical history and physical status
7. Hearing and vision screening

The first three screening activities listed may be performed by the psychologist and the remainder must be cross-referred to other members of the multidisciplinary team. Some of the relevant data the psychologist may wish to collect include: records of previous referrals; the child's attendance record; past records of school success; a comparison of behavior in the academic versus the non-academic setting; group achievement data; and any options tried and their results. In summary, much of the required information may be collected through informal and formal observation, a review of school records, an analysis of work products, and interviews with parents and teachers. A helpful schemata for conceptualizing preassessment screening activities can be found in Table 1.

For more information about informal assessment strategies useful in preassessment screening see Moran (1978) or Guerin & Maier (1983).

Having satisfied the exclusionary criteria for the identification of a potentially LD child, the psychologist should next proceed to actively specify the behaviors

TABLE 1

The Focus and Content of Preassessment Screening

STUDENT CHARACTERISTICS	APPROPRIATENESS OF INSTRUCTION
Skills or deficiencies in academic or special competency	Goals and objectives specified
Behavior in class and outside	Materials matched to skill level
Personality characteristics	Teaching methods
Interests & hobbies	Style of teaching
Ability to perform academically	Method of reporting grades
Learning style	Competence of teachers
Student history	

CLASSROOM SETTING	INFLUENCES OUT OF SCHOOL
Grouping (large, small, one-to-one)	Adaptability of students
Peer relationships	Relationships with parents
Friendships	Community cooperation
Accessibility of school facilities	Influence of religion
Appropriateness of school regulations	Cultural differences
	Peer relationships
	Nutritional needs met
	Socioeconomic status of family
	Student employment
	Recreational activities

indicative of possible learning difficulties. Through incidental observation the teacher may be able to report to the psychologist whether the child evidences the following signs: fails to complete assigned seat work within a reasonable time period; fails to follow directions; requests frequent teacher aid; demonstrates many word-recognition errors; approaches tasks in a slow and disorganized fashion; loses the place in the text; exhibits tremors; appears excessively inattentive; cries or tantrums when frustrated; speaks or uses language atypically; requires many trials for task completion; regularly confuses signs on math operations.

A review of school records should reveal a pattern of grades in previous years, the date of onset of academic problems, any prior testing, and whether special services were provided. The psychologist should be careful to compare the pattern of grades with the attendance record and number of schools attended in recent years. One should also make a comparison of group achievement test results and group IQ scores with class grades. A student with a superior IQ score who achieves one to two years below grade level may be demonstrating the effects of a learning disability. Anecdotal comments made by previous teachers may also provide insights into the onset and history of the problem. Of course, all such informal data from school records should be considered tentative and useful only in developing working hypotheses about the referral problem.

Student work products represent a third valuable source of preassessment information. These include written work, worksheets, homework, tests, and art projects. Work products may be analyzed for copying skills; organization; reversals; letter formation; spatial relationships; failure to follow directions; amount of work produced in a given time interval; learning style; and types of errors.

In some cases a learning problem may go undetected at school and be evident only at home to the child's parent. By interviewing the parents the psychologist may obtain valuable information about recent changes in a child's behavior or routine and their affects on school performance. For example, a parent interview may uncover that the child dislikes school and does not want to attend; acute instances of disruptive behavior at home may begin to occur more frequently; or the child may recruit the parents to intervene with the teacher about an academic or social problem. Interviews may also be conducted with the child and the teacher to verify the parent's concerns.

One instrument that holds great promise for streamlining the preassessment process is the Barclay Classroom Assessment System (BCAS) (Barclay, 1983). The BCAS assesses children in grades three through six from three viewpoints: self-report, peer judgments, and teacher expectations. Teachers are also requested to include achievement stanine scores. The purpose of the instrument is to aid in the identification of those children who are at risk for learning problems because of academic deficits or personal-social problems. These data can be integrated via computer analysis into six factor scores, and a printout describing the characteristics of each child can be provided along with a list of those children who may have problems sufficient for psychological inspection or consultation. Children scoring high on Factor 1 may be typified as "thinkers" in that they are internally oriented, process information slowly, and are good achievers and responsible citizens in the classroom. Factor 2 describes those individuals who possess much support from others, process information quickly, are usually good students, and are seen as "leaders" in the classroom setting. Factor 3 represents a group of children who have multiple problems in either achievement or interpersonal relationships. These children process information slowly but inaccurately. Individuals with high scores on Factor 4 are characterized by impulsivity, acting-out behavior, and under-achievement. There are two other groups that represent middle areas between the four groups already described, but they will not be discussed here. Normative data in the examiner's manual was based on approximately 9000 children. Over 80 studies, including reliability and validity research, have been conducted using this instrument.

As a result of preassessment screening the psychologist should be prepared to make one of two decisions, either that the child does not meet the criteria for LD or that the child should be referred for a comprehensive diagnostic evaluation for learning disabilities. If the decision is to "not refer" then the psychologist should provide consultative assistance to the teacher regarding modifications in teaching materials, instructional techniques, and classroom environment. If the decision is "refer" for diagnostic evaluation, then the psychologist should be careful to choose instrumentation that will meet the criteria set forth in the PL 94-142 guidelines for LD assessment.

DIAGNOSIS AND CLASSIFICATION OF LEARNING DISABLED CHILDREN

False Diagnostic Strategies

The number of LD diagnostic strategies which have been attempted and have failed closely parallels the number of different LD definitions which have been proposed through the years. This is to be expected since test selection and usage always depends on a clear problem specification—unfortunately unavailable in the case of learning disabilities. It is difficult to discuss how tests and behavioral data should be used to determine whether a child is LD without also addressing the question, "Is the child validly LD?" There are several diagnostic strategies prevalent even today that are patently invalid. A brief discussion of these failed strategies is presented so that the psychologist will not repeat such misuses.

An underlying assumption of many past and present definitions of LD, including the current federal definition, has been that an auditory or visual perceptual processing disorder is at the core of most learning disabilities. A wide array of diagnostic instruments have been developed to identify these processing deficits so that they could be remediated in LD resource rooms. Two of the more prominent tests developed to measure processing deficits have included the Illinois Test of Psycholinguistic Ability (ITPA) (Kirk, McCarthy, & Kirk, 1968) and the Developmental Test of Visual-Motor Integration (VMI) (Beery, 1967). For years these tests were standard components of an LD diagnostic battery before the disconcerting facts about their psychometric properties were known. After careful research it was discovered that the subtest reliabilities on the ITPA were so low that no credible foundation for profile interpretation could be built (Lumsden, 1978). In addition, the skills measured on the ITPA appeared to overlap with those tapped on standard IQ tests despite the fact that diagnostic inferences drawn from the ITPA assumed good discriminant validity (Larsen, Rogers, & Sowell, 1976). In the case of the VMI, it is interesting to note that 46% of the LD teachers and 55% of the psychologists asked to rate the reliability and validity of tests for LD diagnosis rated the VMI as "having adequate research evidence for its validity in diagnosing LD" even though no empirical evidence has been published to support this use (Shepard & Smith, 1981).

Equally popular has been the proclivity of psychologists to interpret subtest scatter on the Wechsler Intelligence Scale for Children-Revised (WISC-R) as an indicator of learning disabilities. Several approaches to measure scatter have been attempted without success, such as verbal-performance scale score discrepancy, pattern analysis of subtest scores, and range of scatter. When two different scales or subtests within a test composed of different types of tasks show that a child has extremely different levels of abilities, this is called "scatter." The problem with trying to use scatter as a diagnostic tool is that it appears too often in normals (Salvia & Ysseldyke, 1978). When a clinician works mainly with "at-risk" children, it is easy to lose sight of the wide range of scatter typically found in the profiles of average and normal children. Using a criterion of 15% in the WISC-R standardization sample as the cutoff for abnormal occurrences, Kaufman (1976) concluded that a 10-subtest range of 9 points would not be considered unusual. A significant verbal-performance discrepancy would require a 12-point difference, but a discrepancy worthy of being labeled abnormal statistically should be a 26-point difference (Kaufman, 1979).

Similarly, the Bannatyne (1968) recategorization of WISC-R subtests was particularly promising because the four patterns (Spatial, Conceptual, Sequential and Acquired Knowledge) were empirically derived. Under closer scrutiny, the recategorization has not been successful in differentiating children with visual-perceptual learning disorders from those with auditory-perceptual disabilities (Miller, 1977), nor have the Bannatyne patterns been found to differentiate LD from normal students (Henry & Whitmann, 1981).

Despite these damaging accounts of attempts at pattern analysis some clinicians may think, "I know one when I see one." To examine whether school personnel could differentiate the test patterns of learning disabled from low achievers, 65 school psychologists, 38 special education teachers, and a "naïve" group of 21 university students enrolled in programs unrelated to education or psychology, were provided with information on 41 test or subtest scores of 9 school-identified LD students and 9 non-LD students. These three sets of judges were asked which profile patterns showed learning disabilities and which were non-learning disabled. The results were that all three groups identified approximately the same number of students as LD. Also, although the naïve group had no specific training in psychoeducational decision-making, they were significantly more accurate in identifying those students already classified as LD using five definitions of LD. In summary, neither pattern analysis nor process analysis have increased the psychologist's ability to discriminate LD from non-LD children. Consequently, there has been a shift away from these methods toward assessment of discrepancies in achievement areas (Harber, 1981).

Current Best Practices in Formal LD Diagnostic Assessment

The principle of *discrepancy* or disparity is the essential criterion for learning disabilities cited in the PL 94-142 federal definition. For a discrepancy to exist there must be some way of measuring the difference between the child's present level of achievement and ability to achieve. Given that ability-achievement discrepancy provides the foundation of the LD construct, it follows that the assessment of learning-disabled children should have three major aims. The first aim is to obtain an accurate measure of general intelligence to determine whether the child has the ability for higher achievement despite past or present school grades. The second is to assess areas of low achievement significantly discrepant from the child's measured intellectual ability. The third aim is to identify areas of strength that may represent useful instructional channels.

Physical Functioning: No discussion of assessment for instructional planning would be complete without some consideration of the role of sensory processing tests such as the Auditory Discrimination Test (Wepman, 1973) or the Frostig Developmental Test of Visual Perception (Frostig, Maslow, Lefever, & Whittlesey, 1964). Disappointingly, only 5% of the nineteen tests used most frequently in this endeavor have met the minimum standards set by the American Psychological Association (Shepard & Smith, 1981). If the psychologist wishes to assess sensory process deficits at all that data will probably have to be collected informally. The processing deficits informally observed on a test like the Detroit Tests of Learning Aptitude can be carefully compared to the process dysfunctions found on the child's IQ and achievement tests for similarities.

Intellectual Functioning: For the purposes of assessing intellectual functioning there are several excellent individually administered and nationally normed instruments from which to select. Depending on the age of the child the choices would include the Wechsler Intelligence Scale for Children-Revised (WISC-R, ages 6-0 to 16-11) (Wechsler, 1974), the Wechsler Preschool and Primary Scale of Intelligence (WPPSI, ages 4 to 6-1/2) (Wechsler, 1967), the Wechsler Adult Intelligence Scale-Revised (WAIS-R, ages 16-0 to 74-11) (Wechsler, 1981), the Stanford-Binet Intelligence Scale (Form L-M, ages 2 to adult) (Thorndike, 1973), or the Kaufman Assessment Battery for Children (K-ABC, ages 2-1/2 to 12-1/2) (Kaufman & Kaufman, 1983). It may be tempting for practitioners to substitute brief "measures of IQ" for the standard instruments mentioned above. These might include the Detroit Tests of Learning Aptitude (Baker & Leland, 1967), the Slosson Intelligence Test (Slosson, 1963), or the Peabody Picture Vocabulary Test-Revised (PPVT-R) (Dunn & Dunn, 1981). Such action would surely result in misclassification since the Detroit has neither adequate subtest reliabilities nor evidence of validity; the Slosson has unknown reliability and was normed on a small clinical sample of retarded individuals; and the PPVT-R is clearly a measure of receptive vocabulary, not general intelligence.

Educational Achievement: An individually administered and norm-referenced achievement measure, whether it be reading, mathematics, language, or spelling, will also need to be selected based on the referral to determine whether a significant discrepancy between expected achievement and actual achievement exists. Two of the very few examples of technically adequate achievement tests include the Woodcock-Johnson Psycho-Educational Battery: Achievement Section (ages 3-adult) (Woodcock, 1977) covering ten achievement areas and the Woodcock Reading Mastery Tests (grades K-12) (Woodcock, 1973) with five subtests covering Letter Identifcation, Word Identification, Word Attack, Word Comprehension, and Passage Comprehension. Sattler (1982) provides an excellent discussion of the psychometric qualities of these and other achievement tests. Two currently popular achievement measures, albeit deficient for diagnostic purposes, include the Wide Range Achievement Test (WRAT) (Jastak & Jastak, 1978) and the KeyMath Diagnostic Arithmetic Test (Connolly, Nachtman, & Pritchett, 1971). The wide range of curricular content covered in the WRAT is its boon and its bane. Because there are so few items at any given grade level, its content validity is reduced. While the KeyMath has somewhat better content validity, important normative data are missing such as standard deviations for grade equivalent scores.

Discrepancy Formulas: Many formulas, often available through state departments of education, exist to measure the discrepancy between intellectual ability and achievement, but none is intended to stand as the sole criterion for LD diagnosis. This is only one factor in the multidisciplinary team decision whether a child is LD or not and should serve as a guide for interpreting the magnitude of the differences. Neither the federal guidelines nor DSM-III indicate how a severe discrepancy should be determined, which is why each state has had to develop its own discrepancy formula. Practitioners will be obliged to use the state's formula, most likely, if the objective is to place a child in an LD resource room in the public schools. Under these circumstances it makes good sense for the psychologist to know a bit more about the existing discrepancy models.

The least valid but most often used discrepancy model consists of simply computing the extent to which a child's achievement level in a subject area is below chronological age, mental age, or grade level (Cone & Wilson, 1981). This method ignores the child's own IQ score and the test score variability that naturally increases with grade level; in other words, it ignores the fact that being a year behind in grade one with an IQ score of 98 is much more serious than at grade nine with the same IQ score.

Another model provides for a comparison of standard scores on IQ and achievement tests (Reynolds, et al., 1984). The problem is that this model neglects to take into account the regression of IQ on achievement. This kind of oversight would result in many more children being falsely identified as LD with IQ scores over 100 than justifiable, and also would result in many children being missed with IQ scores below 100.

No matter what their discrepancy model, some states have made the arbitrary decision that all children with grade-appropriate achievement scores are automatically excluded from LD consideration regardless of any aptitude-achievement discrepancy. The net result in these cases is that children with IQ scores above 100 will be systematically denied services even though they may stand a better chance of benefiting from an LD program than a borderline mentally handicapped child.

A more technically adequate procedure than those already mentioned entails establishing a frequency of regression prediction discrepancy (Reynolds, et al., 1984). This formula addresses the question, "Is there a severe discrepancy between the obtained achievement score of this child and the average achievement score of all other children with the same score?" This however is not necessarily the "perfect" discrepancy model. Every model forces the user to make choices about certain characteristics of the children to be identified as LD.

With whatever discrepancy model a psychologist is using it is important to understand its implications for the educational goals of the community being served. Some discrepancy models cover a wide range of intellectual functioning from IQ scores of 70 to 130 + . Others exclude very low or very high ability students. Some proposed models provide for *intra*-individual comparisons of aptitude-achievement discrepancy while others make *inter*-individual comparisons. The inter-individual model takes base rates into consideration; the intra-individual model does not. Some models set the criterion for a severe discrepancy very strictly and others very loosely. The result is that some formulas make it very difficult to qualify a child for LD services and others make it very easy. Some models may identify educationally significant groups and others may not. Educational significance of identified groups may be estimated by asking these two questions: "What are the characteristics of the students referred, but not identified?" and "What are the educational needs and possible educational alternatives for those referred but found not to qualify for LD services?"

Psychometrically sound discrepancy models that are well understood by their users can be of great assistance in establishing minimum standards for the identification of LD children. Discrepancy should be considered under most circumstances a necessary but not sufficient criterion for LD. There are those in which the observed IQ could be depressed, such as in the case of a language disability serving to hide a potential discrepancy (Danielson & Bauer, 1978). By no means should it be construed that every low IQ score be dismissed as invalid so that a particular child can fit the discrepancy criterion. Already, too many "slow learners" are in LD. To corroborate a claim of depressed IQ there should be some other indication of higher intellectual ability such as a very high verbal or performance scale score *and* at least average performance in one or more achievement areas with deficiencies in the remaining achievement areas. The clinician is also cautioned not to overtest a referred child. Due to the normal variation of skill development within individuals, the more tests given, the greater the probability of finding a significant discrepancy just by chance.

Severe discrepancies may also be masked when testing minority group children for LD. Even tests that are technically adequate to assess children from the dominant culture may not be valid for some minority children. The test results may represent biased underestimates of the child's ability, due to poor test-taking skills, lack of motivation, and lack of exposure to the kinds of skills being tested. The psychologist must take such factors into consideration when interpreting the discrepancy of some minority students. Some clinicians may also need to rethink their position that all LD placements are "safe;" overidentification of minority students as LD can be just as harmful as underidentification.

It should be clear at this point that there are multiple-step decision points in the process of LD identification. Does the referred child fit any of the exclusionary criteria? If not, then have technically adequate tests of ability and achievement been selected to test for a severe discrepancy? What are the characteristics of LD children identified with the severe discrepancy method in use? Is the discrepancy formula valid for its intended use? Are the test results used in computing the discrepancy biased against some minority groups or do the results represent underestimates of ability? If these decision points have been addressed and a severe discrepancy has been found, a tentative diagnosis of LD might be considered. The diagnostic label called LD is not a cure-all, however; it provides very little insight into the presumed cause or etiology of an individual child's learning problems. Besides the formal standardized test results used in the computation of discrepancy, other informal assessments conducted by the psychologist can assist the multidisciplinary team in deciding whether the child is LD and what instructional changes should be considered. This is the third aim of LD assessment mentioned earlier in this section—to analyze how a prospective LD student best learns.

Linking Informal Assessment with Intervention Plans

Much of informal assessment has its foundation in impression formation simply because these are not norm-referenced techniques. Three informal assessment strategies in common use include observations of behavioral indicators, testing of the limits, and criterion-referenced testing. When interpreting the results of these informal assessments several sources of bias can intrude and distort the psychologist's impressions. The referring teacher can exert a strong influence on the psychologist to positively identify the child as LD. For example, 95% of all referrals in New York City result in placement in special education (Ysseldyke & Algozzine, 1981). This is why it is of paramount importance that signs of LD be based on informal assessments that are both pervasive and consistent in their presence.

Behavioral Indicators: Behavioral indicators on an intelligence or achievement test represent observable behaviors that may contribute supporting evidence of a learning disability. Numerous lists of behavioral indicators including such items as "poor coordination," "short attention span," "difficulty following directions," "letter reversals," "figure rotations," and "perseverations" have been offered. See Sattler (1982) for examples. Many can be traced back to Clements' (1966) list of symptoms sifted from 100 studies of children with minimal brain dysfunction. The problem with Clements' landmark survey and many of the behavioral indicators a psychologist might observe is that they often fail to discriminate LD from normal children. Even though these symptoms lack diagnostic utility, they are still essential components of a comprehensive LD evaluation because they provide important information for instructional intervention planning and may provide supporting evidence of a learning disability when used in the context of a multifactored, multisourced assessment.

An alternative does exist to clinically observing behavioral indicators during testing. Instead of only observing the subject's performance directly, the examiner might interpret the results of subtest performance in the light of shared abilities or the skills required for the child to be successful across these tests. For example, Picture Completion, Picture Arrangement, and Object Assembly on the WISC-R all involve the manipulation of meaningful stimuli, whereas Block Design and Coding involve abstract stimuli. Children who perform poorly on Block Design and Coding may have difficulty in assimilating abstract stimuli. Such a hypothesis could provide new insights into the kinds of concrete, meaningful instructional materials and strategies this child may require. Kaufman (1979) has elaborated many similar paradigms for clinically comparing and contrasting subtest performance on the WISC-R.

Testing of the Limits: Having noted some behavioral indicators of possible learning disabilities in the course of formal assessment, the examining psychologist may have begun to formulate some clinical hypotheses about how these behavioral indicators might affect achievement. These hypotheses can be tested informally through a procedure called "testing of the limits." Testing of the limits is undertaken only after formal testing is completed. It involves going beyond or modifying the standard test procedures in order to gain additional information about causes for the child's errors and under what conditions the child could be successful. Limits may be tested by providing additional cues. How much and what kinds of assistance are necessary for the child to answer a question correctly? Another limit-testing technique involves asking a child to describe the strategies used to solve a problem. Some children will have a plan and others will not; some will respond impulsively to a problem situation or will show signs they do not comprehend the task. Finally, limits may be tested by giving the child additional time to complete a task in order to determine if the rate of performance affects task outcome.

Criterion-Referenced Testing: In addition to observing behavioral indicators and "testing the limits," a third informal approach a psychologist might employ in

LD assessment would be criterion-referenced testing. In contrast to norm-referenced testing, criterion-referenced tests assess the presence or absence of observable, hierarchical skills in mathematics or reading that can be compared to a predetermined criterion for success. Furthermore, the student's own abilities can be judged and compared to others. Items on these tests can be linked to instructional objectives and enable the specification of starting points for the instruction of sequential skills. This kind of information can be very valuable for a learning disabilities teacher beginning to shape a program for an incoming student.

Both commercially and examiner-constructed criterion-referenced tests are available. An informal criterion-referenced test of reading skills might cover the range from simple letter recognition to reading paragraphs fluently. The KeyMath Test is an example of a commercially prepared test that is best used as a criterion-referenced instrument of mathematical skills, especially since the manual gives a behavioral objective for each item in the test. Behavioral indicators and testing of the limits may be used to great advantage in criterion-referenced testing to analyze patterns of persistent errors and the performance style of the student.

Instead of taking the time to develop their own criterion-referenced tests, psychologists might consider using the breadth and scope skills hierarchies that most often accompany primary reading series and elementary mathematics texts. Otherwise, the examiner should consider using one of the several samples of criterion-referenced tests of reading, written expression, mathematics, and learning style prepared by Zigmond, Vallecorsa, & Silverman (1983).

Case Illustration of an LD Psychoeducational Assessment

The following case study intends to illustrate how a psychological examiner might proceed to identify a learning disabled child by following the federal guidelines of PL 94-142.

The parents and reading teacher of 10-1/2-year-old Jim were concerned that he was not doing as well in fifth grade as they expected he should. Jim had been a good student in the first and second grades but his performance in reading became increasingly poorer as he progressed through elementary school. Jim's teacher reported that in most subjects he seemed to enjoy school, worked hard, and had several good friends. This stood in sharp contrast to his behavior in reading. In the past six weeks Jim had started to exhibit classroom misbehaviors and his motivation to work hard was waning. He would often say, "I just can't read that," or "I don't know what that sentence means." It was clear to the reading teacher that Jim's self-concept as a learner was beginning to suffer even in subjects other than reading, so she made a referral for a psychoeducational assessment.

Review of the health history showed no specific developmental disorders or other medical problems that might precipitate such a reading problem. Jim did have glasses, which he wore regularly, and his corrected visual activity was good. His educational folder revealed that he had performed well in preacademic reading skills such as letter recognition. It was not until the third grade that anyone noted any problems in reading. Apparently, Jim's good verbal reasoning skills helped him compensate for his word decoding deficit. In consultation with the teacher the psychologist discovered that appropriate modifications had been made already in Jim's instructional program in reading. No clear reason for the observed reading problem could be discerned other than a possible learning disability.

Individual psychological examination revealed a friendly, well-dressed, yet anxious boy who was concerned about his ability to perform well on the tests. His WISC-R full scale IQ score was in the high average range. There was no significant difference between his verbal and performance scale scores. Jim appeared especially to enjoy the verbal response items and would give long but very complete answers. He was given the Woodcock-Johnson Psycho-Educational Battery (Part II) and scored at the grade levels 1.8 in reading and 4.8 in spelling. A severe discrepancy between his ability and achievement in reading was identified. When asked to read a passage aloud from one of his classroom readers he was observed substituting words, generally choosing words with appropriate meanings that did not resemble the correct word visually or phonetically. For example, he read "building" for "church" and "picked up" for "lifted." Despite his occasional reversals in the order of words his comprehension was good. Jim became visibly upset during the reading test. He appeared to have very limited word attack skills. In most cases he either recognized the word immediately on sight or would guess.

Jim's difficulties were apparently limited to reading. He had above-average intelligence and fairly normal scores on an achievement test of spelling, but a markedly low score for reading. Jim appeared to be a well-adjusted boy from a supportive home environment. His severe discrepancy between ability and reading achievement could not be explained by any of the exclusionary criteria of the federal definition of learning disabilities. Pertinent observations were made through informal testing and testing of the limits, which helped identify and clarify the reading problem. For example, Jim had no difficulty on the Arithmetic subtest of the WISC-R until he was asked to solve word problems that he had to read. He was observed to lose his place and substitute words, and his reading rate was very slow and laborious. On testing of the limits Jim was asked to put into his own words what he thought the passage meant. It was clear he comprehended portions but certainly not enough to complete any word problems correctly. In contrast, Jim appeared to have an excellent fund of background knowledge, a well-developed vocabulary, and good verbal reasoning skills, as demonstrated by his performance on the WISC-R subtests called Information, Vocabulary, and Similarities. This is not always the case with reading disabled children and might be attributed to stimulation and language interactions taking place in Jim's home. Keeping in mind the LD classification criteria, the results of the psychological assessment seemed to point to a diagnosis of LD, which of course would need to be discussed further and confirmed by the multi-disciplinary staffing team.

It has been said as a diagnostic category, LD suffers from the "Statue of Liberty Effect." Even if a referred child is not "truly LD" it is difficult to deny special educational services to one who is having trouble coping in school. The knee-jerk response may be to continue testing until the "real" source of the learning problem is found. In a simulation study of special education placement decision-making (Ysseldyke, 1980), when specialists were presented with a normal profile on a child their response was to "continue testing," often using psychologically poor measures rather than stop and conclude that the child was normal.

Who are the learning disabled? To a large extent the answer to that question depends on the skills of practicing psychologists to apply exclusionary and discrepancy criteria found in the federal definition of LD. The intent of this chapter has been to sharpen those skills by making the criteria for the accurate assessment of LD children as explicit as possible.

References

American Psychiatric Association. (1980). *Diagnostic and statistical manual of mental disorders*. (3rd ed.). Washington, DC: Author.

Barclay, J.R. (1983). Moving toward a technology of prevention: A model and some tentative findings. *School Psychology Review, 12,* 228-239.

Bannatyne, A. (1968). Diagnosing learning disabilities and writing remedial prescriptions. *Journal of Learning Disabilities, 1,* 242-249.

Clements, S.D. (1966). *Minimal brain dysfunction in children* (NINDS Monograph No. 3, U.S. Public Health Service Publication No. 1415), Washington, DC: U.S. Government Printing Office.

Coles, G.S. (1978). The learning disabilities battery: Empirical and social issues. *Harvard Educational Review, 48,* 313-340.

Cone, T.E., & Wilson, L.R. (1981). Quantifying a severe discrepancy: A critical analysis. *Learning Disability Quarterly, 4,* 359-371.

Danielson, L.C., & Bauer, J.N. (1978). A formula-based classification of learning disabled children: An examination of the issues. *Journal of Learning Disabilities, 11,* 50-63.

Federal Register. (1977, Aug. 23). *Regulations Implementing Education for All Handicapped Children Act of 1975, 42,* 42474-42518.

Federal Register. (1975, Nov. 16). Public Law 94-142. *Education for All Handicapped Children Act, 40,* 20762-21948.

Guerin, G.R., & Maier, A.S. (1983). *Informal assessment in education.* Palo Alto, CA: Mayfield Publishing Co.

Harber, J.R. (1981). Learning disability research: How far have we progressed? *Learning Disabilities Quarterly, 4,* 372-381.

Hewett, F.M., & Forness, S.R. (1974). *Education of exceptional learners.* Boston: Forness, Allyn & Bacon.

Henry, S.A., & Whitmann, R.D. (1981). Diagnostic implications of Bannatyne's recategorized WISC-R scores for identifying learning disabled children. *Journal of Learning Disabilities, 14,* 517-520.

Johnson, D.L., & Johnson, C.A. (1971). Comparison of four intelligence tests used with culturally disadvantaged children. *Psychological Reports, 28,* 209-210.

Kaufman, A.S. (1976). A new approach to the interpretation of test scatter on the WISC-R. *Journal of Learning Disabilities, 9,* 160-168.

Kaufman, A.S. (1979). *Intelligent testing with the WISC-R.* New York: John Wiley & Sons.

Kirk, S.A. (1963). Behavioral diagnosis and remediation of learning disabilities. *Proceedings of the Annual Meeting of the Conference on Exploration into Problems of the Perceptually Handicapped Child, 1.*

Larsen, S.C., Rogers, D., & Sowell, V. (1976). The use of selected perceptual tests in differentiating between normal and learning disabled children. *Journal of Learning Disabilities, 9,* 90-95.

Lumsden, J. (1978). Review of Illinois Test of Psycholinguistic Abilities, Revised Edition. In O.K. Buros (Ed.), *The Eighth Mental Measurement Yearbook, Vol. 1.* Highland Park, NJ: The Gryphon Press.

Marsh, G.E., II, Gearhart, C.K., & Gearhart, B.R. (1978). *The learning disabled student: Program alternatives in the secondary school.* St. Louis, MO: C.V. Mosby Co.

Miller, M.D. (1977). Discrimination between two types of learning disabilities by Wechsler Intelligence Scale for Children subtest patterns. *Dissertation Abstracts International, 37,* 5747A.

Moran, M.R. (1978). *Assessment of the exceptional learner in the regular classroom.* Denver: Love Publishing Co.

Phye, G.D., & Reschly, D.J. (1979). *School psychology: Perspectives and issues.* New York: Academic Press.

Poplin, M.S. (1981). The severely learning disabled: Neglected or forgotten? *Learning Disabilities Quarterly, 4,* 330-335.

Reynolds, C.R., Berk, R.A., Boodoo, G.M., Cox, J., Gutkin, T.B., Mann, L., Page, E.B., & Wilson, V.L. (1984). *Critical Measurement Issues in Learning Disabilities.* Washington, DC: United States Department of Education.

Salvia, J., & Ysseldyke, J.E. (1978). *Assessment in special and remedial education.* Boston: Houghton-Mifflin.

Sattler, J.M. (1982). *Assessment of children's intelligence and special abilities* (2nd ed.). Boston: Allyn & Bacon, Inc.

Schumaker, J.B., Deshler, D.D., Alley, G.R., & Warren, M.M. (1980). *An epidemiological study of learning disabled adolescents in secondary schools: The relationship of family factors to the condition of learning disabilities.* (Research Report No. 17). Lawrence, KS: The University of Kansas Institute for Research in Learning Disabilities.

Shepard, L., & Smith, M.L., with Davis, A., Glass, G.V., Riley, A., & Vojir, C. (1981). *Evaluation and the identification of perceptual-communication disorders in Colorado Laboratory of Educational Research.* Boulder, CO: University of Colorado.

Ysseldyke, J.E. (1980). Technical adequacy of tests used by professionals in simulated decision making. *Psychology in the Schools, 17,* 202-209.

Ysseldyke, J.E., Algozzine, B., Shinn, M.R., & McGue, M. (1982). Similarities and differences between low achievers and students classified learning disabled. *The Journal of Special Education, 16,* 73-85.

Ysseldyke, J.E., & Algozzine, B. (1981). Diagnostic classification decision as a function of referral information. *Journal of Special Education, 15,* 429-435.

Ysseldyke, J., Algozzine, B., Regan, R., & Potter, M. (1980). On "unenlightening data" and "bogus problems": A response to Dan Wright. *Psychology in the Schools, 17,* 543-544.

Zigmond, N., Vallecorsa, A., & Silverman, R. (1983). *Assessment for instructional planning in special education.* Englewood Cliffs, NJ: Prentice-Hall, Inc.

8

Psychological Evaluation of Children with Speech and Language Disorders

JEAN C. ELBERT, PH.D., DIANE J. WILLIS, PH.D.

Disorders of speech and language represent the most frequent type of handicapping condition in children (Cartwright, Cartwright, & Ward, 1981). Because these children constitute one of the largest categories of exceptionalities requiring special education (12-15%), they are likely to be referred for psychological evaluation. The psychologist must be able to tease out possible etiology or etiologies of the speech and language disorder; determine whether the child's disorder is secondary to mental retardation, emotional problems, a lack of environmental stimulation, or to a specific language disorder; and suggest recommendations for academic placement or treatment. The method of assessment is of critical importance.

This chapter will review definitions and classifications of common types of speech and language disorders, issues regarding history-taking and psychological test selection, approaches to assessment, interpretation and integration of results, and appropriate ways of communicating the test findings to parents, teachers, and others.

NORMAL SPEECH AND LANGUAGE FUNCTIONING

The spoken word is basic to human communication, but there are many forms of communication other than sending or receiving information by speaking. Communication can be written or imparted by a smile, a gesture or a warm hug, but for the purposes of this chapter only human verbal communication will be discussed.

Language as well as speech comprise oral communication. Lively (1979) states that normal language functioning involves speaking and listening; i.e., the person must be able to comprehend the spoken words of others as well as have the ability to express oneself meaningfully and effectively (p. 255). On the other hand, speech is a motor act; that is, the actual production of language.

As a motor act, speech involves the coordination of four major processes: (1) respiration, or the act of breathing to provide the airstream used for speaking; (2) phonation, or the production of sound by the larynx and vocal

104

folds; (3) resonance, or the vibratory response of the air-filled cavity above the vocal folds which changes the quality or identity of the sound wave; and (4) articulation, or the use of the lips, tongue, teeth, and hard and soft palates to produce speech sounds such as vowels and consonants (Lively, 1979, p. 255).

Oral communication is absolutely vital to our functioning, and when children or adults present with difficulties in oral communication a number of personal problems can develop. Therefore, it is critical that the speech and language disorder be identified early and that professionals initiate appropriate intervention and treatment procedures. Out of the 12-15% of school-aged children presenting with speech and language problems, *articulation disorders* constitute the largest group of children with a speech problem (see Table 1). Oral language disorders often occur in connection with other handicapping conditions such as learning disabilities, cleft palate, mental retardation, emotional disturbances, and cerebral palsy, and constitute the next largest group of disorders in the school-aged population. The incidence of problems in communication is invariably much higher in multihandicapped children. Voice disorders and stuttering occur less frequently, with these two disorders having higher incidence in males than females.

PRE-DIAGNOSTIC STAFFING AND SCREENING

Etiology

Causes of communicative problems have generally been classified as either organic or functional, and in many cases communication disorders have multiple

TABLE 1

Specific Handicapping Conditions of Children
*Professionally Diagnosed as Speech Impaired**

Specific Conditions	*Percentage of Total*
Severe articulation difficulties	46.1
Expressive or receptive language disorder	44.7
Severe stuttering	2.4
Voice disorders	2.3
Cleft palate, cleft lip	1.8
Other speech disorders	2.7
	100.0

*1983 statistics. *Government Affairs Review, 5,* No. 1, March 1984. Reprinted by permission of American Speech-Language-Hearing Association.

etiologies. Organic factors contributing to speech and language impairment include such areas as neurological and muscular disorders, structural deviations, mental retardation, and sensory handicaps. The neurological and neuromuscular disorders may involve generalized brain injury such as cerebral palsy, which may result in partial paralysis of the speech musculature (dysarthria), or impaired ability to program the motor pattern for forming speech sounds (dyspraxia). More localized brain injury or dysfunction may result in impaired ability to comprehend and/or express language orally. Structural deviations such as nasal obstruction, removal or paralysis of the larynx, and facial deformities of the mouth or jaw such as cleft palate, maloccluded teeth, and other dental irregularities, may all cause communicative difficulty. Mental retardation, since it is often associated with diffuse brain damage, may be considered the cause of speech and language impairment in many cases. Finally, hearing impairment may be regarded as the etiology in selected children.

Functional, or nonorganic, factors constitute a large proportion of speech and language problems, and those contributing to communication disorders also include social and psychological factors. For example, children from abusive or severely neglected homes or children with poor parental models for speech will likely experience inadequate or delayed speech development. Children infantalized by parents who anticipate all of their child's needs and do not reinforce and stimulate oral communication frequently have immature patterns of speech. In essence, there are large numbers of children who present with impaired oral communication, and many problems have both functional and organic components present. A thorough history is important in determining the possible etiological factors.

Need for Interdisciplinary Evaluation

Evaluation of a child's verbal and nonverbal abilities requires the efforts of both a psychologist and a speech and language pathologist, but other specialists may also be involved. The child with a cleft palate will need plastic surgery and perhaps oral surgery and dentistry as well as the care of a general physician. Since most young children experience a high incidence of otitis media, they need not only a general physician but on occasion an audiologist or otorhinolaryngologist. One should keep in mind that a speech and language disorder may not be as straightforward or simple as it looks. Since anatomical, psychological, educational, and sociological factors can all contribute to speech problems, the child may require the expertise of numerous disciplines to correct the speech impairment.

Establishing History and Symptoms

In order to best serve the child referred for assessment, the clinician must interview the parent(s) and obtain a developmental and medical history. Table 2 offers suggestions for history taking and a checklist of symptoms and pertinent history.

TABLE 2

Checklist of Symptoms and Pertinent History

History   YES   NO

1. History of frequent and/or severe ear infections   ☐   ☐
   (otitis media)?
2. Myringotomy procedure (tubes in the ear)?   ☐   ☐
3. History of hearing loss?   ☐   ☐
4. History of medical/physical problems (cleft lip/palate,   ☐   ☐
   seizures, cerebral palsy, etc.)?
5. Has had audiological evaluation?   ☐   ☐
6. Has had speech or language evaluation?   ☐   ☐
7. Has been seen by ORL?   ☐   ☐
8. Impoverished home environment?   ☐   ☐
9. Lack of stimulation of oral communication?   ☐   ☐
10. Evidence of child abuse or neglect?   ☐   ☐
11. Bilingual communication in the home?   ☐   ☐
12. Parents or guardians present with good speech?   ☐   ☐

Symptoms

1. Does not seem to want to talk.   ☐   ☐
2. Relies on gestures to communicate needs.   ☐   ☐
3. Sounds continually congested.   ☐   ☐
4. Sounds nasal.   ☐   ☐
5. Has inappropriate loudness or pitch.   ☐   ☐
6. Stammers or stutters.   ☐   ☐
7. Difficult to understand.   ☐   ☐
8. Speaks in single words or short phrases.   ☐   ☐
9. Has difficulty following verbal directions.   ☐   ☐
10. Seems embarrassed about his/her speech.   ☐   ☐
11. Asks for repetition and/or watches speaker's face   ☐   ☐
    closely.
12. Watches people's lips as they talk.   ☐   ☐
13. Understands gestures but not verbal commands.   ☐   ☐
14. Uses gestures spontaneously.   ☐   ☐
15. Sounds hoarse and has a gravelly rough sounding   ☐   ☐
    voice.

If the child is referred for assessment by the school or family and the question of hearing problems arises, the clinician will want to bear in mind that ruling out physical causes for communication problems is necessary and refer the child to both an audiologist and a speech pathologist. When hearing is judged normal by an audiologist, the clinician can more safely interpret test results.

Other characteristics that the clinician needs to observe during the assessment process include the pitch (high or low), intensity (loud or soft), quality, and resonance of the voice. Whether the child sounds nasal or denasal must also be noted (e.g., cleft-palate children commonly sound nasal), and it is wise to have a speech pathologist look at and listen to the child who does sound nasal. Finally, when assessing a child the clinician must also attend to patterns of speech and, particularly, to any abnormal vocal characteristics. A child who sounds hoarse yet has no cold or allergies, and whose voice has a rough, abnormal, low-pitched, and gravelly quality to it must be referred to either a certified speech pathologist or to an otorhinolaryngologist. Children presenting with a voice disorder may be abusing their voices or there may be underlying laryngeal pathology. In the latter case a physician must be one of the professionals involved in the care of the child.

Generally, developmental milestones, with the exception of speech, are normal in children whose sole problem is communication. Children whose speech and language disorder is secondary to mental retardation frequently will have a history of delayed development in other areas. Children with physical disorders such as cerebral palsy will often have a history of delayed motor development as well as a speech and language disorder, but the intellectual capacity of this group can vary from above normal to severe retardation. Thus the major question for the clinician concerned with the etiology of a child's speech and language impairment is whether the disorder is secondary to mental retardation, emotional problems, a lack of environmental stimulation, or to a specific language disorder.

FORMULATION OF ASSESSMENT AND DIAGNOSTIC STRATEGIES

Objectives and techniques must be carefully outlined and planned in advance to insure that one obtains the information needed for an appropriate assessment. An assessment may consist of both formal and informal tests, and procedures should be selected that will allow the clinician to observe and describe an adequate sample of the child's verbal and nonverbal behavior. The following sections briefly describe the major types of speech and language problems that the psychologist is likely to encounter.

Phonological Disorders

At the most basic level of verbal communication, some children exhibit problems in their ability to learn the sound system of language. The development of speech articulation was once viewed in isolation, and attention was given to the remediation of isolated speech articulation errors. However, phonology is an integral aspect of the overall language system and phonological disorders consist of two primary types: disorders in speech sound perception (input disorders), and disorders in speech sound production (output disorders).

Children with difficulty in perceiving phonological differences may be unable to distinguish acoustically similar words such as *cup/cub* and *pin/pen*. They often misperceive words, either in isolation or in context, and such a difficulty has obvious implications for their ability to comprehend language and learn phonetic approaches to reading and spelling.

Disorders in speech sound production (articulation) refer primarily to the clarity, intelligibility, and accuracy of speech sounds and words. Articulation disorders consist of three major types: omission of sound(s) (e.g., "-oup"/soup; "sumin"/something); substitution of sound(s) (e.g., "wabbit"/rabbit; "dese"/ these); and distortion of sound(s). Such speech production problems may range in severity from mild difficulty in articulating several isolated sounds to severe problems which render oral speech relatively unintelligible. In those children with mild to moderate articulation problems, speech is generally adequate for most verbal tests. However, in the child with poor intelligibility, measures must be selected which minimize verbalization.

Receptive Language Disorders

Beyond the fundamental perceptual level of the speech-sound system, disruptions in verbal communication can occur at the level of comprehension and meaning. It is generally accepted that the ability to understand verbal symbols and linguistic rules precedes the ability to produce verbal messages. A receptive language difficulty (input disorder), such as poor understanding of individual vocabulary words or specific grammatical constructions, phrases, or sentence forms, can occur at several levels of language processing. Children with impaired receptive language fail to process the entire sentence and lose critical information or instructions. Some children have difficulty in auditory attention, perception, and memory, which affects their ability to process and comprehend oral language. Difficulty in auditory figure-ground perception may prevent the child from isolating speech sounds from background noise. Such children may be auditorily distractible, and the additional concentration required in listening may result in fatigue. Many of these children appear to require additional time to process language or they need repetitions; consequently, their responses are often delayed. Others have very short memory spans, which prevent them from retaining lengthy sentences or a series of verbal directions. Children with severe receptive language problems might be erroneously diagnosed as mentally retarded or emotionally disturbed, because they may produce phrases which are echolalic and stereotyped, but have no meaningful context (Myklebust, 1954).

Expressive Language Disorders

Although some children have adequate comprehension of language, as evidenced by their ability to follow verbal directions, they may be delayed in the expression of oral language. Others demonstrate more generalized impairment in both understanding and production of language. Such children generally are delayed in the development of basic vocabulary; they may have limited conceptual understanding and make semantic errors, or use words in inappropriate context. Their communication attempts may be cryptic, omitting necessary grammatical and semantic elements. While capable of responding appropriately to test items involving a high degree of linguistic structure, their spontaneous generation of language may be quite limited. Children with expressive disorders frequently make numerous grammatical errors and often cannot generate appropriate word forms. Still others may produce generally adequate grammatical forms, but exhibit problems in recalling correct word order.

Children with difficulty in producing fluent sentences often exhibit word-finding problems or the inability to recall specific words spontaneously or on demand. The clinician should be aware that this may reflect more generalized problems in retaining and recalling verbal information. Word retrieval difficulty often results in numerous pauses, gestures, repetition of words, and a restricted range of available vocabulary. Such poverty of expression may be revealed in stereotyped phrases (e.g., "you know," "whatcha'ma call it," "dealie"), imprecise word choices, and circumlocutions.

Other children may demonstrate generally adequate grammar and vocabulary, but have poor facility in language production and formulation (i.e., organizing verbal units and formulating ideas in a logical sequence).

Elective Mutes

Occasionally the clinician will be asked to assess children who either will not talk or present with partial speech avoidance. A thorough history demonstrates that these children generally communicate at home but elect not to speak at school. When the history clearly indicates *selective* communication (i.e., the child speaks at home or at the grandparents' house or with the neighbors, but not at school), then the child is likely an elective mute. Most elective mutes receive secondary gain from not talking, since much attention is focused on their mutism. These children tend to be shy and anxious, and some present with speech problems that embarrass them. For a more detailed discussion of elective mutism, the clinician should refer to the article by Halpern, Hammond, & Cohen (1971).

ADMINISTRATION OF TESTS AND PROCEDURES

Comprehensive evaluation of language function, precise characterization of the speech or language deficits, and diagnosis or speech or language disorder must be undertaken by the trained speech and language pathologist. The psychologist's contribution to the evaluation of speech- and language-impaired children generally involves the following areas:

1. Assessment of intellectual functioning, which provides data concerning the child's relative competence in verbal and nonverbal areas. The clinician can contribute valuable information about whether verbal abilities are selectively impaired, or whether the speech or language impairment exists in the context of a generalized cognitive delay (e.g., secondary to mental retardation).
2. Assessment of adaptive behavior and personality, and determination of the extent to which a speech and language impairment affects the child's social and emotional development.
3. Identification of behaviors that suggest inadequate language skills, and screening of possible language impairment.
4. Assessment of educational achievement in areas which may be expected to relate to speech and language disorders.

Assessment of Intelligence

It must be recognized that no specific tests can reliably distinguish between specific language disorder, generalized cognitive delay, and/or environmental deprivation. Such distinctions involve clinical judgment, which is based on an understanding of the complex interrelationships among language and intelligent thought.

Initially, assessing the intelligence of children with impaired verbal comprehension or expression must include measures that are specifically designed to evaluate nonverbal thinking and problem-solving. A severely language-impaired child will obviously experience difficulty with verbal tasks, and the level of cognitive ability could be seriously underestimated in such a child. If the evaluation is to be used for determining school placement, appropriate measures are all the more critical. The clinician should base the selection of one or more tests of mental ability on an informal observation of the response modalities a child has available. For those children who appear to have some limited comprehension of oral language but severely limited verbal output, measures may be selected that involve pointing or following simple verbal instructions. For those whose verbal comprehension is severely impaired, the selection of measures that do not require verbal instructions is critical. Table 3 lists formal measures for the assessment of nonverbal cognitive abilities. Such scales as the Leiter International Performance Scale and the Hiskey-Nebraska Test of Learning Aptitude can aid the clinician in discriminating between children who have generalized cognitive delays and those whose poor performance is specific to verbal language. However, it must be recognized that these scales are not as predictive of later school performance as tests which include the assessment of verbal skills (Anastasi, 1976).

TABLE 3

Assessment of Intelligence

Nonverbal Reasoning	Age Range	Measures Including A Nonverbal Scale	Age Range
Hiskey-Nebraska Test of Learning Aptitude	2½-18½	Wechsler Adult Intelligence Scale Revised (WAIS-R)	16-adult
Arthur Point Scale of Performance, Form I	4-adult	Wechsler Intelligence Scale for Children-Revised (WISC-R) (Performance Scale)	6-16
Arthur Point Scale of Performance Tests: Revised Form II	5-15	Wechsler Preschool and Primary Scale of Intelligence (WPPSI) (Performance Scale)	4-6¼
Leiter International Performance Scale (Arthur Adaptation)	2-18	McCarthy Scales of Children's Abilities (Perceptual Performance Scale)	2½-8½
Coloured Progressive Matrices	5-11; adults	Kaufman Assessment Battery for Children (K-ABC) (Nonverbal Scale)	2½-12½
Advanced Progressive Matrices	adolescent, adult		
Pictorial Test of Intelligence	3-8		
Merrill-Palmer Scale	18 mo.-4		
Columbia Mental Maturity Scale	3½-10		

For those children who have sufficient language to respond to verbal items on a standard measure of intelligence (e.g., Wechsler Intelligence Scale for Children-Revised (WISC-R); Wechsler Preschool and Primary Scale of Intelligence (WPPSI); McCarthy Scales of Children's Abilities), their performance on the nonverbal subtests may be a more accurate reflection of underlying reasoning and problem-solving ability.

A verbal IQ score significantly inferior to the nonverbal or performance IQ score, given that hearing is normal, is generally considered to be a hallmark of the language impaired child. However, it should be noted that on several "nonverbal" subtests, linguistic or verbally mediated strategies may be required. For example, the Wechsler Adult Intelligence Scale-Revised (WAIS-R) or WISC-R Picture Arrangement subtest involves a verbal story sequence; Object Assembly is often performed more efficiently when the child can recognize and covertly label the intended figure, thus resulting in conceptually directed organizational skills. Therefore, Verbal-Performance discrepancies may present only borderline significance in some cases. Significant clues to the child's language impairment may be obtained from responses to verbal test items; therefore, verbatim recording of responses is encouraged so that exact language samples can be evaluted.

The child's performance on verbal subtests should provide insight into the specific communication problems. At this point in the evaluation, the clinician can generate hypotheses for further screening. Examples of specific indicators which should alert the clinician to problems in language reception or expression may be observed from a child's responses to verbal test items:

Phonology:
1) misperception of vocabulary items—e.g., responding to the item "join" as "you be happy and stuff" (joy/join); to "gasoline" as "that sticky stuff your mom puts on you" (vaseline/gasoline); to "letter" as "a thing that you climb" (ladder); to "fable" as "a place where horses live" (stable)
2) misarticulation of sounds— "wed"/red

Sequencing:
1) transposition of sounds within words—e.g., "aminals"/animals; "shun sines"/ sun shines
2) transposition of words within sentences—e.g., stove: "you can cook on food"

Word Retrieval:
1) circumlocutions and imprecise terms—e.g., unable to recall the word "stems," says "they have stickups to carry;" referring to "cactus," says "that plant thingie with sticker things"
2) substitutions of semantically-related words in oral reading—e.g., house/home

Syntax:
1) inappropriate grammatical constructions—e.g., "Them boy ain't go."

2) immature constructions for a child's chronological or mental age—e.g., "Where that man go?"

Assessment of Behavior and Personality Functioning

A child with a communication disorder is frequently at high risk for social and emotional problems. Those who cannot adequately express their needs become easily frustrated. Past failure experiences often lead to increased vulnerability; children who cannot verbalize negative emotional experiences may tend to show heightened irritability, moodiness, and acting-out behavior. The child with language processing difficulty may demonstrate a short attention span and irritability when tasks involve only auditory stimuli; in contrast, improved interest and concentration may be observed when visual stimuli or manipulatable objects are introduced. Many language-impaired children appear uncooperative, withholding, guarded, or impulsive. The failure to establish covert language may result in delayed development of modulation of emotional experience and inner control.

In the child with severely impaired language skills, carefully observing behavior, noting parent interview data, and using objective behavioral scales may all be appropriate in the evaluation of the child's emotional status. Measures of the child's level of adaptive behavior (e.g., Vineland Social Maturity Scale; AAMD Adaptive Behavior Scale, School Edition) may prove very useful as the clinician determines the degree to which a communication disorder may have interfered with the normal development of independent self-help skills. Nonverbal techniques, such as drawing and play interviews, may be necessary in order to evaluate the emotional behavior of severely language impaired and/or nonverbal children.

For language-impaired children who have sufficient language expression to respond to projective tests, particular consideration is necessary in interpreting their responses. Thematic tests such as the Children's Apperception Test (CAT) and Thematic Apperception Test (TAT) are generally used to assess an individual's interpersonal attitudes. It is suggested that the psychologist record and transcribe the responses to thematic tests since they can provide a valuable language sample for analysis. Although pathological modes of thinking are thought to be reflected in projective responses, it is important to note that language-disordered children often produce deviant responses. Children with problems in oral formulation may have extreme difficulty in producing logically coherent stories or their responses may be concrete and descriptive; they may misperceive or mislabel figures or their stories may be impoverished, vague, and imprecise. Often these children require much more encouragement, probes, and even models from the examiner (e.g., "Once upon a time . . ."). Emotional experiences may not be conceptually differentiated by these children; consequently, they may not possess a vocabulary to describe feeling states (e.g., "lonely," "disgusted," "embarrassed," "excited") and may globally categorize affect into positive ("happy") or negative ("sad") experiences.

Use of the Rorschach Psychodiagnostic Test with language-impaired children requires even more cautious interpretation, for responses to this instrument require a complex integration of perception, concept formation, and organization skills. Children with word retrieval problems may fail to label their perceptions accurately, and their inability to describe or articulate answers may result in apparently impoverished records. Thus, the clinician must exercise extreme care lest impaired language production be misinterpreted as a significant indicator of disturbed emotional functioning.

Screening Assessment of Selected Language Skills

For children who have already been evaluated by a speech and language pathologist, no additional assessment of language skills is indicated. However, in cases where the clinician suspects an oral communication problem from the child's history and/or the pattern of results obtained during intellectual assessment, additional data may be helpful. In general, a goal for the clinician is to obtain a representative sample of the child's oral language during spontaneous conversation as well as in response to structured verbal items. Tape recording and/or verbatim recording of the child's verbal responses, as well as noting the use of gesture, are recommended.

Following the establishment of the child's cognitive ability, the clinician may wish to further assess specific areas of language competence. Table 4 lists measures which may provide additional information regarding phonology, receptive language, expressive language, and verbal memory.

For the child who has been observed misperceiving words in conversation or on verbal items, further screening for a possible auditory discrimination problem may be indicated. The Auditory Discrimination Test (Wepman) and the Goldman-Fristoe-Woodcock Test of Auditory Discrimination are appropriate measures for assessing this aspect of auditory functioning. The clinician must recognize that both a mild hearing loss and impaired auditory attention can contribute to problems in the phonology of speech. The child with speech articulation errors should be referred directly to the trained speech pathologist; however, the clinician can provide useful referral data by recording the sounds/words which are obviously misarticulated.

Assessment of language comprehension is essential in the child who has a severe expressive language disorder. Although several intelligence tests include items/subtests that assess receptive abilities (e.g., McCarthy Scales: Picture Vocabulary; Stanford-Binet Intelligence Scale: Oral Commissions), most verbal items require an oral response; thus, the psychologist's ability to assess the child's comprehension may be confounded by the expressive or output disorder. One should select tasks that require merely pointing or marking a response, or following directions. Table 4 lists formal measures that will enable the clinician to establish developmental levels for vocabulary comprehension (Peabody Picture Vocabulary Test-Revised), and comprehension of word forms and grammar (Northwestern

TABLE 4

Assessment of Auditory Language Skills

Area Assessed	Test	Age Range	Description
PHONOLOGY			
Auditory Discrimination/ Perception	Auditory Discrimination Test (Wepman)	5-8	Discrimination of word pairs presented orally
	Goldman-Fristoe-Woodcock Test of Auditory Discrimination	3-Adult	Discrimination of word pairs presented pictorially
RECEPTIVE LANGUAGE			
Single Word Vocabulary	Peabody Picture Vocabulary Test-Revised (PPVT-R)	2½-40	Pictorial multiple-choice test of vocaulary
	Test of Language Development (TOLD-Primary): Picture Vocabulary	4-8	Pictorial multiple-choice test of vocabulary
	Boehm Test of Basic Concepts	5-7	Pictorial multiple-choice test that measures concepts considered to be necessary for school achievement
Comprehension of Grammatical Forms (Morphology and Syntax)	Test for Auditory Comprehension of Language (TACL)	3-7	Pictorial multiple-choice test of grammar units
	Northwestern Syntax Screening Test (NSST): Receptive	3-7	Pictorial multiple-choice test of grammatical constructions
	Test of Language Development (TOLD-Primary): Grammatic Understanding	4-8	Pictorial multiple-choice test of grammatical constructions
Comprehension of Paragraphs	Durrell Analysis of Reading Difficulty (Listening Comprehension)	6-11	Child answers questions after listening to short stories ranging in difficulty level from 1st to 6th grade
EXPRESSIVE LANGUAGE			
Labeling Vocabulary	Expressive One-Word Picture Vocabulary Test (Primary) (Intermediate)	2-12	Labeling of pictures representing concrete nouns and class nouns
Word Association	Illinois Test of Psycholinguistic Abilities: (ITPA): Auditory Association	2-10	Child provides a word after hearing incomplete analogy
	Detroit Tests of Learning Aptitude (DTLA): Verbal Opposites	3-Adult	Producing an antonym or opposite to the target word
Morphology	Illinois Test of Psycholinguistic Abilities: (ITPA): Grammatic Closure	2-10	Child completes stimulus sentence with inflected or derived word forms using verbal stimuli and picture cues
	Test of Language Development (TOLD): Grammatic Completion	4-8	Child completes stimulus sentence with inflected or derived word forms using only verbal stimuli
Syntax	Northwestern Syntax Screening Test (NSST): Expressive	3-7	Sentence repetition with picture cues
	Test of Language Development (TOLD-Primary): Sentence Imitation	4-8	Sentence repetition with verbal stimuli only
VERBAL MEMORY			
	Detroit Tests of Learning Aptitude (DTLA): Auditory Attention Span for Unrelated Words	3-Adult	Word repetition
	Detroit Tests of Learning Aptitude (DTLA): Auditory Attention Span for Related Syllables	3-Adult	Sentence repetition
	Detroit Tests of Learning Aptitude (DTLA): Oral Directions	7-Adult	Paper and pencil task requiring following verbal directions

Syntax Screening Test: Receptive; Test of Language Development (TOLD); Grammatic Understanding Test of Auditory Comprehension of Language (TACL).

In order to evaluate further a child's language expression, tasks which require direct verbal responses are required. Much valuable information about a child's competence with language expression will have been obtained from the verbal test items in a test of intelligence. Additional formal measures for assessing word labeling and retrieval (Expressive One-Word Picture Vocabulary Test), word association and meaning (Illinois Test of Psycholinguistic Abilities (ITPA): Auditory Expression), and grammatic usage (TOLD: Grammatic Completion; ITPA: Grammatic Closure) are listed in Table 4.

Finally, impaired language comprehension and expression in many children is related to poor verbal memory span. Often these children cannot remember a verbal unit long enough to process it sufficiently, or cannot retrieve verbal information well. Table 4 lists several measures of short-term memory for words, sentences, and oral directions, which may provide the clinician with useful information.

Assessment of Educational Achievement

Children with impaired speech and language are at risk for significant problems in school achievement; therefore, assessment of academic levels in these children is an important prerequisite to devising an appropriate educational program. Johnson & Myklebust (1967) have described the areas of reading and written language as visual symbol systems superimposed on a preestablished oral language system. In this hierarchical development of language systems, one can expect problems in oral language comprehension or expression to be reflected in the child's ability to learn written language skills. Children with a phonological disorder may have great difficulty discriminating individual letter sounds, are often delayed in learning letter names and sounds, and may experience significant problems in learning beginning phonics skills. Poor oral language comprehension is generally reflected in poor reading comprehension. If children do not comprehend the spoken word, they will likewise have difficulty understanding the vocabulary sentences or paragraphs they read. Children with expressive language disorders may fail to attend to word endings and be unable to benefit from the contextual cues that aid comprehension in the child with adequate oral language competence. Because of the complex processes involved in written expression, the language-impaired child can often be expected to experience difficulty in language arts and subjects involving written language. Poor verbal comprehension may also reflect in the child's math achievement, particularly when word problems are encountered. Therefore, assessment of reading recognition, reading comprehension, spelling, written language, and mathematics is recommended for the school-aged language-impaired child. Suggested tests for assessing these areas are the following: 1) *reading recognition:* Peabody Individual Achievement Test (PIAT): Reading Recognition; Wide Range Achievement Test (WRAT): Reading; 2) *reading comprehension:* PIAT: Reading

Comprehension; 3) *spelling:* WRAT: Spelling; 4) *written language:* Test of Written Language (TOWL); and 5) *mathematics:* PIAT: Mathematics.

Auditory or language-based learning disabilities must be considered in the context of educational achievement in the speech- or language-impaired child. Harrington's chapter in this book provides additional information regarding assessment procedures for these children.

DIAGNOSTIC DECISIONS

The competent diagnostician must be able to integrate information gathered from: history and background information; parent interview; behavioral observations of the child; and objective psychometric data. In instances where conflicting data exist (i.e., the child is observed to perform at a developmental or language level below that described by the parent), the clinician may often need to exercise considerable judgment. Lack of parental objectivity may need to be weighed against the possibility of underestimating a child's ability from a single observation. The psychologist must consider a child's response to cuing, careful behavioral structuring, and modeling procedures when estimating an optimal level of performance.

In essence, the clinician looks for consistent patterns of strengths and weaknesses, which both describe current functioning and provide a sound rationale for recommending additional assessment or developing treatment strategies. Both quantitative and qualitative information need to be considered in formulating the diagnostic impressions. Such indices as Verbal vs. Performance scores and clustering of verbal-conceptual, perceptual-organizational, and freedom-from-distractability factors (Kaufman, 1979) are useful and important. Equally relevant is the quality of verbal responses with regard to articulation, word retrieval, grammar and word order, and formulation. Some questions that the clinician should raise in analyzing test performance and formulating diagnostic impressions are: Did the child fail the item because of difficulty or poor verbal comprehension of directions? Is the problem at the level of input, output, or both? Is a delay or deficit in the child's performance restricted to verbal tasks, or generalized to verbal and nonverbal tasks?

With the speech- or language-impaired child, a valid differentiation among children with low intelligence, specific language disorder, or environmental disadvantage may often prove very difficult. Careful consideration must be given to the child's development of skills that are not dependent on oral communication (i.e., fine and gross motor skills, object manipulation, sensorimotor activities, visual-spatial perceptual abilities). As a rule, the language-disordered child is expected to have relatively intact nonverbal abilities, while the cognitively delayed child will evidence more generalized decrements in performance. However, the child with borderline intelligence may have developed adequate verbal abilities to cope with the task that demands simple repetition or association and not abstract conceptualization. Environmental disadvantage may interact with a language disorder or cognitive delay to compromise more seriously the child's performance.

In regard to young children who present with complex disorders involving impaired cognition, language, and behavior, the clinician must exercise caution in premature classification, which could result in inadequate or inappropriate placement. Many of these children may require periodic re-evaluations to assess their rate of cognitive growth and/or to evaluate their response to treatment or programming.

With toddlers and preschool-age children, the clinician may wish to refer to developmental norms as guidelines for expected levels of speech and language development. Suggested references are Berry (1969) and Weiss & Lillywhite (1981).

COMMUNICATION OF RESULTS

As emphasized throughout this chapter, the child with impaired speech or language must always be referred to the trained speech and language pathologist for the diagnosis of speech or language disorders. It is equally essential for the psychologist to refer the nonverbal child, the child with a history of otitis media, and any child suspected of hearing sensitivity, to an audiologist.

The clinician's role in determining whether the child's impaired speech or language is specific or consistent with generalized cognitive delay has been addressed. Additional roles include aiding in the early identification and prevention of oral communication problems, and communicating findings to parents, teachers, and other professionals who may be involved with the child.

Both the child's current levels of language and verbal abilities, as well as the relationship between language and intelligence, should be carefully explained to parents. They need to understand the importance of verbal skills as predictors of later school achievement. Some parents of young children may have decided or been advised that the child will "grow out of" the communication problem. They need to be apprised of the importance of early remediation for improved prognosis. Information about the child's strengths and weaknesses should be given along with general suggestions for language stimulation if indicated. Some parents and teachers may require feedback regarding appropriate speech modeling, establishing motivation for the child to communicate orally, reducing length and complexity of verbal directives, and expanding the child's utterances. Additional information regarding the effect of a severe communication disorder on the child's social and emotional development should sensitize the parents to their roles in shaping a child's maturity, independence, self-esteem, and general emotional security. In the child for whom psychological treatment, behavioral management, and/or psychotherapy seems indicated, the clinician should exercise judgment in making a referral. Traditional, verbally oriented psychotherapy may be inappropriate for the child with severe oral communication difficulty.

In conclusion, the psychological assessment of children with speech and language impairment requires particular attention to the selection of appropriate measures, an understanding of the relationship between language and cognition, and the awareness that the involvement of other professionals is crucial if adequate identification and intervention are to occur for these children.

REFERENCES

Anastasi, A. (1976). *Psychological testing* (4th ed.). New York: The Macmillan Company.
Berry, M. F. (1969). *Language disorders of children.* New York: Appleton-Century-Crofts.
Cartwright, G. P., Cartwright, C. A., & Ward, M. E. (1981). *Educating special learners.* Belmont, CA: Wadsworth Publishing Company.
Halpern, W. I., Hammond. J., & Cohen, R. (1971). A therapeutic approach to speech phobia: Elective mutism reexamined. *Journal of the American Academy of Child Psychiatry, 10,* 94-107.
Johnson, D. & Myklebust, H. (1967). *Learning disabilities: Educational principles and practices. New York: Grune & Stratton.*
Kaufman, A. S. (1979). *Intelligent testing with the WISC-R.* New York: John Wiley & Sons.
Lively, M. A. (1979). Speech and language disabled children and youth. In B. M. Swanson & D. J. Willis (Eds.) *Understanding exceptional children and youth.* New York: Houghton-Mifflin Co.
Myklebust, H. (1954). *Auditory disorders in children: A manual for differential diagnosis.* New York: Grune & Stratton.
Weiss, C. E. & Lillywhite, H. S. (1981). *Communicative disorders: Prevention and early intervention.* St. Louis, MO: C. V. Mosby Co.

9

Psychological Evaluation
of Hearing-Impaired Children

MARY MIRA, PH.D.

Approximately 90,000 school-age children may be considered hearing impaired (Cantor & Spragins, 1977), and a large number of them will be referred for psychological evaluation in order to receive special educational services. Other children will be referred because the language deficits resulting from the hearing loss will raise concerns about their overall development.

Few psychologists are trained in any aspect of hearing impairment (Levine, 1974), raising concern about the quality of psychological services these children receive. It is recognized that in many instances the examination must of necessity be conducted by a psychologist with little previous experience with the hearing impaired. The purpose of this chapter is to familiarize psychologists who may be called upon occasionally to see a hearing-impaired child with accepted procedures for planning and conducting a psychological evaluation. Other sources of information for the psychologist unfamiliar with this population include Cantor & Spragins, 1977; Kretschmer, 1983; Levine, 1981; and Rogers & Soper, 1982.

This chapter will address evaluation procedures designed to examine cognitive functioning, language development, academic achievement, and minor behavior problems. It is recommended that one refer a hearing-impaired child in whom the primary psychodiagnostic issue is the presence of an emotional disorder to a clinician more experienced with the hearing impaired.

PRE-EVALUATION CONSIDERATIONS

Defining the Referral Question

The first step in planning an assessment may involve a clarification of the referral question, since the presenting problems that prompted the referral may be couched in devious ways. The psychologist may need to go back to the referring person or to observe the child in the classroom if this is where the referral originated. A question such as, "Does this child belong in my classroom?" may mask the teacher's request for assistance with a behavior disorder. Most referral problems resolve into one of the following:

1. Hearing loss aside, how is the child's cognitive development progressing? The referring professional or the family may wonder if the language delays reflect only the hearing impairment or if they indicate the presence of additional developmental problems.

2. What has been the impact of the hearing loss on the child's language- and vocabularly-based knowledge? Is the language problem consistent with the degree of hearing loss?

3. How is the child doing academically? Is the child progressing as well as can be expected considering the hearing loss? Are there some areas of academic deficiency out of line with expected achievements?

4. What is the most appropriate educational placement and program for this child? What is the child ready to learn and how should this be programmed? In what setting should the child be taught? What are realistic educational goals that the parents and child can set?

5. How can the family or school deal more effectively with problem behavior? Although a hearing-impaired child need not present any greater number of behavior disorders than one who hears well, the presence of a hearing loss may make it difficult for adults to decide how best to deal with them when they do arise.

Development of a Case History

A comprehensive case history provides a vital component of the evaluation. This information not only helps the examiner understand how the child's current functioning evolved, but is also necessary for interpreting evaluation findings and making educational or treatment recommendations. Data making up the case history may come from previous records, but ideally should be supplemented by a current interview with the child's parents. The following areas should be included in the case history.

Description of the hearing loss. Even though the psychologist plans to use an interpreter or nonverbal assessment procedures, a comprehensive picture of the child requires an understanding of the dimensions of the hearing impairment.

1) *Type of loss.* The child may present with a *conductive* hearing loss in which sounds are not transmitted completely to the inner ear and auditory pathways because of problems, generally, in the middle ear. Common causes for conductive impairments are: inflammation in the middle ear resulting in fluid or scar tissue build-up that prevents normal transmission; damaged eardrums; infection or blocking of the Eustachian tube; problems with the bones of the middle ear, preventing them from moving normally and transmitting sound to the hearing mechanism; and blockage of the ear canal. A conductive hearing loss, as a rule, does not exceed a moderate loss. The auditory signal is not distorted, but merely reduced in intensity. A conductive impairment is the type most helped by a hearing aid, and is not always

permanent. Because a conductive loss may be associated with a chronic middle-ear infection, it may fluctuate with the course of the infection, which makes evaluation difficult. A conductive loss may be mild enough to be missed by parents and teachers while still having a deleterious effect on language development and behavior.

The child may have a *sensorineural* hearing loss. These losses are associated with damage to the inner ear, sensory receptors, or to the auditory pathways to the brain. These losses are irreversible, although their effects may be modified by hearing aids. Sensorineural losses may be congenitally related to either genetic or intrauterine factors, or may be acquired at any time due to such factors as trauma, infections, or drugs. With a sensorineural loss, in addition to reduced hearing sensitivity, the auditory signal even though amplified may be distorted, making discrimination of speech more difficult. Children with sensorineural losses may also have a conductive impairment resulting in a *mixed* loss. In these cases, the conductive component may or may not be amenable to improvement.

2) *Degree and extent of hearing loss.* Hearing losses are classified according to the level of intensity across the speech range that the child can hear. These losses generally are categorized as follows:

MILD—15-30 decibel (dB) loss. This degree of loss is often not recognized unless the child begins showing language or attention problems and is referred for audiological evaluation.

MODERATE—30-50 dB loss. The child with a moderate loss may appear to hear most speech in a one-to-one situation but will miss much of what is said in class.

SEVERE—inability fo hear sounds less than 50-80 dB in intensity. These children are more readily identified, especially at the time of expected speech emergence. They will hear only the loudest speech sounds and their articulation, vocabularly, and voice quality will be affected.

PROFOUND—greater than 80 dB. These children will not hear speech and will hear few other sounds.

It is also important to know the extent of the hearing loss in terms of the frequency ranges affected. A hearing loss is rarely of equal severity across all sound frequencies. Occasionally, conductive losses are flat across the frequencies. Sensorineural losses generally become more severe as one goes up the frequencies. The important information consists of the child's hearing sensitivity within those frequencies which encompass most speech sounds.

3) *History of the loss.* Information about the course of the child's hearing loss includes age of onset, when it was identified, how it has been managed, the child's prior training to use residual hearing, and if and for how long an aid has been worn. Obtaining information about the possible cause of the hearing impairment cues the examiner to the possibility of other physical or congenital problems. This history

information will assist in the interpretation of findings, since the impact of the loss on articulation and language is greater the earlier the onset.

It is suggested that historical information gleaned from the interview be documented by records obtained from previous evaluation and training programs.

4) *Child's social history.* The psychologist must also understand the child's current psychosocial situation. This includes the parents' expectations for language competence and educational attainment, and whether these aspirations are consistent with what is known about the child's abilities. Also useful is information about the child's place in the family, experiences in the world such as opportunities for recreation, and the degree of exposure to the hearing world. One should also note the family history of compliance with previous programs.

5) *Current communication skills.* Prior to the evaluation, it is helpful if the psychologist has information about the child's speech-reading competence, ability to interact with speaking adults, use of speech, manual communication, and response to gestural communication.

6) *Health status.* This information should help identify factors that may impose stresses on the child or impede optimal functioning. Current information about the child's vision is vital, not only because this is the child's primary mode of learning, but because of the high incidence of visual problems in the hearing impaired.

ADMINISTRATION OF TESTS AND PROCEDURES

"All Deaf Children are Created Equal"

From the above, one can appreciate that hearing-impaired children do not represent a homogeneous population. A child with a mild loss may superficially function as a hearing child, but no matter how mild the loss, we can assume an effect on language development. Thus, a verbal test reflects a hearing-impaired child's speech-reading and language competence, not cognitive skill. Because of this, even when a hearing-impaired child can interact verbally with the examiner, the clinician must choose assessment techniques appropriate for a child with a severe loss and should not assume that the child fully comprehends the instructions. At no point is it appropriate for the psychologist evaluating basic competencies to assume that the child has enough language to be accurately assessed by verbal means.

There are several reasons for advocating this approach. First, even psychologists skilled in working with the hearing impaired cannot judge how well the child comprehends all of the concepts. Second, if the child has a sensorineural hearing loss, there is a good probability it existed prior to the emergence of speech. Considerable evidence shows that such a prelinguistic loss, however mild, will have an effect on language development. Third, the child with a sensorineural loss may also have a discrimination deficit affecting the ability to correctly hear speech sounds. Fourth, a mild hearing loss, which may not impede one-to-one verbal interchanges, affects what the child can hear in noisy classrooms. Thus, the child with even a mild hearing loss has not had the same exposure to language as the normative sample population for most tests. Since there is no comparability with the normative population, one cannot ethically use verbally based tests as the basis for assessing the cognitive competencies of the hearing impaired.

Communicating with the Child During the Evaluation

The psychologist who is unfamiliar with hearing-impaired children may wonder how to behave with them. These children live in a speaking world and expect that people will talk around them, if not to them. Thus, it is appropriate for the examiner to use speech when greeting the child, indicating where to sit, etc. The clinician should use simple sentences combined with gestures. Generally, the child will be attentive to the examiner's face, expressions, and verbal comments. Interacting this way allows an informal assessment of the child's responsiveness to the verbal components of the interaction, efforts to respond to it, and vocal responses. Almost all hearing-impaired children grasp the approval when the examiner smiles and says, "Good work." An example of an informal verbal interaction with the child, while conforming to standardized nonverbal instructions, would go as follows: If one intends to present a block-building task, the examiner may talk about getting out the test material, asking if the child wishes to open the box, naming what is in the box, and giving the child a chance to label the blocks. This is no different from the informal interaction that goes on during any assessment; it does not affect the instruction, and if the child cannot comprehend any of the above, then performance is not penalized. At this point, the examiner proceeds with the pantomimed or pictorial instructions according to the test procedure. It is important, however, not to carry out an informal verbal interchange with the child while simultaneously presenting the gestural instructions for the item. The hearing-impaired child can only attend to one set of stimuli and should not be penalized because competing visual stimuli are available.

Even if the psychologist has manual communication skills, it is inappropriate to attempt to translate verbal test instructions to the child. Because a hearing-impaired child understands some signs does not indicate comprehension of all the concepts in the instructions. Also several manual communication systems exist, and the psychologist and child might not use the same one. In addition, the clinician should not present the instructions in writing; changing the nature of instruction changes the test. Also, one cannot assume that the ability to read the words of the instructions means that the child grasps all of the concepts.

Many hearing-impaired children have been trained from infancy to be attentive to adults' facial cues. The examiner may not be aware that subtle facial cues are giving the child clues to the correct response, especially on matching tasks. A potential means of counteracting this with a child who seems unduly attached to examiner feedback is to use practice items when available to train the child to take a self-monitoring set.

Supplemental Observation in Other Environments

Whenever possible, the direct examination should be supplemented by an observation of the child in other settings. For the preschool child, the significant environment is the family setting, and the clinician can generally gain information about the child in such interactions by observations structured in the clinic. As with normal hearing children, the observations should include information about: 1) the child's method of engaging family members; 2) use of play materials; 3) communication strategies with family members; 4) the presence of deviant behavior; 5) parental skills in engaging the child in play, encouraging activities, and methods of communicating with the child; and 6) parental strategies for gaining compliance and dealing with behavior problems.

For the school-age child, classroom observation provides valuable information about the child's study skills and work habits, social interactions with peers and teachers, and the presence of behaviors that interfere with learning.

Evaluation of Cognitive Development

A frequent concern about hearing-impaired children relates to cognitive competence in terms of functioning level and patterns and the presence of generalized or specific deficits. There are three strategies for selecting instruments to address these questions. First and most appropriate involves the use of instruments that sample a range of cognitive functions, have been standardized on a hearing-impaired population, and provide standardized instructions appropriate for the population. The second is to select instruments developed on a normal hearing population that have been adapted specifically for the hearing impaired. The third strategy relies on the use of nonverbal tests standardized on the hearing population without any alteration. This section describes examples of each.

Tests standardized on the deaf. Unfortunately, only a few instruments developed for use with hearing impaired children exist, and often these are not readily available to psychologists who do not usually evaluate hearing-impaired children. However, these instruments are the most valid for assessing the hearing impaired and for predicting their academic performance. It is recommended that those practitioners in a clinic or school setting who will occasionally evaluate hearing-impaired children have these instruments available.

1) *Smith-Johnson Nonverbal Performance Scale.* This scale was developed for hearing-impaired children ages 2 through 4 years, and includes 65 items grouped into 14 categories with items arranged with increasing difficulty in each category. The child's performance in each category is compared to his age peers and is rated in each as Above, Below, or within the Average performance level.

2) *Central Institute for the Deaf Preschool Performance Scale.* This nonverbal scale is a restandardization of the Randall's Island Performance Test, which has been used with hearing-impaired preschoolers for many decades. The revision was standardized on hearing-impaired children ages 2 to 5½ years, and correlates with performance on nonverbal scales administered in later years. There are six subtests: Manual Planning; Manual Dexterity; Form Perception; Perceptual/Motor Skills; Preschool Skills; and Part-Whole Relationships. The individual subtests will be familiar to psychologists who have experience with preschool children.

3) *Hiskey-Nebraska Test of Learning Aptitude.* This is the most widely used of the tests standardized on the hearing impaired, and the normative population included children ages 4 to 10. The test has two sets of norms, one for the hearing impaired and one for normal hearing children. The latter set of norms are useful for normal hearing chilren with communication deficits. The test includes 12 subtests, only 7 of which are appropriate for children below age 7. The child's performance on each subtest is assigned an age level, with the resulting score representing a median of subtest scores. The Hiskey-Nebraska samples a broader range of skills than do the performance subtests of the Wechsler scales. There are tasks that require matching pictures in terms of identity, generic association, and analogous reasoning. The test also contains tasks of memory and attention span. Because of the complexity of the tasks, the examiner should not administer this test without first getting supervision in its administration.

4) *The Ontario School Abilities Examination.* This instrument assesses hearing-impaired children across a range of tasks. The test is out-of-print but may be available at centers that have been serving the hearing impaired for a number of years.

Standardized intelligence tests adapted for the hearing impaired. There have been some adaptations of the Wechsler Performance Scales for use with the hearing impaired. Anderson & Sisco (1977) developed norms based on a hearing-impaired school-age population; however, there is no information provided on how the instructions were modified for the normative group or what modifications in instructions the examiner should make.

Another problem in interpreting Wechsler Performance Scale results is that there is generally no information about whether the examiner attempted to use manual communication, whether the child was allowed to practice, or how the examiner conveyed the idea of efficiency on timed test items.

To counteract these deficiencies, Ray adapted the administration of the Wechsler Intelligence Scale for Children-Revised (WISC-R) (Ray, 1979) and the Wechsler Preschool and Primary Scale of Intelligence (WPPSI) (Ray & Ulissi, 1982). In these adaptations, some of the lexical and syntactical features of the instructions were changed so that they can be communicated in each of the sign/symbol systems. Demonstration items were added to Picture Completion, Mazes, and Animal House on the WPPSI, and to Picture Completion, Mazes, and Block Design on the WISC-R. By utilizing these changed procedures, the resulting distribution of scores and mean scores for the hearing-impaired population did not differ from those of Wechsler's normal population.

Despite these adaptations of the Wechsler Performance Scales, the psychologist must keep in mind that this assesses a restricted range of behavior, that Wechsler did not intend the Performance Scale to stand alone, and that prediction of school achievement is not as good as with the Verbal Scales. Thus, these adaptations of the Wechsler Performance Scales must be supplemented by other instruments.

Nonverbal tests standardized on the hearing population. This is the strategy most frequently used by psychologists who evaluate hearing-impaired children (Levine, 1974). The test reported as most frequently used was the WISC-R Performance Scale with the Leiter International Performance Scale the second most widely reported. The Kaufman Assessment Battery for Children (K-ABC) provides a Nonverbal Scale with gestural instructions and motor responses, which is offered as a valid measure of the functioning of the hearing impaired. The instrument is new and has not yet had extensive use with this population.

There are limitations to this strategy for assessing hearing-impaired children. The use of a single performance scale unduly restricts the behavior sampled. Secondly, the child's performance is being compared to that of a population with a different history of experience with language, which means that one cannot draw the same implications from the resulting scores as with hearing children. Performance on nonverbal tests may well be affected by the hearing impairment; it influences the ability to understand the instruction, which are generally verbal, and to understand concepts such as "as quickly as you can." Also, no one has yet demonstrated that the lack of hearing and resulting lack of normal language does *not* change one's problem-solving strategies. Normal hearing children may use language to help them solve nonverbal tests. Different processes may be called into play and, thus, different cognative skills may be measured when assessing the hearing impaired than when assessing those with normal hearing.

It is recognized that on some occasions the psychologist may have no alternative to using nonverbal tests standardized on hearing children, but certain psychological practices will reduce the negative aspects of this. First, the interpretation of the findings must take into account that the resulting scores may represent different functions for the hearing impaired than for the normal hearing child and, thus have different predictive values. Secondly, the use of battery of several instruments is recommended. Depending on the child's age, the psychologist may choose the K-ABC Nonverbal Scale, the WPPSI, the WISC-R, the Merrill-Palmer Scale with the verbal items omitted, the Leiter and the Arthur Adaptation of the Leiter Scales, and the Standard Progressive Matrices.

A "bits and pieces" approach to assessing hearing-impaired children, which would select nonverbal items from a range of tests, cannot be condoned. The individual test items were not constructed to stand by themselves and the resulting range of scores would be meaningless.

Evaluation of Adaptive Ability

As with normal hearing children, a comprehensive psychological evaluation of the hearing impaired may require the administration of other types of evaluations. Frequently of value is information about children's adaptive ability or the ability to use their skills to care for themselves. Adaptive measures should be used when there is a question of retardation, since a valid determination of retardation requires demonstrated deficits in that area as well. The most widely used scale is the Vineland Social Maturity Scale, a parent-directed interview. Hearing loss has little impact on functioning on this scale in the early years except in language skills. Because the hearing loss affects social experiences, the loss does begin to influence adaptive skills in adolescence.

Assessment of Language Skills and Vocabulary-Based Knowledge

Another major area of concern is the impact of the hearing loss on a child's language skills. This information becomes vital when mainstreaming is being considered. If the psychologist can work cooperatively with a speech and language clinician, a comprehensive assessment based on their unique and overlapping competencies can result.

In addressing the child's verbal abilities, one must distinguish between describing the child's competencies and deficits revealed by evaluation results, comparing the child's skills to those of peers (which is necessary for educational placement decisions), and categorizing the child by using verbal test scores as measures of intelligence. The last is not appropriate for reasons that will be discussed in the Interpretation and Communication sections that follow.

Results from the administration of standardized intelligence measures such as the Verbal Scale subtests of the WPPSI and the WISC-R can be one way of providing a measure of vocabulary-based knowledge.

Specific measures of speech and language for preschool children include the following:

1. The Bzoch-League Receptive-Expressive Emergent Language Scale (REEL). This is an interview-format procedure using parental report or examiner observation for ages birth to 3.

2. Peabody Picture Vocabulary Test-Revised (PPVT-R). This is a measure of single-word comprehension requiring a pointing response.

3. Utah Test of Language Development. This is a checklist providing a measure of expressive and receptive language skills betwee the ages of 1 and 15 years.

4. Houston Test for Language Development. This measures receptive, expressive, and conceptual development in children ages 6 months to 6 years. For school-age children, measurements of language competence include:

1. The Peabody Picture Vocabulary Test-Revised (PPVT-R).
2. The Illinois Test of Psycholinguistic Abilities (ITPA). This is useful for ages 2 to 10 years. There are 10 subtests of which Auditory Recognition, Auditory Association, Auditory Sequential Memory, and Grammatic Closure are particularly useful in evaluating specific features of language.
3. Detroit Tests of Learning Aptitude. Although this is a global measure of school-related skills, several subtests provide standardized procedures for evaluating children's verbal skills: Orientations; Verbal Opposites; Oral Expressions; Auditory Attention Span for Related Syllables; and Oral Directions.
4. Woodcock-Johnson Psycho-Educational Battery. This global achievement and ability scale includes several subtests that provide standardized measures of children's language: Picture Vocabulary; Antonyms-Synonyms; Analogies; Memory for Sentences; Visual-Auditory Learning; Blending; Quantitative Concepts; Numbers Reversed; Science; and Social Studies.
5. Kaufman Assessment Battery for Children. This is a measure of intelligence and achievement in standardized format for ages 2½ to 12½. The Expressive Vocabulary, Riddles, Faces and Places, Magic Window, Gestalt Closure, and Number Recall subtests provide useful information about children's language (German, 1983).

Other information about a child's language skills is provided by the child's responses other than to the test material. The examiner may note the child's awareness of verbal and gestural messages as well as willingness to attend to them, attempts to understand them, and efforts to respond in like manner. The child's intelligibility in verbal interchanges and creative efforts to communicate can be noted. In other words, in spite of the hearing impairment, does the child make use of the auditory/vocal components of the communicative interaction?

Assessment of Academic Achievement

For children of school age, information about achievement level is important for making placement and programming decisions. Achievement tests are generally given as group tests. Their interpretation in hearing-impaired children lies open to question if the tests are administered in the standard way since these children probably will not understand the instructions and what is expected of them. One effort to deal with this problem resulted in the development of a specialized edition for hearing impaired students of the 1973 Stanford Achievement Test (Trybus & Karchmer, 1977). This adaptation provided three features. First, the adaptation included a short screening pretest since neither grade placement nor teacher judgment predicted which level of the SAT to use, and because the children varied in the levels among the subtests, it was also necessary to screen them for each of the subtests. The second feature of the adaptation provided practice materials, because hearing-impaired children had difficulty marking in the specified locations on the test blank. The third aspect utilized teacher-dictated items at the lower levels, because the hearing-impaired children's reading limitations hindered comprehension of the printed test items. The authors of this adaptation suggest that if psychologists use achievement tests other than the special edition of the SAT, they must make similar concessions in presenting the material.

The individual achievement measure used most frequently with hearing-impaired children is the Wide Range Achievement Test, 1976 edition (Levine, 1974). This provides three measures: 1) Reading, which is the ability of the child to correctly pronounce unrelated visually presented words; 2) Arithmetic, solving written numerical problems; and 3) Spelling, writing single words from dictation.

Other tests frequently used with the hearing impaired include the Stanford Achievement Test, 1973 edition (discussed previously), and the 1978 edition of the Metropolitan Achievement Test, both of which are comprehensive, well-designed tests standardized on normal hearing children. Another test used is the 1957 California Achievement Test. Again, the cautions outlined for any test used with hearing impaired children based on normal hearing norms apply here.

Assessment of Behavior Patterns

Certain information about the child's behavior should be included in the evaluation since data about the child's noncognitive learning styles are important for educational programming. This includes noting the child's attention during the evaluation and in class, the ability to self-monitor and self-correct, the dependence on examiner or teacher feedback, and where the child fits on the thoughtful to impulsive continuum.

Psychologists may be asked to assess an identified behavior disorder and to make recommendations for management. One cannot complete a diagnostic assessment of the school-age child posing behavior problems without observation in the classroom. A useful way of evaluating such problems includes an assessment that alternates observation of the child's behavior and observation of the teacher's behavior while interacting with that child and other class members.

The direct observation of the child's behavior may be assisted by using a structured behavioral observational tool to quantify, summarize, or compare the resulting data. An example of such a behavioral observation format is the Werry-Quay Classroom Observational System, in which the observer codes certain specified categories of deviant class-behavior and records these in a continuous fashion (Werry & Quay, 1969).

A comprehensive observation of the child's behavior problem in class should include information about the teacher's style of eliciting and reinforcing classroom behavior:

1. The teacher's method of giving instructions. Are the instructions clear or vague? Are they given directly to the hearing-impaired child? Are the instructions direct or indirect? Does the teacher use one-step instructions or a series of instructions? How frequently are they repeated?

2. The response of the teacher to the hearing impaired child's compliance with instruction. Is there feedback to the child indicating approval? What is the time delay of that feedback?

3. Perhaps most important is recording the teacher's response to the child's noncompliance with classroom instruction, and noting the way in which the teacher responds to any inappropriate child behavior.

It is not recommended that a psychologist unfamiliar with the hearing impaired make use of personality tests. A major problem with their use is that the child's language difficulties interfere with communicating instructions. Also, the clinician should not employ play techniques in an evaluative manner, because the child may interpret the task differently and have a different set of expectations of what to do with the toys than would a normal child. Interpretation of personality measures administered to the hearing impaired is best left to psychologists with specialized training in the psychological evaluation and treatment of the hearing impaired.

INTERPRETATION AND INTEGRATION OF FINDINGS

Interpreting the results of the examination of a hearing-impaired child should include consideration of data in the case history. This section discusses ways in which the clinician should integrate evaluation findings in order to respond to the most common referral questions.

1. Are there developmental disabilities other than those imposed by the hearing loss?

In many cases, this question derives from the fact that the child has significant language delays and these raise concerns about whether the delays reflect only the effects of the hearing loss or of other disabilities.

The psychologist should first address the child's overall level of functioning as determined by the evaluation. One must exercise caution when interpreting test findings since in some populations studied, means on performance tests were somewhat lower for the hearing impaired than for normal children (Anderson & Sisco, 1977; Hirshoren, Hurley, & Kavale, 1979) unless special adaptations to insure comprehension of instruction are made (Ray, 1979; Ray & Ulissi, 1982). Once the examiner is sure that evaluation conditions were optimal and the tests were appropriate for the child's hearing impairment, if resulting scores are considerably lower than the average range it becomes likely that developmental delays exist in addition to language delays. Examination of the case history material may provide cues about the origin of these delays.

Another issue to consider in the integration of findings is that of the child's performance pattern. If the psychologist has employed appropriate nonverbal measures such as the Wechsler Performance Scales, hearing loss alone will not cause wide scatter among the scores. Should significant deviations appear, these must be interpreted in light of the basic skills tapped by the tasks, and the examiner should consider further in-depth evaluation of the deficit areas.

2. What is the impact of the hearing loss on the child's language?

When integrating the findings of the evaluation to deal with this question, the psychologist will want to stress a description of the child's functioning in expressive and receptive language areas. Sorting out the differential effects of the hearing impairment and general development requires a comparison between the child's verbal and nonverbal skills. Unless the child's performance on the nonverbal tasks lies within the expected range for his chronological age, it is difficult to attribute any language deficits solely to the hearing loss. Another dimension one should consider is the extent to which the resulting language deficiencies have a functional impact on the child in interpersonal relations, classroom functioning, and social and adaptive areas.

3. What is the impact of the hearing loss on the child's achievement?

The interpretation of achievement test data with hearing-impaired children is extremely difficult. A certain amount of achievement delay is attributable to the hearing impairment. In a recent survey (Trybus & Karchmer, 1977), the median reading comprehension of young hearing-impaired adults was at the 4.5 grade level, indicating that half of these individuals read below or just at newspaper literature level. At best, only 10% of hearing-impaired 18-year-olds can read at or above the eighth-grade level. At no age does even the 90th percentile group of hearing impaired read at the mean level for hearing subjects. The influence of the hearing impairment on these reading comprehension values was revealed by the fact that there was an inverse relationship between reading comprehension and degree of hearing loss. The survey also noted that children who did not enter school until after age 5 did more poorly on reading comprehension scores. For math computation, the achievement levels were somewhat better in that 10% of the hearing impaired scored as well as the hearing mean, with the median math computation level for 20-year-old hearing-impaired adults being at the eighth-grade level. In light of this very strong relationship between hearing impairment, early educational history, and achievement, it may prove difficult for the psychologist not directly involved with hearing-impaired populations to understand the influence of each. It is recommended therefore that psychologists exercise caution about interpreting achievement test data as indicating the presence of learning disabilities over and above those disabilities imposed by the hearing loss.

4. What should be done about educational placement?

Perhaps with no other referral issue is it as vital to integrate findings from the case history and cognitive, language, and achievement evaluations. Ideally, the psychologist comprises only one member of a team of specialists who are integrating their findings to arrive at a placement recommendation. The most important variable determining educational placement involves the degree of the child's hearing loss. A major placement issue for children with severe to profound hearing losses concerns the ideal method of communicating instructional material, whether it should be oral communication or a total communication technique (oral plus manual language). Considerable material exists on the advantages of each approach. Unless the psychologist is familiar with this material and the comparison results, it would not be advisable to make independent recommendations about the preferable approach for a particular child.

The degree to which the hearing loss has affected the child's language is another important determinant of placement. The child who has no speech and language skills learned through hearing requires a different educational program from one with good residual hearing and speech-reading skills.

5. What can be done about the identified behavior problems?

Hearing-impaired children as a group do not demonstrate a greater frequency or degree of behavior disorders than other children. However, any child whose deficit is not completely understood and who receives inappropriate educational programming or family management is at risk for behavior problems. The psychologist, in pulling together the evaluation results should consider: 1) whether all those who deal with the child adequately understand the hearing impairment; 2) whether other previously unidentified cognitive, language, or achievement problems are present; 3) whether any lack of congruence exists between the child's educational needs and the current educational program; and 4) whether the relationship with significant adults contributes to the maintenance of a behavior disorder.

COMMUNICATING THE RESULTS OF THE EVALUATION

There are sound clinical practices for communicating findings that the psychologist should follow when reporting the evaluation of a hearing-impaired child, as with any other child. Issues such as addressing the reliability and validity of findings, preparing timely reports that are comprehensible to the audience, protecting clients' rights to privacy, etc. need not be reiterated here. Some specific suggestions related to the evaluation of hearing-impaired children and children with other disabilities might be mentioned, however.

Prior to evaluating the child, the clinician should make the family aware of the questions that will be addressed and how they will be answered, and should allow the family to observe remotely if possible. Also, parents should know before the evaluation when the results will be available to them.

Whenever possible, the psychologist should communicate directly (face-to-face) with the person who originated the referral, giving the written report as a follow-up. This is particularly true when the referral originated with a teacher who would appreciate the opportunity to exchange ideas about the implications of the findings and strategies for carrying out recommended programs.

When the school is involved in the evaluation and interpretation, the clinician should first make the interpretation to the family, followed by an interpretation to the school in which the parents may participate. It is not good practice to bypass the first interpretation for the parents alone because they may be reluctant to raise certain questions if others are present.

A written report of the findings should be addressed to the referring question. This sounds self-evident, but all too frequently a referral requests help with a behavior problem in the classroom and the psychological report only presents summarized test data.

There is one feature of reporting that is unique to the evaluation of hearing-impaired children. When the psychologist has used verbal tests to study the effects of the loss on the child's ability to master verbal material or to predict how the child would function in a mainstreamed program, the child's performance on such tests should be described in detail with discussion of its implications for training. In some cases, it may be appropriate to indicate age levels for the results, but the scores should not be converted to quotients. If the scores are reported as IQ scores, the examiner violates the precept of using only those tests in which there is comparability of normative sample. This issue arises because psychologists have no control over who handles the reports once they are sent out. Even if the psychologist clarifies reported scores with caution and indicates that a resulting IQ score does not represent cognitive competency but merely language skill, it is too easy for someone in subsequent settings to scan, select, and report figures out of context.

This chapter describes the procedures for evaluating children with hearing impairments in the areas of development, achievement, and behavior. At each step of the evaluation there are considerations that the clinician needs to make to insure that this is done in a valid and ethical manner.

Before beginning the examination, it is important for the psychologist to consider the nature of the hearing impairment, its history, and how it has been managed. The direct examination tools should ideally be selected from those standardized on the hearing impaired (with instructions appropriate to their comprehension) and which sample a broad range of skill areas. In addition to the direct examination of the child, it frequently proves useful to carry out observations in other settings such as with family members or in the classroom.

Care must be taken when integrating and communicating evaluation findings so that the resulting quantitative measurements are not presented in a manner that allows for erroneous interpretation.

REFERENCES

Anderson, R. J., & Sisco, F. H. (1977). *Standardization of the WISC-R Performance Scale for deaf children* (Series T, No. 1). Washington, DC: Gallaudet College, Office of Demographic Studies.

Cantor, D. W., & Spragins, A. (1977). Delivery of psychological services to the hearing-impaired child in the elementary school. *American Annals of the Deaf, 122,* 330-335.

German, D. (1983). Analysis of word finding disorders on the Kaufman Assessment Battery for Children (K-ABC). *Journal of Psychoeducational Assessment, 1,* 121-133.

Hirshoren, A., Hurley, O. L., & Kavale, K. (1979). Psychometric characteristics of the WISC-R Performance Scale with deaf children. *Journal of Speech and Hearing Disorders, 44,* 73-79.

Kretschmer, R. E. (1983). Assessing the hearing impaired child. In S. Ray, M. J. O'Neill, & N. T. Morris, (Eds.), *Low incidence children: A guide to psychoeducational assessment* (pp. 91-140). Sulphur, OK: Steven Ray Publishing.

Levine, E. S. (1974). Psychological tests and practices with the deaf: A survey of the state of the art. *The Volta Review, 76,* 298-319.

Levine, E. S. (1981). The ecology of early deafness: Guides to fashioning environments and psychological assessments. New York: Columbia University Press.

Ray, S. (1979). *Manual for the adaptation of the Wechsler Intelligence Scale for Children-Revised for deaf children.* Sulphur, OK: Steven Ray Publishing.

Ray, S., & Ulissi, S. M. (1982). *An adaptation of the Wechsler Primary and Preschool Scale of Intelligence for deaf children.* Sulphur, OK: Steven Ray Publishing.

Rogers, S. J., & Soper, E. (1982). Assessment considerations with hearing impaired preschoolers. In G. Ulrey & S. J. Rogers (Eds.), *Psychological assessment of handicapped infants and young children* (pp. 115-122). New York: Thieme-Stratton, Inc.

Trybus, R. J., & Karchmer, M. A. (1977). School achievement scores of hearing impaired children: National data on achievement status and growth patterns. *American Annals of the Deaf, 122,* 62-69.

Werry, J. S., & Quay, H. C. (1969). Observing the classroom behavior of elementary school children. *Exceptional Children, 35,* 461-470.

10

Assessing the Visually Handicapped Child

MARCIA S. COLLINS-MOORE, PH.D.,
KATHLEEN N. OSBORN, PH.D.

Most psychologists have had few opportunities to study the effects of visual impairment or total blindness on child development or to interact with visually handicapped persons. Attention is rarely given to specialized assessment procedures for visually handicapped children during undergraduate and graduate training in psychological assessment, yet psychologists are responsible for psychoeducational and psychosocial assessments of visually handicapped and multi-handicapped visually impaired children.

This chapter is designed to provide practical information to increase the knowledge and comfort level of professionals who are asked to evaluate visually handicapped children. An overview of terminology and the impact of visual impairment on child development provide a framework for discussion of comprehensive assessment. Special considerations relevant to each phase of the assessment process are also presented.

The subjects of this chapter are children with moderate and severe visual impairment who may possess one or more additional handicaps but are not severely multi-handicapped. Information in this chapter may be considered an introduction to assessment of all visually handicapped children. However, additional considerations are necessary for competent assessment of severely multi-handicapped visually impaired children.

TERMINOLOGY AND DEMOGRAPHICS

The following definitions are adaptations of terminology in *Visual Handicaps and Learning*, 2nd ed. (Barraga, 1983):

Visual acuity: Acuity refers to a clinical measurement of the sharpness and clarity of vision for discrimination of fine details at a specified distance. Measurements for distance vision are noted in feet (e.g., 20/20) or meters (e.g., 6/6), both of which indicate normal vision. The first number refers to what the person sees; the second to what a normally sighted person can see at that same distance. A child with

137

20/100 vision sees at 20 feet what a normally sighted person sees at 100 feet. Near vision is measured in terms of inches away from the eyes, usually 14, that the person can see a particular type-size.

Visual impairment: This term refers to any optically or medically diagnosable condition in the eye or visual system that affects the development and normal use of vision.

Visually handicapped: This term denotes the total group of learners who have impairments in the structure or functioning of the eye, which cause a limitation in visual learning that interferes with incidental or normal learning through the sense of vision. This group does *not* include children with normal visual acuity who have problems with visual perception or interpretation of visual information.

Blind: People who have only light perception without projection or those who are totally without the sense of vision are blind. The term "legally blind" is used to define persons with 20/200 best corrected vision in the better eye or with a field of vision restricted to a diameter no greater than 20°, a definition originally created to determine eligibility for public assistance. "Blind" and "legally blind" are *not* synonymous. Educationally, the blind child is one who learns through senses other than vision, although perception of light may be present and useful in orientation and movement.

Low Vision: This term denotes vision that gives less than normal acuity even with corrective lenses for distance and/or near visual functioning under ordinary conditions. Most low vision children can use vision for many educational activities, but may require the use of some tactual materials to supplement printed and other visual materials.

Visual impairment is a low incidence handicap in the school age population. Approximately 1 child in 2,000 has a moderate to severe visual impairment that requires the use of modifications in educational materials and procedures. The American Printing House for the Blind national registry of visually handicapped children whose visual acuity falls between 20/200 and blindness recorded 34,814 children in 1980. Inclusion of children with acuity after correction of better than 20/200 but less than 20/70 (the approximate acuity that allows a person to read ordinary newsprint) increases the birth-to-21-year-old population with mild visual impairment to about 1 child in 500. Visual acuity usually is sufficient to allow vision to provide the major source of input for learning. In 1980 the National Society for the Prevention of Blindness (NSPB) estimated that only about 1 child in 10,000 will require tactual materials and modifications in the school program to make normal progress in school (NSPB, 1980).

The visually handicapped population is highly heterogeneous with respect to degree of visual impairment, etiological factors, and age at onset. In addition, the presence of other handicaps is not uncommon; current estimates indicate that approximately 50-70% of visually handicapped children have other handicaps (Fine, 1979; Jan, Freeman, & Scott, 1977).

IMPACT OF VISUAL IMPAIRMENT ON CHILD DEVELOPMENT

Meaningful assessment of a visually handicapped child requires a fundamental understanding of the impact of a visual impairment on child development as well as a familiarity with the development of the normally sighted child. Without this basic knowledge, certain inabilities may be attributed to retardation when, in fact, the inabilities may be due to lack of opportunity to experience the world as a sighted child does. Lacking this knowledge, the evaluator cannot determine the appropriateness of assessment measures, adapt them, or interpret the results.

It is estimated that 85% of all information received by people in our culture is visual. Vision is the most dominant sense in development. Sight gives continuous contact with environment and provides constant information, immediate verification, and the means for understanding self and others in space. Vision has been described as the "coordinating sense," which organizes sensory impressions and sequential perceptions into an understandable whole. Visual impairment interferes with and/or interrupts the relatively automatic and spontaneous process of attachment to the environment and imitation of appropriate behavior.

Development of visually handicapped children is modified according to the age at the onset of visual impairment, parental adjustment to the presence and special needs of the visually handicapped child, and the degree of visual impairment.

Age at Onset of the Visual Impairment

A child may be congenitally or adventitiously impaired. Congenital visual impairment is present at birth or shortly thereafter, whereas adventitious impairment occurs after visual learning has begun. The essential difference between congenital and adventitious visual impairment involves the complete lack or limitation, for congenitally impaired children, of visual orientation and input of visual impressions. Congenitally visually handicapped children are not aware that their vision is impaired or that they are any different from others. They believe that everyone experiences the world as they do and "sees" the same things they "see." Their parents need to initiate the process of adjustment and compensation for them with guided sensory stimulation to develop curiosity about the world within and beyond their reach.

Children who become visually handicapped after they have experienced the world visually and have acquired visual memories are able to retain visual concepts such as space and distance, and build on them with encouragement. For example, orientation and movement in space are enhanced immeasurably by retaining the concept of self in relationship to surroundings and objects in the environment.

Effective use of visual memory is strongly affected by attitudes of parents, friends, and professionals. The extent of emotional trauma accompanying loss of sight is usually relative to whether the loss is gradual or sudden, and coping will depend upon the degree of acceptance and adjustment achieved by the parents.

Parental Adjustment to the Child and Visual Impairment

It is normal and generally necessary to mourn a visual loss in oneself or a loved one, particularly when the visual impairment is severe. The mourning process is similar for parents of both congenitally and adventitiously impaired children. Parents grieve for the loss of the "perfect" child, for the missing or defective part of the child, and/or for a perceived loss of personal self-esteem. They also may grieve for the ongoing losses in their lives due to the continuous burden of additional responsibilities and stresses inherent in raising a handicapped child.

Similar to parents of any handicapped child, parents of visually handicapped and multihandicapped visually impaired children experience shock, denial, grief, guilt, inadequacy, anger, and depression in response to the birth, diagnosis, and ongoing life experiences with the child. Specific characteristics of the parent, the child, and the parent's support system affect the occurrence, intensity, and duration of parental reactions. Controversy exists regarding whether parents experience one predictable progression of emotions in the adjustment process, or over time experience and re-experience emotions analogous to mourning (Collins-Moore, 1984).

With respect to blindness and severe visual impairment, the literature supports the premise that the sensory impairment itself need not cause cognitive or affective deficiencies in visually handicapped children. Instead, the cause of such deficiencies, when present, seems to lie with the impoverishment associated with the parents' negative emotional reactions to the handicap and the child. It has been demonstrated that only when parents adequately resolve their normal negative emotional reactions will they be able to provide for the child's needs or benefit fully from the information and professional guidance they may need as the visually handicapped child grows.

Throughout the adjustment process, parents and child are subject to preconceived ideas about blindness and severe visual impairment, ideas that are generally quite negative. Many consider "blindness" the worst handicap, equivalent to death and linked with ideas of punishment. Societal and cultural perceptions of "blind" persons as physical, psychological, moral, and emotional "inferiors" may subtly intensify the initial shock and subsequent emotional reactions. In rehabilitation a familiar, accepted observation is that adjustment will be affected by the extent to which attitudes toward the impairment can be modified.

Degree of Visual Impairment

In addition to the child's age at onset of the visual impairment and parental reactions, child development is significantly affected by the degree of the visual impairment. The blind child has unique sensory and motor development, unique cognitive and language development, and a unique affective development. Much has been written about the development of the congenitally blind child. Only highlights of the impact of blindness and severe visual impairment can be covered in the next few paragraphs.

For the blind infant, the other senses have intermittent input and may appear diminished. The child receives inconsistent, discrete, and generally unverified fragments of information. Hearing is the only distance sense available, but sound without visual verification is only noise coming from nowhere. Only after much tactual, motor, and auditory interaction does sound acquire meaning to provide information about location, cause, or source. Not until ten to twelve months of age will a blind child reach for an object on sound cue alone, and environmental exploration is usually delayed until the child reaches this point (Fraiberg, Siegel, & Gibson, 1966). In addition, purposeful tactile activity is minimal because the absence of visual cues of color, pattern, shape, and location denies the incentive for tactile exploration.

In regard to motor development, the nervous system of the otherwise normal blind infant matures at a normal rate, enabling the development of muscle tone and coordination, as well as postural and balance mechanisms. However, crawling and walking that normally follow postural achievements are delayed in the blind infant. Significant developmental delays in the ability to employ hands result functionally in delayed fine and gross motor development. Without vision, hand and eye do not work together. Ear-hand coordination must substitute, and is achieved much later than normal eye-hand coordination. All motor achievements that require self-initiated mobility are significantly delayed (Adelson & Fraiberg, 1974).

The blind child's difficulty or reluctance in moving around the environment encourages passive behavior such as self-stimulating mannerisms. Persistence of stereotyped manneristic behavior (misleadingly called "blindisms") is much more common in younger children with more severe visual losses, earlier onset, and multiple disabilities including low intelligence (Freeman, 1977).

For most visually handicapped children, motor development is affected to some extent. Their ability to organize movement in response to incoming stimuli is delayed and so is their knowledge of body parts and how they fit together and function. These children lack the feedback of vision in monitoring body movements and the availability of models for appropriate organization of body movements. Their ability to know space and their motivation to move in it are diminished.

The cognitive development of blind infants and children is unique in that they construct a reality that differs from the sighted child's. Their construct of the world differs because blind children have a limited ability to coordinate and organize the inconsistent and discrete information they perceive into higher levels of abstraction, and to verify the information. The process of establishing concept-defining attributes and relationships is more problematic for them and less accessible to guidance (Santin & Simmons, 1977).

In terms of Piaget's theory of cognitive development, the concept of object permanence, which emerges in the sighted child at about 8-12 months of age, develops in a blind child approximately a year later. Since the results of actions cannot be seen, the child may not understand the ability to cause things to happen or to retain pleasurable stimuli. Object constancy is difficult to achieve if one hasn't observed objects in various orientations, realizing that an object is the same regardless of its position in space. Likewise, limited opportunities to explore objects and to see similarities are reflected in blind preschoolers' classification errors. Also, blind children exhibit delays in conservation of substance, weight, volume, length, and liquids (Higgins, 1973).

The language development of these children is often characterized by delay in combining words to make wants known. Without a concrete referent, the child may not grasp the meaning intended by the speaker. Difficulty in moving from labeling to meaningful use of words in sentences is pervasive. Early language seems to mirror knowledge of the language of others more than the child's own developing knowledge of the world. A "verbal veneer" may prevent or delay language development, with use of meaningless words and phrases repeated out of context.

Affectively, blindness delays self-concept and social development. The blind child has an unusual dependence on a sighted person to mediate and help integrate the environment. Such children have diminished control over their environment. They may not understand that a complex world exists outside themselves, that they are separate from it, or that they can both act on it and be the recipient of action. For example, the child's use of personal pronouns may reveal delay in self-concept development. Blind children tend to confuse the use of personal pronouns, extending the use of the second and third person pronouns or even their own name to refer to themselves.

For blind children, social relationships are affected from the initial mother-infant interaction and beyond. Lack of vision alters the attachment process. Separation anxiety, which is normal for all children, is prolonged through the second year. Blind children have difficulties in forming the image of "self" in relation to other "selves." They may appear to have ambivalent emotional involvement and appear to be disinterested, noncommunicative, and uninformed about the rudiments of play with peers. Consequently, blind children may be avoided by peers and rejected or overprotected by strangers and relatives. Social interactions are more complicated because subtle visual cues are missing and facial expressions are unknown.

Finally, regarding social development of self-help skills, many of the skills normally learned by imitation and observation are delayed in blind children. For example, chewing, scooping, and self-feeding skills may be delayed two years or more. Insecurity and inability to locate the bathroom may contribute to delayed toilet training.

Although studies of blind infants and children often are predominant in the literature, approximately 75-80% of all school-age visually handicapped children are either low vision or visually limited. For low-vision children, the developmental problems that characterize blind children are modified according to the degree of the visual impairment and their experiences in learning to use vision effectively. Unrestricted use of vision must be encouraged to maintain and develop optimum visual functioning in low-vision children. These children are *not* blind, and can benefit from vision training to enhance all learning.

Visual functioning and efficiency are contingent on physiological, psychological, intellectual, and environmental factors. Accordingly, the same diagnosis and degree of visual impairment may affect each low vision child uniquely. Furthermore, visual acuity has minimal, if any, relationship to the capacity for visual development or for acutal visual functioning (Faye, 1970). The greater the visual impairment, however, the earlier the child needs special educational services and visual stimulation to insure that cognitive development progresses in relation to capacity.

The child with low vision may have difficulty in developing basic optical skills such as fixation, tracking, focusing, accommodation, and convergence. Likewise, eye-hand coordination and various aspects of visual perceptual development, such as visual memory, visual closure, and visual organization, are affected depending upon the type and severity of the visual impairment (Barraga, 1983). Limitations in quantity and quality of visual information necessitate the child asking questions or discussing visual impressions with normally sighted persons so that valid visual perceptions can be organized and remembered.

When low vision children initially seek active involvement with other children, their differences become apparent and problems in socialization may occur. Learning to read visually, when impaired vision makes it difficult to discriminate and recognize the symbols, will create problems without specialized readiness programs. However, if the visual impairment is moderate, the first signs affecting schoolwork may not appear until the second half of the third grade or at the fourth grade level. It is then that the size of type in the average school book becomes smaller than what the low vision child needs to read easily. If the child must strain to read, emotional problems may develop.

Adolescence presents difficult challenges for the low-vision child. In addition to the usual teenage problems, the strain of being physically different from one's peers provokes anxiety. A sense of personal "limbo" between the "sighted" and "blind" worlds may develop as a result of circumstances such as sufficient sight to perform most tasks but inadequate vision to drive an automobile. The use of large-print books or special magnifying devices and prescription optical aids may further "single out" the low-vision student. The low-vision adolescent keenly feels individual differences from classmates, and may withdraw from active participation when feeling slighted or misunderstood. Acceptance of personal limitations and unique strengths is crucial for all visually handicapped children.

PRE-DIAGNOSTIC STAFFING

Soon after receiving a referral for the assessment of a visually handicapped child, a pre-diagnostic staffing should be held to design an overall plan for assessment. A comprehensive assessment will necessarily include information from a variety of sources, representative samples of the child's behavior in numerous situations, and both observational and objective data from parents, medical specialists, teachers, and other professionals who provide services to the child and family.

First, the referring question(s) should be determined. What is the objective of the assessment? Possible objectives may be: 1) to determine appropriate class placement and types of special services needed; 2) to compare the child with a reference group; 3) to evaluate the child's rate of learning; 4) to evaluate the effectiveness of an intervention strategy; or 5) to determine the child's competencies and *how* the child functions. Specific content areas and questions are identified by the examiner's review of available records, consultation with the parent(s) and all professionals working with the child, and observation of the child prior to assessment. The objective of the assessment and the referring question(s) guide the examiner throughout the assessment process.

Physical History and Current Functioning

In reviewing the records of the visually handicapped child's physical history and current functioning, a primary consideration is the child's visual condition. Physiologically, visual functioning may be affected by reduced visual acuity, restricted field of vision, defective color vision, and fixation problems. Information about these and other aspects of the visual impairment are usually provided by an eye report from an ophthalmologist. This information has implications for evaluating and educating the child.

Information in an eye report is highly variable, depending on the thoroughness of the examination and the child's ability to cooperate during the eye exam. This is particularly true if the child is severely handicapped. A comprehensive eye report should provide the following information: cause of visual impairment; age at onset; family history of similar eye problems; stability of the impairment (progressive or non-progressive); medical treatment required; use of glasses or contact lens and under what circumstances; distance and near visual acuity; presence of color vision; field of vision; restrictions on the child's activities; and time for re-examination. (See Napier, et al. (1981) for glossary of terms and further information.)

Often various aspects of the previous list will be omitted from the report. Also, children's functioning during an eye examination seldom indicates their full visual abilities. Although the eye examination can provide a great deal of information, the critical variable for school personnel is the way the child uses vision (i.e., visual efficiency). This is best determined by a functional low vision exam (Barraga & Morris, 1980; Langley & Dubose, 1976), a patient interview focused on the child's experiences in using vision, and observation of the child. With this information, the knowledgeable examiner may develop hypotheses about the learner's perceptual base (e.g., whether totally tactual/kinesthetic or some degree of visual), and about potential use of visual materials during assessment.

The examiner also needs to know the presence and effect of other handicapping conditions. It cannot be overemphasized that with visual impairment, the presence of other handicaps increases the child's disability geometrically rather than additively. In other words, the effect of additional handicaps is not merely visual impairment *plus* deafness or *plus* mental retardation, but rather visual impairment multiplied *times* deafness or mental retardation. The interaction effects create increased complexities in dysfunctions.

Other necessary physical information includes lighting preferences and habits, use of glasses or other low vision aids, and the effects of medicines being taken. For younger and multi-handicapped children, the examiner also must determine motivational and directional cues used by teachers and parents, positions facilitating maximum visual and hand function, and the child's most alert times of the day.

The psychologist can best obtain much of this information by observation of the child prior to the formal assessment. Observation assists in: refining and/or adding to the questions that will guide assessment; structuring the environment for assessment; selecting appropriate assessment instruments; and adapting material as necessary. Pre-assessment observation is generally unstructured observation in the natural learning situation, although it also may be semi-structured or structured. Screening is a form of structured observation, which the examiner may wish to use to determine more accurately which tests will most appropriately evaluate the child's skills.

Intellectual

For purposes of discussion, assume that the objective of assessment is to determine the child's competencies and how the child functions. The examiner's knowledge of the impact of visual impairment on child development will guide the review of available records as well as guiding inquiries during the interviews to obtain information relevant to the child's physical, intellectual, educational, emotional, and social (P-I-E-E-S) functioning.

During the pre-diagnostic staffing, information from school records, hospital charts, and previous psychological reports should be reviewed. Also, preparation for observation of the child and consultations with parents and professionals who serve the child and family should be discussed.

Emotional

Information about the child's relationship with parents, siblings, and extended family members and the child's responsibilities in the home provide insight into possible rejection and/or overprotection, which are two common emotional responses to a visually handicapped child in the family. Likewise, the child's experiences with other children in play, church, neighborhood, and community activities are relevant to determining the family's acceptance of the child and the range of life experiences. The parents' perception of the severity of the visual impairment and their long term wishes/goals for the child are also important.

Educational

A teacher of visually handicapped children always should be consulted prior to assessing a visually handicapped child. Of course, it is preferable to interview a teacher who has had experience with the child. The teacher may advise the examiner about the availability of appropriate assessment materials and should be asked to perform screening tests, as necessary, to determine the child's communication medium (braille, large print, auditory) and visual efficiency. The teacher can provide information about the child's attitude toward the visual impairment, orientation and mobility skills, use of vision and other senses in schoolwork and play, light preferences, and use of low vision aids for near and distance visual tasks. In addition, a teacher familiar with the child should be asked about the current educational program, general developmental level, attention span, listening skills, play behaviors with other children, and reinforcements/rewards valued by the child.

Social

Prior to assessment the examiner should consult with the person(s) who referred the child, with the parent(s), and with the professionals providing services to the child and family. Consultation with and cooperation from the child's parent(s) and the teacher of the visually handicapped take primary importance.

In consulting with the parents of a visually handicapped child, the examiner should be sensitive to apprehensions and expectations that parents often bring to meetings with "professionals." The parents undoubtedly have had encounters with physicians and a variety of other "helping professionals" since the diagnosis of the visual impairment, and previous experiences will influence their attitudes toward the examiner and the assessment.

It is advisable to begin by informing parents about the assessment process and inquiring about their immediate concerns. The psychologist should elicit specific questions of particular interest to the parents regarding their child's current functioning and potential. Thereafter, obtaining the following information is especially relevant. The developmental history should include questions about the child's attainment of developmental milestones that are dependent on vision, and questions about the child's functional use of vision in a variety of environments. The educational history should include inquiries about the child's participation in infant and preschool programs that provide special services for visually handicapped children.

During any pre-assessment observation, relationships with peers should be noted. Potential social adjustment problems may be evident during interactions on the playground or in the lunchroom. Also, the child's orientation in space and movement should be observed. Children with severe visual impairments should be receiving instruction from an orientation and mobility specialist. If necessary, an assessment of the child's functioning in this area should be obtained from that specialist or a certified teacher of the visually handicapped.

ADMINISTRATION OF TESTS AND PROCEDURES

The evaluation of a visually handicapped child is never automatic and therefore presents a professional challenge. Once the examiner knows the objective and specific questions to be answered, one must structure the session to gain rapport with the child and to gather sufficient data on the various aspects of the child's functioning. This section presents the environmental considerations, selection of evaluation procedures, selection of tests, and modification of procedures and materials necessary for assessment.

Environmental Considerations

Assessment of a visually handicapped child involves environmental considerations that are essential in obtaining an accurate and useful evaluation. Considerations for establishing and maintaining a comfortable affective environment or rapport with a visually handicapped child may be identified as follows: 1) speak as you approach so that the child will be aware of your presence; 2) offer the child your arm or hold the younger child's hand before proceeding to the examining room; 3) speak in a normal tone of voice, unless the child also has a hearing loss; 4) do not feel uncomfortable about using sight-oriented words such as "look" or "see;" and 5) use tactile and verbal reinforcements frequently (Genshaft, Dare, & O'Malley, 1980).

The examiner provides the key stimulus in the assessment environment, and as such needs to avoid inadvertently interfering with the child's performance. The examiner's personal attire is an important factor. Bright or patterned clothes and dangling, glittery jewelry create visual distractions that may interfere with the child's attention. Likewise, heavy colognes or perfume may interfere and should be avoided.

The must be control of auditory noise such as music, telephone, intercom interruptions, and other loud sounds that create competition for the child's attention. Visual distractions, such as the clutter of irrelevent objects in the room, should be kept to a minimum. It is advisable to have only essential furniture, necessary for the evaluation and arranged to give adequate space and mobility for the child. The child should be given ample time to explore and become familiar with the surroundings prior to beginning the evaluation.

The examiner must determine the child's particular lighting preferences and should provide the most favorable lighting conditions unique to each child. In general, low vision learners may require three to ten times the usual room illumination even when working in familiar surroundings and with known materials. One child may prefer diffused white light at a low level of intensity, and another may need high intensity light. Children with visual disorders such as albinism, aniridia, and some cataracts may require minimum light, whereas those with optic atrophy and macular degeneration usually require more.

Glare should be avoided since it reduces visibility and interferes with visual efficiency. Directed light should come from a closed-hood lamp with an adjustable stand, which is placed in back of the child or at the side of the better eye so that the shade directs the light only on the task. The child should face away from the bright light of windows. The best ways to determine a child's lighting needs involve inquiring of the child's teacher, observing the child, experimenting with the placement of materials, desk, chair, and lights, and asking the child what is most comfortable.

For low-vision children, the use of optical and non-optical visual aids during assessment may be necessary. For example, a bookstand or raised surface helps to reduce postural fatigue by bringing test materials closer to the child's eyes. Line guides and reading windows may be especially helpful for low-vision children who find it difficult to focus on individual words or lines of print. Spectacles and magnification devices normally used by the child should be available during assessment. Encouragement and permission to use vision and visual aids as the child chooses are essential.

Low-vision children may experience visual fatigue during assessment more quickly than sighted children. Scheduling short breaks at regular intervals may avoid excessive fatigue, or the examiner may rely on behavioral cues such as rubbing eyes or evident strain to focus as guidelines.

The working surface for the test materials must provide adequate contrast for test objects. Black construction paper can be used with light objects, or a non-glare white construction paper or flannel fabric would be appropriate with dark objects or testing materials. In addition, the type of paper used makes a difference; written work should be done with a black or blue felt-tip pen on glare-free white or manila paper (Swallow, 1977). The examiner should hold test materials against a plain background rather than near one's own body, which could be distracting to the visually handicapped child.

For any performance activity, the examiner needs to define the space for work. One solution is to place all the materials on a tray that provides the perimeter of the work space. Alternately, a large piece of construction paper outlined with masking tape or strips of sandpaper provides a flat surface for cards and booklets.

Selection of Evaluation Procedures

The purpose of the evaluation is one factor in the selection of the appropriate procedures and tests. The amount and quality of vision (i.e., acuity and function) further determines what is appropriate for a particular child. For instance, the Perkins-Binet Intelligence Test (an adaptation of the 1972 Stanford-Binet Intelligence Scale) has two versions, one for the child with "usable vision" and the other for the "non-usable vision" child. The child's communication medium (braille, large print, auditory) and level of visual efficiency limits or broadens the choice of tests.

Both formal and informal assessment procedures are necessary in assessing the range of a child's abilities and skills. It may be appropriate to plan the evaluation over a period of days rather than in one or two sessions. This will provide observations over time of a wide range of behaviors.

Children may be observed in a variety of totally unstructured settings, or the environment and the materials available may be semi-structured or structured to require specific types of performance. Observing the following behaviors can provide valuable information about visually handicapped children: 1) awareness of, and attention to, the surrounding environment and persons within it; 2) seeking and exploring patterns of movements; 3) kind and variety of cues used for independent actions; 4) use of language to initiate contact or to respond to others; 5) extent to which the child originates behavior; and 6) adaptations to materials and to people (Barraga, 1983).

Accurate assessment of the visually handicapped child's capabilities and adaptive skills proves difficult because few standardized protocols are available. The examiner must be knowledgeable about the various instruments and how the standardization was obtained. Was the test designed for the sighted, blind, or low-vision child? Often the tests designed for the visually handicapped child have norms based on small numbers or biased by institutional populations. Content-referenced tests are generally more reliable than norm-referenced tests in the educational setting. Diagnostic tests that measure the skills the child has and what needs to be learned have proven valuable in assessing educational needs and problems. The child's approach to each task is as important as whether the answer is right or wrong. Observing *how* the child attempts a task helps the examiner to determine what adaptations or compensatory strategies the child has developed for problem-solving tasks.

It is often advantageous to use portions of numerous instruments that are appropriate for the child's assessment, even when the entire test is not applicable. What many examiners do in practice is select items or subtests from existing tests and consider what skills and processes are involved in performing each task.

Interpretation of isolated items or tasks often proves difficult because they have been separated from other items in the standardized tests. The clinician should analyze the information gained from the selected items/subtests diagnostically, with the focus on what the child can do and how the child adaptively solves problems (i.e., a functional assessment). These portions or selected items can help provide checks and balances on the other assessment measures.

Selection of Tests

Following the P-I-E-E-S mnemonic guideline, areas to assess include physical, intellectual, educational, emotional, and social functioning. This section presents a number of different assessment procedures and instruments that have been used with visually handicapped children. No attempt has been made to create an exhaustive list of instruments or to propose a specific test battery. Since the visually handicapped population is a heterogeneous one with great variations in individual characteristics, suggesting a specific test battery is inappropriate. Also, examiners should use creativity and ingenuity in trying some of their favorite instruments with the visually handicapped children they have been asked to assess. For further discussion and more extensive listings of instrumentation, see the selected references cited in this chapter's bibliography.

Physical Functioning

The assessment of physical functioning should include an evaluation of fine motor skills and manual dexterity. Tests of manual dexterity are useful in assessing pre-vocational and vocational skills.

To assess fine-motor skills, the Developmental Test of Visual-Motor Integration can be administered to some low-vision children without adaptations and good reliability. The Purdue Perceptual Motor Survey evaluates balance and posture, body image and differentiation, perceptual-motor match, ocular control, and form perception. This measure may prove useful when developing a perceptual-motor program for visually handicapped children. Another instrument appropriate for low-vision children is the Motor-Free Visual Perception Test. This test, standardized on motorically impaired and physically handicapped children, measures visual-perceptual abilities without involving motor components. The Body Image of Blind Children assesses body planes, body parts, body movements, laterality, and directionality of blind children ages five to fifteen.

Measures of manual dexterity provide an opportunity to see the child in action, doing rather than verbalizing. Orientation in a work space, ability to follow patterns of movement, ability to maintain attention and effort in a repetitive task, and sheer motivation are demonstrated. Without these action tasks, the examiner would fail to see quite so complete a picture of the visually handicapped child. For the child under age eight, these tasks may be largely informal measures in observing a child manipulate play materials such as pegboards, formboards, puzzles, and blocks. The

Minnesota Rate of Manipulation Tests, the Pennsylvania Bi-Manual Worksample, and the Crawford Small Parts Dexterity Test have norms developed for blind persons ages fifteen and older. All three require the subject to manipulate screws or blocks on a formboard while being timed. Since norms were developed in 1957, they may not be applicable to current visually handicapped persons (Genshaft, Dare, & O'Malley, 1980).

Intellectual Functioning

Intellectual functioning may need to be assessed by developmental measures for the younger and multihandicapped visually impaired children. The Bayley Scales of Infant Development (with adaptations as necessary), Callier-Azusa Scale, Denver Developmental Screening Test, and Developmental Activities Screening Inventory are appropriate instruments for younger and low-functioning children. One commonly used instrument for measuring cognitive abilities is the Perkins-Binet Intelligence Scale, with versions for blind and low-vision children. Many examiners use the Wechsler Revised Verbal Scales or the Slosson Intelligence Test. All items that require visual learning or experience may require additional probing for interpretation. The Boehm Test of Basic Concepts and the Tactile Test of Basic Concepts are content-referenced tests, appropriate for kindergarten and first-grade levels, assessing the child's spatial, temporal, qualitative, and miscellaneous concepts. The Blind Learning Aptitude Test is a tactual test for blind children ages six to sixteen years, designed to assess processes and operations necessary for their learning. For the child age sixteen and older, the Haptic Intelligence Scale is a performance instrument comparable to the performance scale of the Wechsler Adult Intelligence Scale. The Stanford-Ohwaki-Kohs Block Design Intelligence Test for the Blind has norms for blind and low-vision persons at least sixteen-years-old.

Emotional Functioning

In the area of emotional evaluation, familiarity of the psychologist with the instrument is extremely important. When interpretation is done with an awareness of the special problems of visual impairment, personality and emotional maturity measures prove effective tools in the overall evaluation. Bauman's Emotional Factors Inventory and the Adolescent Emotional Factors Inventory, as well as the Anxiety Scale for the Blind, provide items that are largely based upon adjustment behavior as described by visually handicapped persons. Sentence completion tests such as the Rotter Incomplete Sentence Blank, which include items about family, school, peer relationships, fears, and goals, can be adapted to include items reflecting reactions to visual impairment and its impact on the child's life. The Minnesota Multiphasic Personality Inventory may be used selectively. It is recommended that these measures be administered through large print, braille, or tape recording, which guarantees privacy in making the response and improves the predictive value of the results.

Educational Functioning

Educational achievement tests for the visually handicapped child have been available since the early 1900s. There are general achievement measures that offer a test battery for various academic skill areas. The California Achievement Tests, the Sequential Tests of Educational Progress, and the Wide Range Achievement Test are available in both braille and large type. Widely used at the senior high school levels and required for admission to many colleges, the Admissions Testing Program: Scholastic Aptitude Test of the College Entrance Examination Board has been put into braille and oral-presentation form with answers to be typed by the student.

Diagnostic achievement tests are available for specific academic skills. The Diagnostic Reading Scales, Revised, the Gates-McKillop-Horowitz Reading Diagnostic Test, the Gilmore Oral Reading Test, and Stanford Diagnostic Reading Test are available in braille and large-type versions. The Woodcock Reading Mastery Test, which is content-referenced, is suitable for low-vision children. The KeyMath Diagnostic Arithmetic Test, containing 14 subtests, is available in braille form. All of the general achievement tests previously listed have subtests that measure mathematical skills. Spelling tests for the sighted child can be presented for oral responses from the visually handicapped child. Some low-vision children can be assessed by the Spelling subtest on the Peabody Individual Achievement Test, which assesses proofreading of single words. The test of Written Spelling assesses dictated spelling of words that were employed in ten commonly used basic-spelling series.

An auditory assessment is essential for understanding the strengths and weaknesses of an important learning modality. The auditory vocal responses, i.e., decoding, encoding, memory, articulation, and sound discrimination, are the skills that the visually handicapped child needs to understand and communicate with others. Appropriate subtests from the Detroit Tests of Learning Aptitude assess the child's auditory and cognitive thought processes in order to pinpoint specific learning deficits. Other recommended tests include the Auditory Discrimination Test (Wepman) and the Auditory Discrimination subtest of the Gates-McKillop-Horowitz Reading Diagnostic Tests.

Evaluation of the child's language development should include informal observation of spontaneous language as well as formal assessment of linguistic abilities. For infants and preschool children, the Gestural Approach to Thought and Expression (GATE) and The Bzoch-League Receptive-Expressive Emergent Language Scale are appropriate. The Peabody Picture Vocabulary Test can be enlarged for low-vision children. The Illinois Test of Psycholinguistic Abilities contains auditory subtests (i.e., auditory decoding; auditory-vocal association; vocal encoding; automatic-sequential ability; auditory vocal automatic ability; auditory-vocal sequencing ability; and auditory and grammatic closure, which are useful with visually handicapped children in order to develop portions of a listening skills program. The Carrow Elicited Languages Inventory measures a child's morphological and syntactical control of language. For children with low vision, a better test may be Carrow's Test for Auditory Comprehension of Language. The Durrell Analysis of Reading Difficulty, adopted by the American Printing House for the Blind, offers a reading test and a parallel listening test that measures understanding of the spoken word.

Social Functioning

Measures of social competency are usually designed to be administered through an interview with parents or other caregivers. Developmental scales or behavioral checklists can accurately describe the typical behavior of the child, supplemented by interviews with the parent(s), teacher, and other significant caregivers. The Maxfield-Buchholz Social Maturity Scale for Blind Children, standardized on preschool blind children, is used to assess personal, social, and functional development. The AAMD Adaptive Behavior Scale, a criterion-referenced check list, has 2 forms, one for the parent and another for the school. This social development scale, standardized on mentally retarded children ages three to thirteen and older, is divided into two sections: independent functioning and aberrant behavior. This scale proves helpful in determining the child's coping skills, but one should be cautious in interpretation of the results for a visually handicapped child.

Pre-vocational and Vocational Skills and Interests

Methods of evaluating manual dexterity, which were described with regard to assessment of physical functioning, have been used for evaluating pre-vocational and vocational skills. However, normative data do not exist for young children.

For high-school students inventories such as the Strong-Campbell Interest Inventory, which were developed for sighted persons, can be read aloud or audiotaped. The Kuder Preference Record, Vocational, can be administered in braille and has braille sheets available from the Perkins School for the Blind. Bauman developed the PRG Interest Inventory, which is based on the jobs, interests, and hobbies of blind persons.

Since norms for visually handicapped persons are not highly significant predictors of success in a competitive job market, the most significant contribution that an examiner can make analyzes the child's work habits, interpersonal skills, appearance, and degree of independence. This information, gathered primarily through observation and interviews with the child and persons who know the child, proves critically important in reflecting the child's vocational potential (Genshaft, Dare, & O'Malley, 1980).

Modification of Procedures and Materials

A major question that arises when evaluating visually handicapped children is when and how to modify assessment procedures and materials. The objectives of the assessment and the characteristics of the child and the testing materials determine how to resolve this question. If the purpose of the assessment is to compare the child's current functioning in a specified area strictly with the normal child, one should not employ modifications (Scholl, 1983). Similarly, if the test materials were designed for and normed with visually handicapped children, modifications are unnecessary. However, when the objective is to determine the child's competencies and how the child functions, modifications are often necessary and appropriate.

Since no two visually handicapped children respond the same way to their impairment, modifications are often individualized. In modifying the presentation of assessment items, one must exercise care to avoid altering the intent and purpose of the original item. It is important to remember that any changes from the standardized procedures must be recorded for later inclusion in the written report.

Standard instructions used with sighted children may be inappropriate and confusing to the visually handicapped child. Word choice should be clear, concise, and precise. The examiner needs to provide verbal and tactile information about the test materials and procedures that a normally sighted child would observe visually during the assessment.

Response modifications include: allowing gesturing or pointing; responding orally, brailling, or typing answers; and lengthening the response time permitted for those tests not normed for visually handicapped children. The general rule for increasing the time allotments is one-and-a-half times for the large-print readers and twice the time for braille readers. Audiotaping sentence completions or true-false questions for the evaluation of social and emotional functioning affords privacy to the older child when expressing personal feelings.

Modifying visual designs for tactual presentation to the child with non-usable vision can be accomplished by using geometric shapes or designs with simple structure and only essential details. The psychologist can trace the design and then outline it with a line of glue to produce a raised line drawing. Also, thermaform copies of tactual material may be obtained from a teacher of the visually handicapped.

Large-print words and adequately enlarged pictorial materials can be utilized for the child with usable vision. One can enlarge pictures through clear, bold reproduction with a copying machine or by hand. Visual aids, such as a large lighted magnifier or a closed circuit television, may be used to enlarge printed materials from one to sixty times the original size. The examiner should choose pictures with only clear and essential details to eliminate the confusion of many small unimportant lines.

The use of concrete objects for the assessment is better than models or miniatures. For the blind child, the examiner should encourage tactual exploration of the testing materials as they are described. It may be appropriate to guide the child's hands, allowing ample time to become acquainted with materials. The examiner may also follow these procedures with low-vision children as necessary.

INTERPRETATION AND INTEGRATION OF FINDINGS

Interpreting and integrating the assessment data into a clear and concise psychological report should yield information that is meaningful and immediately useful. Therefore, more than one written report may be necessary according to who will receive the information.

Content of the report should address the original referring question(s) as well as subsequent questions that were determined during pre-diagnostic observations and consultations. The examiner must carefully construct the report to provide factual statements from which others can make inferences and judgments. Behavioral descriptions are reported in objective terms to indicate what the child did under specific conditions at a given time (Swallow, 1981). Such reporting enables both current and future users of the information to gain insight into the child as an individual.

Since the visually handicapped population is so heterogeneous and test modifications are individualized, it is essential to include specific descriptions of all modifications of standardized procedures or materials. The rationale for deviating from standard procedures and the effect anticipated on resulting data should be documented in the report.

Physical

Assessing the degree to which a visual handicap interferes with test performance is at best a judgment matter. It is very difficult, perhaps objectively impossible, to separate visual reception from visual perception, cognitive functioning, and language skills. Therefore, the clinical judgment of the examiner is especially critical in the interpretation of assessment data. Without appreciating variables such as the child's past cultural opportunities, the presence and characteristics of siblings, the emotional atmosphere of the home, and the impact of visual impairment on child development, the examiner will be unable to differentiate between failures related to a history of visual impairment and those that truly reflect limited ability and potential (Genshaft, Dare, & O'Malley, 1980).

As the examiner interprets and integrates the data, several general considerations related to the presence of visual impairment are noteworthy. The recency of the diagnosis of adventitious visual impairment (i.e., disease process or trauma), the stability of the visual impairment and visual acuity (i.e., stable or progressive impairment; fluctuating vision), recent or anticipated surgery, and the presence of chronic or intermittent pain (i.e., poorly controlled congenital glaucoma) will affect the child's global functioning. These factors should be included in the report and taken into account.

Intellectual and Educational

Visually handicapped children rarely master all developmental milestones on time. Therefore, concepts of chronological age norms based on a sighted population are inappropriate, especially for understanding a very young or multihandicapped visually impaired child. For accountability and prediction, it is best to measure the child's skills and knowledge along an achievement continuum rather than to compare performance to a normative sample. One can use standardized tests as content-referenced tests to interpret scores in terms of content sampled by the test. Describing the child's range and patterns of functioning in specified areas is much more reliable and valid than any "score" or "label."

Often visually handicapped children have a wealth of stored rote facts, but exhibit poor problem-solving strategies. Their frame of reference for sorting, organizing, and relating sensory impressions to construction and assimilation of complete precepts is limited in scope (Barraga, 1983). A repertoire of splinter skills rather than behavior reflecting concept acquisition is not uncommon, especially with younger children. These children may demonstrate apparent understanding by higher performance on selected tests of information, but have poor ability to apply the "knowledge." A "verbal veneer" may obscure their inaccurate understanding of both visual and nonvisual concepts.

Emotional

Congenital blindness affects interpersonal relationships, since eye contact is denied and facial expressions are unknown without training. The fine nuances of facial expression are abnormal in most congenitally blind children. Therefore, it is hazardous to diagnose depression on the basis of apparently flat affect or facial expression (Freeman, 1977).

Likewise, the low-vision child may not maintain direct eye contact during communication. For example, a visual field defect may necessitate using peripheral vision to obtain the best view. The child's unusual visual behavior is not an indication of social or emotion problems.

The stereotyped behaviors demonstrated by some congenitally blind children, such as rocking, finger flicking, and eye poking, may be misunderstood as necessarily indicative of severe emotional disturbance or low intellect. Instead, these behaviors may merely represent self-stimulation and can be unlearned. The examiner should observe when the behavior occurred and specify the circumstances, the activity, and whether the behavior interfered with or prevented the child from performing tasks.

Social

With the low-vision child, one may frequently find adjustment problems because of ambivalent feelings with family, friends, and teachers who expect behavior incompatible with visual functioning. The child's visual impairment may not be readily apparent to laymen and can be mistaken for stupidity, inattention, or indifference (e.g., not recognizing friends in the hall at school).

Since blindness and severe visual impairment carry a significant social stigma in our culture, it is wise for the examiner to consider any personal biases or fears brought to the assessment process. Observation and interpretation of the child's performance may be influenced subtly by the examiner's own attitude toward visual impairment.

Consideration of these issues affecting interpretation and integration of assessment data will assist the examiner in providing meaningful information to professionals, the family, and the visually handicapped child. It also will assist in making appropriate referrals for evaluation or treatment by specialists in other areas, such as speech and language or occupational therapy.

COMMUNICATION OF ASSESSMENT RESULTS

Assessment results may be communicated through the written psychological report, professional staffing, and personal conferences. One or more of these feedback methods may be appropriate according to the recipient's knowledge of psychological assessment and involvement with the child. With a parent's permission, the written report usually is given to medical personnel and other professionals providing services to the child and family. The written report also serves as the basis for information presented during a professional staffing and the personal conferences with parents and child.

Psychological reports frequently are sent to the medical personnel responsible for the management of the visually handicapped child's health. Results from the evaluation provide the physician with more complete knowledge of the child's functioning. Ideally, the information may assist medical personnel in interacting with the child during necessary medical procedures, monitoring the child's development, and consulting with the family about the child's medical management and lifestyle.

The most frequent users of psychological assessment data are school personnel. Before holding a professional staffing, the examiner should ascertain what special classes and programs are available for visually handicapped children in the school system, the equipment and visual aids provided, and the availability of counseling services as needed. All school personnel involved in the child's daily program should have access to the written report and, whenever possible, should attend the professional staffing.

Involving the classroom teacher, special teachers of the visually handicapped, school counselor, principal, and other specialists (such as a speech and language therapist or a physical therapist) in the interpretation of the test results facilitates the development of a more comprehensive and unified program for the child. It is imperative for the examiner to explain clearly the test results and the implications of the data for each school staff member in planning curricular activities and learning strategies to match the child's unique needs.

The examiner's responsibilities also may include interpreting the assessment data to vocational rehabilitation counselors. A close working relationship between educational and rehabilitation personnel enables the vocational rehabilitation counselor to have more thorough information for vocational planning with the student.

Assessment data is usually interpreted to parents through a personal conference with the examiner. Most parents are not knowledgeable about psychometric instruments and terminology; therefore, the examiner must avoid the use of psychological jargon and provide basic explanations about the assessment instruments. One must explain to the parents what learning processes are being assessed and give concrete examples of the child's performance. The child's developmental and functional status across affective, psychomotor, and cognitive dimensions should be presented in terms that parents can understand. The information must be meaningful to the parents for them to support the recommended educational programs and make practical judgments and decisions about providing a home environment that promotes the child's maximum development and independent living.

As the visually handicapped child passes through the normal problems of childhood and adolescence, professionals must be prepared to help the parents cope with the visual impairment's unusual overlay on those usual problems. The examiner must assist the parents in facing the limitations of the child while still maintaining a realistic appraisal of capacities and abilities. It is often helpful to refer them to parents' groups that assist in facing these realities and also provide ongoing support.

As an integral part of the evaluation process, the examiner also has an obligation to discuss the assessment with the child. Appreciation for efforts during the assessment sessions could be expressed to the young preschooler. The examiner can give the school-age child general information about personal abilities, stressing the importance of becoming actively involved in the learning opportunities of the school program. At the secondary level, more information should be provided. Data regarding potential for higher education or specific vocational training, as well as personal management skills, help the student to identify suitable educational and vocational goals.

In summary, effective psychoeducational and psycho-social assessment guides the visually handicapped child, the family, and the involved professionals toward the future. It furnishes a profile of functional abilities and deficits that is useful for the prescriptive planning of learning experiences. The assessment process challenges the psychologist by demanding keen observation, creativity, and careful clinical judgment.

REFERENCES

Adelson, E., & Fraiberg, S. (1974). Gross motor development in infants blind from birth. *Child Development, 45,* 114-126.

Barraga, N.C. (1983). *Visual handicaps and learning* (2nd ed.), Austin, TX: Exceptional Resources.

Barraga, N.C., & Morris, J.E. (Eds.). (1980). Diagnostic assessment procedure. In *Program to develop efficiency in visual functioning.* Louisville, KY: American Printing House for the Blind.

Collins-Moore, M.S. (1984). Birth and diagnosis: A family crisis. In M.C. Eisenberg, L.C. Sutkin, & M.A. Jansen (Eds.) *Chronic illness and disability through the lifespan: Effects on self and family.* New York: Springer Publishing Co.

Faye, E.E. (1970). *The low vision patient.* New York: Grune & Stratton.

Fine, S.R. (1979). Visual handicap in children. In V. Smith & J. Keene (Eds.) *Clinical Developmental Medicine, 73*(40).

Fraiberg, S., Siegel, B., & Gibson, R. (1966). The role of sound in the search behavior of a blind infant. *The Psychoanalytic Study of the Child, 21,* 327-357.

Freeman. R.D. (1977). Psychiatric aspects of sensory disorders and intervention. In P. Graham (Ed.), *Epidemiological approaches in child psychiatry.* New York: Academic Press.

Genshaft, J.D., Dare, N.L., & O'Malley, P.L. (1980). Assessing the visually impaired child: A school psychology view. *Journal of Visual Impairment and Blindness, 74*(9), 344-350.

Higgins, L.C. (1973). *Classification in congenitally blind children.* New York: American Foundation for the Blind.

Jan, J.E., Freeman, R.D., & Scott, E.P. (1977). *Visual impairment in children and young adolescents.* New York: Grune & Stratton.

Langley, M.B., & DuBose, R.F. (1976). Functional vision screening for severely handicapped children. *New Outlook for the Blind, 70,* 346-350.

Napier, G.D., Kappan, D.L., Tuttle, D.W., Schrotberger, W.L., Dennison, A.I., & Lappin, C.W. (1981). *Handbook for teachers of the visually handicapped.* Louisville, KY: American Printing House for the Blind.

National Society to Prevent Blindness. (1980). *Vision Problems in the U.S.* New York: Author.

Santin, S., & Simmons, J.N. (1977). Problems in the construction of reality in congenitally blind children. *Journal of Visual Impairment and Blindness, 7*(12), 425-429.

Scholl, G.T. (1983). Assessing the visually impaired child. In S. Ray, M.J. O'Neill, & N.T. Morris (Eds.), *Low incidence children: A guide to psychoeducational assessment.* Natchitoches, LA: Steven Ray Publishing.

Swallow, R. (1981). Fifty assessment instruments commonly used with blind and partially seeing individuals. *Journal of Visual Impairment and Blindness, 75* (2), 65-72.

Selected References Regarding Methods and Assessment Instruments:

Bauman, M.K., & Kropf, C.A. (1979). Psychological tests used with blind and visually handicapped persons. *The School Psychology Digest, 8,* 257-270.

Genshaft, J.D., Dare, N.L., & O'Malley, P.L. (1980). Assessing the visually impaired child: A school psychology view. *Journal of Visual Impairment and Blindness, 74* (9), 344-350.

Langley, M.B. (1979). Psychoeducational assessment of the multiply handicapped child: Issues and methods. *Education of the Visually Handicapped, 10* (4), 97-115.

Scholl, G., & Schnur, R. (1976). *Measures of psychological, vocational and educational functioning in the blind and visually handicapped.* New York: American Foundation for the Blind.

Swallow, R. (1981). Fifty assessment instruments commonly used with blind and partially seeing individuals. *Journal of Visual Impairment and Blindness, 75* (2), 65-72.

Swallow, R. (1977). *AFB Practice Report: Assessment of visually handicapped children and youth.* New York: American Foundation for the Blind.

11

Assessing Childhood Anxiety and Depressive Disorders

ROBERT G. HARRINGTON, PH.D.

Twenty years ago it was customary for child psychologists to criticize certain parenting styles that seemed to encourage children to grow up spoiled by giving them too many personal possessions too early. In the 1980s, children are being subjected to a new wave of pressures. The "future shock" of which Alvin Toffler (1978) spoke is upon us. Children are not allowed time to explore the wonder and excitement of discovery that epitomizes childhood. Instead, they are rushed through their formative years so that they may assume the responsibilities of fully matured adults at increasingly earlier ages. This prevailing attitude has given new life to the old saw that "Youth is wasted on the young." David Elkind (1981) refers to these miniature adults as "hurried children." Children are being required to make rapid and major physical, psychological, and social adjustments in order to cope with the demands foisted on them by a fast, competitive, adult society. The megatrends forecasted for society seem to include many more sweeping changes in the future too (Naisbitt, 1982). These sweeping life changes and constantly rising adult expectations can produce stresses in children for which their tender years and limited experiences may not have prepared them.

Parents, schools, and the media all contribute to the hurried lifestyle of children today. The preschool years have not been left to be wasted on the "frivolity" of play; instead, forced precocity is the order of the day. For some parents, individualized instructions for their children has taken on a new and unintended meaning. Many toddlers and early preschoolers are either extensively tutored by their parents at home or are sent to learn "essential" preacademic skills at expensive private preschools. The apparent purpose of all this early education is for parents to give their children a head start, a competitive edge in the race to achieve in elementary and secondary school. Unfortunately, in the midst of all the hurry these young scholars may experience early failures or much undue pressure to succeed. Their young intellects simply may not be ready to assimilate and comprehend these more advanced concepts.

161

Current trends in junior fashions also may serve to accentuate children's rush to adult status. Children's clothing styles have become blurred with those of adults to the extent that some young teenagers may appear physically developed well beyond their actual years. The net result has been that not only do these children try to behave like adults but some adults may tend to treat them like peers. Despite appearances, children have vastly different psychological needs than adults. Children's distinctly different clothing used to cue adults to be sensitive, even protective, of young children; not so anymore. For adults to treat children as equals constitutes a false democracy, because it fails to take into account their inherent intellectual, social, and emotional differences.

Examples of hurried children can be drawn from almost all quarters of children's lives today. A new phenomenon in the airline industry is the "unaccompanied minor." Of necessity, children may travel alone from one end of the country to the other to visit divorced or separated parents. In the process of traveling alone these children may be exposed to new people, situations, decisions, and experiences with which they have no previous experience. Even many children's summer camps are no longer the idyllic settings for camping, hiking, swimming, and games they once were. The imposed adult perspective on camp life seems to dictate that sheer fun has no intrinsic value. These precious months at camp need to be filled with more productive activities like computer literacy, competitive sports taught by a real pro, or accelerated educational opportunities. Consequently, the natural proclivity of children to play and fantasize is devalued in preference to more adult activities.

The media, including movies, television, books, and magazines, all contribute to this attitude toward prematurity by choosing to depict children in sexually explicit scenes, drinking alcohol, smoking, and otherwise cavorting in situations well beyond their abilities to handle them. The consequence is that many adults may expect children to speak, behave, and respond like other adults even when they lack the prerequisite years of experience. Some lawyers may also exacerbate this situation when they inappropriately persist in trying to resolve children's problems in courtrooms rather than in these children's own homes. For example, Elkind (1981) has described one case in which a sixteen-year-old child legally divorced his parents in 1980 under a new Connecticut state law.

One has to question whether this kind of adult treatment of children's problems is in the best interests of the child. In fact, as these combined sources of stress continue to increase in frequency and intensity many more children may be at greater risk for adjustment reactions or other forms of psychopathology. Of course, it is impossible to attribute all childhood psychopathology to the "hurried child" phenomenon, but the social psychology of the hurried child should serve to exemplify in a practical manner the kinds of stressors that could precipitate the disorders known as childhood anxiety and childhood depression. This chapter will address both of these topics in two separate sections: Part I—Childhood Anxiety; and Part II—Childhood Depression.

DSM-III AND THE DIAGNOSIS OF CHILDHOOD PSYCHOPATHOLOGY

The overall purpose of this chapter is to: 1) describe the symptomatology of the diagnostic categories of childhood anxiety and childhood depression; 2) explain the diagnostic criteria for childhood anxiety and childhood depression; and 3) describe psychological instrumentation helpful in the diagnosis of these childhood psychological disorders.

Before launching into a discussion of childhood anxiety and depression it may be useful to differentiate the various definitions of the terms "anxiety" and "depression" in order to avoid later confusion over diagnostic terminology. The terms "anxiety" and "depression" have been used to refer to four distinct diagnostic levels. Each level may hold diagnostic significance depending on its definitional differences. The four levels of diagnostic analysis include the level of the *symptom, syndrome, disorder,* or *disease.* Behavior analysts often make diagnoses at the level of *symptoms,* or in other words, target behaviors (Kazdin, 1983). Symptomatic diagnoses of anxiety or depression may be made on the basis of *overt* behavior (e.g., anxious tics or depression-based withdrawal), *affect* (e.g., anxious or depressed mood), *cognition* (e.g., irrational beliefs), or *vegetative functioning* (e.g., somatic concerns). In contrast to the independent functioning of symptoms, the term *syndrome* implies that certain of the above behaviors may co-vary or occur regularly in combination (Edelbrock, 1979). The significance of a syndrome is that, in treatment, it may be possible to alter several related behaviors simultaneously by treating one target behavior (Wahler & Fox, 1980). When a syndrome cannot be accounted for by some more pervasive condition, a *disorder* may be said to exist. Childhood anxiety or childhood depression may be considered disorders when these patterns of behavioral symptoms cannot be explained by other disorders of which they are a part. Sometimes specific symptoms may be interpreted as indicative of a *disease* when the etiology of the abnormality has a biological base.

Behavioral approaches and the school-based classification system associated with Public Law 94-142 equate childhood anxiety and childhood depression with related symptom identification. In contrast, the *Diagnostic and Statistical Manual of Mental Disorders* (DSM-III) (American Psychiatric Association, 1980) utilizes the first three levels of analysis, including symptoms, syndromes, and disorders, in arriving at a diagnosis. DSM-III must be acknowledged as the most extensive, detailed, and careful attempt in psychiatric history to develop a comprehensive diagnostic system. Furthermore, this diagnostic system represents an attempt at universal agreement on the criteria to be used to identify certain child and adult psychopathological disorders. Not only is reliable classification important to insurance companies for reimbursement purposes, but relatively homogeneous categories such as these may also be important for research purposes, determination of etiology and epidemiology, treatment specification, and the identification of social, biological, or other factors that may exacerbate or mitigate the effects of the disorder. As a consequence, the child psychologist has an intellectual responsibility to examine this system with great care rather than simply to dismiss the notion of traditional diagnosis in favor of behavioral assessment. For this reason, the diagnostic assessment of childhood anxiety and depression disorders will be discussed primarily in relation to the criteria specified in DSM-III.

PART I: CHILDHOOD ANXIETY DISORDERS

Symptomatology and Classification

According to DSM-III the disorders of childhood can be subdivided into five broad categories: Intellectual, Behavioral (overt), Emotional, Physical, and Developmental. Anxiety disorders of childhood can be found under the heading of Emotional Disorders. Separation anxiety, avoidant disorder, and overanxious disorder are included under this classification. In the cases of separation anxiety and avoidant disorder the anxiety is localized to specific situations. In the case of overanxious disorder, the anxiety is generalized to a variety of situations. In addition, it is possible to apply to children any of the DSM-III classifications describing adult anxiety disorders that seem appropriate to the examiner. This is a controversial point since some researchers fail to recognize child counterparts in the major adult anxiety disorders (Achenbach, 1980; 1982). The fact that it is possible to classify children using diagnostic categories designed for adult psychopathology tends to corroborate Elkind's (1981) position that some adults, psychologists included, may tend to hurry children by failing to take into consideration the essential developmental differences between adults and children in using the DSM-III diagnostic categories. Only the three childhood anxiety disorders specified in DSM-III will be discussed in this chapter.

Separation Anxiety Disorder

The diagnostic criteria for the separation anxiety disorder classification according to DSM-III include the following:

A. Excessive anxiety concerning separation from those to whom the child is attached, as manifested by at least three of the following:
   (1) unrealistic worry about possible harm befalling major attachment figures or fear that they will leave and not return
   (2) unrealistic worry that an untoward calamitous event will separate the child from a major attachment figure, e.g., the child will be lost, kidnapped, killed, or be the victim of an accident
   (3) persistent reluctance or refusal to go to school in order to stay with major attachment figures or at home

(4) persistent reluctance or refusal to go to sleep without being next to a major attachment figure or to go to sleep away from home

(5) persistent avoidance of being alone in the home and emotional upset if unable to follow the major attachment figure around the home

(6) repeated nightmares involving the theme of separation

(7) complaints of physical symptoms on school days, e.g., stomachaches, headaches, nausea, vomiting

(8) signs of excessive distress upon separation from major attachment figures, e.g., temper tantrums or crying, pleading with parents not to leave (for children below the age of six, the distress must be of panic proportions)

(9) social withdrawal, apathy, sadness, or difficulty concentrating on work or play when not with a major attachment figure

B. Duration of disturbance of at least two weeks.

C. Not due to a Pervasive Developmental Disorder, Schizophenia, or any other psychotic disorder.

D. If 18 or older, does not meet the criteria for agoraphobia.

Children exhibiting the symptoms of separation anxiety disorder may experience anxiety well beyond that expected at the child's developmental level, even to the extent of panic in a wide variety of circumstances including separation from parent figures, or from home or other family surroundings. It is not uncommon for these children to shadow a close parent around the house. They may refuse to run errands or attend school. These children may worry that their parents are going to die while they are gone, that they will be lost and never see them again, or that they will be devoured by some imaginary monster. These children may have frequent night-terror dreams combined with an irrational fear of the dark and rush for the comfort of their parents' bedroom. When forced to separate for purposes such as school, the child may resist at first then become homesick, may fantasize reunions, and also may manifest psychosomatic complaints such as stomachaches, headaches, nausea, and vomiting. In addition to these symptoms, adolescents may exhibit palpitations, dizziness, and faintness. Generally, as children get older their separation anxieties become more specific and less amorphous. Some adolescent boys may deny their feelings of anxiety over separation yet overt behaviors and physical symptoms belie their anxiety. Depending on the previous status of the parent-child relationship, some overwhelmed parents may falsely interpret their child's separation anxiety as nothing more than another episode of demanding, intrusive behavior. Other parents may view their children as overly conscientious, conforming, and eager to please. In many cases, separation anxiety may closely follow some personal life stress, such as the death of a relative or pet, a family illness, or a major life change such as a move to a new school or neighborhood. These children typically come from close-knit families and much less often from neglectful families.

Avoidant Disorder of Childhood

The critical distinction between the avoidant disorder of childhood and separation anxiety is that instead of excessively worrying about separation, the avoidant child withdraws from socializing with peers and meeting new people while simultaneously desiring to build these social relationships. In this way, an approach-avoidance dissonance is established. These children may cling tenaciously to their parents and hide behind them when introduced to strangers. Anxiety may be manifested in terms of embarrassment, timidity, stuttering, and articulation difficulties. These children often are unassertive in peer relationships and lack confidence. Consequently, they may fail to form social bonds beyond the family and suffer feelings of isolation, anxiety, and depression. These children often are initially identified in preschool or kindergarten, where preschool teachers have a basis of comparison to evaluate children's social behaviors.

The DSM-III criteria for the avoidant disorder of childhood or adolescence classification include:

A. Persistent and excessive shrinking from contact with strangers.
B. Desire for affection and acceptance, and generally warm and satisfying relations with family members and other familiar figures.
C. Avoidant behavior sufficiently severe to interfere with social functioning in peer relationships.
D. Age at least 2-1/2. If 18 or older, does not meet the criteria for Avoidant Personality Disorder.
E. Duration of the disturbance of at least six months.

Overanxious Disorder

The third disorder in the subclass of anxiety disorders of childhood or adolescence is called overanxious disorder. The principle feature that differentiates overanxious disorder from separation anxiety and avoidant disorder of childhood or adolescence is that the anxiety, worry, and fear is not focused on any particular situation or object and cannot be attributed to a recent psychosocial stressor. Instead, the anxiety is generalized and directed toward future events or hypothetical situations. The child may worry about performance on some yet-to-be announced examination, needlessly fear possible injury, or shrink from meeting expectations such as homework deadlines, doctors appointments, or small household chores. Such a child may become so preoccupied with worrying about the terrible outcome of some particular action that even routine activities like visiting the doctor for a check-up become exasperating and overwhelming. Some teenagers may fear peer judgment, doubt their athletic ability, envision social rejection, worry about school grades, or even cringe at the normal behavior of other family members they believe might embarrass them. At the basis of this anxiety is a concern with what others will think. Physical manifestations of the overanxious disorder may include headache, upset stomach, speech anxiety, shortness of breath, nausea, fainting spells, or insomnia. Behavioral symptoms may consist of restlessness, or nervous habits such as tics, nail-biting, or hair-pulling. The child might complain of feeling "embarrassed" or "nervous" about an upcoming event. An adult who enlists such a child's participation in a dreaded activity may be described as "mean" or "critical" by the child. At first these children may appear very mature, even precocious. In order to gain adult and peer approval they may actively avoid confrontations and conform to social mores almost excessively in order to avoid attention. These children may exhibit perfectionistic tendencies while being simultaneously overwhelmed by self-doubt and the possibilities of success. Overanxious disorders appear to be more prevalent among boys, first-borns, small families, upper socioeconomic groups, families where self-worth is tied to performance, or families where no level of performance is reinforced (only criticized).

According to DSM-III overanxious disorder may be identified when the following criteria have been met:

A. The predominant disturbance is generalized and persistent anxiety or worry (not related to concerns about separation), as manifested by at least four of the following:
    (1) unrealistic worry about future events
    (2) preoccupation with the appropriateness of the individual's behavior in the past
    (3) overconcern about competence in a variety of areas, e.g., academic, athletic, social
    (4) excessive need for reassurance about a variety of worries
    (5) somatic complaints, such as headaches or stomachaches, for which no physical basis can be established
    (6) marked self-consciousness or susceptibility to embarrassment or humiliation
    (7) marked feelings of tension or inability to relax
B. The symptoms in A have persisted for at least six months.
C. If 18 or older, does not meet the criteria for Generalized Anxiety Disorders.
D. The disturbance is not due to another mental disorder, such as Separation Anxiety Disorder, Avoidant Disorder of Childhood or Adolescence, Phobic Disorder, Obsessive Compulsive Disorder, Depressive Disorder, Schizophrenia, or a Pervasive Developmental Disorder.

PSYCHOLOGICAL ASSESSMENT OF CHILDHOOD ANXIETY DISORDERS

Current best practice in the psychological assessment of childhood anxiety disorders would suggest that the clinician not restrict the selection of assessment techniques to either a psychometric or a behavioral model (Harrington, 1984). In fact, a multi-method approach probably provides the most comprehensive view of a particular child's anxiety disorder, the underlying assumption being that anxiety affects not just one but multiple channels of behavior or emotion (Rachman, 1978). This conceptualization of anxiety assessment has been called "triple response mode" (Cone, 1979), "multiple response components" (Nietzel & Bernstein, 1981), or the "three-response system" (Kovacs & Miller, 1982). The three channels affected by anxiety are the *cognitive channel,* the *physiological channel,* and the *motor channel.*

These three response channels can be ordered along a continumn of directness and objectivity according to how well each one measures a target response of clinical relevance at the time and place of its occurrence (Cone, 1979). The *cognitive channel* is the most subjective and indirect system of the three because it relies on the individual's ability to self-report an accurate perception of feeling. Self-reports may take several different forms. The psychologist might ask the child to respond to inquiries about anxiety-arousing situations in the context of an interview. Alternatively, the child may be taught to collect and report personal data through self-monitoring of anxiety attacks. Finally, one can easily and efficiently collect self-report data by having the child complete either an anxiety scale or some questionnaire in which anxiety is a factor.

The effects of anxiety on the *physiological channel* may be assessed by measuring changes in the sympathetic portion of the autonomic nervous system (Nietzel & Bernstein, 1981; Paul & Bernstein, 1973). Anxiety may affect heart rate, blood pressure, and galvanic skin response (GSR) differentially in individual children, and this is why more than one physiological measure is used to define anxiety in the physiological channel (Haynes, 1978). These techniques are much more objective and direct than the self-report techniques used to assess the cognitive channel, but may not be feasible for typical clinicians to assess because of lack of training, equipment, or the situation specificity of the anxiety-arousing stimuli.

The third channel, the *motor channel,* focuses on the measurement of actual overt or motor behavior of the child. The motor channel may be assessed directly or indirectly. For the clinician to directly evaluate the motor channel of anxiety there must be observable evidence of some physiological arousal in the child. For example, a child might visibly tremble at even discussing separation from the mother in order to attend school. A more indirect way to observe the motor manifestations of physiological arousal in the child might be for a parent to carefully observe the correspondence of avoidance behavior with certain stimuli. For example, a child experiencing an avoidant disorder might choose to "hide out" for the evening rather than talk with peers phoning him to attend a party.

Although the modes of measurement in the three-channel system for assessing anxiety seem to be independent, in fact they are not. For example, it may be possible to measure any one of the three behavioral content areas using a technique or device whose measurement channel is cognitive. To illustrate, the clinician might assess the motor component of separation anxiety through an interview in which the child is asked questions regarding approach behaviors toward attending summer camp. Interviews structured in this way may permit the clinician to assess motor behavior indirectly in situations where it might be impossible to witness the child's anxiety upon leaving home. Likewise, the child might be asked specific questions about the physiological arousal experienced under these same circumstances. In this manner, many questionnaires and rating scales may actually measure the cognitive, physiological, and motor channels all in one self-report instrument.

SELF-REPORT INSTRUMENTS TO MEASURE CHILDHOOD ANXIETY

A number of self-report instruments exist to measure childhood anxiety. It should be made clear at the outset that these more subjective measures may be susceptible to the demand characteristics of social desirability, with a consequent reduction in reliability and validity. In defense of child self-report instruments, Finch, Nelson, & Moss (in press) have argued that vital data from which treatment goals may be drawn are lost when a person's own perception of reality is ignored. Furthermore, self-report inventories may provide data complementary to, albeit different from, other data sources (Ollendick & Cerny, 1981).

Unlike adults, some children may be unwilling or unable to verbalize their subjective feelings and reactions to stress and anxiety within the context of a behavioral interview. Self-report inventories permit the child to respond in written form and in privacy. Probably the major benefit of self-report inventories in the assessment of childhood anxiety disorders is that they help the child label and describe many facets of the anxiety disorder, regardless of the child's ability for self-expression. This feature of self-report inventories is especially useful in the assessment of young children. Two prominent self-report inventories designed specifically to evaluate childhood anxiety will be described first. Next, two broader child personality inventories that both contain scales useful in the assessment of childhood anxiety will be described.

The original Children's Manifest Anxiety Scale (CMAS) (Castenada, McCandless, & Palermo, 1956) has been widely used for almost thirty years. Reynolds & Richmond (1978), however, criticized the CMAS for the following reasons: 1) a lack of coverage in terms of the areas of anxiety assessed; 2) many items too difficult for elementary school-age and mentally retarded children to read and comprehend; 3) an insensitivity to the developmental changes in anxiety; and 4) less than one-third of the 42 items met the criteria for a good test item recommended by Flanigan, Peters, & Conry (1969). For these reasons Reynolds & Richmond (1978) revised the CMAS. The Revised Children's Manifest Anxiety Scale (RCMAS) contains 28 Anxiety items and 9 Lie items, and was normed by race and sex on a sample of 4,972 school-age children ages six to nineteen (Reynolds & Paget, 1982). The response dimension is a simple "yes" or "no" depending on whether the child believes each statement is like him or her. The readability of the RCMAS was set at the third-grade level with the possibility of first- and second-graders understanding the content if read to them. Only scale items that met the criteria established by Flanigan, et al. (1969) were included in the RCMAS (i.e., difficulty index .30 ≤ P ≤ .70, and biserial correlation of that test item to test score, r ≥ .40).

In a large-scale investigation to develop norms for the RCMAS, Reynolds & Paget (1982) administered the scale to 4,972 children (2,208 white males; 2,176 white females; 289 black males; and 299 black females) between the ages of six and nineteen from thirteen states and eighty school districts. Alpha reliability coefficients ranging from .42 to .87, with the majority above .80, were calculated by age, race, and sex. Reynolds (1981) reported a nine-month test-retest correlation of .68 for 534 fourth-, fifth-, and sixth-graders. These levels of internal consistency and test-retest reliability are within acceptable ranges. In order to evaluate the concurrent validity Reynolds (1980) administered both the RCMAS and the State-Trait Anxiety Inventory for Children (STAIC) (Spielberger, 1973) to forty-two children referred for psychological evaluation. A significant correlation (r = .85, P < .001) was found between only the RCMAS and the A-trait scale of the STAIC, and not between the RCMAS and the A-state of the STAIC. This finding led Reynolds (1980) to conclude that the RCMAS may constitute a measure of trait anxiety but not state anxiety. It is also interesting to note that the RCMAS correlated positively with teacher observations of classroom behavioral problems (Reynolds, 1982). In a factor analysis of the RCMAS three factors were identified: Physiological Anxiety, Worry and Oversensitivity, and Concentration Anxiety. These factors held across sex and race (Reynolds & Paget, 1981) with reliability coefficients for each factor in the .60-.80 range except for young black females with several coefficients in the .15-.25 range.

Another popular scale useful in the measurement of childhood anxiety is the State-Trait Anxiety Inventory for Children (STAIC) (Spielberger, 1973). As its title suggests the STAIC consists of two separate 20-item self-report inventories, one measuring trait anxiety and the other state anxiety. Trait anxiety refers to the child's general level of anxiety or how the child typically feels, while state anxiety is that anxiety specific to certain situations. The STAIC was intended for children in the 9-12 age range. Both scales of the STAIC were normed on samples of normal and child guidance children, while the norms for elementary school children were based on 1,554 Florida elementary school children in grades four, five, and six. 35-40% of this sample were black.

At first inspection the reliability data for normal and emotionally disturbed children seem discrepant. The test-retest reliabilities of 246 normal school children on the A-trait scale were .65 for males and .71 for females (Spielberger, 1973). On the state scale Spielberger (1973) reported coefficients of .82 for males and .87 for females. In contrast, Finch, Montgomery, & Deardorff (1974) found higher levels of test retest reliabilities on the state scale (.63) and lower for the trait scale (.44) for thirty emotionally disturbed children in residential treatment. Finch, et al. (1974) attribute this discrepancy to the constantly high levels of anxiety experienced by emotionally disturbed children at any given moment, and to the higher reporting inconsistency by emotionally disturbed children compared to normals.

The correlations showing concurrent validity between the A-trait scale and the CMAS (Castenada, et al., 1956) and the General Anxiety Scale for Children (Sarason, Davidson, Lightfall, Waite, & Ruebush, 1960) are .75 and .65 respectively (Spielberger, 1973). To establish construct validity Montgomery & Finch (1974) administered the STAIC to sixty emotionally disturbed and sixty normal control children. The cut-off scores they established correctly discriminated 65% of the disturbed group using the A-State, 63% using the A-trait, and 65% with a combined score. To study the use of the STAIC in the evaluation of test anxiety, Spielberger (1973) sampled 900 fourth-, fifth-, and sixth-graders using the A-state scale under two conditions: 1) standardized administrations, and 2) how they thought they would feel just before taking a major final exam. The two conditions were discriminated on the A-State scale for both males and females. These results were substantiated in a study by Newmark, Wheeler, Newmark, & Stabler (1975). In contrast Finch, Kendall, Montgomery, & Morris (1975) found increases in anxiety ratings on not only the A-state scale but also the A-trait scale when they tested emotionally disturbed children in the midst of failure experiences. These discrepant results may suggest that personality traits, such as A-trait anxiety, are not as firmly established in emotionally disturbed children as compared to normal children.

In summary, both the RCMAS and STAIC appear to have the necessary levels of reliability and validity to support their use as measures of childhood anxiety. Clinicians will most probably find themselves shifting from one test to the other because of the relative advantages of each. That is, the RCMAS has the strength of spanning from kindergarten to age nineteen; the STAIC was intended for nine-to-twelve-year-olds. The STAIC was normed on both normal and emotionally disturbed children; the RCMAS was normed only on normal children. Finally, the STAIC measures both state and trait anxiety; the RCMAS is a measure of chronic manifest anxiety only. The final choice will depend on the case history of the child under consideration and whether the presenting symptomatology and the DSM-III classification under consideration require a state-trait distinction.

The RCMAS and the STAIC are considered narrow-band measures because they focus on only one dimension of personality: childhood anxiety disorders. The benefit of more global instruments containing multiple scales is that they provide a broader description of personality functioning. Even if some childhood anxiety disorder has been identified using the RCMAS or the STAIC, that anxiety disorder may also affect functioning in some related areas. For example, an overanxious disorder may cause a child to become a social isolate with a concomitant reduction in social skills, and a scale with broader coverage might identify these accompanying problems. That same scale could also be used to identify personal competencies of the child helpful in the development of treatment regimens. Finally, if these scales are completed by teachers and parents they may introduce two new perspectives derived from distinctly different settings, the home and the school; the two alternative viewpoints may then be compared to those self-reported by the child. If similarities are uncovered, then the anxiety disorder may be more pervasive than if significantly different personality profiles are reported. Two instruments suitable for these purposes are the Behavior Problem Checklist (BPC) (Quay, 1977; Quay & Peterson, 1975) and the Personality Inventory for Children (PIC) (Wirt, Lachar, Klinedinst, & Seat, 1977).

The BPC is a factor analytically derived dimensional rating scale assessing 55 problem areas, each of which is rated on a three-point dimension in regard to its severity. The checklist measures four primary constructs: Conduct Problems, Personality Problems, Inadequacy-Immaturity, and Socialized Delinquency. Inter-rater and test-retest reliabilities have been high, and numerous validation studies have been performed using the BPC (Speer, 1971; Touliatos & Lindholm, 1975; Victor & Halverson, 1976). A major advantage of the BPC is that it may be completed by the child's parents and/or teachers. The PIC, on the other hand, has sixteen separate scales for males and females and seventeen supplemental scales to be completed by the parents. The supplemental scales were intended to identify more specific areas of parental concern. Each profile contains three validity scales, one screening scale for general maladjustment, and twelve clinical scales. The clinical scales are: Achievement; Intellectual Screening; Development; Somatic Concern; Depression; Family Relations; Delinquency; Withdrawal; Anxiety; Psychosis; Hyperactivity; and Social Skills. The PIC test manual provides a considerable amount of information about test development and profile analysis, including empirical validity data for most but not all of the scales.

A FUNCTIONAL ANALYSIS OF CHILDHOOD ANXIETY DISORDERS

Child self-report inventories and parent/teacher rating scales have limits to their utility. Such screening instruments can only identify in gross ways those children manifesting excessive anxiety to the extent that it interferes with their ability to function. When these tests are used in conjunction with the DSM-III criteria to identify accurately a particular childhood anxiety disorder, such as separation anxiety, avoidance disorder, or overanxious disorder, psychological examiners may automatically increase their understanding of the problem. This can be accomplished by referring to the descriptions of predisposing factors, associated features, age of onset, course, impairment, prevalence rates, sex ratio, familial patterns, and differential diagnosis, which accompany all three childhood anxiety disorders described in DSM-III. Certainly these bits of information can prove helpful in conceptualizing the nature of anxiety disorder, but they provide no idiographic data about which specific situations, objects, or people are stressful for the child. Identification of these idiographic data is important in the determination of a final diagnosis and treatment planning. For this purpose an informal interview with the child may offer the most efficient approach, especially with adolescents. The psychologist might pose a variety of hypothetical anxiety-inducing circumstances and ask how the adolescent would respond. One may have to employ a less direct approach with younger, less verbal children. Kelly (1976) has advocated a "fear thermometer" to assess young children's fears and anxieties. The young child is asked simply to color-in various levels of fear on a simulated thermometer, indicating degree of discomfort with a variety of objects, events, or people.

Next, each identified anxiety-arousing situation must be functionally analyzed to determine the antecedent and consequent events associated with the anxious behavior. The psychologist may conduct interviews with parents, teachers, or the child, but the two most direct approaches involve either observing the child role-playing a response in a fictitious anxiety-arousing situation or using a Behavioral Avoidance Test (BAT) (Lang & Lazovik, 1963). Simply put, the BAT requires the clinician to observe and record the circumstances of the child's anxious behavior under real conditions. The BAT usually proves more reliable than simulations and allows the psychologist to contrast the controlling variables in those situations in which the anxiety response does or does not occur.

The interrater agreement for childhood anxiety disorders according to DSM-III is 50% (Mattison, Cantwell, Russell, & Will, 1979); much room for improvement exists. Consequently, the differential diagnosis of the three classifications of childhood anxiety disorders requires a holistic approach that does not rely on any single assessment procedure. Because children may be reticent in the clinical interview, and because direct observation of the anxiety response may be impossible, the psychodiagnostician may find it necessary to rely heavily, but not solely, on child self-report inventories or parent/teacher rating scales. By administering these behavior rating scales to various informants in different environments, the clinician may obtain data regarding the situation specificity of the child's behavior. This information is useful in discriminating separation anxiety and avoidance disorders from overanxious disorders. Furthermore, when two different informants (i.e., mother and father, or two different teachers) complete behavioral rating scales in the same setting and the clinician compares these to more direct observations or measures of behavior in that setting, a number of different treatment implications may arise. If the parents and/or teachers do not agree on their ratings, then the child may be adjusting the behavior depending on which adult is present. Alternatively, one parent may perceive the child's behavior inaccurately, and by comparing and contrasting ratings to direct observations and child interview responses, the clinician may be able to infer this. An accurate classification of a childhood anxiety disorder according to the DSM-III criteria and the development of the most effective treatment program for a child require this kind of careful comparison of data from several different assessment instruments, informants, and stimulus situations.

PART II: CHILDHOOD DEPRESSION

A controversy exists in the psychodiagnostic literature regarding whether childhood depression constitutes a depressive syndrome equivalent to adult depression, or whether it is simply an affective symptom accompanying some other psychiatric diagnosis. The typical behavioral manifestations of avoidance disorder of childhood, for example, often may include depressive symptoms. If regularly avoiding social encounters with peers, a child may not only appear worried or anxious but also seem "blue," "sad," or "withdrawn." It has been argued that such depressive symptoms could be misidentified instead of the underlying anxiety disorder.

Conversely, a second perspective maintains that depression may exist in children but its external manifestations may be altered or masked. Almost all non-psychotic symptoms have been identified as possible masking symptoms, including enuresis, temper tantrums, hyperactivity, delinquency, truancy, phobias, hypochondriasis, and, interestingly, learning disabilities. In fact, one recent study (Colbert, Newman, Ney, & Young, 1982) investigated the incidence of depression in 282 children admitted to a child and family psychiatric unit. The study identified 153 children, or 54%, as depressed. Only eleven, or 7.2%, of these 153 children were identified by the psychiatric staff as having a learning disability. In comparison, fifty-three of these children were considered to have learning disabilities by previous teachers or previous educational/psychometric reports. The point arises that certain depressed children may remain unidentified because depressive symptomatology may be manifested by such a wide variety of behavioral problems, such as learning disabilities. A third position feels that depression in childhood is a transitory phenomenon from which most children spontaneously recover and should not therefore be considered psychopathological (Lefkowitz & Burton, 1978). In truth, all three of these perspectives are debatable, and what should be obvious is that much more research needs to be conducted on the psychological construct called childhood depression, and the criteria for the differential diagnosis of childhood depression need to be more discriminating.

The major consensus in the child psychopathology literature is that depression in children is parallel to adult depression, with the addition of some developmentally appropriate symptoms. The position taken by DSM-III is that the essential features of depression in children are the same as in adults; therefore, the adult diagnostic criteria are appropriate for children. Two problems arise when these DSM-III criteria are adopted for children. First, the reliability and validity of these criteria may be lower when applied to children than to adults. Second, when psychologists use adult criteria to classify childhood psychopathology, they overlook the developmental perspective and in fact reinforce a perspective that sees these "hurried children" as miniature adults. Despite these problems the current accepted practice is to diagnose a child as having a major depressive disorder using the same DSM-III criteria specified for adult depressive disorders.

The only current alternative to DSM-III is one that psychologists working in public-school settings may have to consider. According to the federal guidelines contained in PL 94-142 for the identification of behaviorally disordered children in the public schools, the child must exhibit one or more of the following characteristics over a long period of time and to a marked degree: 1) an inability to learn that cannot be explained by intellectual, sensory, or health factors; 2) an inability to build or maintain satisfactory interpersonal relationships with peers and teachers; 3) inappropriate types of behavior or feelings under normal circumstances; 4) a general pervasive mood of unhappiness or depression; and 5) a tendency to develop physical symptoms or fears associated with personal or school problems. Only the fourth characteristic makes any mention of depression, let alone provides criteria for its identification in children. Until recent efforts to define operationally the components of the federal definition are completed (McCarney, Leigh, & Cornbleet, 1983), the DSM-III system will represent the most specific criteria currently available for the identification of childhood depressive disorders.

SYMPTOMATOLOGY AND CLASSIFICATION

Almost any disturbing behavior a child manifests may be the impetus for a parent or teacher to refer that child for a psychological assessment of what they perceive to be depressive symptoms. Many of these referrals will be excluded from consideration as depressive disorders, yet the symptomatology of childhood depression is wide-ranging. In practice, the clinician should recognize the range of presenting symptomatology associated with actual cases of childhood depression (Poznanski, 1982).

Depressed affect of course provides a primary symptom. These children may seldom smile and may appear somber. The child may not talk spontaneously even over the course of several interviews. Depressed children may have difficulty recalling any recent experiences that were fun for them. They may spend excessive amounts of time staring blankly at TV programs. Self-esteem may be quite low, describing themselves as "stupid" or "unpopular," and they may express overwhelming guilt feelings. Friendships with peers may have disintegrated only recently. One major distinction between a learning-disabled child and a depressed child is that the depressed one was probably performing at an acceptable level in school prior to the depression. A depressed child may also show more variability in school achievement depending on mood vascillations. These children may appear detached and preoccupied with their own inner concerns. Complaints of excessive fatigue are common to the extent that they may be even too tired to play. Slumped and inactive, the depressed child may not move throughout the interview. Rate of speech and language expression may be retarded. They may respond to questions with no elaboration. Reductions in sleeping and eating may be reported by the parents. Morbid ideations or suicidal thoughts may be expressed during the course of an interview. Parents may also report frequent outbursts of irritability. Children may describe episodes where they feel like crying and complain of somatic concerns such as stomachaches, leg pains, and headaches.

Many of the symptoms present in the adult syndrome of depression with its affective, cognitive, motivational, and somatic components are identical to the symptoms of depression identified in children (Leon, Kendall, & Garber, 1980). Apparently only certain developmentally based differences in symptomatology separate the adult from the childhood form of depression. The problem is that the unique symptoms reported to be present in childhood depression differ from author to author. Irritability, low self-esteem, social withdrawal, and aggressive behavior have all been mentioned as unique features of childhood depression (Clarizio, 1984); it is not clear whether these unique aspects represent "essential" or "associated" features (Cantwell, 1982). Furthermore, it is not clear how childhood depressive symptoms change with age (Weissman, Orvaschel, & Padian, 1980). For instance, while slowed speech, psychomotor retardation, lack of eye contact, and thought disturbances are not common symptoms in childhood depressives, they are in adults. Several differences between the unique characteristics of adolescent and adult depression have also been identified. A poor body image seems to be more closely related to depression in adolescents than in adults. There is a positive relationship between assertiveness and depression for adolescents and an inverse relationship between assertiveness and depression for adults. Family and peer relationships do not seem to impact adolescent depression as much as adult depression. The area of overlap between the symptomatology for childhood depression and adult depression may be great, but the unique developmental differences are still unclear and hinder the diagnostic process. A closer look at the specific DSM-III criteria for the identification of depression may help to elucidate the current situation. Only the DSM-III criteria for unipolar exogenous depression will be presented. Bipolar depression has been excluded from the discussion because the prevailing belief is that bipolar depression is rare in children (Anthony & Scott, 1960; Nissen, 1981). Likewise, endogenous depression will not be discussed because current theory suggests that the etiology of childhood depression is only infrequently biologically based (Graham, 1981).

According to DSM-III, the diagnostic criteria for a major depressive episode include:

A. Dysphoric mood or loss of interest or pleasure in all or almost all usual activities and pastimes. The dysphoric mood is characterized by symptoms such as the following: depressed, sad, blue, hapless, low, down in the dumps, irritable.

The mood disturbance must be prominent and relatively persistent, but not necessarily the most dominant symptom, and does not include momentary shifts from one dysphoric mood to another dysphoric mood, e.g., anxiety to depression to anger, such as are seen in states of acute psychotic turmoil. (For children under six, dysphoric mood may have to be inferred from a persistently sad facial expression.)

B. At least four of the following symptoms have each been present nearly every day for a period of at least two weeks (in children under six, at least three of the first four.)

   (1) poor appetite or significant weight loss (when not dieting) or increased appetite or significant weight gain (in children under six, consider failure to make expected weight gains)

   (2) insomnia or hypersomnia

   (3) psychomotor agitation or retardation (but not merely subjective feelings of restlessness or being slowed down) (in children under six, hypoactivity)

   (4) loss of interest or pleasure in usual activties, or decrease in sexual drive not limited to a period when delusional or hallucinating (in children under six, signs of apathy)

   (5) loss of energy; fatigue

   (6) feelings of worthlessness, self-reproach, or excessive or inappropriate guilt (either may be delusional)

   (7) complaints or evidence of diminished ability to think or concentrate, such as slowed thinking, or indecisiveness not associated with marked loosening of associations or incoherence

   (8) recurrent thoughts of death, suicidal ideation, wishes to be dead, or suicide attempt

C. Neither of the following dominate the clinical picture when an affective syndrome (i.e., criteria A and B above) is not present, that is, before it developed or after it has remitted:

   (1) preoccupation with a mood-incongruent delusion or hallucination

   (2) bizarre behavior

D. Not superimposed on either Schizophrenia, Schizophreniform Disorder, or a Paranoid Disorder.

E. Not due to any Organic Mental Disorder or Uncomplicated Bereavement.

The *Diagnostic and Statistical Manual* (DSM) is in its third edition, and with each revision advances have been made to specify more precisely the diagnostic criteria and decision rules. Nevertheless, DSM-III should be considered a work "in progress." Interrater agreement for the diagnosis of childhood depressive disorders has been found to be still only 42% (Mattison, Cantwell, Russell, & Will, 1979). Furthermore, the construct of "masked" depression has been omitted from discussion in the DSM-III criteria for a major depressive episode. Finally, when comparing DSM-III criteria for diagnosing childhood depression with the "depressed" factor on the Child Behavior Checklist (CBCL), minimal overlap has been found (Achenbach & Edelbrock, 1979). Only two of the thirteen items that appeared on the "depressed" factor overlapped significantly with DSM-III. These two symptoms were the presence of depressed mood and excessive guilt feelings. This discrepancy highlights the limitations of a rational consensus rather than an empirical basis for the construction of the diagnostic categories in DSM-III.

PSYCHOLOGICAL ASSESSMENT OF CHILDHOOD DEPRESSIVE DISORDERS

In order for the assessment of childhood depressive disorders to be multi-factored and multi-sourced, three factors must be considered: Who can provide the most reliable and valid information about the disorder? What are the most relevant environmental contexts? Which kinds of assessment methods are available and are most suitable? To begin, the clinician may use interview and self-report methods regarding the child's perceptions of the problem as it relates to home and school. Parents and teachers may serve as informants on behavior rating scales and interviews to report their perceptions of the problem as it is manifested at home and school. Finally, peers may complete peer nomination scales to identify those children who may evidence symptoms associated with childhood depression in their daily social interactions.

The Kiddie-SADS (K-SADS) (Chambers, Puig-Antich, & Tabinzi, 1978) is one of the most widely used child psychiatric interviews available to assess the symptoms of depression, conduct disorders, neurosis, and psychosis in children ages six to sixteen. The parents are interviewed first, followed by the teachers and then the child alone. Summary data are then compiled based on all three sources of information. Each symptom is rated separately for its severity, based not only on specific criteria but also on its occurrence in the previous week and for past and current episodes. Despite the clinical judgment involved in guiding the interview and in scoring, relatively high interrater reliabilities (r=.65 to .96) have been reported for the presence of specific symptoms and overall diagnosis. Content validity of Kiddie-SADS may be assumed since it samples the criteria for affective disorders, including depression. The Interview Schedule for Children (ISC) (Kovacs & Beck, 1977), the Bellevue Index of Depression (BID) (Petti, 1978), and the Children's Depression Rating Scale (Poznanski, Cook, & Carroll, 1979) represent examples of other interview formats to assess childhood depression.

Having specified the symptomatology using the Kiddie-SADS, the clinician might consider administering a child self-report inventory to substantiate the initial findings. The Children's Depression Inventory (CDI) (Kovacs, 1981; Kovacs & Beck, 1977) is the most widely used. It is a 27-item severity measure of overt depression in children between ten and seventeen years old. Each of the 27 items consists of three sentences ranging from normalcy, to mild symptomatology, to severe and clinically significant symptoms. Each item is read aloud to the child, and the child marks the answer based on feelings experienced over the previous two weeks. Each item is then scored on a 0 to 2 point scale resulting in a range of scores from 0-54.

Interrater consistency estimates range from .71 for a sample of pediatric-medical outpatients to .87 for a sample of normal children (Kovacs, 1978). Correlations of individual items to the total score appear generally good (Kovacs, 1983). Test-retest reliability of the CDI is fair to excellent depending on the retest interval and characteristics of the sample. The lowest values were found for normals over a one-week interval (r=.38) (Saylor, Finch, Spirito, & Bennett, 1983). Kovacs (1978) found that the CDI could discriminate between those emotionally disturbed children diagnosed as depressed and those who are not, and between depressed and normal children. The CDI, however, has not been found to be sensitive enough to discriminate less severe forms of depression from psychiatric conditions not in the depressive domain.

The Children's Depression Scale (CDS) (Tisher & Lange, 1978) represents another self-report measure of depression in children, albeit less well investigated than the CDI. The CDS contains 48 items focusing on depressive symptoms and reactions ("Often I feel I am not worth much") and 18 items focusing on more positive experiences ("I enjoy myself most of the time"). The 48 depressive items have been divided into five subscales: affective response, social problems, self-esteem, preoccupation with own sickness and death, and guilt. The format of the CDS is novel and enjoyable for young children. Each item is presented on a separate card, which the child is asked to place in one of five boxes ranging from "very right" to "very wrong." Another unique feature of this scale is that parallel items can be answered by parents and teachers to describe the child. Overall, the psychometric qualities of the CDS as reported by its developers are better than for other similar scales. They report high internal consistency reliability, and that scores on the CDS distinguish depressed children from both normals and other diagnostic groups. Further cross-validation studies of the CDS need to be conducted by independent researchers.

In summary, the use of child self-report inventories in the assessment of depression should be conducted with great caution. In some cases further psychometric data are required; in others, it is not always clear how resulting data should be interpreted. For example, children may rate themselves as less depressed across various measures of depression than do their parents (Kazdin, French, & Unis, in press). Children's self-reports can also sometimes reflect what happened in that child's life five minutes ago rather than representing a consistent pattern of behavior over time. Finally, because all these instruments are modeled after adult scales and assess adult symptomatology analogues, they fail to take into account differences in the child's developmental level. Future scales need to incorporate age specific norms and items pertinent to different developmental levels.

The depression scale of the Personality Inventory for Children (PIC) (Wirt, et al., 1977) already mentioned in this chapter represents a vehicle by which parents can specify their concerns about a child's depressive symptomatology. The PIC can be administered to the parents of children ages three to sixteen. There are 46 items on the Depression Scale that deal with moodiness; social isolation; lack of energy; crying spells; pessimism; serious attitude; concern with death and separation; indecisiveness; sensitivity and criticism; and uncommunicativeness. High test-retest reliability on this scale has been reported for psychiatric outpatients (r=.94) and normal children (r=.93). More validity data need to be gathered for the scale. One advantage of the PIC is that the multiple scales, such as the Withdrawal Scale and Social Skills Scale, may prove to be helpful in understanding the impact of the depression on other areas of the child's life. Another scale the examiner might consider as a means of assessing childhood depression through parental report is the Child Behavior Checklist (CBCL) (Achenbach & Edelbrock, 1982).

A newly developed and innovative approach to the assessment of childhood depression is the Peer Nomination Inventory of Depression (PNID) (Lefkowitz & Tesiny, 1980). Peers represent a ready source of direct observational data about a targeted child's level of energy and social involvement, not only in school situations but in numerous other settings. The PNID also takes advantage of the increased reliability derived from multiple peer ratings and the fact that these peers probably are directly familiar with many of the behaviors covered on the scale. The PNID contains 20 items covering four areas related to depression: affective, cognitive, motivational, and vegetative. In a group setting children are asked to nominate other classmates for questions like, "Who doesn't have much fun?" and "Who plays alone?" 452 boys and 492 girls from fourth- and fifth-grade classrooms in New York City comprised the norm sample. Adequate levels of internal consistency (r=.85) and test-retest reliability (r=.79) have been reported. The scale items are represented by three factors: loneliness, inadequacy, and dejection. The PNID appears to be predictive of school performance, self-concept, teacher rating of work, skill and school behavior, peer rating of happiness and popularity, and loss of control. One unresolved discrepancy is that the correlation between scores on the PNID and ratings of depression by teachers, parents, and child self-report have not been high (Tesiny & Lefkowitz, 1982). The utility of the PNID should be restricted to school setting and not used in clinical settings because accurate ratings require a stable peer group familiar with the target child.

Childhood depression is a psychological construct that is not very well understood. This situation compounds the challenges for the psychologist seeking to assess this affective disorder, and consequently several recommendations are in order. First, childhood depression should always be evaluated from multiple perspectives and not based on child self-report or interview, parent/teacher rating, or peer nomination alone. Situational specifity of the problem behavior should always be considered.

Clinical evidence for childhood depression should be based on evidence derived from instruments such as the Kiddie-SADS, the CDI, the PIC, and the PNID. If symptomatology of childhood depression is discovered, the examiner should question whether these symptoms represent a depressive syndrome or are secondary effects of some other major childhood disorder, such as childhood anxiety disorder. If identified, then these other major disorders should be treated first before developing a treatment program targeted at specific depressive disorders. The assessment of childhood depression and childhood anxiety disorder proves difficult at best, but if the clinician becomes aware of the issues and assessment alternatives, useful assessment information can be obtained.

REFERENCES

Achenbach, T.M. (1979). The Child Behavior Profile: An empirically based system for assessing children's behavioral problems and competencies. *International Journal of Mental Health, 7,* 24-42.

Achenbach, T.M., & Edelbrock, C.S. (1982). *Manual for the Child Behavior Checklist and Child Behavior Profile.* Burlington, VT: Child Psychiatry, University of Vermont.

Achenbach, T.M., & Edelbrock, C.S. (1979). The Child Behavior Profile: II. Boys aged 12-16 and girls aged 6-11 and 12-16. *Journal of Consulting and Clinical Psychology, 47,* 223-233.

American Psychiatric Association. (1980). *Diagnostic and statistical manual of mental disorders* (3rd ed.). Washington, DC: Author.

Anthony, J., & Scott, P. (1960). Manic-depressive psychosis in childhood. *Journal of Child Psychology and Psychiatry, 1,* 53-72.

Cantwell, D. (1982). Childhood depression: A review of current research. In B. Lahey & A. Kazdin (Eds.), *Advances in clinical child psychology* (Vol. 5). New York: Plenum.

Castenada, A., McCandless, B.R., & Palermo, D.S. (1956). The Children's Form of the Manifest Anxiety Scale. *Child Development, 27,* 317-326.

Chambers, W., Puig-Antich, J., & Tabinzi, M. (1978). *The ongoing development of the Kiddie-SADS (Schedule for Affective Disorders and Schizophrenia) for school-age children.* Presented at the American Academy of Child Psychiatry, San Diego, CA.

Clarizio, H.F. (1984). Childhood depression: Diagnostic considerations. *Psychology in the Schools, 31,* 181-197.

Colbert, P., Newman, B., Ney, P., & Young, J. (1982). Learning disabilities as a symptom of depression in children. *Journal of Learning Disabilities, 15,* 333-336.

Cone, J.D. (1979). Confounded comparisons in triple response mode assessment research. *Behavioral Assessment, 1,* 85-95.

Edelbrock, C. (1979). Empirical classification of children's behavior disorders: Progress based on parent and teacher ratings. *School Psychology Digest, 8,* 355-369.

Elkind, D. (1981). *The hurried child.* Reading, MA: Addison-Wesley Publishing Company.

Finch, A.J., Jr., Kendall, P.C., Montgomery, L.E., & Morris, T. (1975). The effects of two types of failure on anxiety of emotionally disturbed children. *Journal of Abnormal Psychology, 84*, 583-585.

Finch, A.J., Jr., Montgomery, L.E., & Deardorff, P. (1974). Reliability of State-Trait Anxiety with emotionally disturbed children. *Journal of Abnormal Child Psychology, 2*, 67-69.

Finch, A.J., Jr., Nelson, W.M., III, & Moss, J.H. (In press). A cognitive-behavioral approach to anger management with emotionally disturbed children. In A.J. Finch, Jr., W.M. Nelson, III, & E.S. Ott (Eds.), *Cognitive behavioral approaches to treatment with children*. Jamaica, NY: Spectrum Publications.

Flanigan, P.J., Peters, C.J., & Conry, J.L. (1969). Item analysis of the Children's Manifest Anxiety Scale with the retarded. *Journal of Educational Research, 62*, 472-477.

Graham, P. (1981). Depressive disorders in children: A re-consideration. *Acta Paedopsychiatrica, 46*, 285-296.

Harrington, R.G. (1984). A holistic approach to the assessment of emotionally disturbed children. In M.J. Fine (Ed.), *Systematic intervention with disturbed children*. New York: SP Medical & Scientific Books.

Haynes, S.N. (1978). *Principles of behavioral assessment*. New York: Gardner Press.

Kazdin, A. (1983). Psychiatric diagnosis, dimensions of dysfunction and child behavior theory. *Behavior Therapy, 14*, 73-99.

Kazdin, A., French, N., & Unis, A. (In press). Child, mother and father evaluations of depression in psychiatric inpatient children. *Journal of Abnormal Child Psychology*.

Kelly, C.K. (1976). Play desensitization of fears of darkness in preschool children. *Behavior Research and Therapy, 14*, 79-81.

Kovacs, M. (1983, April). *The Children's Depression Inventory: A self-rated depression scale for school-aged youngsters*. Unpublished manuscript.

Kovacs, M. (1981). Rating scales to assess depression in school-aged children. *Acta Paedopsychiatrica, 46*, 305-315.

Kovacs, M., & Beck, A.T. (1977). An empirical-clinical approach toward a definition of childhood depression. In J.G. Schutterbrank & A. Raskin (Eds.), *Depression in childhood: Diagnosis, treatment and conceptual models*. New York: Raven Press.

Kovacs, M.J., & Miller, G.A. (1982). Hypothetical constructs vs. intervening variables: A re-appraisal of the three-systems model of anxiety assessment. *Behavioral Assessment, 49*, 309-318.

Lang, P.J., & Lazovik, A.D. (1963). Experimental desensitization of phobia. *Journal of Abnormal and social psychology, 66*, 519-525.

Lefkowitz, M.M., & Burton, N. (1978). Childhood depression: A critique of the concept. *Psychological Bulletin, 85*, 716-726.

Lefkowitz, M.M., & Tesiny, E.P. (1980). Assessment of childhood depression. *Journal of Consulting and Clinical Psychology, 48*, 43-50.

Leon, G., Kendall, P., & Garber, J. (1980). Depression in children: Parent, teachers, and child perspectives. *Journal of Abnormal Child Psychology, 8*, 221-235.

McCarney, S., Leigh, J., & Cornbleet, J. (1983). *Behavior Evaluation Scale*. Columbia, MO: Educational Services.

Mattison, R., Cantwell, D.D., Russell, A.T., & Will L. (1979). Comparison of DSM-II and DSM-III in the diagnosis of childhood psychiatric disorders-II. Interrater agreement. *Archives of General Psychiatry, 36,* 1217-1222.

Montgomery, L.E., & Finch, A.J., Jr. (1974). Validity of two measures of anxiety in children. *Journal of Abnormal Child Psychology, 2,* 293-298.

Naisbitt, J. (1982). *Megatrends: Ten new directions transforming our lives.* New York: Warner Books, Inc.

Newmark, C.S., Wheeler, D., Newmark, L., & Stabler, B. (1975). Test-induced anxiety with children. *Journal of Personality Assessment, 39,* 409-413.

Nietzel, M.T., & Bernstein, D.A. (1981). Assessment of anxiety and fear. In M. Hersen & A.S. Bellack (Eds.), *Behavioral assessment: A practical handbook* (2nd ed.). Elmsford, NY: Pergamon.

Nissen, G. (1981). Classification of depressions in childhood. *Acta Paedopsychiatrica, 46,* 275-284.

Ollendick, T.H., & Cerny, J.A. (1981). *Clinical behavior therapy with children.* New York: Plenum Press.

Ollendick, T.H. & Hersen, M. (Eds.). (1984). *Child behavioral assessment.* New York: Pergamon Press.

Paul, G.L., & Bernstein, D.A. (1973). *Anxiety and clinical problems: Systematic desensitization and related techniques.* Morristown, NJ: General Learning Press.

Petti, T. (1978). Depression in hospitalized child psychiatry patients: Approaches to measuring depression. *Journal of the American Academy of Child Psychiatry, 17,* 49-59.

Poznanski, E.O. (1982). The clinical phenomenology of childhood depression. *American Journal of Orthopsychiatry, 52,* 308-313.

Poznanski, E., Cook, S., & Carroll, B. (1979). A depression rating scale for children. *Pediatrics, 64,* 442-450.

Quay, H.C. (1977). Measuring dimensions of deviant behavior: The Behavior Problem Checklist. *Journal of Abnormal Child Psychology, 5,* 277-287.

Quay, H.C., & Peterson, D.R. (1975). *Manual for the Behavior Problem Checklist.* Unpublished manuscript.

Rachman, S. (1978). *Fear and courage.* San Francisco: Freeman Press.

Reynolds, C.R. (1982). *Convergent and divergent validity of What I Think and Feel: The Revised Children's Manifest Anxiety Scale.* Unpublished manuscript.

Reynolds, C.R. (1981). Long-term stability of scores on the Revised Children's Manifest Anxiety Scale. *Perceptual and Motor Skills, 53,* 703.

Reynolds, C.R. (1980). Concurrent validity of What I Think and Feel: The Revised Children's Manifest Anxiety Scale. *Journal of Consulting and Clinical Psychology, 48,* 774-775.

Reynolds, C.R., & Paget, K.D. (1982, March). *National normative and reliability data for the Revised Children's Manifest Anxiety Scale.* Paper presented at the annual meeting of the National Association of School Psychologists, Toronto, Canada.

Reynolds, C.R., & Richmond, B.O. (1978). "What I Think and Feel": A revised measure of children's manifest anxiety. *Journal of Abnormal Child Psychology, 6,* 271-280.

Reynolds, C.R., & Paget, K.D. (1981). Factor analysis of the Revised Children's Manifest Anxiety Scale for blacks, whites, males, and females. *Journal of Consulting and Clinical Psychology, 49,* 352-359.

Sarason, S.B., Davidson, K.S., Lightfall, F.F., Waite, R.R., & Ruebush, B.K. (1960). *Anxiety in elementary school children.* New York: Wiley.

Saylor, C.F., Finch, A.J., Jr., Spirito, A., & Bennett, B.A., (1983). *A systematic evaluation of the Children's Depression Inventory.* Manuscript under review.

Speer, D.C. (1971). The Behavior Problems Checklist (Peterson-Quay): Baseline data from parents of child guidance and non-clinic children. *Journal of Consulting and Clinical Psychology, 36,* 227-228.

Tesiny, E., & Lefkowitz, M. (1982, August). *Assessing childhood depression: Cumulative data.* Paper presented at the Annual Meeting of the American Psychological Association, Washington, D.C.

Tisher, M. & Lange, M. (1978). *Children's Depression Scale* (Research Edition). Palo Alto, CA: Consulting Psychologists Press.

Toffler, A. (1971). *Future shock.* Miami, FL: Bantam Books.

Touliatos, J., & Lindholm, B.W. (1975). Relationships of children's grade in school, sex, and social class to teacher's ratings on the Behavior Problem Checklist. *Journal of Abnormal Child Psychology, 3,* 115-126.

Victor, J.B., & Halverson, C.F., Jr., (1976). Behavior Problems in elementary school children: A follow-up study. *Journal of Abnormal Child Psychology, 4,* 17-29.

Wahler, R., & Fox, J. (1980). Solitary toy play and time out: A family treatment package for children with aggressive and oppositional behavior. *Journal of Applied Behavior Analysis, 13,* 23-29.

Weissman, M., Orvaschel, H., & Padian, N. (1980). Children's symptom and social functioning self-report scales: Comparison of mothers' and children's reports. *Journal of Nervous and Mental Disorders, 168,* 736-740.

Wirt, R.D., Lachar, D., Klinedinst, J.K., & Seat, P.D. (1977). *Multidimensional description of personality.* Los Angeles: Western Psychological Services.

12

Considerations in Physical and Health-Related Disorders

DIANE J. WILLIS, PH.D., JAN L. CULBERTSON, PH.D., & RUTH ANN MERTENS, PH.D.

Approximately 10% of the children and youth in the United States are afflicted with physical or health-related disorders. The disabilities can be caused by a variety of factors, including: 1) genetic-related disorders such as diabetes, cystic fibrosis, or hemophilia; 2) prenatal and postnatal complications, which can cause seizures or cerebral palsy; 3) diseases and systemic health disorders; and 4) congenital anomalies such as cardiovascular problems or cleft lip/palate.

With the advances in medical technology the incidence of genetic disorders as a physical and health-related problem has more than doubled in the last 10 years. Additionally, more premature infants are surviving the neonatal intensive care unit, thus adding to the incidence of physically related disorders. This presents a unique challenge to the clinician evaluating children with these disorders in that the clinician will need to become knowledgeable about the cognitive and behavioral attributes of this population.

This chapter discusses selected physical and health-related disorders, specifically genetic disorders, chronic health disorders, and physical disorders such as cerebral palsy. The clinician will be instructed on the ways of assessing children presenting with these problems, on the integration and interpretation of test data, and on the communication of results to family, school, and other professionals.

DEFINITIONS AND INCIDENCE

In Swanson & Willis (1979), physical and health disabilities are defined as those medical conditions that "limit the alertness, vitality, or strength of the individual to such an extent that his or her educational performance is adversely affected. Depending on the severity of the condition the child's social and emotional status is also affected" (p. 379). Table 1 lists some of the physical disabilities that the clinician may encounter. It is important to remember that the cognitive, language, motor, academic, and social-emotional abilities of children with these disabilities may range from average or above to severely and profoundly impaired. Although

TABLE 1

Physical and Health-Related Disabilities

Physical and/or Neurological	Genetic, Endocrine, and Metabolic	Musculoskeletal	Other
Cerebral Palsy	Down's Syndrome	Muscular Dystrophy	Leukemia
Convulsive Disorders (seizures)	Turner's Syndrome	Scoliosis	Congenital Heart Defects
Spina Bifida	Phenylketonuria	Juvenile Rheumatoid Arthritis	Asthma
	Hurler's Syndrome		Rheumatic Fever
	Neurofribromatosis	Osteogenesis Imperfecta	
	Cystic Fibrosis		Sickle Cell Anemia
	Hemophilia		
	Diabetes		

approximately 10% of children in the United States are afflicted with physical and health-related disorders, the incidence *requiring special education* is approximately one to two percent of the school-aged population.

PRE-DIAGNOSTIC STAFFING AND SCREENING

General Considerations

The child with a known physical or health-related disorder may be referred for assessment to determine appropriate academic placement and programming. If the physical or health-related disorder is chronic, such as hemophilia, leukemia, cardiovascular disorders, and so forth, the child may be underachieving because of secondary neurological involvement. Although children with chronic health-related disorders have had numerous medical examinations, none of these examinations may have recognized or even addressed potential cognitive deficits. Therefore, the clinician plays an important role in addressing the cognitive strengths and weaknesses of these children as well as the social-emotional issues and how any one child may be affected by the disorder. The impact of social and emotional factors, such as poor self-esteem, lack of motivation, and anxiety regarding the physical disorders, may result in poorer academic performance.

Since the chronically ill or physically disabled child is often misperceived as less bright, and because the teacher or parents may not expect as much from this group, their achievement and learning may be deficient. The evaluation then takes on greater meaning since the clinician can provide a more accurate measure of intellect and learning potential.

Gathering Information Prior to Planning the Assessment

The first steps prior to evaluation of the child consist of obtaining: a thorough history from the parents; medical information from the physician(s), including prohibitions or precautions placed on the child because of the child's health-related disorder; and past and present school information.

First, the history from the parents can provide important premorbid data concerning the child's development and behavior prior to onset of the illness or health problems. If the child's health problems are congenital, such as with genetic disorders, cerebral palsy, and other neuromuscular disorders, the clinician should determine how these disorders have affected the child's early developmental progress or learning opportunities. For example, has the child been delayed in reaching all early developmental milestones, or only those involving motor development? Was the child hospitalized or confined to a bed frequently during early childhood, precluding normal opportunities for exploring and learning from the environment? How did the physical/health disorder affect the child's opportunities for involvement with peer groups, family members, and structured learning situations? Answers to these and other questions provide essential baseline information which will help the clinician understand and interpret the assessment data obtained on the child.

Next, medical information obtained from the child's physician is useful both in providing a medical diagnosis and also listing any restrictions or precautions placed on the child because of health or physical problems. Once a medical diagnosis is made, the clinician should attempt to learn what, if any, effect the medical problem may have upon the child's learning and behavior. For the clinician unfamiliar with the impact of a genetic, physical, or other health-related disorder upon a child's cognitive and academic functioning, it is wise to review material on the disorder. For example, children with genetic disorders show a wide range of intellectual variabilities, and also can have accompanying problems such as hearing loss, heart problems, etc. Children with Down's Syndrome for instance may well demonstrate IQ scores more closely resembling their parents and siblings, contrary to the popular belief that this group of children is always severely to moderately retarded. The interested clinician will want to order resource books for his or her office and the following are recommended. *The Handbook for the Practice of Pediatric Psychology* edited by June Tuma (1982) has two excellent chapters, one on the "Psychological Effect of Physical Illness and its Concomitant" (Willis, Elliot & Jay) and another on "Assessment Techniques in Pediatric Psychology" (Magrab & Lehr).

The Encyclopedia of Pediatric Psychology (Wright, Schaefer, & Solomons, 1979) lists many health-related disorders and reviews intellectual and social/emotional literature. The book *Understanding Exceptional Children and Youth* (Swanson & Willis, 1979) reviews a host of educational and psychological effects of physical/ health and other exceptionalities on the developing child. The clinician will need to seek out a variety of genetic texts (generally in a medical library) to review genetic-related disorders.

Medical information from the child's physician may also provide important information regarding the child's sensory capabilities. For instance, have visual and auditory acuity problems been ruled out? This is especially important to know in a child with severe motor problems, who may not be able to speak or manipulate test items. Medical information regarding the child's auditory, visual, and motor skills and deficits provides the basis for selection of cognitive and academic test instruments. The physician may also be a resource regarding the effects of certain medications, such as anticonvulsants or stimulant drugs, on the child's behavior and learning abilities. An excellent book on this topic for the clinician is *Children on Medication* by Gadow (1979). Finally, the clinician can obtain information from the child's physician regarding any restrictions or precautions necessary for the child to undergo testing. For example, children with motor handicaps or other physical/ health disorders may tire easily. Thus, the fatigue factor is an important consideration in the assessment. It is frequently advisable to have the child return for testing on a number of different days for relatively short periods each time. Frequent rest breaks should also be built into the daily schedule, and facilties should be available to allow the child to lie down or to change positions when needed. Children with cerebral palsy or other motor problems often need special supportive chairs or special positioning of their bodies before they are able to respond to testing. The clinician must assure that proper facilities and equipment are available before attempting to assess a child with motor disability.

A third area of information gathering involves the child's past and present school history, including the number of schools attended, grades repeated, special classes and/or related services received, and any special equipment or facilities needed in the school environment. It is important to differentiate whether the child's school problems result from the handicapping condition itself or from frequent absences related to illness.

Thus, a comprehensive family, medical, and school history will provide the necessary background from which to understand and interpret the child's test performance.

Planning the Assessment

Several basic premises should underlie the assessment of any child, but particularly children with handicapping conditions. In addition to obtaining a comprehensive family, medical, and school history, those premises include:

1) clearly defining the referral question; 2) obtaining information on the child's stimulability through various sensory channels; 3) using an hypothesis-testing approach to planning the assessment; and 4) finally obtaining a profile of strengths as well as weaknesses for each child.

The clear definition of the referral question is an important guide to the clinician in selecting a test battery. For instance, if information is requested on the intellectual functioning of a child with mild cerebral palsy, the clinician must choose a test instrument which circumvents the child's motor handicaps and measures knowledge and problem-solving abilities through the child's strongest channels. On the other hand, if the referral question asks the extent to which the child's motor handicaps affect academic performance, the clinician should include some academic tests with motor requirements and some without in order to assess the relative differences in performance. It is also essential to note whether the referral question comes from the parents, physician, or school. For example, the physician may not have included tests of fine motor dexterity and speed or graphomotor ability in the medical examination, and may find this information from the clinician very useful. The school may wish to have suggestions regarding the child's strongest learning channels and the best approaches to teaching the child, in addition to a description of intellectual functioning. The clearly defined referral question can help the clinician focus the assessment directly on the most important questions regarding a particular child, and thus avoid duplication or irrelevant testing.

One of the first steps in selecting a test battery involves asking how the child best receives information. The child's physician should have provided information on visual and auditory acuity as well as the extent of any motor or physical deficits. However, even if acuity deficits are ruled out, the clinician must still examine stimulability through the various sensory channels to ascertain how the child best receives and perceives information. Does the child learn best through the auditory, visual, or tactile modalities, or through some combination of these modalities (e.g., auditory-visual, visual-motor, etc.)? Simple tasks should be selected which allow the clinician to examine the relative differences in the child's performance through various information processing channels.

An hypothesis-testing approach is an important premise to the assessment because it places the clinician's focus first on the child rather than the tests. Children with physical and health disorders present with various strengths and weaknesses, and thus no one battery of tests is appropriate for all. Neither is the child's age the most important criterion in test selection. Rather, the clinician should form hypotheses regarding the child's strengths and weaknesses as measured through verbal and nonverbal material, through various sensory modalities, and through academic areas and social and adaptive areas. The goal of assessment should be to test out these hypotheses by selecting test instruments which measure the various skill areas of interest. Since no "standard" test battery exists for all motor-handicapped children, all genetically disordered children, etc., the clinician must *task analyze* each test, asking:

1) What does the test purport to measure? (e.g., intelligence, spelling ability, self-help and adaptive skills, handwriting skill)
2) How is information presented to the child? (e.g., through verbal directions, pictures, pantomime)
3) What is the child required to do in order to demonstrate knowledge? (e.g., give lengthy verbal responses, answer "yes" or "no," point to a picture, manipulate blocks or puzzle pieces, write an answer, nod head)

Once these questions are answered, the clinician may then ask if the test allows information to be presented to the child through a strong sensory channel rather than a weak one, or if the response mode required by the test is appropriate for the child. Modifications *can* be made in test administration and the required response mode, if these modifications are described specifically in the test report and interpretation of results.

The final premise to the assessment, that of providing a profile of strengths and weaknesses for each child rather than a global score, follows naturally from the hypothesis-testing approach. Certain intelligence and academic tests provide global scores that summarize across a variety of skill areas, often masking significant strengths and weaknesses. This pattern of strengths and weaknesses is infinitely more valuable to educational programming than the global scores, and thus should comprise the primary goal of assessment. For further discussion of this approach to assessment, see Culbertson & Ferry (1982) and Culbertson (1981).

Finally, pervading every aspect of the assessment is the social-emotional functioning of the child. Social-emotional factors may affect the child's general style of responding to the testing and thus influence scores even on cognitive and academic tasks. In fact, depressed scores on standardized tests of academic achievement may largely reflect the atypical, relatively restricted educational experiences of some of these children rather than actual skill deficits in the areas the tests attempt to measure. These children also may not have had adequate opportunity to learn the basic classroom-related skills involved in test-taking procedures per se, which one would assume the average child of school age had acquired; therefore, they may require a significant amount of training to the task. Adequate demonstration of the testing procedure and opportunities for practice trials should be allowed. Only when it is clear that the child understands the nature of the task should testing proper begin; otherwise, the resulting poor performance may be inappropriately attributed to cognitive or skill deficits.

ADMINISTRATION OF TESTS AND PROCEDURES

The content areas of an assessment battery typically include measures of cognitive ability, communication style, perceptual modes of learning (including auditory, visual and motor modalities), specific academic skills, and social-emotional functioning. Each of these areas will be discussed in the following section. The reference book *Tests* (1983) lists many intellectual and educational tests, behavioral rating scales and questionnaires, and projective instruments, providing a useful resource in evaluating children with physical/health-related disorders.

Cognitive Assessment

Cognitive assessment of children with most health and genetic-related disorders is possible using measures such as the Wechsler Preschool and Primary Scale of Intelligence, Wechsler Intelligence Scale for Children-Revised (WISC-R), McCarthy Scales of Children's Abilities, etc. The profiles provided by these scales are especially useful in comparing verbal with nonverbal abilities, and examining the specific pattern of strengths and deficits. Assessment of children who present with moderate to severe speech and language disorders, hearing impairment, or visual impairment may require modifications of these tests or may require other procedures outlined in the respective chapters on these disorders. It should also be noted that the Wechsler Scales include subtests which reflect academic achievement (e.g., Information, Arithmetic, Vocabulary), and these subtest scores may be depressed in children with prolonged school absences due to illness.

Assessing the cognitive functioning of the nonverbal, severely physically handicapped child with cerebral palsy requires the selection of an instrument which minimizes motor and speech requirements. The Pictorial Test of Intelligence, appropriate for 3- to 8-year-old children, is designed to allow the child to indicate an answer by "eye-pointing," or merely looking at the correct response from among alternatives widely spaced on a large card. Other tests of intellectual functioning which may be appropriate for motorically handicapped children include the Columbia Mental Maturity Scale, the Full Range Picture Vocabulary Test, the Coloured Progressive Matrices, and the Quick Test.

Of critical importance in evaluating the child with cerebral palsy is correct positioning of the child's body and of the testing materials. In children with cerebral palsy, it is known that certain positions of the body elicit primitive reflex movements that obviate purposeful motor activity. Proper positioning may allow some children to accomplish at least grossly adequate manipulations on certain tasks. In this regard, the clinician is required to become acquainted with the muscle-tone abnormalities of motor-handicapped children (i.e., hypertonia, hypotonia, etc.) and/or to obtain the consultation of a physical therapist for suggestions about proper positioning. See Rogers (1982), among others, for an excellent discussion of primitive reflex movements in cerebral palsy and other motor abnormalities.

The psychologist will frequently need to present materials in a vertical rather than horizontal orientation in order to accurately monitor the child's responses when "eye-pointing" is employed. Thus, special arrangements are sometimes necessary to allow for proper display of materials, such as placing printed material on a large, upright easel. The child's use of a head wand or other device will also influence the manner in which test materials may be appropriately presented. For information about various devices and techniques to aid individuals with physical disabilities, see Bigge (1976).

Assessment of Communication Ability

Children with severe motor handicaps often have disorders in the oral musculature needed for control of speech. Language deficits may also be apparent, and are usually related to the degree of mental retardation present. Although it is not the clinician's role to diagnose speech and language disorders, much useful information can be obtained about a child's language in the course of the evaluation. For instance, many opportunities arise for taking verbatim language samples during the assessment of cognitive abilities. Those samples allow one to attend to the child's sentence structure and length, syntax, and vocabulary. The clinician may also note whether the child misperceives similar-sounding words, misunderstands oral directions, verbalizes very little, or verbalizes with obvious physical effort. These observations provide useful information for making a referral to a speech and language pathologist. For children with severe deficiencies in speech musculature control, alternative communication methods must be used and the clinician should become familiar with these. Some children may use only "yes/no" responses, while others use picture or communication boards, or electronic devices. If necessary, one may adapt those alternative communication devices for use during the testing.

Perceptual and Perceptual-Motor Assessment

For children with language ability, tests of auditory discrimination and auditory memory may be chosen from various subtests of the Illinois Test of Psycholinguistic Abilities, Detroit Tests of Learning Aptitude, or McCarthy Scales of Children's Abilities.

Children with health-related disorders such as seizures, diabetes, leukemia, asthma, etc. may be administered the Bender Visual Motor Gestalt Test or the Developmental Test of Visual-Motor Integration (VMI). Children with seizures often have visual perceptual problems and need to be assessed in this area. Of course, children who present with serious motor impairment may have difficulty manipulating a pencil to complete drawing tests, but their visual perceptual skills may be examined by use of the Motor-Free Visual Perception Test.

Assessment of Achievement Levels

Another strategy for the assessment of motorically impaired children is available to the clinician through the modification of standard tasks. For example, in assessing academic achievement, one may modify the items of the Peabody Individual Achievement Test (PIAT) by cutting out and placing the response choices at opposite extremes on a large piece of cardboard to allow for response by "eyepoint." Many questions or concepts allow for presentation in yes/no, agree/disagree, or multiple-choice format, where some signal may be arranged for responding (such as eye-pointing or even blinking of the eyes) to indicate choice of an alternative when it is presented either verbally or pictorially. These items may be modifications of items from existing standardized concepts, and even higher-level abstract reasoning abilities.

Timed tasks should typically be modified by dispensing with time limits when working with motor-handicapped children, particularly where the task has any motor component. Of course, the clinician should note this departure from standardized testing procedure in both oral and written reports of test results.

Children with health-related problems may be underachieving due to school absences, so it is important to measure their achievement accurately. Tests such as the PIAT and the Wide Range Achievement Test can be given to most of these children under normal test conditions.

Assessment of Social-Emotional Functioning

Many children with chronic illness or motor handicaps present with social-emotional problems secondary to their disability. When children are dependent upon caretakers to perform daily tasks for them, attendant problems in separation-individuation, low self-esteem, and depression frequently develop. Guilt, resentment, and anger are also many times a part of the family dynamics in such cases. In cases of multiple sclerosis and other terminal illnesses, the impact on the child and family of the child's impending early death is enormous. Thus, assessment of the child's social-emotional functioning, of parent-child relationships, and of the coping abilities and strategies of all those involved represent important dimensions of the psychological evaluation.

When the child is verbal, standard verbal techniques for assessing social-emotional functioning may be suitable, such as the Rorschach Psychodiagnostic Test, sentence completion forms, and The Children's Apperception Test (CAT-A; CAT-H; CAT-S). The CAT-S contains items involving physical disability and prolonged illness, which may be particularly appropriate for tapping into the child's thoughts and feelings about the handicapping condition. Additionally, the Child Anxiety Scale can be used to assess the level of anxiety a child might be experiencing due to the physically or health-related disorder. Self-concept measures or negative self-statements, as well as behavior rating scales that screen for possible behavior problems and aid in making treatment decisions, can provide important data. Walls, Werner, Bacon, & Zane (1977) list both descriptive and prescriptive instruments that the clinician can employ to screen and identify behavior disorders.

When the child does not have adequate speech/language, the clinician may need to rely primarily on the reports of caretakers, teachers, and other individuals familiar with the child. One may request that those individuals fill out various adaptive rating scales, such as the Burks' Behavior Rating Scales, the Vineland

Social Maturity Scale, and others, describing the child's social-emotional functioning.

INTEGRATION AND INTERPRETATION OF DATA

The more comprehensive and informative report consists of four main areas. First, the background information including details of the history and the clinician's impressions of the interview with parent(s) and child must precede the actual reporting of test results. Second, behavioral observations of the child both during assessment and in the classroom or on the playground permit the clinician to know the child better and to interpret test results in a manner that benefits the child. For example, one must look for evidence of motor weakness, physical fatigue, or impulsive, distractible behavior that may adversely influence the child's test scores and school performance. These behaviors must be so noted in the clinician's report and allowances made (such as pro-rating the Performance IQ on the WISC-R by omitting the Coding score for a child with mild to moderate cerebral palsy), so the IQ measures are more accurate and the recommendations or suggestions on behalf of the child reflect the child's weakness. The third area should include actual interpretations of test data in view of the history and behavioral observations, with statements regarding the strengths and weaknesses that the child presents in the test profile. The fourth area includes suggestions for classroom placement and other diagnostic recommendations.

Due to the wide variation in cognitive and academic abilities, there is no "typical" profile of test results for children with motor handicaps, other than generally depressed scores on tests with motor components. An appropriate selection of tests for administration to these children will minimize the effects of their motor handicaps on test results. When these children are severely affected and/or have led dependent lives that restrict their experiences, there may be an accompanying depression of scores on tests involving knowledge acquired from the environment and practical judgment tasks. Such lowered scores do not indicate that these children have deficits in their ability to learn, but merely reflect their restricted opportunities for experience in these areas. As previously discussed, physically handicapped children also frequently have atypical school experience, and this may be reflected in lowered scores on tests of academic achievement. Again, this does not necessarily represent a true skill deficit, but rather the effect of the child's handicaps on academic experiences.

The assessment battery of the child with chronic health-related problems must be integrated to demonstrate strengths and weaknesses and the academic level of the child. Differentiating academic underachievement due to health problems (with subsequent lack of energy or vitality) from a specific learning disability is a difficult but necessary challenge. Children with seizures, hemophilia, leukemia, or cardiac problems may well have a learning disorder secondary to either their illness or the effects of the medical treatment. They may thus require special remedial services

DIAGNOSTIC DECISIONS AND RECOMMENDATIONS

The basic effect of physically or health-related disorders on the child's cognitive, academic, and social-emotional function must be clearly delineated in the clinician's report. The primary responsibility of the clinician is to make a clear and definitive diagnosis that provides the basis for appropriate academic placement and programming.

COMMUNICATING RESULTS

The clinician's report of the assessment profile must be communicated to the parents, school personnel, and other professionals involved with the child, such as physicians, speech and language pathologists, etc. The psychologist must exercise care in interpreting results to parents. For parents of physically handicapped children, the clinician must explain in detail the special arrangements taken and the task modifications made in order to maximize the child's opportunities to demonstrate abilities. This approach can help the parents accept with greater confidence the validity and reliability of the test findings, and they can also make good use of these ideas in working with the child at home. Focusing on the child's strengths is important. Often parents will ask what they can do to "help" their child, so the clinician must anticipate this question and be prepared to respond in a specific and sensitive manner. Specific comments to school personnel can also be helpful, such as focusing discussion on the positioning of the physically handicapped child or on the fatigue aspect of a child with cardiac problems or leukemia. With the physically handicapped child, the clinician can also assist by conveying in detail to school personnel the types of task modifications necessary in working with the child, as these may prove quite useful in the child's classroom instruction.

In conclusion, clinicians who assess many children each month must continually remind themselves that each child is unique and each requires special thought regarding the test battery to be administered. The uniqueness of the child may be found in the history, interview data, behavioral observations, and psychological profile. The psychologist must always keep in mind that test scores alone tell us nothing about a child.

REFERENCES

Bigge, J. L. (1976). *Teaching individuals with physical and multiple disabilities.* Columbus, OH: Charles E. Merrill Publishing Company.

Culbertson, J. L. & Ferry, P. C. (1982). Learning disabilities. *Pediatric Clinics of North America, 29,* 121-136.

Culbertson, J. L. (1981). Psychological evaluation and educational planning for children with central auditory dysfunction. In R. W. Keith (Ed.), *Central auditory and language disorders in children.* Houston: College-Hill Press.

Gadow, K. D. (1979). *Children on medication: A primer for school personnel.* Reston, VA: Eric Clearinghouse on Handicapped and Gifted Children.

Rogers, S. J. (1982). Assessment considerations with the motor-handicapped child. In G. Ulrey & S. J. Rogers, *Psychological assessment of handicapped infants and young children.* New York: Thieme-Stratton, Inc.

Swanson, B. M. & Willis, D. J. (1979). *Understanding exceptional children and youth.* New York: Houghton-Mifflin.

Sweetland, R. C., & Keyser, D. J. (Eds.). (1983). *Tests: A comprehensive reference for assessments in psychology, education and business.* Kansas City, MO: Test Corporation of America.

Tuma, J. (Ed.). (1982). *Handbook for the practice of pediatric psychology.* New York: John Wiley & Sons.

United Cerebral Palsy Association. (1976). What is cerebral palsy? New York: Author.

Walls, R. T., Werner, T. J., Bacon, A., & Zane, T. (1977). Behavior checklists. In J. O. Cone & R. P. Hawkins (Eds.), *Behavioral assessment: New directions in clinical psychology.* New York: Brunner/Mazel.

Wright, L., Schaefer, A., & Solomons, G. (1979). *Encyclopedia of pediatric psychology,* Baltimore: University Park Press.

13

Legal Aspects of Psychological Testing

J. RAY HAYS, PH.D., J.D.

This chapter deals with those issues that affect the psychological examiner from a legal and ethical perspective. The practice of any profession stems from a model generated within a social community and professional school, which defines that practice. Professional practice of any sort is increasingly recognized as having a legal context, and because of the intrusion of this legal framework into practice, the psychological examiner requires some knowledge of both the legal vocabulary and the legal procedures and requirements that are placed on practice.

Professional practice must meet certain requirements to satisfy the multiple demands of different constituents. States have particular requirements for minimum evaluations which affect school placement of children. Tests vary in their reliability and validity with different cultural groups. The psychologist must choose tests appropriate to the referral questions, which also satisfy the requirements of the law. A narrow view of the professional's role will often compromise the best possible outcome for the client. The psychological examiner must integrate the psychological requirements that best serve both the client and society. This chapter will provide some of the basic information necessary for the psychologist to understand concerning the legal context of practice and the extent to which some of these legal issues affect practice.

The law that applies in a specific setting, of course, depends upon the law of the state in which the practice occurs. No attempt will be made here to illustrate comprehensively the law of specific jurisdictions, because the law on any issue is dynamic and may change each time legislatures meet or the court decides a case. Issues that underlie the current expression of the law, however, do not change so rapidly. This chapter discusses issues with which the psychologist should be familiar in order to know, in the absence of specific legal guidelines, not only the professional aspects of serving clients but the legal context as well.

A chapter such as this provides no substitute for competent local legal advice. Knowledge of local practice must be gathered from individuals in the community who deal with these issues regularly. Practitioners need a local resource (an attorney

197

or law school professor) who can give specific advice when a problem arises for which there is no other guidance. Our society, unfortunately, has become increasingly litigation-conscious toward professionals, as evidenced by the dramatic rise of malpractice insurance premiums in the 1970s. Practicing within legal constraints, and going outside them only after careful thought and consideration, will do much to forestall legal problems.

LAW, MORALS, AND ETHICS

One guiding principle of all ethical codes of the helping professions is the concern for the welfare of clients. For example, in the Oath of Hippocrates, physicians swear to follow systems or regimens that will benefit patients, and to abstain from whatever is mischievous and deleterious. The principle is best embodied in the proscription *primum non nocere,* "first do no harm." The ethical code of psychologists tells them to "respect the dignity and worth of the individual and strive for the preservation and protection of fundamental human rights" (American Psychological Association, 1981). In the ethical standards of the American Personnel and Guidance Association, the members are described as dedicated to the enhancement and uniqueness of each individual and thus to the service of society.

Psychological practice has a moral, ethical, and a legal context as well as a psychological one. Although this chapter is limited in scope to legal issues, it is appropriate first to define the differences between morals, ethics, and the law. Psychologists who understand these relationships and the differences between them are better equipped to help their clients resolve conflicts and identify priorities for themselves.

Legal codes are derived from the broad ethical consensus of a community. Legal standards comprise the formal rules—legislative, administrative, or those derived from judicial decisions—that reflect a society's consensus on the conduct of relationships. Morals may refer both to the code of conduct adopted by an individual and to the rules which the community has adopted to give its members a clear idea of their specific duties and obligations. Ethics, on the other hand, are the standards by which we judge actions as right or wrong. As one uses the terms here, morals are a statement of one's value system; ethics are the values that underlie the statements of morals (Hare, 1967; Frankena, 1963).

THE DUTY OF INFORMED CONSENT

Before beginning to examine any individual, the psychologist must obtain the legally adequate informed consent of the client. Failure to do so might result in the examination being considered a battery (*Natanson* v. *Kline*) or an invasion of the right to privacy. "Legally adequate consent" has been defined as consent by a person who has the following characteristics: legal capacity, comprehension of information, and voluntary agreement. *Legal capacity* means that the person giving consent is of minimum legal age and has not been adjudicated as incompetent to manage his or her affairs. In the absence of required minimum age or competency, a guardian or parent may give consent to an evaluation. Comprehension of information means that one must give the prospective client the information that a reasonable and prudent person would require to make a decision about whether to be evaluated, and the client must show that he or she comprehends the information. *Voluntary agreement* means that there must be no undue coercion or undue inducement to undergo the procedure. There are four elements which must be present in informing the client about any proposed procedures, and these are: 1) the risks, and 2) the benefits of the proposed procedure; 3) the risks of foregoing the procedure; and 4) the alternative procedures available instead of the proposed treatment. Exceptions to the requirement of informed consent occur under emergency circumstances and with minor children or incompetent persons.

Standard for Disclosure

According to *Natanson* v. *Kline*, "the duty of the physician to disclose, however, is limited to those disclosures which a reasonable medical practitioner would make under the same or similar circumstances." This is a relative standard, which has been gradually replaced by an absolute standard that requires a professional to disclose all "material" information. In *Canterbury* v. *Spence*, the court defined material information as relating to "the inherent and potential hazards of the proposed treatment, the alternatives to that treatment, if any, and the results likely if the patient remains untreated." Generally, there are no hazards to psychological tests. There are disadvantages to not using them, including failure to diagnose problems and to formulate remedial programs. There are no acceptable alternatives to standardized psychological tests.

Consent by Children

Children do not generally have the right to consent to any form of treatment or evaluation, although many states give minors the right to seek treatment for pregnancy, venereal disease, and psychiatric problems without parental consent. These laws arose from the belief that requiring parental consent might inhibit minors from seeking treatment that was in the best interest of the individual and society. In general, consent by either parent is effective for providing psychological evaluation. The *assent* of the child should be obtained since the individual's cooperation in any procedure aids both treatment and its outcome (Schectman, Hays, Schuham, & Smith, 1982). Assent is defined as the affirmative agreement by a person who, due to age or mental incompetency, may not give consent.

Unless adjudicated as incompetent, adults are considered competent to consent to evaluation. Patients have the capacity to consent when they have the "mental ability to make a rational decision, which includes the ability to perceive, appreciate all relevant facts and reach a rational judgment upon such facts" (*State Department of Human Services* v. *Northern*). If the psychologist believes that the proposed client does not understand the suggested procedures or is incompetent, a guardianship proceeding should be initiated. This will result in the appointment of a guardian who can provide consent for the client.

Consent by the spouse or next of kin may be sufficient in some states to treat incompetent persons. The more cautious approach seeks a guardianship before conducting any evaluation or initiating any type of treatment.

Emergencies

When a patient is presented in an unconscious state because of illness or trauma, a physician may treat the patient without consent. Consent to the application of life-saving measures when the patient cannot communicate is implied in the theory that a reasonable, ordinary, and prudent person would consent to the procedures.

There are few instances in which a person would require a psychological evaluation in emergency circumstances and could not consent to the procedure. The only situation where that might arise involves the case of a person so severely disturbed that they are unable to consent, and an evaluation is requested to determine the extent of psychopathology. Any potential harm to a person, other than inconvenience, is slight enough to be outweighed easily by the potential benefit from an evaluation. Permission to conduct such an evaluation would ordinarily be given by a reasonable person.

PRIVILEGED COMMUNICATION AND CONFIDENTIALITY

Confidentiality and privilege are frequently confused (Hays, 1981; Everstine, Everstine, Heymann, True, Frey, Johnson, & Seiden, 1980). *Confidentiality* refers to information obtained that is not to be revealed outside of a relationship, such as that between a priest and penitent. Revealing such information without the client's permission is a breach of confidentiality. *Privilege* is a narrower concept and concerns the admissibility of information in a court of law. One can distinguish the terms by their scope: confidentiality covers any information obtained in confidence, while privilege relates only to courtroom testimony. Bersoff & Jain (1980) have written an excellent guide on privileged communication. The confidential relationship between psychologists and their patients is a tradition at least as old as the psychological profession. Psychologists, like lawyers, physicians, and other members of learned professions, do not reveal information about their clients to others who have no need or right to know, and may be held liable for revealing such information without the permission of the patient.

A professional's testamentary privilege exists, if it exists at all, as a result of statute or case law. Testamentary privilege rests with the patient and not with the professional; that is, the information becomes admissible in court when the patient or client desires it to be admitted. Once the client wants the information revealed, the professional must provide the testimony.

Two California cases illustrate this point. *In re Lifschutz* involved a psychiatrist found in contempt of court and jailed after he repeatedly refused the court's order to answer questions concerning a former patient. His patient was suing someone, claiming that person had caused him severe mental and emotional distress. Clearly, information about previous treatment could be relevant to such a suit. The psychiatrist believed that there was an ethical obligation not to reveal the information, and that the information was irrelevant because of the time that had elapsed between treatment and the suit. The court ordered the psychiatrist to testify.

In *Caesar* v. *Mountanos*, the psychiatrist was held in contempt and sentenced to jail for refusing to disclose information about a patient who had sought financial damages as a result of an automobile accident. The patient was seeking therapy for emotional problems that she believed resulted from the accident. Dr. Caesar, the psychiatrist, refused to answer questions about his treatment of her, claiming that such revelations would be harmful to her psychological well-being. The court concluded that the competing interests to be weighed were the patient's interest in privacy and the state's compelling interest in ascertaining the truth. Because the plaintiff, Dr. Caesar's patient, was attempting to recover damages for a psychic injury, and information about her treatment was therefore relevant and material to the decision, the court required Dr. Caesar to provide the information. Professional interests in the client's well-being must thus give way, in the presence of the state's compelling interest, to a full and fair disclosure in court. In this case the interest of the group overrode the interest of the individual.

The Duty to Warn

The matter of privileged communication between a professional and a client has several general exceptions. One is the duty to warn an intended third-party victim of the threat of harm by a mentally disturbed client. The doctrine came to dramatic public attention in *Tarasoff* v. *Board of Regents of the University of California*. A student at the university had revealed to a counselor that he intended to kill his girlfriend. The therapist called the campus police, who held the student for a few hours and then released him. Two months later, after the woman returned from a visit out of the country, the student killed her. Her family sued the therapist and the university for failure to warn their daughter or them of the threat.

The California Supreme Court ruled that a confidential relationship must yield when disclosure is essential to avert danger to others; the privilege ends where public peril begins. The duty to warn occurs when a therapist has reason to believe that a third party is in imminent danger.

The doctrine of duty to warn has been considered in a number of jurisdictions, at legislative and judicial levels. Several states have acknowledged that such a duty exists; other states have either rejected the notion completely or taken a neutral approach. The practitioner should seek local consultation to discover the local status of the duty to warn.

Child Abuse and Neglect

Mira & Herman provide, in their chapter in this book, an excellent guide to evaluation and testimony in cases of child abuse and neglect. In certain settings psychological evaluations will be required of children who are suspected of being abused and neglected, and of their parents. Because of the nature of these cases, the examiner frequently knows that the results of the evaluation will carry much weight in the decisions that are reached, both in determining placement of the child and in possibly terminating the rights of the parents. Such cases often are not decided without resort to court proceedings; this then increases the burden of the examiner's responsibility to insure that the rights of the various parties are protected.

Case example: A school refers a child to a psychologist's office for evaluation and consultation on a behavior problem and poor school performance. The child has bruises in varying degrees of healing and scars from other cuts in various places on her body. She is also fearful and cowed during the evaluation. The psychologist does not obtain any further information nor does he tell the school that there is a concern about child abuse. The psychologist, however, believes the child may have been abused and reports this belief to the local child welfare authorities. The parents then sue the psychologist for violation of their right to privacy, interference in the parent-child relationship, and intentional infliction of mental suffering. Should the psychologist have reported the case? Are there any penalties for a failure to report?

Child-abuse reporting laws comprise another general exception to the rules on confidentiality and privilege. Most states require any person who has knowledge of or observes child abuse or neglect to report it to the community agency responsible for children's protective services. Abuse or neglect includes the psychological as well as physical health of children. Failure to report child abuse is generally a misdemeanor crime. The responsible agency will investigate the complaint and determine whether to initiate termination of parental rights. These agencies have the right to intervene rapidly to protect children from life-threatening situations, and most statutes provide immunity to individuals who report in good faith under such laws. Thus the reporting person should have no fear of libel, or slander, or other suits by accused parents. In the case mentioned, the psychologist would not have to worry about an adverse judgment if the report of potential child abuse was made in good faith.

The prudent practitioner must inform parents and agencies such as schools of the limits of confidentiality afforded to the professional by legal constraints. One of these limits is that, in life-threatening situations, the professional has a duty to protect family members who cannot protect themselves, as in the case of child abuse.

Rape and Sexual Abuse

The current view of rape maintains that this is a crime of violence, in which the act of sexual contact is used to play out the violence of one person toward another. For the purpose of this chapter, rape is defined as heterosexual intercourse without the female's consent. Sexual abuse is any other type of forcible attempt at sexual gratification, including sexual abuse of a child, homosexual contact, deviant sexual intercourse, and other forms of abnormal sexual activity.

Whenever the psychologist is confronted with evidence of rape, concern should focus on at least two issues: proper medical treatment of the victim, including counseling, and the legal preservation of evidence. Rape victims are most frequently seen by emergency room personnel, who should be sensitive to the perceptions of the crime victim. Special training programs are available for emergency-room staffs to aid them in working with rape victims. Rape evidence kits should be kept in stock and staff members trained in the use of these kits.

Counseling of a rape victim should commence with the first persons from whom treatment is sought. Because of the nature of the act, long-term consequences of the rape should be anticipated. Physical healing may take only a short time, but the psychic wounds may last much longer. Because the long-term consequences of rape are now well known, long-term counseling should be recommended. The clinician obviously cannot force counseling on an unwilling victim, but good professional practice calls for offering treatment for problems we believe exist.

Many psychologists will see patients whose sexual lifestyles are not the norm, and these lifestyles have certain implications (for example, the incidence of acquired immune deficiency syndrome (AIDS) is relatively higher in promiscuous homosexual men). So-called deviant sexual habits also have legal implications, because they are frequently proscribed by law. The professional must exercise care with information concerning these habits that is written into the patient's record of treatment. The best method for handling sensitive information is to regard the patient's record as a legal document. The author of this chapter was told in training, "Every chart goes to court." Keeping that in mind may help guide the psychologist in record-keeping. Records should be accurate and complete, but should not contain speculation, conjecture, and unfounded hypotheses. This is true not only for sex-related cases but for all patients.

When sexual abuse of a child seems to have occurred, the psychologist is obliged to report this to child protective services or to the police. From the standpoint of the reporting requirement, no difference exists between physical abuse and sexual abuse of a child, but there is a difference in the support and counseling that may be required. Children who have been abused, whether physically or sexually, are generally secretive about it. They fear that they have done something wrong and that their life will be worse if they reveal what happened to them. Sometimes the adult involved makes overt threats to the child. The psychologist should help young victims to understand that they will be supported in coping with the problems that are revealed. In doing so the psychologist should be familiar with available resources and how to use them.

Appearing in Court

Testimony in court and the role of the expert witness are the subject of other chapters in this book. However, it is important for psychologists to understand how a witness is summoned to testify and how that request must be treated. There are two basic ways in which a person will appear as a witness; either voluntarily or by subpoena. In the case of a voluntary witness, the attorney requesting the testimony will explain to what the witness is to testify. The details of the testimony should be worked out with that attorney beforehand.

A subpoena is a command for a person to appear at a certain time and place to give testimony in a certain matter. There are two types of subpoenas: the *subpoena ad testificandum,* which is the ordinary subpoena, and the *subpoena duces tecum,* which commands the person to produce certain records and documents under that person's control. Attorneys are becoming more sophisticated regarding psychological testimony and are issuing more of the latter type of subpoenas than in the past.

When a subpoena is issued the psychologist must respond, whether or not believing that the information produced would be harmful to the client or that the information is privileged and confidential. The psychologist may raise the issue of a statutory privilege for the information and assert that on behalf of the client. Once the court has ruled on the admissibility of the testimony, however, the psychologist should be guided by the directions of the judge. If the court rules that the information is not privileged and is admissible, the psychologist must testify or run the risk of a contempt finding from the court. Psychologists confronted with testifying when they thought they should not have asked this author for advice, and were advised to testify rather than risk going to jail. If the court errs in allowing the testimony, then that error will be found upon appeal.

WHO IS THE CLIENT?

In working for agencies, such as schools, each psychologist must recognize the competing alliances between employers, families, and the client. Professional ethics require that our first allegiance be with the client. When conflicts arise between the requirements of the agency in which the psychologist works and the needs of the client, which should prevail? Clear cut answers to such dilemmas are frequently lacking, since the competing needs of agencies and clients may often lead to unpredictable results. The psychologist should simply be aware of the potential for conflict and insure that everyone involved understands how the work should proceed. A professional can determine somewhat how his or her work product will be used by setting limits with clients and agencies before work begins. Having each party agree at the beginning about how to proceed can do much to forestall difficulty later.

MALPRACTICE

Malpractice is a civil legal action and refers to the professional's civil liability for providing services. An aggrieved person who perceives a transgression on the part of the psychologist has several avenues for obtaining relief (Hare-Mustin, Marecek, Kaplan, & Liss-Levinson, 1979). Four factors must be present and proved before a client may "recover." Recovery refers to the award of money to a party or compensation for the wrong suffered. The first element in a malpractice action is *standard of care,* which refers to that minimum level of care a reasonable and prudent practitioner would have provided under the same or similar circumstances. The standard of care is that care which is the generally accepted or standard practice of the profession. Second, the practitioner must have *breached* that standard of care in some way. A breach refers to any failure to live up to the established standard of care. Such failure may include breach of a fiduciary or trust relationship with a patient (Hays, 1981). The breach of care must be the *proximate cause* of *damages* suffered by the patient, which are the third and fourth elements of any malpractice action. Simple negligence or malpractice suits outnumber all other actions against professionals, comprising about two-thirds of all cases (Hogan, 1979).

An example of malpractice in a psychological evaluation would occur if the evaluator failed to score properly the instruments used in the evaluation, and as a result misclassified the examinee. The failure of the examiner to score the tests properly is a breach of the examiners' duty of care. The standard of care provides that examinations be correctly scored. If the misclassification of a child caused this examinee to suffer failure in school then the fourth element of malpractice would have occurred. In any malpractice suit, all four elements of professional negligence must be present and proved; if any element of the requisite four is missing, there is no recovery by the examinee.

One apt statement about malpractice says that there is not so much malpractice in the professions as there is bad psychology. Obviously, the better the relationship between practitioner and patient, the less the likelihood of a malpractice action, regardless of treatment outcome for the patient.

ADVERSE IMPACT OF TESTS

The psychologist should be aware that the Equal Employment Opportunity Commission (EEOC) has adopted rules that outline the use to which tests can be put in employment. These rules are found in 45 C.F.R. §1607. These rules define "test" as any paper and pencil instrument or performance measure used as the basis for any employment decision, such as hiring, promotion, or transfer. The use of tests that adversely affect any employment decision of any protected group constitutes discrimination unless the tests have been validated, shown to be job related, *and* alternative procedures to testing are unavailable. The EEOC adopted these rules because the Commission believed that in many instances tests were used as the basis of employment decisions without evidence that they were valid predictors.

The Congress has passed an act which provides for protection of the privacy of parents and their school-age children in the educational records of the student (PL 93-380). This public law was designed to insure that these educational records would be confidential. The law provides that the contents of the record will not be revealed to third parties without the express authorization of the parents. Under PL 93-380, parents may also inspect their child's educational record and make copies of it.

The law also provides a procedure whereby the parents can request that the educational record of their child be amended. Parents have a right under this law to a hearing on their request to amend the child's educational record, and this law sets the standards for the conduct of such a hearing. From a practical standpoint, PL 93-380 means that parents have the right to see what any educator, including educational psychologists, writes about their child and to review the protocols of their children's evaluations.

SUMMARY

At the very least, the foregoing chapter implies the need for training and education that address the issues of interaction between the clinician and the law. The following specific suggestions are designed to reduce the clinician's risks at the points of interface with the law, and to promote the treatment relationship within the confines of the law:

1. Obtain the informed consent of clients before beginning any evaluation or treatment. This includes parental permission for children.

2. Establish clear guidelines for yourself and your clients about how to proceed if conflicts occur between the use of an evaluation in an agency setting, and professional standards, legal duties, and obligations.

3. Make certain your employer and your examinees and their families know exactly who is the client and know the extent of your professional involvement with the client, the family, and the agency.

4. Communicate the extent of privileged communication, if any, and confidentiality to your client.

5. Be familiar with the statutes that have implications for practice in your state.

6. Consider retaining an attorney to be on call for opinions or clarifications.

7. Develop a close working relationship with members of your profession's local ethics committee. In those marginal situations that do not involve a legal decision, advice from committee members who have a current working knowledge of professional ethics may be helpful in resolving problems.

8. Keep abreast of new developments concerning statutes that affect clinical practice (for example, patients' rights law, licensing laws, limitations on research activities).

9. From the clinical standpoint, straightforwardness and honesty remain excellent guides to avoid legal difficulties with clients.

The practice of psychology occurs within a society which places legal constraints on our actions as professionals. The psychologist must be aware of the extent to which we are free to operate within a legal context and within the bounds of professional practice. Clients deserve to have the information revealed to their psychologists kept private. Adhering to ethical and legal standards will enhance the standing of the profession and engender the respect of the consumers of psychological services.

REFERENCES

American Psychological Association. (1981). Ethical principles of psychologists. *American Psychologist, 36,* 633-638.
Bersoff, D., & Jain, M. (1980). A practical guide to privileged communication for psychologists. In G. Cooke (ed.), *The role of the forensic psychologist.* Springfield, IL: Charles C. Thomas.
Everstine, L., Everstine, D., Heymann, G., True, R., Frey, D., Johnson, H., & Seiden, R. (1980). Privacy and confidentiality in psychotherapy. *American Psychologist, 35,* 828-840.
Frankena, W. K. (1963). *Ethics.* Englewood Cliffs, NJ: Prentice-Hall.
Hare, R. M. (1967). Ethics. In J. Macquarrie (ed.), *Dictionary of Christian ethics.* London: SCM Press.
Hare-Mustin, R., Maracek, J., Kaplan, A., & Liss-Levinson, N. (1979). Rights of clients, responsibilities of therapists. *American Psychologist, 34,* 3-16.
Hays, J. Ray. (1981). Privacy and confidentiality. *American Psychologist, 36,* 914.
Hogan, D. B. (1979). *The regulation of psychotherapists* (Vol. 1.). Cambridge, MA: Ballinger.
Schectman, F., Hays, J. R., Schuham, A., & Smith, R. (1982). Accountability and confidentiality in psychotherapy with special reference to child treatment. *Clinical Psychology Review, 2,* 201-211.

CASES

Canterbury v. Spence, 464 F.2d 772 (D.C. Cir. 1972).

Natanson v. Kline, 350 P.2d 1093 (Kansas 1960).

State Department of Human Services v. Northern, 563 S.W.2d 209.

Tarasoff v. Board of Regents of the University of California, 529 P.2d 533 (Calif. 1974) 551 P.2d 334 (Calif. 1976).

14

Evaluation and Testimony in Child Neglect

MARY MIRA, PH.D., MARC S. HERMAN, PH.D.

With increasing frequency the legal system is calling on psychologists as expert witnesses, requesting opinions about diagnostic issues, psychological bases of behavior, the probability of future behavior, and recommended treatments. In order to be effective participants, psychologists must not only be competent in evaluation procedures, but must become sophisticated about the legal process and capable of modifying their traditional stance to courtroom circumstances. Although a number of publications orient psychologists to the role of the expert witness (e.g., Anderton, Staulcup, & Grisso, 1980; Brodsky, 1977; Brodsky & Robey, 1972; Hays, 1983; Poythress, 1977; Poythress, 1980), most deal with civil commitments and cases involving insanity pleas. Psychologists are becoming increasingly involved through the juvenile courts with issues involving children and families. Child neglect is one type of case in which child psychology can play a major role. This chapter will explore the special demands of the juvenile court on the psychologist as an expert witness in cases of child neglect. Before outlining the specific evaluation procedures, some dimensions of these which the psychologist must consider before conducting an evaluation will be discussed. These issues relate to the legal system and its procedure for handling child neglect cases.

How the Legal System Deals with Child Neglect

A neglected child is one whose caretakers failed to provide for basic survival and emotional needs. Neglect may be defined as:

> a condition in which a caretaker responsible for the child either deliberately or by extraordinary inattentiveness permits the child to experience avoidable present suffering and/or fails to provide one or more of the ingredients generally deemed essential for developing a person's physical, intellectual, and emotional capacities. (Polansky, Hally, & Polansky, 1975, p. 5)

Statutory definitions of the neglected child are broad and this lack of precision makes it difficult for a naïve psychologist to determine the guidelines for making decisions about the status of a child.

Child neglect proceedings are conducted within the juvenile court system, which operates differently from the more familiar criminal court. Thus, prior to conducting an evaluation, the psychologist should become familiar with the juvenile court, which was set up both to provide for the safety of the child and to remediate the family and reduce the risk of any present or future harm to the child. Determining the guilt of a party, assigning punishment for wrongdoing, and arranging reparations to injured parties, all of which characterize the criminal justice system, have never been a part of the concept and operation of the juvenile court. The statutes which define neglect do so in terms of the child's characteristics, rather than the criminality or illegal nature of parental behavior. In the criminal courts, witnesses participate in an adversarial system in which the interests of two parties, often client versus state, are presented and debated to arrive at a win-lose decision (Anderton et al., 1980). The psychologist as an expert witness in juvenile court often takes an advocacy stance, seeking to understand the status and needs of the child based on clinical/scientific evidence rather than on what the child or family's interests may be. Changes in the statutes regarding rights of children and guaranteeing them increased due process rights similar to adults heighten the adversarial nature of the juvenile courtroom situation. This will require a corresponding accommodation on the part of the psychologists, making it necessary to balance the position of an ethical and objective stance with being prepared to handle the cross examination by the parents' and the child's attorneys.

The civil proceedings relating to neglect are initiated by the filing of a petition that alleges the child is receiving inadequate care or is neglected. Anyone can start the process which leads to filing of a petition; many states require professionals, including teachers, social workers, and psychologists, to report their suspicions of child neglect. In most states the child and the parents are notified of a hearing and of their right to counsel. At the hearing the judge makes a determination about the status of the child after hearing testimony from professionals about the child's health, developmental, and emotional status, and about the caretakers' parenting capabilities. Because of psychologists' special skills, they are frequently called upon to give evidence in such cases. The format of the juvenile court in which the expert witness may appear as "friend of the court" affords the psychologist an opportunity to present an integrated picture of the child's status and needs, the parents' capabilities and needs, and to propose a relevant treatment package and set of recommendations corresponding to the assessment.

THE PSYCHOLOGIST'S ROLE IN THE DISPOSITION OF CASES OF CHILD NEGLECT

The juvenile court judge, in order to make decisions about what is best for the child, hears evidence from social agencies that may have investigated the case and from professionals who have examined the child and the family. There are three areas in which psychologists can provide expert opinion which will prove useful to the juvenile courts. First is a comprehensive assessment of the child's developmental, behavioral, and emotional status, and this includes identifying any deficits or special needs in educational, developmental, or emotional areas, stating probable causes of these problems, and giving an estimate of their future impact on the child's life. The second area covers assessment of the stimulating and nurturing properties of the caregiving environment. The third is the evaluation of capacity for change in the caregiving environment, including an assessment of parents' ability to learn new techniques, their responses to previous training, and judgments about the adequacy or appropriateness of past intervention offered them.

Having considered these issues related to the legal aspects of neglected children, a consideration of the actual psychological assessment follows. The remainder of this section is devoted to descriptions of some of the behavioral dimensions to study and some useful assessment tactics.

Evaluating the Child's Status

An assessment of the child's developmental and emotional status provides a baseline record of the child's response to the caregiving environment. Many children whose status is of concern are young and thus developmentally pliable, rendering them vulnerable to the impact of their environment. It is also important to identify whether the child has special needs or disabilities, since these children are most at risk for neglect. Children who need specialized treatments at home or in clinics, or who require frequent trips for treatment, will try the resources of even adequate parents.

A comprehensive evaluation of the child addresses cognitive and motor competence, language skills, educational functioning, and social and behavioral characteristics. These assessments can be carried out through the administration of appropriate tests, the examination of school records, the use of behavioral surveys completed by teachers and/or caretakers, and through direct observation of the child interacting with significant people in a familiar environment. If the psychologist identifies special problems, it is helpful to provide the court with a thorough description of these and other associated problems, and the long-term effects and treatments required. Whenever possible, the parents' ability to meet these special needs should be assessed. Many times the identified special needs will be in areas such as sensory functioning or neuromotor development, which are not generally within the psychologist's province; however, the psychologist should have the interdisciplinary skills to evaluate the impact of these deficits on the child's total psychosocial status and to assess the likelihood that the parents will understand and secure the necessary treatments.

Often the psychologist will be asked to address the question of the cause of any identified deficits. Even if it is not possible to identify the specific etiology, the psychologist can make a contribution by summarizing for the court the current scientific evidence about the correlation between caregiving or environmental variables and the presence of these deficits.

Assessing the Caregiving Environment

A problem in the evaluation of neglectful situations, in addition to lack of well-defined standards, is that neglectful behavior on the part of parents may stem from pernicious and chronic acts of omission rather than from the commission of prohibited acts. However, dimensions of parenting skill can be differentialted and measured independently. Psychologists have the knowledge to describe parenting skills as they occur on a day-to-day basis and, by clearly describing parents' knowledge and actions, provide the courts with useful information about parental adequacy in meeting their children's needs.

This section will review the dimensions of behavior necessary to take into account when determining parental neglect and will describe some procedures for assessing significant environmental features.

The determination that parenting is inadequate to the degree of neglect is based on findings of haphazard scheduling of child care, parental substance abuse, uncertain and chaotic setting, and minimal parental attention, involvement, or stimulation (Wald, 1975). Hertz (1979) has characterized such deficits as those that relate to 1) love and affection, 2) housekeeping, 3) meeting the child's physical needs for health and nutritional care and meeting standards of cleanliness, and 4) providing stimulation for intellectual development. Although psychologists focus primarily on assessment of the quality of parent/child interaction and generally do not address issues such as housekeeping conditions, in developing testimony about a child's neglected status it may be helpful to include observations about these dimensions.

The evaluation of the caregiving environment is often carried out by the use of a systematic method of observation of parents, possibly supplemented with direct psychological evaluation conducted by interviews or standardized evaluation formats.

The evaluation of the caregiving environment includes consideration of several aspects of parental function, and the psychologist should at least screen the following areas:

Child management skills. This includes systematic and direct observation of parent-child interactions at the clinic in unstructured or play settings, noting how parents deal with positive and negative behavior, their ability to offer stimulation for intellectual development, and their strategies for problem-solving and for teaching their child.

Parental knowledge of child development. This may be studied through brief interviews or short questionnaires, and includes both parental knowledge of child development and their expectations for their children.

Parental ability to handle stress, anger, and uncertainty. This area also includes a screening for psychopathology through interviews, psychological testing, and background information garnered from other agencies.

Parental supports. This focuses on an evaluation of the degree of the families' isolation from the rest of the community, and the nature of supports available to them. One should also include an assessment of the marital relationship and the overall family environment, because it provides information about parental capacity to adequately care for the child.

The observation of parental interactions with the child should be quantified by using one of the several structured methods for coding observations of parent-child interaction (Forehand & Peed, 1979; Mash, Terdal, & Anderson, 1973). A reliable, quantifiable observation system is indicated when it is likely that the observations will form part of the psychologist's testimony in court.

In addition to direct observation of parent-child interaction, it is useful to include quantified information about the other dimensions of the caregiving environment. There are several scales available for quantifying the observations of essential elements of caregiving. The Urban Childhood Level of Living Scale (Hally, Polansky, & Polansky, 1980) was developed as a method of scaling significant elements of child care in cases where children were suspected of being neglected. The Urban form of the scale, one of several forms developed, was standardized on low-income white families. The scale covers nine areas, five related to the child's physical care and four to psychological care. The 99 items are grouped into the following categories: 1) general positive child care; 2) state of house repair; 3) negligence; 4) quality of household maintenance; 5) quality of health care and grooming; 6) encouragement of competence; 7) inconsistency of discipline and coldness; 8) encouragement of super-ego development; and 9) material giving. Each item is scored as "Yes" or "No" and the resulting percentile scores can be grouped into five levels, ranging from Severely Neglectful to Good Child Care.

Another useful scale is the Home Observation for Measurement of the Environment (HOME) (Caldwell & Bradley, 1979), which quantifies information obtained through parent interview. There are two forms, one for children from birth to age 3 and one for preschoolers. The Infant Scale provides information about the home in the following areas: 1) emotional and verbal responsivity of mother; 2) avoidance of restriction and punishment; 3) organization of the physical and temporal environment; 4) provision of appropriate play materials; 5) maternal involvement with the child; and 6) opportunities for variety in daily stimulation. The Preschool HOME Scale provides scores in these areas: 1) stimulation through toys, games, and reading material; 2) language stimulation; 3) safety and cleanliness of the physical environment and how conducive it is to development; 4) pride, affection, and warmth; 5) stimulation of academic behavior; 6) modeling and encouragement of social maturity; 7) variety of stimulation; and 8) physical punishment. The HOME scale provides reliable, easily obtained information about dimensions of the caregiving environment that have significant correlations with later child development (Bradley & Caldwell, 1976; Bradley & Caldwell, 1980; Elardo, Bradley & Caldwell, 1977).

The evaluation of parents suspected of being neglectful raises some ethical issues for the psychologist. Generally, this parent is a reluctant client, often directed by the courts to seek evaluation. In order to work with such parents, psychologists must frequently restate that their role is primarily one of child advocacy, and stress that the goal of the evaluation is to make recommendations to the court about how the caregiving environment can be modified for the benefit of the child.

Another professional issue regards the confidentiality of information elicited from the parents during the evaluation. If a dilemma arises between respecting the confidential nature of the information and the requirement to provide complete testimony, the concensus is that the rights of the child and the need both to protect and consider the child's welfare take precedence over the issues of confidentiality between client and psychologist (Guyer, 1982). Also, psychologists need to keep in mind that they can be held liable for failing to report material that can be used as evidence.

Determining Potential for Change

In addition to evaluating the status of the child and the quality of the home environment, psychologists may be asked whether the environment has potential for change. If the child is found to be neglected, the court must make a decision regarding the disposition of the case. The child may be taken into legal custody of the designated state agency, physical custody may continue with the natural parents, or the child may be placed in foster care. At this point the court makes recommendations for treatment or training designed to correct the identified deficits so the child may be returned to parental custody.

There are at least three types of questions that the psychologist may need to address in making recommendations for the disposition. For cases new to the courts, one may be asked if the family can benefit from intervention and what kind of treatment would be appropriate. Neglect may stem from deficits in parental knowledge, judgment, or motivation (Cantwell, 1980), and the psychologist's assessment of the parents can both address this and lead to recommendations for appropriate intervention. One should also consider here whether special concessions will be required regarding the type or intensity of the intervention due to the parents' unique characteristics (i.e., illiteracy, lack of mobility, or poverty).

For families who have been in treatment previously, the psychologist may be asked if and to what extent they have responded to the intervention. The ease with which this question can be answered will depend on whether the psychologist has access to information about parental competencies at the time of the original hearing, and to the findings of those who have been working with the family in the interim. In order to have ready access to such information, the psychologist must maintain a cooperative relationship with those professionals who generally handle treatment of neglectful parents in the community.

A third question that psychologists may be asked to address relates to the adequacy or appropriateness of the intervention that has been provided to the family. This is of particular concern in cases where the families have made such minimal progress over a period of time that the courts are considering permanent severance of their rights to the child. If it is determined that the family's inadequacy is persistent and unyielding, there must be assurances that their rights have not been violated either because the treatment was inappropriate or was not truly made available to them. The issue here concerns whether or not a reasonable effort has been made to improve the child's care and whether the remediation was appropriate for the family.

PREPARING FOR AND TESTIFYING AT THE NEGLECT HEARING

Throughout the evaluation of the child and the caregivers, several things can be done that will smooth the process of presenting testimony. It is helpful to maintain accurate records documenting the procedures used to collect information on which testimony is based. Psychologists rely on a variety of data sources, including direct evaluation of child or parents, information from staffings with other professionals involved in the case, and review of available records. The psychologist should be prepared to name the information sources and to state whether these procedures are commonly used by other psychologists in making similar kinds of judgments. It is also useful to document the amount of time spent in the evaluation of the case, and the psychologist should know if this is the amount typically allotted by others for similar evaluations.

Following the evaluation a formal report is prepared, which the psychologist will be asked through the subpoena to bring to the hearing. Any records used during testimony can be requested as evidence; they are read by lawyers for the state, family, and child, and will be used by the judge in making decisions about disposition. Since the audience will have varying degrees of psychological sophistication, the report should be written in language understandable to a lay audience.

Another practice that will ease the courtroom procedure consists of the principals involved in the evaluation of the child and family arranging a pre-trial conference to review their findings and their recommendations. It is also helpful if, prior to the hearing, the psychologist meets with the lawyer who will be presenting the case in order to clarify what questions the psychologist is prepared to address on the witness stand. If these procedures are followed, the hearing should not offer any surprises to the expert witness. The judge will wish to hear all of the evidence that will help with decision-making, and may overrule defense-attorney ploys that interfere with testimony. In some cases, following the presentation of evidence the judge might directly question the expert witness on the stand.

Psychologists can expect to be asked certain kinds of questions about their qualifications, the examination procedures, and the findings. Table 1 presents examples of the kinds of questions that a psychologist can expect at a neglect hearing.

In many ways, the action of the neglect hearing will be familiar to the psychologist who has previously testified in court. Certain procedures are similar to other courts, including the swearing-in of the witnesses, the order of questioning and cross-examination, and the general professional conduct expected of the principals. In the juvenile court, witnesses who have not yet testified may be required to remain outside the courtroom until called to the witness stand. The psychologist is testifying as an expert witness and should be prepared to state his or her credentials. The expert witness is asked to present the findings and can expect to have the findings questioned and perhaps even challenged.

One feature of the hearing that might prove disconcerting to the psychologist testifying for the first time is the presence of the parents in the courtroom, hearing all of the evidence. It could happen that the psychologist presents findings of major significance to parents who are strangers.

The authors recognize that their responsibility in cases of child neglect is to the court and that they, together with the court, assign priority to the safety and well-being of the child; however, we accept a professional responsibility to communicate to the parents all assessment results that they will need to know in order to meet the child's needs. A history of parental neglect does not justify dealing with them as if they were not interested in their child's welfare. Therefore, if parents are available at the time of the child's evaluation one should apprise them of the findings regarding the child's status, any special needs, and recommendations for meeting those needs. If the parents are not available, as when the child is in foster care, the psychologist can approach them via their caseworker and offer them the findings prior to the court hearing.

RESPONSIBILITIES OF PSYCHOLOGISTS TESTIFYING IN CASES OF CHILD NEGLECT

The preceding description of the psychologist's role in child neglect cases points out the need for skills in addition to those involved in child evaluation and treatment. First, a knowledge of the legal process in juvenile court is vital. Understanding this process makes the job easier and improves the psychologist's effectiveness as spokesman for the neglected child.

Second, it is important that the psychologist appreciate the knowledge of the other professionals involved in the case and work with them as a team prior to the court hearing. Interprofessional communication increases the information base necessary for understanding the child and caregivers.

TABLE 1

Examples of Questions Addressed to Psychologists during Child Neglect Hearings

Professional Qualifications of Witness
Describe your training, experience, and professional credentials.
Where are you employed? What are your major job functions?
How long have you worked in this field?

Evaluation of the Child
How and when did you become involved in this case?
Number of appointments scheduled, number kept and missed.
Describe the appearance and behavior of the child.
What is your assessment of the child's current functioning?
Describe any special needs or limitations of the child.
How does the child function in school? With peers?
Specifically, what does the caregiver need to do for this child to meet his special needs?
What are your specific recommendations to meet the child's special needs?
What is the probable cause of any limitations noted?
What are the implications of the identified problems for the child's education, living arrangements, and care?
How long term are these problems?

Evaluation of the Parents
Number of appointments scheduled and missed.
What was the parent's explanation for missed appointments?
What were your objectives or treatment plans with these parents?
What were your findings with respect to the parents' abilities, interests, and concerns?
Describe any special deficits in the parents' ability to meet their own needs, to meet the child's needs, or to comprehend and act on any information and training supplied to them.
How will parental deficits influence the child?
What specific changes must parents make before the child can reside with them?
Do the parents agree with your findings?
What remediation do you recommend for this family?
Where is this remediation available?
How has this family used the resources you have recommended to them?
What kind of supervision will be required if the child is to reside with the family?
Describe the family's proposal for child care. Is it adequate?
Is it possible for the parent to provide for one or more of the children, but not for all?

Evaluation of Parent/Child Relationship
Describe the behavior observed between parent and child.
What is the nature of the relationship? Its strengths and weaknesses?
How does the child's behavior differ when with the parent and with others?
Describe the ways in which continuation of this relationship would be constructive/destructive to the child.
What risks are there to the child by remaining in this relationship?
In what specific ways must this relationship change?
How can this change be affected?
How long will this change take?

Third, psychologists who evaluate neglected children must have an understanding of those factors which influence a child's behavioral development. In many cases of child neglect there are multiple problems, involving both the child and the caregiving environment. The psychologist must become sufficiently familiar with these problems and be able to consider and weigh their influence on the child. The authors' experience shows that psychologists can evaluate neglected children most effectively when they have acquired those interdisciplinary skills that determine if all aspects of the child have been adequately evaluated.

In many cases, the evaluation of the caregiving environment will reveal deficits leading to the recommendation of intervention in these areas. The psychologist should become familiar with all of the local resources for neglectful parents, in order to state for the court what intervention is required and whether it is realistically available in the community.

REFERENCES

Anderton, P., Staulcup, V., & Grisso, T. (1980). On being ethical in legal places. *Professional Psychology, 11*, 764-773.

Bradley, R.H., & Caldwell, B.M. (1976). Early home environment and changes in mental test performance in children from 6 to 36 months. *Developmental Psychology, 12*, 93-97.

Bradley, R.H., & Caldwell, B.M. (1980). The relation of home environment, cognitive competence, and IQ among males and females. *Child Development, 51*, 1140-1148.

Brodsky, S.L. (1977). The mental health professional on the witness stand: A survival guide. In B.D. Sales (Ed.), *Psychology in the legal process* (pp. 269-276). New York: Spectrum Publishing.

Brodsky, S.L., & Robey, A. (1972). On becoming an expert witness. *Professional Psychology, 3*, 173-176.

Cantwell, H.B. (1980). Child neglect. In C.H. Kempe & R.E. Helfer (Eds.), *The battered child* (3rd ed.) (pp. 183-197). Chicago: University of Chicago Press.

Elardo, R., Bradley, R., & Caldwell, B.M. (1977). A longitudinal study of the relation of infants' home environments to language development at age three. *Child Development, 48*, 595-603.

Forehand, R., & Peed, S. (1979). Training parents to modify the noncompliant behavior of their children. In A.J. Finch, Jr., & P.C. Kendall (Eds.), *Clinical treatment and research in child psychopathology* (pp. 159-184). New York: Spectrum Publishing.

Guyer, M.J. (1982). Child abuse and neglect statutes: Legal and clinical implications. *American Journal of Orthopsychiatry, 52*, 73-81.

Hally, C., Polansky, N.F., & Polansky, N.A. (1980). *Child neglect: Mobilizing services* (DHHS Publication No. OHDS 80-30257). Washington, DC: LSDS, Department 76.

Hays, J.R. (1983). *The psychologist as an expert witness*. Dallas: Wilmington Press.

Hertz, R. (1979). Retarded parents in neglect proceedings: The erroneous assupmtion of parental inadequacy. *Stanford Law Review, 31*, 785-805.

Mash, J., Terdal, L.G., & Anderson, K. (1973). The response-class matrix: A procedure for recording parent-child interactions. *Journal of Consulting and Clinical Psychology, 40,* 163-164.

Polansky, N.A., Hally, C., & Polansky, N.F. (1975). *Profile of neglect: A survey of the state of knowledge of child neglect.* Washington, DC: Department of Health, Education and Welfare, Community Services Administration.

Poythress, N.G. (1977). Mental health expert testimony: Current problems. *Journal of Psychiarty and the Law, 5,* 201-227.

Poythress, N.G. (1980). Coping on the witness stand: Learned responses to "learned treatises." *Professional Psychology, 11,* 139-149.

Wald, M. (1975). State intervention on behalf of neglected children: A search for realistic standards. *Stanford Law Review, 27,* 985-1040.

15

The Expert Witness:
Techniques and Skills

KAREN L. WESTPHAL, PH.D., STANLEY H. KOHN, J.D.

(Editor's Note: The considerations offered in this chapter comprise the format of witness workshops that Dr. Westphal and Mr. Kohn give to groups of mental health professionals. This material is reprinted by permission of the authors. © Copyright Karen L. Westphal, Ph.D. and Stanley H. Kohn, J.D.)

Psychologists are increasingly being called upon to testify in a variety of administrative and judicial proceedings. The advent of Public Law 94-142 hearings, the heightened emphasis on need for psychological input in child-abuse and custody cases, the rise in numbers of elderly persons in the population with concomitant growth of competency hearings, and the necessity for psychological testimony in criminal defenses have all increased the likelihood that at some time during a psychologist's career, a request will come to testify as an expert witness.

For convenience, the terms "hearing" and "trial" are used interchangeably in this chapter. Hearings usually include administrative proceedings and some non-jury judicial proceedings. A trial is the formal adversarial-type judicial hearing that requires a judge and a jury. In some states many of the types of hearings or trials discussed will be actual trials with juries; in others, all of these matters are heard by a judge without a jury, and the judge is the judge of both the law and the facts. In any event, the techniques used in testifying will always be the same.

The difference between lay testimony and expert testimony is depicted here, with greater emphasis placed on expert testimony. The best methods to employ in responding to direct-examination and cross-examination, and some techniques that might be used to strengthen the credibility and impact of a professional's testimony are offered. Finally, this chapter will recognize the traps and pitfalls that all witnesses must face.

WITNESSES IN GENERAL

There are two types of witnesses: lay witnesses and expert witnesses. Lay witnesses have no specialized knowledge or skill in the subject matter or controversy. Expert witnesses, because of their experience and/or training, are called

220

upon to give testimony about the aspects of a controversy that lie within their fields of expertise. The same person may be a lay witness in some contexts and an expert in others.

The major difference between a lay witness and an expert is that *the expert witness can give opinion testimony and draw inferences* from the facts concerned with the controversy. A lay witness is required to have firsthand knowledge of the facts about which testimony is sought, knowledge that has been personally acquired through perception of one of the five senses. The witness either saw it, heard it, felt it, tasted it, or smelled it. Thus, the general rule emerges that a lay witness is prohibited from testifying about anything other than that gained from personal perception. Because an expert witness has the special ability to aid the court or the hearing officer in deciding the facts of the controversy, this general rule doesn't apply to them.

The legal definition of an expert witness, as set forth in Rule 702 of the Federal Rules of Evidence, follows:

If scientific, technical, or other specialized knowledge will assist the trier of fact (the judge, the hearing officer or a jury) to understand the evidence or to determine a fact in evidence, a witness qualified as an expert by knowledge, skill, experience, training or education may testify thereto in the form of an opinion or otherwise.

Before allowing an expert witness to state an opinion or to draw an inference, the judge must be satisfied on two points: that the opinion is necessary to a full understanding of the issue in controversy, and that the witness possesses the requisite skill, knowledge, training, or experience with which to deal with the matter.

Most hearing officers and judges have a rather liberal approach to the first requisite; instead of the opinion being necessary, they frequently will require only that the opinion be helpful.

The practical differences between lay testimony and expert testimony follow.

TESTIMONY BY LAY WITNESSES

Lay witnesses cannot testify about inferences or conclusions they have drawn from the facts they actually observed, no matter how obvious the conclusion may seem. If it is truly an inescapable conclusion, the jury or the trier of fact will reach that conclusion. An example of lay testimony follows:

Q: Did you have an opportunity to see the child, Charles Brown, at school on Tuesday, February 19, 1984?
A: Yes, I did.
Q: Describe his physical appearance.
A: He had a large purple bruise on his right cheek, and a similar bruise on his upper right arm.

Q: From your observation, what caused those bruises?

A lay witness would not be permitted to comment on the cause of the bruises, because the answer requests an opinion from the witness. The lay witness has not been qualified to offer opinions, inferences, or conclusions, which can only be offered by an expert competent in the specific scientific field. The theory behind the rule prohibiting lay testimony from offering a conclusion is that reaching a conclusion serves as the function of the hearing officer or the jury.

Just a single statement such as "the parent was uncooperative" may be inadmissible as lay testimony, yet clearly would be proper testimony for an expert. One should limit lay testimony to the perceived facts concerning that parent's uncooperative behavior. To illustrate this point, an example follows:

Q: Did you attempt to contact the mother?
A: Yes, I telephoned her several times, but she would not return any of my calls.
Q: Did you make any other efforts to contact her?
A: Yes, I twice sent notes home setting up appointments, but she failed to keep both appointments.
Q: Were there any other efforts at communication?
A: I sent her two consent forms, at her request, and neither was returned.

So far the line of questioning elicited proper lay testimony, but suppose the attorney asked an additional question:

Q: What were you able to determine from the mother's conduct?
A: She was a very uncooperative parent.

A jury, having heard those initial questions and answers, could draw the inference that the mother was very uncooperative; thus that final answer, since it would not help the jury, is unnecessary. Most judges would not allow a lay witness to respond to the last question above.

The previous series of questions and answers also demonstrates that an attorney must lay the proper groundwork for opinion testimony. One accomplishes this by securing facts from which the inference of "uncooperative behavior" can be drawn. An expert witness could not take the witness stand and testify that the mother was uncooperative without having first detailed all of the efforts at communication.

PRIVILEGED COMMUNICATIONS

One erroneous belief held by most professionals must be addressed. Most professionals believe that, in all instances, any information gained from a client or patient is absolutely privileged and the professional cannot be required to give testimony concerning that information. This is just not true.

The only privilege that exists in every state concerns the attorney-client privilege: an attorney can never be required to divulge information learned from a client, except if the client reveals plans to commit a crime to the attorney. In most of those states that may have otherwise already established privilege for physician-patient or therapist-patient relationships, that privilege is often abrogated by specific statutes for particular types of cases. For example, most states have statutes that specifically negate any privilege in child-abuse cases, except for the lawyer-client privilege and the priest-penitent privilege.

In a highly publicized South Carolina case, a psychologist who counseled an abusive parent and later refused to testify at the criminal trial for the murder of her child, served eight days and nights in jail for his refusal. He was released only after the jury had returned a verdict of guilty.

Every psychologist therefore should seek the advice of an attorney regarding those instances when one has the right to refuse to testify.

How to Qualify as an Expert

When an expert's testimony is to be presented, the lawyer must qualify the witness as an expert by asking questions that demonstrate the educational background, skills, and experience of the witness. The attorney should be provided with a copy of the expert's vita in order to formulate questions about one's undergraduate education, practica, fellowships, assistantships, research areas, thesis field, publications, work experience, papers presented, graduate degrees, and community activity. All of the above may relate to the field of expertise in which the attorney wants to secure expert testimony.

An expert need not be world famous, nor the author of a book on the subject, nor a preeminent authority in a field. The expert's opinions need only be consistent with those reasonably held by others in the same field. For instance, the testimony of an expert carpenter in his sixties who could neither read nor write, but had over forty years of experience in using a carpenter's framing square, was the key to victory in a negligence lawsuit. After fully explaining the framing square and the observable facts concerning the steep and dangerous angle of a stairway, the carpenter was allowed to give his opinion of the negligent design and about the construction of a safer design in the same space.

Expert Testimony Subject Matter

The proper subject matter for an expert witness is that which is so intimately bound up in a science, profession, business, or occupation that it is beyond the knowledge of the average lay person. When the subject involves one where an expert is necessary to investigate the facts, but where an ordinary person can reach an independent conclusion once those facts are made known, the expert cannot testify about opinion or inference.

For example, only specially trained professionals can interpret x-ray films. They can point out abnormalities and give an opinion regarding what sort of force produced the abnormalities. Whether or not the abnormality was caused by child abuse is a matter for the jury, and is not a proper opinion or inference to be sought from expert testimony.

LIMITATIONS ON EXPERT TESTIMONY

In areas where the psychologist is qualified by both experience and training, it is possible to testify as an expert witness in a number of areas. A school psychologist may be called on to testify as an expert witness in child custody matters and in child abuse cases. The psychologist may offer opinion testimony to assist the court in determining the ultimate custodial placement of a child. Expert opinion is often necessary in school-related matters, such as expulsion proceedings and due process hearings pursuant to Public Law 94-142.

A psychologist may be called upon to testify regarding testing and evaluations performed by another psychologist. The testimony will be permitted if supplemental knowledge is gained from the expert witness' files based on firsthand knowledge. For example, if the testifying psychologist interviewed or counseled the child or the parents independently, or interviewed the child's teachers prior to testifying, such firsthand knowledge together with file information may be used to form the expert's opinions.

TECHNIQUES FOR EFFECTIVE TESTIMONY

Preparation is vital. Thorough preparation alleviates nervousness while in the courtroom and forms the basis of effective performance, and is therefore *mandatory* before going to court. The steps to take before going to the hearing follow:

1) If testimony will relate to agency records or files, the psychologist must become totally familiar with these files. The files should be read several times and handwritten notes made regarding dates, test results, and personal perceptions of the child. It is essential to be familiar with the location of every file document that one may need to produce in court.

If the expert witness did not create the file personally, the attorney may require one to testify that it is an ordinary and usual record kept in the normal course of the agency's business. The psychologist should therefore talk to the person who actually created and maintained the file in order to become familiar with the entire record-keeping process, including the location of the records within the agency.

As mentioned before, the psychologist should always develop handwritten notes to use while testifying. Testifying from personally prepared handwritten notes is much safer if material exists in the file that is otherwise confidential or would be embarrassing to the expert or to the client if publicized at the hearing. Documents used on the witness stand or taken into the courtroom are discoverable by the adverse party immediately following the testimony. The expert witness should expect to be required to turn over to the opposing attorney all documents taken into the courtroom for the purpose of cross-examination.

Whenever a witness testifies from notes it captures the attention of the opposing attorney who may want to create excitement about this at the hearing. Testifying from notes is perfectly proper. The lawyer who has asked the psychologist to testify may want the psychologist to explain that although the files were reviewed a number of times, it was not possible to remember all of the dates and times of contact with the parent or to recall the specific perceptions of the child formed during counseling sessions; thus, all of the information needed to be summarized into comprehensive handwritten notes.

2) When testifying about some event that happened months earlier, the psychologist's memory should be refreshed. One technique that works well involves actually returning to the place where the event occurred, envisioning the scene as it was then, and taking notes about the many small things that will be recalled.

3) The expert witness should dress appropriately and neatly. A good deal of useful information exists on the impact of attire on perceived credibility. Judges, juries, and hearing officers tend to be conservative and since part of a witness' purpose is to exemplify professional stature, one should wear professional clothing (preferably dark colors, and blue is better than black). Men should wear a conservative coat and tie, avoiding more stylish clothing such as pink shirts. Women should wear a coat or a jacket and leave it on in the courtroom. Women should, however, avoid going overboard with masculine-type clothing; it results in being perceived as cute, not competent.

Gum chewers should not even carry a pack of gum into the courtroom. Very often through nervousness or during a lull in court activity, a stick of gum will be unconsciously unwrapped and put into the mouth.

4) The psychologist should never try to memorize any part of the testimony; it just won't work. Just trying to stay calm in a courtroom is very difficult and memory is often the first thing to go. Further, since questions will not come in any foreseeable order, the witness may become lost.

If the attorney asks something that the witness cannot remember but knows is in the file, it is acceptable to ask permission to look the item up. However, others thereafter have the right to look in your file as well.

5) Prior to trial, the attorney for the other side may want to discuss testimony with the expert witness. Although proper, you should notify your attorney of the request. The psychologist should never turn over any records or documents.

COURTROOM BEHAVIORS

A number of simple techniques makes the actual courtroom appearance more comfortable.

If the psychologist receives a subpoena to testify, it should be brought to the courthouse on the day of the hearing. This may prove helpful since the subpoena usually states in which courtroom the witness is to appear. After arriving at the courtroom, if the expert witness does not know the attorney who issued the subpoena, one should seek out this attorney and become introduced. If a hearing or trial is in progress, it is best for the witness to remain outside the courtroom until called.

The psychologist should expect to feel anxious from the time of entering the courtroom. It is important to remember that the judge and jury will observe the witness approaching the witness chair. The expert's every move and total appearance are factors that jurors often use to assist them in forming an opinion about the profession and the professional's credibility. The expert witness usually feels a special kind of nervousness when taking the witness stand. The most common symptoms of courtroom nervousness include: perceptual problems, especially of sight and hearing; lowering of the voice, speaking rapidly or in a monotone; slumping in the witness chair; and an inability to recognize anyone in the courtroom.

The witness can take some steps to alleviate these possible effects. To avoid perceptual problems, one can feel more oriented by looking around, first at the walls and windows, then at the furniture, and then at the other people present. It helps to concentrate on speaking and to strive to speak a little more slowly and loudly than usual, making each word heard but avoiding long pauses between words. Moderation is the key word in the effort to overcome nervousness. The witness should try to sit with a straight back and avoid nestling down in the chair. A curled-up witness does not make as favorable an impression on the jury as one with erect posture. If nervousness creates shaky hands, they can be folded in the lap or steadied against one's leg or the side of the chair. The witness should not clasp the armrest.

How to Answer the Questions

While on the witness stand, the psychologist is sworn to tell the truth. One should speak to the examiner frankly and openly, as if speaking to a friend or neighbor. The psychologist should take care not to fidget, cover the mouth, or make other nervous gestures while speaking. While it may be appropriate in a speech to inject a little humor in order to overcome nervousness, one should never try to be humorous in court. The image the witness must project consists of sincerity or dignified warmth.

Every case is not only a serious one, it is also a human one in which the expert witness should have a genuine concern for all of the people involved. The projection of a humane attitude may assist the judge toward evaluating the witness' credibility in a positive manner. A concerned appearance on the stand usually makes a better impression than does a frozen, calculating one, or an attitude of detached professionalism.

The witness must give a spoken answer. Nodding, head shaking, gesturing, and other nonverbal responses are not acceptable. It is important for the expert to listen carefully and understand each question completely before starting to answer. If the witness does not understand the question, one may ask to have it repeated or rephrased.

The question should be considered within the context in which it was asked. For example:

Q: You stated that you are a psychologist. Where did you go to school?
A: General William Moultrie High School.

While high school may have been one of the happiest times in the psychologist's educational career, it is not the proper response in the context of one's profession as a psychologist.

Suppose the question was "What did you and Mrs. Jones talk about during your first interview?" While the topics may have included the weather or the price of steak, the answer sought is in relation to the case. The psychologist's response should include the date, time, and place of the conversation, which should be recorded in one's handwritten notes. The witness should then describe the substance of the conversation or the topics discussed. The witness must be alert to the kind of responses desired. Direct examination usually calls for narrative responses; cross-examination normally requires a "yes" or "no" or some other short response. While the witness should avoid volunteering additional information when responding, one always has the right to fully explain an answer.

The "yes" and "no" problem can be difficult to handle during cross-examination because very often the lawyer wants a definite answer that doesn't fully answer the question. For example:

Q: Answer me "yes" or "no," was the home investigation completed in the time required by the law? Answer me "yes" or "no."
A: Yes, *we are always careful to do that.*

Avoid the superfluous portion of this response. No additional explanation was necessary. Now, the same question again:

Q: Answer me "yes" or "no," was the home investigation completed in the time required by the law? Answer me "yes" or "no."
A: No, his parents went on a three-week vacation and it was not possible to interview them.

Without the full explanation the answer would have been harmful. A full explanation is always permissible.

A common witness error involves double-thinking or overthinking questions. Lawyers do not usually have a devious purpose or hidden agenda, but rather only try to develop their cases in an orderly fashion. To avoid overthinking, the witness may pause before answering the question.

The expert witness should not offer overly technical answers in attempting to draw meaning from the question. One should not respond by giving a review of the literature or by explaining statistical premises, unless of course that is what the attorney specifically asked for.

The English language does not change just because it is spoken in a courtroom. For example, if the lawyer asks, "Were you at the home of Mrs. Smith on February 3, 1984?" it does not mean "Were you inside the home" or "Did you remain inside any significant length of time?" The question simply asks if the witness was at that home—inside, outside, or on the street in front of the house at any time on that day.

Let the attorney develop the testimony. The lawyer has a theory about the case and a plan to develop the witness' testimony. For example: "Do you remember an interview with Mrs. Jones on Tuesday, February 3, 1984, at 10:00 a.m.?" The best response to this would be "yes" or "no." In the next question the examining attorney may ask for the substance or the circumstances of that interview. The purpose of the first question may have been to prepare a foundation before introducing the significant part of the testimony, which is the lawyer's job. If the expert witness gets wrapped up in helping the case by exhibiting a super memory, one may never get around to answering the question.

Many witnesses, when asked a question like "Did you talk to B.B. Weems on April 15, 1980?" will respond, "Oh, yes, I remember talking to B.B. on the 15th; that was a Saturday and I'm not too busy on Saturdays, so I just strolled across the Square to B.B.'s place. It wasn't raining, which was sort of unusual because it had rained almost every weekend for the past month and a half, so I didn't have to take my umbrella with me." This is an example of not only answering the question, but also providing so much additional information that no one wants to listen to anything else the witness has to say.

If the psychologist does not know the answer to a question, it is best simply to say so. If the witness cannot remember, it is better to admit it than to guess or speculate. A witness is not required to have an answer to every question. But should one remember an answer later during the testimony, the questioner may be interrupted as follows: "Excuse me, but you asked me previously if I remembered any conversations I had with Johnny concerning contacts with his grandfather prior to the reported sexual assault, and I said that I didn't remember. Well, I just remembered that Johnny described a family picnic, at which his grandfather was present, in very positive terms when I asked him to report his early childhood recollections."

The psychologist should never use "I don't remember" or "I don't know" simply to avoid answering difficult or indelicate questions. If the witness truly does not remember an event or know the answer to a question, it is much better to say so than to guess at an answer.

If the witness gives an incorrect or unclear answer, it should be clarified as soon as possible. It is always better to correct a mistake than to have the opposing attorney discover the error. Once a witness realizes an error, it is best to say, "May I correct something I said earlier?" or "I just realized that something I said earlier should be corrected."

The psychologist's testimony need not conform to the testimonies one may have heard previously. The expert is expected to testify regarding personal observations, opinions, or inferences. Even eyewitnesses can have different impressions of the same event. The expert witness is never expected to agree with or parrot someone else's testimony, and attempts to do so may be discredited.

When responding to a question, the psychologist should look at the questioner. However, during lengthy explanations, it may be best to look directly at the jury or the judge. The purpose of testifying is to impart important and necessary information. Looking at the lawyer or other trial participants before responding to the opposing attorney's question gives the appearance of waiting for a signal or of being coached.

The witness should do nothing that could impart the impression of bias for or against any party, although one is obviously the proponent or opponent of some position in the case. Expert opinion must always be based upon professional judgment, not designed to fit the desired outcome of the case.

A slight shift in emphasis during cross-examination in an attempt to advocate an expected outcome can backfire, giving the opposing counsel a basis to argue that a witness is biased, which diminishes that witness' credibility. For example:

Q: Answer me "yes" or "no," was the home investigation completed in the time required by law?
A: Yes, *we are always careful to do that.*
Q: And following the evaluation of the home, did you notify the parents of the results within fourteen days and invite them to a staffing?
A: Of course, we always follow the exact procedure.

While the answers may be technically correct, one can see here the witness' mistake in emphasizing a particular position, which gives the opposing attorney an opportunity to argue that the witness is biased. It is the function of the attorney to argue the case; the expert only reports facts, information and opinion.

In the event that one or more truthful answers damages the position of the client for whom the psychologist is testifying, the lawyer will handle it in a professional manner.

How to Survive Cross-examination

Cross-examination is a necessary part of both the judicial system and due process protections in all adversarial procedures. The Constitution declares that all people have the right to confront their accusers, and under this system, the attorney for each side of a controversy is obligated to attempt to throw a different light on the testimony of opposing witnesses.

Different attorneys practice various techniques of cross-examination and the methods vary for different witnesses. A number of guidelines help the expert witness survive. Only what the witness actually remembers should be stated. The cross-examiner may attempt to suggest details that the witness does not remember and did not state on direct examination. The witness should not follow the cross-examiner's leading question into an answer that is suggested by the question.

For example, the cross-examiner, donning the nicest smile, may lean over and say, "Wouldn't you agree that these nice parents have the best interests of their own daughter, little Eloise here, at heart?" A seemingly innocuous question, but on direct examination the witness answered a number of questions that demonstrated the parents were unconcerned and uncooperative. The psychologist should not be lulled into a conflicting answer on cross-examination just because of the lawyer's smile or because the answer sounds reasonable. The correct response might be, "Oh, I believe they love little Eloise, but as I perceive it they have not been acting in her best interests."

Another example:

Q: You saw blood flowing from Harold's arm after he was struck, didn't you?
(The witness thinks, "Well, I saw Harold get violently struck. I don't remember blood, but with the violence of that blow, there must have been some blood. Besides, this lawyer says there was blood. I'll say . . .")
A: Yes.

The witness, in fact, may have been too far away to have seen the blood, which is precisely why one would not remember seeing any. This distance-perception problem would be argued by the cross-examiner attempting to impeach the witness' credibility or believability. In reality, the skin on Harold's arm may not have been broken at all because the force was not great enough and there *was* no blood. In this instance, the witness would be impeached because the testimony of others would show there was no loss of blood.

The psychologist should be careful of a question in cross-examination that asks, "Nothing else happened?" After some thought or another question the expert may remember something else. One's response to "Nothing else happened?" should reserve the right to remember more later, as: "That's all I recall at this time," or "That's all I remember happening."

If a question has two parts requiring different answers, the witness should answer in two parts. Cross-examiners sometimes use the technique of asking compound questions. The witness should not respond to a compound question that is only partially true with a simple "yes." Compound questions should be divided into appropriate parts and then answered. For example:

Q: Is it not true that you drove to the Smith's home on February 3, 1984, stormed inside, and immediately picked up their child, Mary?

A: There are three parts to that question, and each part has a different answer. I did go to the Smith home on February 3, 1984, but I spoke with Mrs. Smith on the front porch for about 15 minutes. She then invited me inside and we spoke in the living room for another 15 minutes. After that, Mrs. Smith allowed me to take Mary to school.

A good habit for the expert witness to acquire involves responding in a positive manner. Answers should not begin with qualifiers, such as "I think," "I believe," "to the best of my recollection," or "I guess." The witness can be forthright and positive about the important things without remembering all of the little details. If the attorney asks about little details that the psychologist does not remember, it is best to respond, "I do not recall."

A common mistake of otherwise-competent expert witnesses occurs when the psychologist does not offer opinions about the psychological data. Constantly deferring to the literature or to various schools of psychological thought makes it appear that the witness is uncertain of personal beliefs. For example, when relating data from psychological interviews, the expert witness may be asked the following:

Q: So you believe the information you obtained in your interview with Susan indicates that she has been abused by her mother?
A: That would be the interpretation of those following the behaviorist or Adlerian schools of thought; however, the Freudians believe that such statements might only be evidence of an Oedipal conflict.

The question should simply have been answered "yes," as the question asked for only the psychologist's personal expert opinion. The explanation of the basis of one's determination is not required until an attorney asks for it.

Expert witnesses should admit their beliefs and sympathies honestly, and explain their reasons. It would be absurd to deny an obvious sympathy, and an honest admission of favoritism does not discredit a witness. For example:

Q: Do you have a feeling about how you would like this hearing to come out?
A: Yes, I do.
Q: You would like to see Johnny taken permanently from his family, wouldn't you?
A: I'm sorry that the family will continue to be separated, but my evaluation indicates that it is not in his best interests to be returned home at this time.

This response is very different from coloring answers because of favoritism. Only when an attorney can show the judge that a witness will change or tailor testimony because of personal feelings about the case is credibility destroyed.

LOOK OUT FOR TRICK QUESTIONS

The most popular of this type of question is, "Are you being paid to testify?" In many types of cases it is acceptable for witnesses to be paid, particularly experts. In some states even lay witnesses are allowed a statutory witness fee and mileage allowance. An example of a proper explanation is, "I am being paid a fee of fifty dollars an hour. This is my normal consultation rate."

Sometimes the question arises, "Who told you to say that?" The answer should be, "I was only told to tell the truth." Another unnerving question is, "Have you talked to anyone about this case?" The response would almost always be "Yes," and the witness should identify all of those persons (lawyers, parents, teachers, the child, colleagues).

A witness should always be polite on the stand, even if the attorney conducting the examination is not. The psychologist should never appear argumentative or sarcastic. The attorney always has the advantage by asking the questions, but the honest witness has nothing to fear on cross-examination.

If an expert's testimony has not been harmful to a case or if the cross-examiner believes that further questioning will be fruitless or counterproductive, cross-examination may consist of only a few perfunctory questions or be waived entirely. When an expert has made a very credible and professional presentation, a lawyer is often not adequately prepared to attack a witness through cross-examination. The attorney may refrain from any questions because of being intimidated by the appearance and ability of the witness, and might just say, "No questions."

More frequently, when testimony has damaged the opposition's case, the attorney will want to argue for the jury that they should not believe the expert. This argument requires that through cross-examination the attorney show that either the witness is lying or incompetent. The attorney may try to get the witness to say things that are not completely true. Hence, the attorney uses compound questions, tries to lull the witness into following response-suggesting questions, bombards the witness with those "yes" or "no" situations, demands answers, and wants to examine handwritten notes. In such instances, the lawyer is searching for some little inconsistency with which to argue for the judge or the jury that since the witness lied or was totally incorrect on a particular point, the entire testimony is unworthy of belief.

Testifying for a substantial period of time is surprisingly tiring and can cause fatigue, crossness, nervousness, anger, carelessness, and a willingness to say anything in order to get off the witness stand. If the witness feels such symptoms, it is best to ask the judge for a five-minute break to have a glass of water or to go to the bathroom.

Testifying in court can be a difficult experience; however, through preparation, effort, and understanding, appearing as a witness can be an educational and satisfying experience.

Appendix:
Test Directory and Index

Refer to page(s):	*Test Title*

AAMD ADAPTIVE BEHAVIOR SCALE, SCHOOL EDITION (ABS)   *K. Nihira, R. Foster, M. Shellhaas, H. Leland, N. Lambert and M. Windmiller*

Assesses children ages 3-16 years old whose adaptive behavior indicates possible mental retardation, emotional disturbance, or other learning handicaps. Used for screening and instructional planning.

Ninety-five item paper-pencil scale, completed by the examiner, measures social and daily living skills and behaviors. Completion of the scale requires approximately 30 minutes. Scores are converted to profiles which are used in diagnostic and placement decisions and in formulating general educational goals. Examiner required and evaluated. Not suitable for group use. A starter set including manuals, two assessment booklets, two each instructional and diagnostic profiles, and two parent guides costs $21.00. *Publisher:* CTB/McGraw-Hill

ADAPTIVE BEHAVIOR INVENTORY OF CHILDREN (ABIC)   *Jane R. Mercer and June F. Lewis*

Measures the social role performance of children ages 5-11 years old in their family, peer group, and community.

Two hundred forty-two item inventory (interview format) measuring six aspects of adaptive behavior including: family, community, peer relations, non-academic school rules, earner/consumer, and self-maintenance. Items are divided into two sections. The first section applies to children of all ages, while the second consists of age-graded questions. The interview, conducted by a trained professional, varies in time of administration. This is one component of the System of Multicultural Pluralistic Assessment (SOMPA). Examiner required and evaluated with the aid of a hand key. Not suitable for group use. Available in Spanish. The basic kit includes the manual, six scoring keys, and 25 record forms for $30.00. *Publisher:* The Psychological Corporation

ADMISSIONS TESTING PROGRAM: SCHOLASTIC APTITUDE TEST (SAT)

Measures verbal and mathematical reasoning abilities of high school juniors and seniors that are related to successful academic

233

performance in college. Used to supplement secondary school records and other information in assessing readiness for college level work.

One hundred thirty-five item paper-pencil multiple-choice computer scored test measures reading comprehension, vocabulary, and mathematical problem solving ability involving arithmetic reasoning, algebra, and geometry. The test consists of 85 verbal questions arranged in two sections including 25 antonyms, 20 analogies, 15 sentence completions, and 25 reading questions; and 50 mathematical questions arranged in two sections including approximately two-thirds multiple-choice and one-third quantitative comparison questions. Timed administration requires two and one-half hours. Examiner required. Suitable for group use. Contact publisher concerning time and place of administration and cost. *Publisher:* The College Board Publications

76, 82

ADOLESCENT AND ADULT PSYCHOEDUCATIONAL PROFILE (AAPEP) *Mesibov, Schopler and Schaffer*

Measures learning abilities and characteristics in autistic and communications handicapped adolescents and adults. Used by service-providers, teachers, and parents in preparing and maintaining autistic and communications handicapped individuals in community-based programs. Used with individuals previously regarded as untestable.

This multiple item task performance test varies in time of administration. The test results comprise a profile reflecting the characteristics and abilities of the individual being tested. The profile is translated into an appropriately individualized set of goals and objectives which provide a basis for instructional planning and placement. Examiner required and evaluated. Not suitable for group use. The test kit includes the following materials required for uniform administration of the test: nerf ball and basket, checkers and board, pinball game, radio and battery, empty box, playing cards, tape of typical workshop sounds, five magic markers, work box, 100 pencils, erasers, target board with balls, magazine, catalog, pad of paper, pen, wooden block, metal plate, nut and bolt, box sorting tray, green buttons, three wing nuts, five bolts, seven washers, five nuts, five sandwich bags, 10 dominoes, sewing block and lace, screwdriver, wrench, four-piece shape board, survival signs, comic book, paperback book, movie ticket, price signs, December calendar, #1, #2, and #3 cards, color jig, four color chips, written instruction cards, alphabet cards, five jig cards, schedule, five paper clips, clock, pill bottles, tops, and 20 markers. The test kit listed above with manual costs $225.00. *Publisher:* Orange Industries

151

ADOLESCENT EMOTIONAL FACTORS INVENTORY *Mary K. Bauman*

Measures emotional and personality factors for visually handicapped adolescents. One hundred fifty item paper-pencil or oral response questionnaire assesses the personal and emotional adjustment of visually handicapped adolescents. Time of administration varies. Provides scores on the following nine scales: sensitivity, somatic symptoms, social competency, attitudes of distrust, family adjustment, boy-girl adjustment, school adjustment, morale, and attitudes concerning blindness. A validation score is also provided. Questionnaires are presented in large print format. Instructions for tape recording the questions are included.

Supplementary materials provided in the test kit include a discussion of personality assessment for blind adolescents and a discussion of the inventory. This test is an adolescent form of the Emotional Factors Inventory. Examiner required and evaluated. Paper-pencil version suitable for group use. The test kit (includes the large print test booklet, set of scoring overlays, 10 IBM answer sheets, supplementary materials and norms) costs $15.00. *Publisher:* Associated Services for the Blind

112   ADVANCED PROGRESSIVE MATRICES (APM-1962)
             J.C. Raven

Assesses the mental ability of adolescents and adults with above-average intellectual ability by means of nonverbal abstract reasoning tasks. Used for school and vocational counseling and placement, as well as research.

Forty-eight item paper-pencil multiple-choice test arranged in two sets. Set I is a practice set containing 12 problems. Set II contains 36 problems, each of which consists of a pattern or figure design which has a part missing. The individual selects one of six possible parts to complete the figure or pattern. Individuals are allowed 40 minutes to complete the test. Examiner required and evaluated with the aid of a hand key. Suitable for group use. Standardized in Great Britain. Ten copies each of sets I and II with 50 answer sheets and a set of scoring keys costs $139.15. *Publisher:* H.K. Lewis & Company Ltd./U.S. Distributor—The Psychological Corporation

151   ANXIETY SCALE FOR THE BLIND   *Richard E. Hardy*

Measures manifest anxiety among blind and partially sighted individuals 13 years of age and older and recently modified adults in a 78 item true-false test. Used for clinical evaluations by psychologists, psychiatrists, and trained counselors.

The individual is given a roll of tickets to be placed to the right or left of the table to indicate true or false as the items are read aloud. Time of administration varies. Originally developed for use in residential schools with students of high school age, it is useful in other contexts as well. The test is still experimental in nature and must be used only by psychologists, psychiatrists, and other qualified counselors. Examiner required and evaluated. Not suitable for group use. The scale costs $4.00. *Publisher:* American Foundation for the Blind

Test Title

ARTHUR POINT SCALE OF PERFORMANCE, FORM I
Grace Arthur

Measures intelligence of children and adults. Used as a non-verbal supplement to the highly verbalized Binet tests, especially with people having language, speech, emotional, or cultural problems.

The ten nonverbal task assessment subtests are: Mare-Foal Formboard, Seguin-Goddard Formboard, Pintner-Paterson 2-Figure Formboard, Casuist Formboard, Pintner-Manikin Test, Knox-Kempf Feature Profile Test, Knox Cube Imitation Test, Healy Pictorial Completion Test 1, Kohs Block Design Test, and Porteus Mazes. Particularly useful in supplementing the Binet scale in cases where the environmental conditions have varied widely from those of the average child. The comparison is of value whether it confirms the Binet ratings or shows a disparity in verbal and nonverbal development. Examiner required and evaluated. Not for group use. Complete kit which includes all tests, 50 record cards and manual costs $395.00. *Publisher:* Stoelting Co.

ARTHUR POINT SCALE OF PERFORMANCE TESTS: REVISED FORM II   *Grace Arthur*

Measures mental abilities in difficult to assess children ages 5-15 years. Used to assess children with reading problems, delayed speech, hearing impairments, and non-English speaking subjects.

The scale of five tests includes: Knox Cube Test (Arthur Revision); Seguin Formboard Test (Arthur Revision); Arthur Stencil Design Test I; Healy Picture Completion Test II; and Porteus Maze Test (Arthur Modification). Supercedes Form 1 of the Arthur Point Scales of Performance, and is more completely non-language. May be used independently or as a supplement to the Arthur Adaptation of the Leiter International Performance Scale. Testing time is 45-90 minutes. Examiner required and evaluated. Not suitable for group use. The complete set which includes all necessary equipment for the 5 tests, 100 record forms and the manual costs $200.00. *Publisher:* The Psychological Corporation

ASTHMA SYMPTOM CHECKLIST (ASC)
Robert A. Kinsman, Katy O'Banion, Philomène Resnikoff, Thomas J. Luparello and Sheldon L. Spector

Measures the subjective symptomology and emotional responses associated with severe asthma attacks. Used with patients suffering from reversible obstructive lung disease (asthma) to determine the manner in which their subjective responses to acute episodes may color the clinical picture, thereby influencing decisions related to hospitalization, prescribed drug regimens, and prognosis.

Seventy-seven item paper-pencil self-report questionnaire assessing subjective responses to acute asthma attacks in the following five categories: airway obstruction symptoms, fatigue, panic-fear, irritability, and hyperventilation-hypocapnia. Thirty-two of the 77 items do not fall within one of these five categories and are presented in the unique symptom category. Each of the questionnaire items states a symptom which is often reported during acute asthmatic episodes. Individuals rate each item according to their own experiences on a five-point scale ranging from one (never) to five (always). Time required to complete the checklist varies. Results provide a profile of the individual patient's subjective symptomology associated with acute asthmatic episodes. Professional training and experience are required for proper use and interpretation of the results. *Source:* (1973). *Journal of Allergies and Clinical Immunology, 52*(5), 284-296: reprint requests to Dr. R.A. Kinsman, Psychophysiology Research Laboratories, Department of Behavioral Sciences, National Jewish Hospital and Research Center, 3800 East Colfax Avenue, Denver, Colorado 80206.

94, 115, 116, 152   AUDITORY DISCRIMINATION TEST, 1973
Joseph M. Wepman

Measures auditory discrimination ability of children ages 5-8 years old. Used to identify specific auditory learning disabilities for possible remediation.

Multiple item oral response test in which children are verbally presented with pairs of words and asked to discriminate between them. Untimed administration requires 10-15 minutes. Predicts articulatory speech defects and certain remedial reading problems. Identical to the 1958 Edition of the same test, except for scoring procedures. Scoring in the 1973 Edition is based on a "correct" score basis rather than the "error" basis of the original edition. The new manual contains: standardization tables on 5, 6, 7, and 8-year-olds, a five point rating scale, interpretive guidelines, reports on research using the test, and selected references. Examiner required and evaluated with the aid of a hand key. Not suitable for group use. The complete kit (includes 20 each forms IA and IIA and manual) costs $13.10. *Publisher:* Western Psychological Services

91   BARCLAY CLASSROOM ASSESSMENT SYSTEM (BCAS)
James R. Barclay

Evaluates children in grades 3-6 in relation to classroom situations, their peers, and their teachers. Identifies gifted children and children with potential learning disabilities. Used by educators and counselors to establish IEP's in compliance with PL 94-142.

Multiple item paper-pencil evaluation booklet is used by the examiner to collect information from the teacher and each child in a class. Completion of the booklet requires 30-45 minutes. A comprehensive computer report is provided for each child based on the data gained from the child, classmates, and the teacher (who pro-

Test Title

vides demographic information and responds to a brief adjective checklist for each child). The computer report provides the following information: factor scores for achievement-motivation, control stability, introversion-seclusion, energy-activity, sociability-affiliation, and enterprising-dominance; narrative report of the child's self-estimates concerning self-competency skills, vocational awareness, reinforcers, and attitude toward school; peer and teacher estimates; suspected difficulties with problem analysis; and general intervention direction and prescriptions. When stanine scores for standardized tests are provided by the teacher, additional relationships between psychosocial variables and academic achievement can be obtained. Examiner required. Intended for group use. The introductory kit for assessing 36 students, including computer processing, costs $120.00. *Publisher:* Western Psychological Services

BAYLEY SCALES OF INFANT DEVELOPMENT
Nancy Bayley

Two multiple item paper-pencil observational inventories assess the mental and psychomotor development of children ages 2-30 months. Diagnoses normal versus retarded development.

The Mental Scale measures sensory-perceptual behavior, learning ability, and early communication attempts. The Motor Scale measures general body control, coordination of large muscles, and skills in fine muscle control of hands. Completion of the two scales requires approximately 45 minutes. Examiner required and evaluated. Not suitable for group use. The complete set which includes all necessary equipment and stimulus materials, manual, 25 each of three Infant Behavior Record forms, and a carrying case costs $250.00. *Publisher:* The Psychological Corporation

BENDER VISUAL MOTOR GESTALT TEST
Lauretta Bender

Assesses the visual-motor functions of individuals from age three years to adulthood. Used in the evaluation of developmental problems in children, learning disabilities, retardation, psychosis, and organic brain disorders.

Nine item paper-pencil test consisting of nine different Gestalt cards. The individual is given the cards one at a time and asked to reproduce on a blank sheet of paper the configuration or design presented on each card. Test administration is untimed and requires 15-20 minutes to complete. Responses are scored according to the following criteria: development of the concepts of form, shape, and pattern; and orientation in space. Analysis of performance may indicate the presence of psychosis or maturational lags. Examiner required and evaluated. Scoring service provided by Koppitz and Grune & Stratton. The nine test cards and instruction book cost $17.00. *Publisher:* American Orthopsychiatric Association

Test Title

BENTON REVISED VISUAL RETENTION TEST
Arthur Benton

Measures visual memory in individuals ages eight years old to adult. Used as a supplement to usual mental examinations and in experimental research.

Ten item paper-pencil test assessing visual perception, visual memory, and visuoconstructive abilities. Items are designs which are shown to the individual one at a time. The individual studies the design and reproduces it as exactly as possible on a blank sheet of paper. Administration is untimed and requires approximately five minutes to complete. Materials include design cards, and three alternate and equivalent forms, C, D, and E. Examiner required and evaluated. Not suitable for group use. The complete set including the manual, design cards (three forms combined), and 50 record forms costs $17.00. *Publisher:* The Psychological Corporation

THE BLIND LEARNING APTITUDE TEST
T. Ernest Newland

Evaluates the academic aptitude of blind children ages 6-16 years old. Sixty-one item verbal-touch test of tactile discrimination involving patterned dots and lines on 61 embossed plastic pages. The examiner guides the child's hand over the pages and they describe what they feel. Administration requires 20-45 minutes. Examiner required and evaluated with the aid of a hand key. Not suitable for group use. The complete set including the examiner's manual, testing book, embossed pages, and 30 record forms costs $50.00. *Publisher:* University of Illinois Press

THE BODY IMAGE OF BLIND CHILDREN
Bryant J. Cratty and Theresa A. Sams

Evaluates the extent to which blind children ages 5-15 years old are able to identify their body parts and respond to requests for various types of movements.

Multiple item oral response and task performance assessment procedure measuring the body image of blind children in the following areas: body parts, body planes, body movements, laterality, and directionality. Time required for administration varies. The manual includes: norms for comparison among various subpopulations of blind children, suggested applications, interpretive guidelines, and a discussion of body-image training for blind children. Examiner required and evaluated. Not suitable for group use. The cost of the manual is $4.50. *Publisher:* The American Foundation for the Blind

BOEHM TEST OF BASIC CONCEPTS   *Ann E. Boehm*

Evaluates the mastery of concepts used in school instruction for children grades K-2. Used for screening for referral to special services.

Fifty item paper-pencil multiple-choice test of concepts related to quantity, space, and time. The child responds to oral instructions by marking one of several pictures. Untimed administration requires 15-20 minutes. Test booklets are available in alternate forms A and B. Examiner required and evaluated with the aid of a hand key. Suitable for individual or small group use. Spanish version available. A complete set of 30 test booklets 1 and 2 (form A or B), directions, class record, scoring key, and manual costs $17.10. *Publisher:* The Psychological Corporation

81

BRIGANCE® DIAGNOSTIC INVENTORY OF EARLY DEVELOPMENT   *Albert H. Brigance*

Measures the development of children from birth to the developmental age of seven years. Diagnoses developmental delays and monitors progress over a period of time. Used to develop IEP's.

Two hundred item paper-pencil, oral response, and direct observation inventory assessing psychomotor, self-help, communication, general knowledge and comprehension, and academic skill levels. Test items are arranged in developmental sequential order in the following sections: pre-ambulatory skills, gross motor skills, fine motor skills, pre-speech, speech and language skills, general knowledge and comprehension, readiness, basic reading skills, manuscript writing, and basic math skills. An introductory section outlines how to administer the tests, assess skill levels, record the results, identify specific instructional objectives, and develop IEP's. Time of administration varies in length. Results, expressed in terms of developmental ages, are entered into the individual record book, which shows graphically at each testing to what point an individual child has progressed. An optional group record book monitors the progress of 15 individuals. Examiner required and evaluated. Not suitable for group use. The assessment book and 10 individual developmental record books costs $67.95; the group record book costs $7.95. *Publisher:* Curriculum Associates, Inc.

193

BURKS' BEHAVIOR RATING SCALES   *Harold F. Burks*

Identifies patterns of behavior problems in children grades 1-9. Used as an aid to differential diagnosis.

One hundred ten item paper-pencil inventory with which a parent or teacher rates the child on the basis of descriptive statements of observed behavior. Nineteen subscales measure: excessive self-blame, anxiety, withdrawal, dependency, suffering, sense of persecution, aggressiveness, resistance, poor ego strength, physical strength, coordination, intellectuality, academics, attention, impulse control, reality contact, sense of identity, anger control, and social conformity. Completion of the inventory requires 15-20 minutes. The Parent's Guide and the Teacher's Guide define each of the scales, present possible causes for the problem behavior, and offer suggestions on how to deal with the undesirable behavior from the point of view of parent or teacher. The manual discusses: causes and manifestations and possible intervention approaches for each of the subscales and use with special groups such as educable mentally retarded, educationally and orthopedically handicapped, and speech and hearing handicapped. Examiner required and evaluated with the aid of a hand key. Not suitable for group use. The complete kit including 20 booklets and profile sheets, the manual, two parent's guides, and two teacher's guides costs $14.00. *Publisher:* Western Psychological Services

129, 152   THE BZOCH-LEAGUE RECEPTIVE-EXPRESSIVE
                    EMERGENT LANGUAGE SCALE (REEL)
                    Kenneth R. Bzoch and Richard League

Assesses emerging factors of expressive and receptive language in children from birth to age 36 months. Identifies children in need of further evaluation.

One hundred thirty-two item paper-pencil inventory measuring the child's overt speech and response behaviors as observed and rated by a parent or individual who has daily contact with the child. Test items consist of statements of language behavior typical of children ages 0-36 months. The evaluator rates each item as being present or absent. Three expressive and three receptive factors are measured for each of 22 age levels. Time required to complete the inventory varies. Three scores are derived: expressive language quotient, receptive language quotient, and overall language quotient. Results also yield receptive, expressive, and combined expressive and receptive language ages. Self-administered by evaluator. Not for group use. A packet of 25 inventories costs $12.95; contact publisher concerning cost of manual. *Publisher:* University Park Press, Inc.

44, 131, 152   CALIFORNIA ACHIEVEMENT TESTS: FORMS C AND D
                    (CAT/C & D)   *CTB/McGraw-Hill*

Assesses achievement in basic academic skills of children grades K-12.9. Used for making educational decisions leading to improvement in instruction.

Multiple item paper-pencil tests measuring basic curricular areas of reading, language, and mathematics. Divided into ten overlapping levels spanning Kindergarten through grade 12. Level 10 is a "readiness" instrument for children in Kindergarten derived from Form S of the Comprehensive Test of Basic Skills. Levels 11-19 are composed of separate tests that combine to yield scores in total reading, spelling, total language, total mathematics, and reference skills. Spelling not available at level 11; reference skills are tested only at levels 14-19. Time of administration varies, depending on level, up to two hours and 48 minutes. Alternate form D available for levels 13-19. Examiner required and evaluated with the aid

Refer to page(s):	*Test Title*

of a hand key; computer scoring available. Suitable for group use. The multi-level examination kit costs $20.00. *Publisher:* CTB/ McGraw-Hill

151

CALLIER-AZUSA SCALE: G-EDITION
Robert Stillman (Editor)

Assesses the development of deaf-blind and severely and profoundly handicapped children. Used to plan developmentally appropriate activities and to evaluate a child's developmental progress, particularly at the lower levels.

Multiple item paper-pencil observational inventory measuring 18 developmental subscales in five developmental areas: motor development (postural control, locomotion, fine motor, and visual-motor); perceptual abilities (visual, auditory, and tactile development); daily living skills (undressing and dressing, personal hygiene, development of feeding skills, and toileting); cognition, communication, and language (cognitive development, receptive communication, expressive communication, and development of speech); and social development (interactions with adults, peers, and the environment). Each subscale is made up of sequential steps describing developmental milestones. Some steps are divided into two or more items describing behaviors which appear at approximately the same time in development. Scale items are rated according to the presence or absence of the specific behaviors listed. The developmental steps described in the scale take into account the specific sensory, motor, language, and social deficits of deaf-blind and severely and profoundly impaired children (scale items differ from behaviors typically observed among normal children at the same developmental level). Administration of the scale is based on at least two weeks of observation of spontaneously occuring behaviors which typically appear in conjunction with classroom activities. The scale must be administered by someone thoroughly familiar with the child's behavior. No specific testing expertise is required other than good observational skills and a knowledge of the child's repertoire of behaviors. Most accurate results are obtained if several individuals having close contact with the child (teachers, aides, parents, specialists) evaluate the child on a consensus basis. Age equivalencies are included only to provide a rough means of comparing functioning levels in different areas of behavior. Interpretation of the scale results is based on the sequence in which the behaviors occur, not the age norms for normal children. A profile sheet is provided for summarizing scale results. Self-administered and evaluated by the examiner. Not suitable for group use. Contact publisher concerning cost. *Publisher:* Callier Center for Communication Disorders

153

CARROW ELICITED LANGUAGES INVENTORY (CELI)
Elizabeth Carrow-Woolfolk

Measures the productive control of grammar in children ages 3.0-7.11 years and diagnoses expressive language delays and disorders. Used to obtain data on a child's grammatical structure.

Fifty-two item test of oral stimuli, based on the technique of eliciting imitation of a sequence of sentences that include basic construction types and specific grammatical morphemes. The stimuli (51 sentences and one phrase) are presented by the examiner. Administration requires approximately five minutes. The child's responses are recorded and transcribed from the tape onto a scoring/analysis form, which provides a format for analyzing errors of substitution, addition, omission, transposition, and reversal. A separate verb protocol sheet provides for analyzing production of verb forms. The test is not appropriate for use with non-verbal children. Examiner required and evaluated. Not suitable for group use. The complete set including the test manual, a training guide with practice exercises, the analysis forms, and a cassette or reel-to-reel training tape costs $53.00. *Publisher:* Teaching Resources Corporation

127   CENTRAL INSTITUTE FOR THE DEAF PRESCHOOL PERFORMANCE SCALE (CID PRESCHOOL PERFORMANCE SCALE)   *Ann E. Geers and Helen S. Lane*

Measures intellectual potential of hearing-impaired and language-impaired preschoolers using completely non-verbal testing procedures. Predicts school achievement.

Multiple item task performance test assessing abilities in the following areas: manual planning (block building, Montessori cylinders, and two-figure formboard), manual dexterity (buttons and Wallin pegs), form perception (Decroly pictures, Seguin formboard), perceptual/motor skills (Knox cube, drawing, and paper folding), preschool skills (color sorting and counting sticks), and part/whole relations (Manikin and Stutsman puzzles). All tests may be administered without requiring a single spoken word from either the examiner or the child (optional verbal clues are provided for use with children who do hear). Time of administration varies. Test materials were selected from existing mental tests for children between two and five years of age, to obtain a broad, clinical picture of the child's abilities, as well as a numerical rating (Deviation IQ) that would correlate with a Stanford-Binet IQ. The test is an adaptation of the Early Randall's Island Performance Series. Examiner required and evaluated. Not suitable for group use. The complete test kit including the manual, record forms, and all manipulatives required for the subtests costs $395.00. *Publisher:* Stoelting Company

43, 193   CHILD ANXIETY SCALE (CAS)   *John S. Gillis*

Diagnoses adjustment problems in children ages 6-8 years. Helps to prevent emotional and behavioral disorders in later life by identifying children who would benefit from therapeutic intervention at an early age. Used for clinical evaluations and educational and personal counseling.

Multiple item paper-pencil test measuring anxiety-based disturbances in young children. Test items are based on extensive research of the form anxiety takes in the self-report of 6-8 year olds. An audio-cassette is used to present the questionnaire items, and brightly colored, easy-to-read answer sheets are specially designed for use with children of this age group. Time required for administration varies. The manual contains: reliability and validity information, scoring instructions, and percentiles and standard scores for both sexes separately and combined. Examiner required and evaluated. Suitable for group use. The professional examination kit costs $19.45. *Publisher:* Institute for Personality and Ability Testing, Inc.

178, 180   CHILD BEHAVIOR CHECKLIST AND REVISED CHILD BEHAVIOR PROFILE   *Thomas H. Achenbach and Craig Edelbrock*

Four paper-pencil inventories assess the behavioral problems and competencies of children ages 4-16 years from four perspectives: the Child Behavior Checklist assesses behavior from the parents' point of view, the Teacher Report Form assesses the child's classroom behavior, the Direct Observation Form employs an experienced observer to rate the child on the basis of a series of at least six 10-minute observation periods, and the Youth Self-Report (for ages 11-18) gathers information directly from the child.

The four-page Child Behavior Checklist contains two pages of questions regarding the child's social history, interests, and school performance. Most items combine free response questions about the child with multiple-choice rating scales for comparing the child with his peers. The last two pages of the checklist present 118 items describing a variety of problem behaviors. Parents rate each item from 0 (not true) to 2 (very true) according to their child's behavior over the past six months (time period may vary). Responses are scored according to the Revised Child Behavior Profile, which yields scores for social competence scales and behavior problem scales as well as internalizing, externalizing, and total problem scores. Norms provided in terms of T-scores.

The Teacher's Report Form is presented in a similar four-page format, gathering background information and assessing 188 items related to classroom behavior. Scoring profile includes: standard scores, four general adaptive characteristics, eight behavior problem scales, internalizing and externalizing problems, and total problem scores. The Direct Observation Form rates 96 problem behaviors from 0 (not observed) to 3 (severe intensity) for a 10 minute period. Also provides for scoring on-task behavior at 1-minute intervals. The observer writes a narrative description of the child's behavior during the observation period and then rates the behavioral items accordingly. Stable scores are obtained by averaging the ratings obtained on six different occasions. Individual item scores, total behavior problem scores, and on-task scores act as direct indices of behavior problems and change over time and provide a basis for group comparison.

The Youth Self-Report form also uses a four-page format to gather firsthand information related to the items on the Child Behavior Checklist. Item scores and total scores act as indices of the child's self-perceived problems and competencies.

The manual for all four instruments (230 pages) discusses: development and construction of the scales; the internalizing-externalizing dichotomy, factor loadings; standardization and norms; reliability and validity; effects of clinical status, socioeconomic status and race; clinical cutoff scores, cluster analyses, profile patterns, and taxonomy; classification of children according to their profile patterns; distribution and correlates of profile types; clinical and research applications; and scoring procedures by hand and computer. Self administered (except for the Direct Observation Form); examiner evaluated. All self-administered forms suitable for group use. A sample packet including all report forms and scoring profiles for the four inventories costs $5.00. *Publisher:* Department of Psychiatry, University of Vermont

44   CHILD BEHAVIOR RATING SCALE   *Russell N. Cassel*

Measures behavior and personality adjustment of children from preschool through the third grade. Used in counseling both normal and emotionally handicapped children.

Seventy-eight item paper-pencil inventory consisting of brief statements about behavior and personality which the evaluator (someone familiar with the child) applies to the child and answers on a six-point scale ranging from "Yes" to "No." The questionnaire can be completed in 30-40 minutes. Provides a total personality adjustment score and a profile of the child's adjustment in five areas: self, home, social, school, and physical. Standardized on 2,000 normal and 200 emotionally handicapped children. Examiner required and evaluated with the aid of a hand key. Suitable for group use. The complete kit including 25 scales and the manual costs $9.60. *Publisher:* Western Psychological Services

75, 83   CHILDHOOD AUTISM RATING SCALE (CARS)   *Eric Schopler, Robert J. Reichler, Robert F. Devellis and Kenneth Daly*

Measures observable behaviors related to childhood autism. Identifies autistic children and differentiates autistic children from other developmentally disordered children.

Fifteen item rating scale assessing the following behaviors and reactions: relationships with people, imitation (verbal and motor), affect, use of body, relation to non-human objects, adaptation to environmental change, visual responsiveness, auditory responsiveness, anxiety reaction, non-verbal communication, activity level (motility patterns), intellectual functioning, and general impressions. Guidelines are presented for a structured diagnostic

Refer to page(s):	Test Title

evaluation session eliciting behaviors and reactions related to the 15 items of the scale. The child interacts with the examiner while additional observers view the procedings through a one-way observation and listening screen. The length and number of observation periods varies. The child's behavior is rated in each of the 15 categories on a four-point continuum from normal behavior (one) to severely abnormal behavior (four). Age is considered in making all evaluations. The total score and the number of items rated moderately abnormal (three) or higher are used to place the child in one of three diagnostic categories: not autistic, mild-moderately autistic, or severely autistic. Examiner required and evaluated. Not suitable for group use. *Source:* (1980). *Journal of Autism and Developmental Disorders, 10* (1), 91-103: address all correspondence, including requests for the appendix containing the complete CARS form, to Dr. Eric Schopler, Director, Division TEACCH, 214 Medical School Wing B 207H, Department of Psychiatry, School of Medicine, University of North Carolina at Chapel Hill, Chapel Hill, North Carolina 27514.

9, 43, 60, 114, 193

THE CHILDREN'S APPERCEPTION TEST (CAT-A)
Leopold Bellak and Sonya Sorel Bellak

Assesses personality in children ages 3-10 years. Used in clinical evaluation and diagnosis.

Ten item oral response projective assessment procedure measuring the traits, attitudes, and psychodynamics involved in the personalities of children. Each test item consists of a picture of animals in a human social context through which the child becomes involved in conflicts, identities, roles, family structures, etc. The child is presented with the pictures one at a time and asked to tell a story about each one. Administration requires approximately 20-30 minutes. Also includes: informational material on the history, nature, and purpose of CAT, Ego Function Graph, test interpretation, use of the Short Form, research possibilities, and bibliography. Examiner required and evaluated. Not suitable for group use. Available in the following foreign languages: Spanish, Indian, French, German, Japanese, Flemish, Portugese, and Italian. The complete kit including pictures and manual costs $14.00. *Publisher:* C.P.S., Inc.

9, 43, 60, 114, 193

CHILDREN'S APPERCEPTION TEST—HUMAN FIGURES (CAT-H) *Leopold Bellak and Sonya Sorel Bellak*

Assesses personality in children ages 3-10 years. Used for clinical evaluation and diagnosis.

Ten item oral response projective assessment procedure measuring the traits, attitudes, and psychodynamics involved in the personalities of children. The test consists of ten pictures of human figures in situations of concern to children: conflicts, identities, roles, family structure, etc. Administration requires approximately

Refer to page(s):	*Test Title*

20-30 minutes. Also included: a review of the literature concerning the use of animal vs. human figures in projective techniques, a discussion of the process of transposing animal figures to human forms, a copy of Haworth's Schedule of Adaptive Mechanisms in CAT Responses, and bibliography. Examiner required and evaluated. Not suitable for group use. Spanish, Portugese, Flemish, and Japanese versions also available. The complete kit including 10 pictures and the manual costs $14.00. *Publisher:* C.P.S., Inc.

9, 43, 60, 114, 193   THE CHILDREN'S APPERCEPTION TEST—SUPPLEMENT (CAT-S)   *Leopold Bellak and Sonya Sorel Bellak*

Assesses personality in children ages 3-10 years. Used for clinical evaluation and diagnosis.

Ten item oral response projective assessment procedure measuring the traits, attitudes, and psychodynamics at work in the personalities of children. The test items consist of ten pictures using animal figures to present the children with family situations which are common, but not as universal as those of the Children's Apperception Test. Situations depicted are: prolonged illness, physical disability, mother's pregnancy, separation of parents, etc. The picture plates are constructed like pieces of a large jigsaw puzzle with irregularly-shaped outlines. Children who do not relate stories readily can manipulate these forms in play techniques. Administration requires approximately 20-30 minutes. Also included: informational material on test techniques and bibliography. Examiner required and evaluated. Not suitable for group use. Spanish, French, Flemish, and Italian versions also available. The complete kit of 10 pictures and the manual costs $14.00. *Publisher:* C.P.S., Inc.

43, 178, 179, 181   CHILDREN'S DEPRESSION INVENTORY (CDI)
Maria Kovacs

Assesses the severity of depression currently experienced by children ages 8-13 years. Used for clinical research in childhood depression.

Twenty-seven item paper-pencil inventory measuring an array of "overt" symptoms of childhood depression such as sadness, anhedonia, suicidal ideation, and sleep and appetite disturbance. Each item assesses one symptom by presenting three related statements such as "I am sad once in a while," "I am sad many times," and "I am sad all the time." For each item, the child is asked to select the statement which best reflects his feelings and ideas during the previous two weeks. Time required for administration varies. The three choices for each item are assigned numerical values from 0-2, graded in order of increasing psychopathology. A total score (ranging from 0-54) is obtained by adding the numerical scores of the individual items. The average score in non psychiatric populations is nine, while a cutoff score of 19 identifies children whose scores deviate significantly from the "normal" population. Examiner required and evaluated. Suitable for use with small groups of children, but individual administration is advisable with psychiatric populations or if there is any question as to the child's ability to remain on task. *Source:* (1981). *Acta Paedopsychiatrica, 46,* 305-315; for further information, please contact Maria Kovacs, Ph.D., Assistant Professor of Psychiatry, Western Psychiatric Institute and Clinic, 3811 O'Hara Street, Pittsburgh, Pennsylvania 15261; (412) 624-2043.

178

CHILDREN'S DEPRESSION RATING SCALE (CDRS)
Elva O. Poznanski, Stephen C. Cook and Bernard J. Carroll

Measures severity of depression in children ages 6-12 years. Used for clinical diagnosis and research in childhood depression.

Sixteen item paper-pencil inventory assessing the following factors which are considered to be symptomatic of depression in children: depressed mood, weeping, self-esteem, morbid ideation, suicide and suicide ideation, irritability, schoolwork, capacity to have fun, social withdrawal, expressive communication, sleep, disturbance of eating pattern, frequent physical complaints, general somatic, hypoactivity, and reversal of affect. The scale is completed by a clinically experienced examiner on the basis of personal observations, interviews with the child and parents, interviews with school personnel, and interview with the nursing staff if the child is hospitalized. Each item consists of statement or paragraph defining one of the factors (symptoms) listed above, followed by three to five statements which provide a range of choices from "not depressed" to "severely depressed." The examiner selects the statement for each item which most accurately describes the child's behavior at the time of the rating. Analysis of individual item scores yields a global rating of depression based on a five-point scale ranging from "definitely not depressed or doubtful depression" to "severe depression." Examiner required and evaluated. Not suitable for group use. *Source:* (1979). *Pediatrics, 64*(4), 442-450: reprint requests to Elva O. Poznanski, M.D., The University of Michigan Psychiatric Institute, Children's Psychiatric Hospital, Ann Arbor, Michigan 48109.

43, 179

CHILDREN'S DEPRESSION SCALE
Moshe Lange and Miriam Tisher

Measures depression in children ages 9-16 years. Identifies depressed children in need of further evaluation.

The 66 test items, 48 "depressive" and 18 "positive", measure six aspects of childhood depression: effective response, social problems, self-esteem, preoccupation with own sickness, of death, guilt, and pleasure. Items are presented on cards which the child sorts into five boxes ranging from "very right" to "very wrong" according to how he feels the item applies to himself. A separate set of cards, identical in content but appropriately reworded is provided for use with parents, teachers, or other adults familiar with the child. Complete set of materials include: two sets of 66 cards, five boxes, record form, and manual. Examiner required and evaluated. Not for group use. For cost information contact publisher. *Publisher:* The Australian Council for Educational Research Limited

42   CHILDREN'S RESPIRATORY ILLNESS AND OPINION
            SURVEY (P-RIOS)   *Irwin Matus, Robert A. Kinsman and
            Nelson F. Jones*

Assesses attitudes and biases of children suffering from reversible obstructive airway disease (asthma) concerning their medical condition, their treatment programs, and their personal role and the roles of others in the management of the disease. Used by physicians and other medical personnel to identify attitudes which may interfere with the progress of the child's asthma treatment program.

Forty-six item paper-pencil questionnaire measuring attitudes toward chronic respiratory illness and hospitalization in a residential treatment program along the following seven dimensions: minimization of severity, passive observance of illness, bravado, expectation of staff rejection, moralistic authoritarianism, stigma, and external control. The seven dimensions are based on questionnaire items which conceptually represent an attitude such as denial of illness, stigma associated with asthma, level of realistic thinking about the illness, level of optimism, expectations about the patient's own role and that of others in its management, and orientation toward treating personnel. The child completes the questionnaire by rating each item on a five-point scale from one (strongly agree with the statement) to five (strongly disagree). Time required for administration varies. Analysis of four of the dimensions (passive observance of illness, bravado, moralistic authoritarianism, and psychological stigma) is unrelated to chronological age. Analysis of the remaining dimensions is related to age and may be used to identify the perpetuation of immature attitudes and conditions of emotional arrest which may hinder the progress of the child's treatment program. The presence of an adult examiner (trained medical personnel) is required to clarify instructions and to help the child to understand puzzling items. The child is encouraged to ask questions as needed. Examiner evaluated. Individually administered to children under 11 years of age; suitable for use with small groups of children 11 years of age and older. *Source:* (1978). *Journal of Chronic Diseases, 31,* 611-618: address reprint requests to Irwin Matus, Pediatric Behavioral Sciences Liaison Team, National Jewish Hospital and Research Center, 3800 East Colfax Avenue, Denver, Colorado 80206.

19, 20   A CLASS PLAY   *E.M. Bower*

Evaluates the peer perceptions and self-images of children grades 3-7. Identifies children with low self-images and children whose self-image does not correspond with the perceptions of their

Refer to page(s):	*Test Title*

peers. Used by classroom teachers to identify children in need of further assistance or evaluation.

Fifty item paper-pencil test consisting of two sections. Section I (20 items) contains descriptions of 20 hypothetical roles in a play, with instructions directing each student to choose the classmate who would be most suitable and natural in each of the roles. Odd numbered items present positive roles such as "a class president" or "a very fair person who plays games fairly," while even numbered items present negative roles such as "a bully who picks on smaller boys and girls." Section II (30 items) consists of multiple-choice questions in which students are presented with four of the roles from the play (two positive and two negative) with instructions such as "which of these four roles would a teacher pick you to play?" Students are asked to indicate roles they would pick for themselves, as well as roles their peers or teacher would (or would not) pick for them to play. Time required for administration varies. Scoring for both sections consists of computing the proportion of positive and negative perceptions for each child within each of the sections. A comparison of the students' peer-perceptions (the score from Section I) with their self-perceptions (the score from Section II) indicates the congruence or incongruence between the students' perceptions of themselves and the way they are perceived by others. Examiner required and evaluated. Suitable for group use. *Source: Bower, E.M. (1969). Early identification of emotionally handicapped children in school. 2nd ed.* Springfield, Illinois: Thomas.

112, 191

COLOURED PROGRESSIVE MATRICES   *J.C. Raven*

Assesses the mental ability of children 5 years of age and older who are mentally subnormal or impaired. Used for school and clinical counseling, and research.

Thirty-six item paper-pencil nonverbal test consisting of design and pattern problems printed in several colors, including the two easiest sets from SPM-1938, plus a dozen additional items of similar difficulty. In each problem, the subject is presented with a pattern or figure design which has a part missing. The subject then selects one of six possible parts as the correct one. Examiner required. Suitable for group use above age eight. Standard norms developed in Great Britain. Single test booklets are $5.50, 50 hand scorable answer documents are $4.15 and scoring keys are $10.00 *Publisher:* H.K. Lewis & Co. Ltd./U.S. Distributor—The Psychological Corporation

112, 191

COLUMBIA MENTAL MATURITY SCALE (CMMS)   *Bessie B. Burgemeister, Lucille Hollander Blum and Irving Lorge*

Assesses mental ability in children 3½ to 10 years old. Used with children having physical or verbal impairments.

Ninety-two item test of general reasoning abilities. Items are arranged in a series of eight overlapping levels. Level administered determined by child's chronological age. Testing time is 15-20

Refer to page(s):	Test Title

minutes. Items are printed on 95 (6″ x 19″) cards. Child responds by selecting from each series of drawings the one that does not belong. Examiner required. Not suitable for group use. Materials include item cards and a Guide for Administration and Interpretation, which includes directions in Spanish for $125. *Publisher:* The Psychological Corporation

43   THE CONNERS PARENT SYMPTOM QUESTIONNAIRE
C.K. Conners

Assesses the behavior problems of children ages 3-17 years as observed by their parents in the home setting. Identifies children with significant behavior problems in need of further evaluation.

The 48 item paper-pencil observational inventory assesses a child's problem behaviors in a variety of home related areas such as family relationships, peer relationships, personal habits, health, and emotional development. Each item describes a problem behavior frequently encountered in the home setting. The parent indicates the degree to which the child exhibits the behaviors by rating each item on a four-point scale from zero (not at all) to three (very much). Yields the following six factor scores: conduct problems, learning problems, psychosomatic problems, impulsivity-hyperactivity, anxiety, and hyperactivity index. Normative data provided by sex and age group for children ages 3-17 years. Self-administered by parents with evaluation by the examiner. Not suitable for group use. *Source:* Barkley, R.G. (1981). *Hyperactive children: a handbook for diagnosis and treatment.* New York: Guilford Press

18, 43   THE CONNERS TEACHER RATING SCALE (TRS)
C.K. Conners

Assesses the classroom behavior of children from preschool to grade 12. Identifies children with significant behavior problems, and indicates children who are potentially hyperactive.

The 28 item paper-pencil observational inventory assesses the conduct problems of children ages 3-17 years. Each item describes a problem behavior frequently encountered in the classroom setting. The teacher indicates the degree to which the child exhibits the behaviors by rating each item on a four point scale from zero (not at all) to three (very much). Yields the following four factor scores: conduct problems, hyperactivity, inattention-passivity, and hyperactivity index. Normative data provided by sex and age group for children ages 3-17 years. Self-administered by teacher. Not suitable for group use. *Source:* Barkley, R.G. (1981). *Hyperactive children: a handbook for diagnosis and treatment.* New York: Guilford Press

43   COOPERSMITH SELF-ESTEEM INVENTORIES (CSEI)
Stanley Coopersmith

Measures attitudes toward the self in social, academic, and personal contexts. Used for individual diagnosis, classroom screening, pre-post evaluations, and clinical and research studies.

Fifty-eight or 25 item paper-pencil test of self-attitudes in four areas: Social Self-Peers, Home-Parents, School-Academic, and General-Self. Related to academic achievement and to personal satisfaction in school and adult life. Testing time is 15 minutes. Materials include three forms: the 58 item School Form (ages 8-15), 25 item School Short Form, and 25 item Adult Form (ages 15-adult). Self-administered. Suitable for group use. Twenty-five School Form booklets are $5.00; 25 Adult Form test booklets $3.25; school scoring keys $2.00; adult keys $1.25; manual also available. *Publisher:* Consulting Psychologists Press, Inc.

CRAWFORD SMALL PARTS DEXTERITY TEST (CSPDT)
John Crawford

Measures fine eye-hand coordination. For use in selecting applicants for jobs such as engravers, watch repairers and telephone installers.

Two part performance measure of dexterity. Part 1 measures dexterity in using tweezers to assemble pin and collar assemblies. Part 2 measures dexterity in placing small screws in threaded holes in a plate and screwing them down with a screwdriver. The CSPDT may be administered in two ways. In the work-limit method, subject completes task and total time is the score. Using time-limit procedure, the score is the amount of work done in a specified time. Examiner required and evaluated. Suitable for group use. Materials include assembly plate, pins, collars, and screws for $134.00. *Publisher:* The Psychological Corporation

DENVER DEVELOPMENTAL SCREENING TEST (DDST)
Wm. K. Frankenburg

Evaluates a child's (ages birth-6 years) personal, social, fine and gross motor, language, and adaptive abilities as a means of identifying possible problems and screening for further evaluation.

One hundred-five item "pick and choose" test taking approximately 10-20 minutes to complete. The items are blocks, a bell, a ball, a bottle, raisins, rattle, yarn and a pencil. Items are presented to the child in chronological step-wise order to permit a more dynamic profile, like a growth curve, of a child's development. The examiner observes what the child does with the items and makes recommendations based on perceived abnormalities. Available in Spanish. Examiner required and evaluated. Not for group use. The kit is $17.00, the manual $14.00 and 100 test forms $9.00. *Publisher:* Ladoca Publishing Foundation

DETROIT TESTS OF LEARNING APTITUDE   *Harry J. Baker*

Measures concentration and comprehension skills for professional diagnosis of individual learning disabilities in children ages 3 and older.

Test Title

Nineteen category, examiner-led and evaluated test, covering pictorial and verbal absurdities, pictorial and verbal opposites, oral omissions, social adjustment, free association, memory for design, number ability, and likenesses and differences. Eight classifications are measured within each category: reasoning and comprehension, practical judgment, verbal ability, time and space relationships, number ability, auditory attentive ability, visual attentive ability, and motor ability. Testing time is 35-40 minutes. Materials consist of record booklets and forms, examiner's handbook and supplement, book of pictorial materials and a sample packet. The examiner, depending upon the subtest, shows response cards or reads to the pupils and records their responses. Must be administered individually by trained professionals. Specimen set is available for $17.95. *Publisher:* Bobbs-Merrill

DEVELOPMENTAL ACTIVITIES SCREENING INVENTORY (DASI) *Rebecca R. Fewell and Mary Beth Langley*

Assesses developmental skills and abilities in infants and young children ages 6 months-5 years. Used for early detection of disabilities for determination of remedial teaching.

Fifty-five item paper-pencil and manual dexterity test. It measures academic/cognitive and basic skills/perceptual motor factors, and can be presented in different sequences in one or two sittings. Instructions are given either visually or verbally. The developmental skills studied include fine-motor manipulation, cause-effect relationships, associations, number concepts, size discriminations, and sequencing. Examiner required and evaluated. Not suitable for group use. Materials include a kit of manipulative materials such as cubes, a peg board and pegs, a form board, beads, rings, an assortment of cards, cups, bowls, and plastic shapes; student response forms for $99.00. The manual suggests instructional programs which can be used before a comprehensive remedial program is developed. The inventory can be modified for use with the visually or hearing impaired. *Publisher:* DLM Teaching Resources

DEVELOPMENTAL TEST OF VISUAL-MOTOR INTEGRATION (VMI) *Keith E. Beery and Norman A. Buktenica*

Identifies children (ages 2-15 years) with problems in visual perception, hand control, and eye-hand coordination

Fifteen to twenty-four item paper-pencil test measures the integration of visual perception and motor behavior. Test items, arranged in order of increasing difficulty, consist of geometric figures which the children are asked to copy. The Short Test Form (15 figures) is used with children ages 2-8 years. The Long Test Form (24 figures) is used with children ages 2-15 years and adults with developmental delays. The manual includes directions for administration, scoring criteria, developmental comments, age norms, suggestions for teaching, percentiles, and standard score equivalents. Supplementary materials include: VMI Monograph and stimulus cards (a 47-page booklet on visual-motor research studies a set of 24 cards for remediation) and assessment worksheets (10 copies each of 40 different worksheets related to tasks on the VMI). Examiner required and evaluated. Suitable for group use. Specimen set is available for $5.48. *Publisher:* Modern Curriculum Press, Inc.

44

THE DEVEREUX CHILD BEHAVIOR RATING SCALE (DCB)   *George Spivack and Jules Spotts*

Assesses symptomatic behaviors of children ages 8-12. Used with mentally retarded and emotionally disturbed children for diagnostic and screening procedures, group placement decisions, and assessment of progress in response to specific programs or procedures.

Ninety-seven item paper-pencil inventory assesses overt behavior patterns of children. The evaluator (parent or childcare worker living with the child) rates each item according to how he feels the subject's behavior compares to the behavior of normal children his age. Testing time is 10-15 minutes. Yields 17 scores: distractibility, poor self care, pathological use of senses, emotional detachment, social isolation, poor coordination and body tonus, incontinence, messiness-sloppiness, inadequate need for independence, unresponsiveness to stimulation, proneness to emotional upset, need for adult contact, anxious-fearful ideation, "impulse" ideation, inability to delay, social aggression, and unethical behavior. Self-administered by evaluator. Not for group use. Examination set (includes 25 scales and manual) costs $10.50. *Publisher:* The Devereux Foundation

9, 152

DIAGNOSTIC READING SCALES, REVISED (DRS) *George D. Spache*

Identifies a student's strengths and weaknesses in reading. Used by educators to determine placement and prescribe instruction.

A multiple item, verbal test consisting of a series of graduated scales containing three word-recognition lists, twenty-two reading selections, and twelve phonics and word analysis tests. The word-recognition list yields a tentative level of performance and is used to determine the student's entry level to the reading selections, which in turn are used to establish three reading levels for the student—instructional level (oral reading), independent level (silent reading and comprehension), and potential level (auditory comprehension). The word analysis and phonics tests measure the following skills: recognition of initial and final consonants, consonant digraphs and blends, short and long vowel sounds, vowels with r, vowel diphthongs and digraphs, common syllables and phonograms, initial

Refer to page(s):	*Test Title*

consonants presented auditorily; auditory discrimination of minimal word pairs; initial consonant substitution; and blending of word parts. Examiner required and evaluated. Not suitable for group use. Specimen set (includes test book, record book, representative pages of the manual, and a test reviewer's guide) costs $12.00. *Publisher:* CTB/McGraw-Hill

116, 153

DURRELL ANALYSIS OF READING DIFFICULTY: THIRD EDITION *Donald D. Durrell and Jane H. Catterson*

Assesses reading behavior in children grades 1-6. Used in diagnosis, measurement of prereading skills, and planning remedial programs.

Multiple item series of tests and situations measures ten reading abilities: oral reading, silent reading, listening comprehension, listening vocabulary, word recognition/word analysis, spelling, auditory analysis of words and word elements, pronunciation of word elements, visual memory of words, and prereading phonics abilities. Supplementary paragraphs are provided for oral and silent reading to be used in supplementary testing or retesting. Examiner required and evaluated. Not suitable for group use. Materials include a spiral-bound booklet containing items to be read and a tachistoscope with accompanying test card for $20.00. *Publisher:* The Psychological Corporation

28

ELIZUR TEST OF PSYCHO-ORGANICITY: CHILDREN & ADULTS *Abraham Elizur*

Differentiates between organic and non-organic brain disorders in individuals age 6 years to adult. Used by neurologists, psychologists, educators, counselors, and researchers.

Multiple item task assessment test using drawings, digits, and blocks to eliminate "unidimensional" measurements. Test tasks are easily performed by subjects so as not to bias the results with intelligence factors. Separate instructions are provided for administering to adults and children. Results yield quantitative and qualitative measures with cutoff points provided for classifying examinees as organic. Testing time is 10 minutes. Examiner required and evaluated. Not for group use. Complete kit (includes 10 protocol booklets, 1 set test materials and manual) costs $27.80. *Publisher:* Western Psychological Services

151

EMOTIONAL FACTORS INVENTORY *Mary K. Bauman*

Measures emotional and personality factors of visually handicapped individuals.

One hundred-seventy item paper-pencil or oral response questionnaire assessing the personal and emotional adjustment of visually impaired individuals. Provides scores on the following seven scales: sensitivity, somatic symptoms, social competency, attitudes of distrust, feelings of inadequacy, depression, and attitudes concerning blindness. A validation score is also obtained. Questionnaires are presented in large print format. Instructions for tape recording the questions are included. Supplementary materials provided in the test kit include a discussion of the inventory, instructions for administering and scoring the inventory, and a comparative study of personality factors in blind, other handicapped, and non-handicapped individuals. Examiner required. Paper-pencil version suitable for group use. Complete test kit (includes large-print test booklet, set of scoring overlays, 10 IBM answer sheets, supplementary materials, and norms) costs $15.00. *Publisher:* Associated Services for the Blind

EXPRESSIVE ONE-WORD PICTURE VOCABULARY TEST: UPPER EXTENSION *Morrison F. Gardner*

Assesses the expressive vocabulary of students ages 12 to 15 as a measure of verbal intelligence. Used to detect speech defects and learning disabilities.

Multiple item oral-response test in which the student demonstrates his ability to understand and use words by naming pictures that range from simple objects to representations of abstract concepts. Each test item consists of one picture stimulus that requires a single word answer. Testing time is 5-10 minutes. Test results yield mental ages, percentiles, stanines, and deviation IQ scores which allow for comparing expressive language skills with other measures of receptive language, for detecting speech defects, identifying learning disorders related to hearing loss and imperceptions of the auditory modality, assessing auditory-visual association ability, and for evaluating a bilingual student's English/Spanish fluency. Examiner required and evaluated. Suitable for use with small groups who respond in writing. Spanish Form available. Test kit (includes manual, test plates, and 25 English Record forms in a vinyl folder) costs $33.50. *Publisher:* Academic Therapy Publications

EYSENCK PERSONALITY QUESTIONNAIRE (EPQ) *H. F. Eysenck and S. B. G. Eysenck*

Measures the personality dimensions of extraversion, emotionality and toughmindedness (psychotocism in extreme cases) in individuals age 7 through adult. Used for clinical diagnosis, educational guidance, occupational counseling, personnel selection and placement, and market research.

The 90 item paper-pencil yes-no inventory measures three important dimensions of personality: Extraversion-Introversion (21 items), Neuroticism-Stability (23 items), and Psychoticism (25 items). Twenty-one items provide data for the falsification scale. The questionnaire deals with normal behaviors which become pathological only in extreme cases, hence use of the term "toughmindedness" is suggested for non-pathological cases. An 81 item

Refer to page(s):	*Test Title*

Junior Form is also available for testing at lower ages. Testing time is approximately 15 minutes. Scores (hand keyed) are provided for E-Extraversion, N-Neuroticism or emotionality, P-Psychoticism or toughmindedness, and L-Lie. College norms presented in percentile form for both Form A and B separately and combined. Adult norms provided for an industrially employed sample. Self-administered. Suitable for group use. Specimen set (includes manual and one copy of each form) is available for $3.25. *Publisher:* Educational and Industrial Testing Service

9, 59

FAMILY RELATIONS TEST-ADULT VERSION
Eva Bene and James Anthony

Assesses memories of early family relationships. Used for evaluation for individual and family couseling and as a research tool.

Multiple item test providing systematic recollection of early family experiences. Subject chooses figures from a large group to represent the family. The subject then assigns item cards indicating like or dislike, love or hate, or jealousy to each of the different figures. Memories regarding parental competence are also explored. Item content facilitates recollection of childhood family feelings. Testing time is 20-25 minutes. Examiner required. Not suitable for group use. Contact publisher for cost. *Publisher:* NFER-Nelson Publishing Company

9, 59

FAMILY RELATIONS TEST-CHILDREN'S VERSION
Eva Bene and James Anthony

Assesses child's (ages 3-15) subjective perception of the interpersonal relationships in the family. Used for individual and family counseling and as a research tool.

Materials include a set of family figures and a pack of cards with a single emotion, attitude or sentiment printed on each card. Family figures are selected by the child to represent every member of the family. An additional figure is called "nobody". The child then assigns each card to a particular family member. Scoring consists of counting the cards for each figure. Results indicate relative psychological importance of each family member, whether feelings are positive, ambivalent or negative, and whether or not feelings are reciprocal. Materials include two item sets, one for ages 3-7 and one for ages 7-15. Testing time is 20-25 minutes. Examiner required. Not suitable for group use. Contact publisher for cost. *Publisher:* NFER-Nelson Publishing Company

94

FROSTIG DEVELOPMENTAL TEST OF VISUAL PERCEP-TION *Marianne Frostig and Associates*

Assesses perceptual skills to help evaluate children (from nursery school-grade 3) referred for learning difficulties or neurological handicaps.

Refer to page(s):	*Test Title*

Forty-one item test of five operationally-defined perceptual skills: Eye-Motor Coordination, Figure-Ground, Constancy of Shape, Positions in Space, and Spatial Relationships. Testing time is 30-45 minutes. Correlated with reading achievement in normal first grade classroom. Materials include 11 demonstration cards showing various shapes and figures. Examiner provides regular and colored pencils, and crayons. Blackboard necessary for group administration. Individual and group administration. Examiner required. Scoring by hand key. Specimen set (includes test booklet, manual, monograph, demonstration cards, and set of score keys) costs $6.00 *Publisher:* Consulting Psychologists Press, Inc.

191

FULL RANGE PICTURE VOCABULARY TEST (FRPV)
R.B.Ammons and H.S. Ammons

Assesses individual intelligence in individuals two years of age and older. May be used for testing special populations such as physically handicapped, uncooperative, aphasic, or very young subjucts.

Fifty item test of verbal comprehension. Items are matched on 16 cards. Subject points to one of four drawings which best represents a particular word. Subject may also respond by indicating yes or no as the examiner points to each drawing. No reading or writing is required of the subject. Testing time is 5-10 minutes. Materials include two parallel forms, A and B, which use the same set of stimulus plates. Scoring is by hand key. Examiner required and evaluated. Not suitable for group use. Set of plates with instructions, norms and sample answer sheets costs $15.00. *Publisher:* Psychological Test Specialists

152

GATES-McKILLOP-HOROWITZ READING DIAGNOSTIC TESTS   *Arthur I. Gates, Anne S. McKillop and Elizabeth C. Horowitz*

Evaluates oral reading, spelling, and writing skills of children in grades 1 to 6, and diagnoses reading difficulties of older students. Used for class grouping and curriculum planning.

Eleven part verbal, paper-pencil test of the following abilities: oral reading, isolated word recognition, knowledge of word parts, recognizing and blending common word parts, reading words, giving letter sounds, naming letters, identifying vowel sounds, auditory blending and discrimination, and an informal writing sample. Testing time is approximately 60 minutes. Not all parts need to be given to every student. Examiner required and evaluated. Not for group use. Materials include a test materials booklet containing a tachistoscope (for word flash tests), pupil record book, and manual at a cost of $5.50. *Publisher:* Teachers College Press

| | *Test Title* |

GESTURAL APPROACH TO THOUGHT AND EXPRESSION (GATE) *M. Beth Langley*

Assesses the communication systems of sensory or physically impaired children from birth to age 36 months. Determines the non-verbal child's most effective means of communication, identifies cognitive/social deficiencies that may be interfering with the child's progression towards a more conventional verbal or non-verbal communication system, and determines which communicative behavior should next be facilitated within a developmental framework.

The 65 item paper-pencil observational checklist evaluates the communication behaviors of children functioning below the developmental age of 36 months. Test items are presented in chronological developmental order in six age groups: 0-4 months, 4-8 months, 8-12 months, 12-18 months, 18-24 months, and 24-36 months. Each test item states a communication behavior which is developmentally appropriate for the age group in which it is listed. The examiner checks each behavior which the child exhibits during an observation period lasting a minimum of three days and a maximum of two weeks. The scoring procedure yields a developmental communication age, while a graphic profile sheet depicts the child's specific strengths and weaknesses. The measurement procedures listed in the test are suggested as only one means of eliciting the behavior required to meet passing criteria for each item. The examiner is encouraged to adapt testing procedures or materials to the child's handicapping condition(s) so as not to penalize the child for sensory or physical impairments. Examiner required. Not suitable for group use. *Source:* M. Beth Langley, c/o 5436 27th St. South, St. Petersburg, Florida 33712

GILMORE ORAL READING TEST *John V. Gilmore and Eunice C. Gilmore*

Assesses the oral reading abilities of students grades 1-8. Used for program planning and academic placement.

Oral reading test measures three aspects of oral reading ability: accuracy, comprehension, and rate. The spiral-bound booklet of reading paragraphs and the manual of directions are needed to administer the test which takes 15-20 minutes. A separate record blank is needed for each child tested. A five-level classification of accuracy, rate, and comprehension is provided, along with stanines and grade-equivalents for accuracy and comprehension scores. Available in two alternate and equivalent forms, C and D. Examiner required and evaluated. Not suitable for group use. Examination kit (includes manual and record blank) costs $5.00. *Publisher:* The Psychological Corporation

---

GOLDMAN-FRISTOE-WOODCOCK TEST OF AUDITORY
DISCRIMINATION   *Ronald Goldman, Macalyne Fristoe and
Richard W. Woodcock*

Assesses ability to discriminate speech sounds in quiet and in noise. Screens for deficiencies in speech-sound discrimination that may contribute to learning difficulties in children ages 3 and up.

Two part test 20-30 minutes in length. Examiner presents test plate containing four drawings to the subject, using an audio cassette for standardized presentation. The subject responds to a stimulus word by pointing to one of the drawings. Total error scores can be converted to age-based percentile ranks and standard scores. An error analysis may be completed to explore further the types of errors made on either subtest. Examiner required and evaluated. Not for group use. Materials include test plates bound in an easel, manual, 50 response forms and test audio-cassette for $38.50. *Publisher:* American Guidance Service

HAPTIC INTELLIGENCE SCALE   *Harriet C. Shurrager and
Phil S. Shurrager*

Measures the intelligence of blind and partially-sighted individuals. Used as a substitute for or supplement to, the Wechsler Adult Intelligence Scale.

The timed test of 90 minutes duration contains seven nonverbal (except for instructions) task assessments. The tests are: Digit Symbol, Object Assembly, Block Design, Plan-of-Search, Object Completion, Pattern Board, and Bead Arithmetic. Wechsler's procedures were followed in establishing age categories and statistical treatment of the data. Examiner required. Not for group use. Complete kit (includes 25 record blanks, testing materials and manual) costs $450.00. *Publisher:* Stoelting Co.

HEADACHE CHECKLIST   *Leonard Epstein*

Assesses the nature and severity of an individual's headache symptoms. The 23 item paper-pencil checklist consists of three parts. Part one (seven items) gathers general background information related to the individual's headaches, such as medical problems, stressful situations which may be related to the headaches, and the frequency and duration of the headaches. Part two (15 items) investigates more specific headache symptoms. Each item describes a symptom often reported by sufferers of severe headaches. The individual rates each item as it applies to his own headaches on a five-point scale from "always" to "never." Part three (one item) requires the individual to indicate on a set of four drawings of a head (front, back, right side, and left side) the location of the headaches. May be administered to children in the form of a structured interview with the child and/or parents. Examiner required and evaluated. Suitable for group use. *Source:* Reprints

| *Refer to page(s):* | *Test Title* |

available from Robert D. Lyman, Ph.D., Executive Director, Brewer-Porch Children's Center, The University of Alabama, P.O. Box 2232, University, Alabama 35486; (205) 556-4141 or 348-7236.

78, 111, 112, 127   HISKEY-NEBRASKA TEST OF LEARNING APTITUDE
Marshall S. Hiskey

Evaluates learning potential of deaf children (ages 2½-18½) and those with hearing, speech or language handicaps. Used to establish how deaf individuals compare with those who can hear.

A battery of 11 subtests measures visual-motor coordination, sequential memory, visual retention or stimuli in a series, visual discrimination and matching. The tests are: Bead Patterns, Memory for Color, Picture Identification, Picture Association, Paper Folding Patterns, Visual Attention Span, Block Patterns, Completion of Drawings, Memory for Digits, Puzzle Block Picture Analogies, and Spatial Reasoning. Testing time is 50-60 minutes. Scales have norms for comparing hearing and deaf children. Examiner required and evaluated. Not suitable for group use. Complete set (includes all materials, manual and record forms) costs $96.00. *Publisher:* The Hiskey-Nebraska Test

213, 214   HOME OBSERVATION FOR MEASUREMENT OF THE ENVIRONMENT (HOME)   *Bettye M. Caldwell, Robert H. Bradley and staff*

Measures the quality of the home environment for infants and preschool children to six years of age. Used for research purposes.

Forty-five or 55 item (depending on which form is used) paper-pencil inventory assesses the following aspects of a child's home environment: frequency and stability of adult contact, amount of developmental and vocal stimulation, need gratification, emotional climate, avoidance of restriction on motor and exploratory behavior, available play materials, and home characteristics indicative of parental concern with achievement. The examiner completes the inventory on the basis of a one hour visit to the child's home (while the child is awake). The parent is interviewed and parent-child interactions are observed during this period. Roughly two-thirds of the items are based on observed behaviors; one-third are based on parental report. All items are scored plus (+) or minus (-) depending on whether or not the behavior is observed during the visit or the parent reports that the conditions or events are characteristic of the home environment.

The form for infants and toddlers (45 items) provides a total score and scores for six subscales; emotional and verbal responsibility of parent, acceptance of child's behavior, organization of physical and temporal environment, provision of appropriate play materials, parent involvement with child, and opportunities for variety in daily stimulation. The form for preschoolers (55 items) provides a total score and scores for eight subscales: learning stimulation, language stimulation, physical environment, warmth and affection, academic stimulation, modeling, variety in experience, and acceptance. Testing time is approximately one hour. Examiner required and evaluated. Contact publisher for cost. *Publisher:* University of Arkansas at Little Rock/Center for Child Development

130

HOUSTON TEST FOR LANGUAGE DEVELOPMENT
Margaret Crabtree

Assesses verbal and nonverbal communication abilities in children from birth to six years of age. Diagnoses problems resulting from emotional deprivation, neurological disabilities, retardation, auditory or visual-motor deficits or environmental linguistic influence. Used to plan specific intervention procedures and to monitor the child's progress.

The multiple item verbal and nonverbal checklist of communication abilities at two age levels takes approximately 30 minutes to complete. The Infant Scale consists of an observational checklist of linguistic and pre-linguistic skills characteristic of normal infants up to 18 months of age. The 2-6 Year test consists of 18 subtests which include both verbal and nonverbal tasks. The 18 subtests include: Self-Identity, Vocabulary, Body Orientation, Gesture, Auditory Judgments, Oral Monitoring with Toys, Sentence Length, Temporal Content, Syntax, Prepositions, Serial Counting, Counting Objects, Imitates Linguistic Structure, Imitated Prosodic Patterns, Imitates Designs, Drawing, Oral Monitoring while Drawing and Telling About Drawing. The manual provides normative data and information on reliability and validity. Individual child record forms serve as a work sheet, score sheet and permanent record of the test performance. Examiner required and evaluated. Not for group use. Complete kit (includes 25 record forms, vocabulary cards, necessary manipulatives and manual) costs $78.00. *Publisher:* Stoelting Co.

28, 92, 116, 117,
130, 152, 192

ILLINOIS TEST OF PSYCHOLINGUISTIC ABILITIES (ITPA)
Samuel A. Kirk, James F. McCarthy and Winifred D. Kirk

Assesses use and understanding of psycholinguistic abilities in children ages 2-10; facilitates assessment of a child's abilities for purposes of remediation.

The 300 item verbal and paper-pencil test evaluates a child's cognitive and perceptual abilities in three areas: communication, psycholinguistic processes, and levels of organization. There are 12 subtests: Auditory Reception, Visual Reception, Auditory Association, Visual Association, Verbal Expression, Manual Expression, Grammatic Closure, Visual Closure, Auditory Sequential Memory, Visual Sequential Memory, Auditory Closure, and Sound Blending. Testing time is approximately 60 minutes. Examiner required; scoring is by hand key. Not for group use. Test kit includes Examiner's Manual, two picture books, chips, picture sequences, picture strips, six objects for the verbal and manual expression test, $33\frac{1}{3}$ rpm record, and carry case for $110.00. *Publisher:* University of Illinois Press

44

IOWA TESTS OF BASIC SKILLS, FORMS 7 AND 8 (ITBS)
A.N. Hieronymous, E.F. Lindquist and H.D. Hoover

Assesses the development of basic academic skills in students Grades K-9. Identifies individual student's strengths and weaknesses and evaluates the effectiveness of instructional programs.

All levels assess combinations of the following skills: vocabulary, reading, language, spelling, capitalization, punctuation, usage, work-study, visual materials, reference materials, mathematics concepts, problem solving, and computation. Listening and word analysis are also measured at the primary level. Levels 5-8 (157-539 items each), for use with Grades K-3.5, comprise the Primary Battery, which uses machine-scorable test booklets. Levels 9-14 (350-465 items each), for use with Grades 3-8/9, comprise the Multilevel Edition, which uses test booklets and separate answer sheets. Testing time varies from 150-235 minutes. Normed concurrently with the Cognitive Abilities Test for reliable comparisons between attained and expected achievement scores. Examiner required. Hand key or computer scoring available. Suitable for group use. Contact publisher for cost. *Publisher:* The Riverside Publishing Company

44

IOWA TESTS OF EDUCATIONAL DEVELOPMENT (ITED):
FORMS X7 AND Y7 *E.F. Lindquist and Leonard S. Feldt*

Measures adolescent and adult learning skills and abilities and general educational development. Identifies strengths and weaknesses in content skill areas (although not a test of specific curriculum areas or minimal competencies) and monitors educational development.

The 357 item paper-pencil test takes 240 minutes to complete. Factors measured include: recognizing good writing, solving quantitative problems, critically analyzing social issues, understanding nontechnical scientific reports, recognizing sound scientific inquiry methods, using common information sources and tools, and perceiving subtle meanings and moods in literature. Available in two levels (Level I for grades 9-10; Level II for grades 11-12) with overlapping items. Norm referenced. Examiner required. Scoring is by hand key or computer scoring. Suitable for group use. Rental and scoring for student $2.30 and a review set is available for $4.10. *Publisher:* Science Research Associates, Inc.

JUNIOR EYSENCK PERSONALITY INVENTORY (JEPI)
Sybil B. G. Eysenck

Measures the major personality dimensions of children ages 7-16. Used as a research instrument.

The 60 item paper-pencil yes-no inventory measures Extraversion-Introversion (24 items), Neuroticism-Stability (24 items). Twelve of the items constitute a falsification scale for the detection of response distortion. Testing time is approximately 10 minutes. Scores (hand keyed) are provided for E- Extraversion, N- Neuroticism and L- Lie. Norms available for selected samples of majority and minority children. Examiner required. Suitable for group use. Available in Spanish. Specimen set (includes manual and one copy of all forms) is available for $3.00. *Publisher:* Educational and Industrial Testing Service

KAUFMAN ASSESSMENT BATTERY FOR CHILDREN
(K-ABC)   *Alan S. Kaufman and Nadeen L. Kaufman*

Measures the intelligence and achievement of children ages 2½-12½. Defines intelligence as ability of children to process information and solve problems. Used for psychological and clinical assessment of the learning disabled and mentally retarded, minority group and preschool assessment, and neuropsychological research.

Sixteen computer scored subtests of mental processing skills and achievement. There are: three subtests of sequential processing, seven subtests of simultaneous processing, and six subtests of achievement (acquired knowledge, reading, and arithmetic). Examiner presents to the child a test plate containing a stimulus item, gives a verbal direction, and the child responds. Directions may be given in the child's native language, or with gestures for the hearing impaired. Battery time varies in length from 35-85 minutes depending on level. Yields four major scores: sequential processing, simultaneous processing, mental processing composite, and achievement. Each score has a mean of 100 and a standard deviation of 15. National percentile ranks, age and grade equivalents, and sociocultural percentile ranks are also available. Standardization is based on 1980 census data. Separate scales for mental processing and achievement were normed on the same sample. Examiner must have necessary qualifications to use the test. Not for group use. Spanish version available. Materials include test plates bound into three easel kits, interpretive manual, 118 photo series cards, seven matrix chips, nine triangles, 25 individual test records, and a container for $135.00. *Publisher:* American Guidance Service

KEYMATH DIAGNOSTIC ARITHMETIC TEST
Austin Connolly, William Nachtman and E. M. Pritchett

Diagnoses childrens' (grades K-6) arithmetic skills to identify areas of weakness for remedial instruction.

The three category test covering: Content, (numeration, fractions, geometry and symbols), Operations, (addition, subtraction, multiplication, division, mental computation, and numerical reasoning), and Applications, (word problems, missing elements, money, measurement and time). The examiner displays a test plate to the student and asks a test question, recording the response on an individual record form. Only those items within the student's functional range are administered. Materials include test plates bound into an easel, manual and a package of 25 diagnostic records. Grade equivalents, grade percentile ranks, and normal curve equivalents for grades 2-6 are available. Diagnostic information provided includes total test performance, area performance in content, operations, and applications, subtest performance, and subtest item performance. A KeyMath Metric Supplement to assess metric measurement skills is available. Examiner required and evaluated. Not for group use. Complete kit costs $46.50. *Publisher:* American Guidance Service

153

KUDER PREFERENCE RECORD, VOCATIONAL, FORM CP *Frederic Kuder*

Evaluates occupational interests of students and adults. Used in vocational counseling and employee screening and placement. Identifies reading subject areas of special interest.

The 168 item paper-pencil test measures interests in ten occupational areas: outdoor, mechanical, scientific, computational, persuasive, artistic, literary, musical, social science, and clerical. Subject uses pin to indicate a "most liked" and "least liked" activity for each group of three activities. High school reading level required. Self-administered and scoring is by hand key. Suitable for group use. Specimen set is $5.50; no charge for manual if requested when ordering. *Publisher:* Science Research Associates

78, 111, 112, 128

LEITER INTERNATIONAL PERFORMANCE SCALE (LIPS)
Russell G. Leiter

Measures intelligence and mental age for all individuals 2-18 years old including the deaf, cerebral palsied, non-English speaking, and culturally disadvantaged in a non verbal task assessment test.

The subject is required to match blocks with corresponding characteristic strips positioned in a sturdy wooden frame. The difficulty of the task increases at each level. The categories measured are: Concretistics (matching of specific relationships), Symbolic Transformation (judging relationships between two events), Quantitative Discriminations, Spatial Imagery, Genus Matching, Progression Discriminations, and Immediate Recall. Test materials include three trays of blocks and strips that make up 54 subtests. Tray 1 covers years 2-7, Tray 2 covers years 8-12 and Tray 3 covers years 13-17. Instructions for all age levels are delivered by easily-

                            Test Title

learned pantomime. Testing time is approximately 45 minutes. The LIPS yields Mental Age and I.Q. The Binet-type year scale has four tests at each year level from Year II through Year XVI and six tests at year XVII. Examiner required and evaluated. The test kit includes all materials, wooden frame, carrying case, 100 record cards and manual for $495.00. *Publisher:* Stoelting Co.

LURIA-NEBRASKA NEUROPSYCHOLOGICAL BATTERY
Charles J. Golden, Thomas A. Hammeke, and Arnold D. Purisch

Assesses a broad range of neuropsychological functions for persons age 15 and older. Used to diagnose specific cerebral dysfunction and to select and assess rehabilitation programs in a 269 item verbal, observational test.

The discrete, scored items produce a profile for the following 14 scales: Motor, Rhythm, Tactile, Visual, Preceptive Speech, Expressive Speech, Writing, Reading, Arithmetic, Memory, Intellectual, Pathognomonic, Left Hemisphere, and Right Hemisphere. The battery (1½-2½ hours in duration) has the ability to diagnose the presence of cerebral dysfunction, as well as to determine lateralization and localization. Test may be computer scored or hand keyed. Examiner required. Not for group use. The test materials include: six stimulus cards, one tape cassette, and a few commonly available items such as a comb, a quarter, and a stopwatch. A manual provides instructions for administering the test, evidence of reliability and validity, interpretive guides, and copies of the *Administration and Scoring Booklet* and the *Patient Response Booklet*. The *Administration and Scoring Booklet* includes the Profile Form and Computation of Critical Level Tables. It is used to record all scores during the administration and provides the verbal instructions to be read to the patient. *The Patient Response Booklet* is provided for those items requiring written answers. Complete kit costs $137.50. *Publisher:* Western Psychological Services

MAXFIELD-BUCHHOLZ SOCIAL MATURITY SCALE FOR BLIND PRE-SCHOOL CHILDREN   *Kathryn E. Maxfield and Sandra Buchholz*

Measures the social maturity of blind children ages 0-8 years. The multiple item paper-pencil observational inventory and parent-interview guide assesses the developmental skills and social maturity of blind infants and pre-school children. The examiner's ratings are based on personal observations in the home setting and supplemented by parent interview. This scale is an adaption of Vineland Social Maturity Scale. Examiner required and evaluated. Not suitable for group use. Twenty-five record blanks and manual costs $7.00. *Publisher:* The American Foundation for the Blind

McCARTHY SCALES OF CHILDREN'S ABILITIES

Assesses intellectual and motor development of children 2½ to 8½ years of age.

Refer to page(s):	*Test Title*

The test measures six aspects of children's thinking, motor, and mental abilities: Verbal Ability, Short Term Memory, Numerical Ability, Perceptual Performance, Motor Coordination, and Lateral Dominance. Verbal, Numerical, and Perceptual performance scales are combined to yield the General Cognitive Index. Items involve puzzles, toy-like materials and game-like tasks. Testing time is 45-60 minutes. Six of the component scales which predict the child's ability to cope with school work in the early grades form the McCarthy Screening Test. Examiner required and evaluated. Not suitable for group use. Complete Set (includes all necessary equipment, manual, 25 record forms and 25 drawing booklets) costs $150.00. *Publisher:* The Psychological Corporation

17   MEMORY-FOR-DESIGNS TEST (MFD)
Frances K. Graham and Barbara S. Kendall

Assesses perceptual-motor coordination in individuals ages 8½ to 60. Used to differentiate between functional behavior disorders and those associated with brain injury.

The 15 items consist of designs on cardboard cards. Subject is shown a design for five seconds, then attempts to draw it from memory. This procedure is repeated for each of the 15 items. Materials include manual which summarizes research with the MFD. Testing time is 10 minutes with scoring by hand key. Diagnostic testing and evaluation should be closely supervised by a clinical or school psychologist, psychiatrist, neurologist, or pediatrician. Examiner required and evaluated. Not suitable for group use. Complete kit costs $17.00. *Publisher:* Psychological Test Specialists

74, 78, 112, 128   MERRILL-PALMER SCALE   *Rachel Stutsman*

Measures intelligence in children age 18 months through four years of age. Used as a substitute for, or a supplement to, the Binet Scale.

The 19 task assessment and oral response test measures language skills, motor skills, dexterity, and matching. The 19 subtests are: Stutsman Color Matching Test, Wallin Pegboards A & B, Stutsman Buttoning Test, Stutsman Stick and String, Scissors, Stutsman Language Test, Stutsman Picture Formboards 1, 2, & 3, Mare-Foal Formboard, Seguin-Goddard Formboard, Pintner-Manikin Test, Decroly Matching Game, Stutsman Nested Cubes, Woodworth-Wells Association Test, Stutsman Copying Test, Stutsman Pyramid Test, Stutsman Little Pink Tower Test, and Kohs Blocks. The test deals directly with the problem of resistance in the testing situation and provides a comprehensive listing of the many factors influencing a child's willingness to cooperate. Refused and omitted items are considered when arriving at a total score which may then be converted to mental age, sigma value, or percentile rank. The test is significant in its complete independence from The Stanford-Binet Scale. All subtests may be ordered separately. Examiner required and evaluated. Not suitable for group use. Complete kit (includes all tests and 50 record blanks) costs $325.00 *Publisher:* Stoelting Co.

131

METROPOLITAN ACHIEVEMENT TEST: 5TH EDITION-SURVEY BATTERY   *Irving H. Balow, Roger Farr, Thomas P. Hogan, and George A. Prescott*

Assesses school achievement of children in grades K.0-12.9. Used for measuring performance of large groups of students.

Multiple item paper-pencil tests are divided into 8 levels: Preprimer, Grade K.0-K.5; Primer, Grade K.5-1.4; Primary 1, Grade 1.5-2.4; Primary 2, Grade 2.5-3.4; Elementary, Grade 3.5-4.9; Intermediate, Grade 5.0-6.9; Advanced 1, Grade 7.0-9.9; and Advanced 2, Grade 10.0-12.9. The Basic Battery for all eight levels consists of tests in reading comprehension, mathematics and language. The Complete Battery for Primary 1 through Advanced 1 adds Social Science and Science tests to the basic three. Scoring is by hand key with options for machine scoring and scoring service. Materials include two alternate and equivalent forms, JS and KS, at Primer through Advanced 2 levels. Metropolitan Reading, Mathematics and Language Instructional Tests provide more in-depth analyses than does the Survey Battery. Examiner required. Suitable for group use. Specimen sets (includes test, Teacher's Manual for Administering and Interpreting—specify level) costs $8.00 each. *Publisher:* The Psychological Corporation

43, 59, 151

THE MINNESOTA MULTIPHASIC PERSONALITY INVENTORY: THE INDIVIDUAL FORM (MMPI) *Starke R. Hathaway and Charnley McKinley*

Assesses individual personality. Used for clinical diagnosis and research on psychopathology.

The inventory is a 550 item true-false test of ten clinical variables or factors of personality: hypochondriasis, depression, hysteria, psychopathic-deviate, masculinity-femininity, paranoia, psychasthenia, schizophrenia, hypomania and social introversion. Scores are also obtained on four validity scales: Question, Lie (L), Validity (F), and Defensiveness (K). Materials include 550 cards to which the individual responds. Computer scoring available; may be hand keyed. Personality scores are plotted on profile sheets reflecting standard deviations from the Mean. Test time is 90 minutes. Old and New Group Forms are also available. Examiner required and evaluated. Available in 45 languages. Cost for 25 recording sheets, item cards and answer keys (includes manual) is $77.00. *Publisher:* University of Minnesota Press—distributed exclusively by NCS Professional Assessment Services

Refer to page(s):	*Test Title*

151

MINNESOTA RATE OF MANIPULATION TESTS
Employment Stabilization Research Institute, University of Minnesota

Measures finger-hand-arm dexterity. Used for employee selection for jobs requiring manual dexterity, and in vocational and rehabilitation training programs.

The five test battery measures: Placing, Turning, Displacing, One Hand Turning and Placing, and Two Hand Turning and Placing. Materials consist of two test boards, each with 60 round holes in four rows, and 60 round blocks, painted orange on the top half and yellow on the lower half. Two blocks are transferred from one board to the other, being turned and moved in various ways. The subject is then instructed to transfer all pegs back to the board using only one hand. In the turning test, the pegs are left in the board and the subject removes each block one at a time with one hand, turns it over, transfers it to the free hand and replaces it in the same position on the board. All tests are timed (10 minutes each) and repeated for four complete trials. The Displacing and Turning Tests are suitable for use with the Blind. Examiner required and evaluated. Suitable for group use. The board, blocks, and 50 individual record forms, and a manual are included in a vinyl carrying case for $167.50. *Publisher:* American Guidance Service

150, 192

MOTOR-FREE VISUAL PERCEPTION TEST (MVPT)
Ronald R. Colarusso and Donald D. Hammill

Assesses visual perception in children (ages 4-8) and older individuals who have motor problems. Used for screening, diagnostic, and research purposes, especially with those who are learning disabled, motorically impaired, physically handicapped, or mentally retarded.

The test is a 36 item point-and-tell test taking 10 minutes to complete. The subject is shown a line drawing and asked to match the stimulus by pointing to one of a multiple-choice set of other drawings. Materials consist of test plates and recording forms. Examiner required; scoring is by hand key. Not for group use. The test kit (includes manual, test plates and 50 recording forms) costs $32.50. *Publisher:* Academic Therapy Publications

43

THE NEONATAL BEHAVIORAL ASSESSMENT SCALE
T. Berry Brazelton

Evaluates selected reflexes, motor responses, and interactive behavioral responses of newborn infants. Predicts cognitive and emotional patterns in the infant. Used by medical professionals and paraprofessionals to teach parents about their newborn's state changes, temperament, and individual behavior patterns and to improve early health and development care.

Test Title

The forty-seven item assessment procedure measures neonatal reflex responses in a behavioral context. Twenty-seven items measure the infant's inherent neurological capacities, as well as responses to certain sets of stimuli. The behavioral section includes: items that assess how soon the infant diminishes responses to stimuli of light, sound, and pinprick to the heel; auditory and visual items that determine how much and when the infant attends to, focuses on, and gives feedback in response to animate or inanimate stimuli; items assessing the degree and organization of the infant's motor coordination and control of motor activities throughout the examination; items assessing the infant's rate and amount of change during periods of alertness and states, color, activity, and peaks of excitement throughout the examination; items assessing how much, how soon, and how effectively the infant uses his own resources to quiet and console himself when upset or distressed (this category includes the graduated efforts of the caregiver to intervene and quiet the infant); and items assessing the infant's smiling and amount of cuddling behaviors. A second section of the scale includes 20 items assessing specific elicited reflexes and movements on a three-point scale (hypoactive, normal, and hyperactive). The assessment procedure can be completed in 20-30 minutes. Proper use of the scale calls for repeated assessments up to the age of one month.

All scale items are scored in a manner which takes into account the infant's state (ranging from deep sleep to intense crying) at the time of testing. Some of the 27 behavioral items are scored during a specific interaction with the infant (such as his head turning in response to a voice), but most are scored according to total continuous observations that are made throughout the entire assessment examination. For example, state changes, color changes, periods of alertness, and peaks of excitement are observed through the examination and scored at the conclusion.

All persons using the scale must be trained in the proper administration of test items, order of examination procedures, optimal condition of treating, and method of scoring. A list of trained examiners who can provide training may be obtained by writing directly to the principal investigator (Brazelton). It is essential that each examiner have a wide range of experience in assessing normal infants as a basis for scoring and interpreting the results of this scale. Examiner required and evaluated. Not suitable for group use. Contact publisher concerning cost and availability of the manual (revised second edition). *Publisher:* Lippincott/Harper Publishers, Inc.

NORTHWESTERN SYNTAX SCREENING TEST (NSST)
Laura L. Lee

Measures a child's (ages 3-7) syntactic development. Used to identify difficient children who need futher evaluation.

The NSST is a screening test in which the child is asked to

respond to short verbal statements by picking out a picture that the statement best describes or by repeating an appropriate statement pertaining to the picture. Testing time is 15-25 minutes. Receptive and expressive language abilities are evaluated. Examiner required. Not suitable for group use. The test and 100 answer forms cost $19.95. *Publisher:* Northwestern University Press

9, 19, 44, 61, 117,   PEABODY INDIVIDUAL ACHIEVEMENT TEST (PIAT)
118, 152, 192, 193   *Lloyd M. Dunn and Fredrick C. Markwardt, Jr.*

Provides an overview of individual scholastic attainment in children ages 5 and up. Used to screen for areas of weakness requiring more detailed diagnostic testing.

The 402 item test consists of mathematics (84 items), reading recognition (84 items), reading comprehension (66 items), spelling (84 items), and general information (84 items), including science, social studies, fine arts and sports requiring 30-50 minutes. Examiner required and evaluated. Not suitable for group use. Materials include two easel kits containing test plates, 25 record booklets, and a manual for $68.50. Derived scores are grade equivalents, grade percentile ranks, age equivalents, age percentile ranks, and standard scores by age or grade. *Publisher:* American Guidance Service

42, 94, 115, 116,   PEABODY PICTURE VOCABULARY TEST-REVISED
129, 130, 152   (PPVT-R) *Lloyd M. Dunn and Leota M. Dunn*

Measures hearing vocabulary for standard American English, estimates verbal ability and scholastic aptitude in children ages 2½ and up. Used with non-English speaking students; to screen for mental retardation or giftedness; as a part of a comprehensive battery; and to screen applicants for jobs requiring good aural vocabulary.

The untimed 175 item "point-to" response test measures receptive vocabulary in English. Test items, arranged in order of increasing difficulty, consist of plates of four pictures. Subjects are shown a plate and asked to point to the picture which corresponds to the stimulus word. Only those plates within a subject's ability range are administered. Age-based norms include: standard scores, percentile ranks, stanines, and age equivalents. Examiner required and evaluated. Complete kit includes: 175 test plates bound in an easel, manual, 25 individual record forms, and shelf box for $31.00. Available in two forms, L and M. Special Plastic Plate Edition available. *Publisher:* American Guidance Service

180, 181   PEER NOMINATION INVENTORY OF DEPRESSION
                           (PNID) *Monroe M. Lefkowitz and Edward P. Tesiny*

Identifies depressed and severely depressed children based on the ratings of their peers. Used for research in childhood depression.

                 Test Title

The 19 item paper-pencil inventory consists of 13 depression, 4 happiness, and 2 popularity items. Each item asks a question such as "who often plays alone?" or "who often smiles?" The items are read aloud to a classroom of children who mark on a class roster each of their peers whom they feel "best fit the question." The children may indicate as many peers for each item as they wish, but may not nominate themselves. Each child receives two scores: an item score reflecting the number of times the child was selected by his peers for each item and a total score reflecting a sum of the item scores. High scores identify children who exhibit depressed intellectual functioning, poor social functioning and diminished ebullience (primary symptoms of childhood depression). Examiner required and evaluated. Suitable for group use. *Source:* (1980). *Journal of Consulting and Clinical Psychology, 48* (1), 43-50: requests for reprints should be sent to Monroe M. Lefkowitz, New York State Department of Mental Hygiene, 44 Holland Avenue, Albany, New York 12229.

PENNSYLVANIA BI-MANUAL WORKSAMPLE
John R. Roberts

Measures manual dexterity and eye-hand coordination in individuals 16-39 years.

It is a multiple-operation manual dexterity test. Individual is presented with an 8 x 24 inch board containing 100 holes (arranged in 10 rows) and a set of nuts and bolts, to test finger dexterity of both hands, whole movement of both arms, eye-hand coordination, and bi-manual coordination. The individual grasps a nut between thumb and index finger of one hand and a bolt between the thumb and index finger of the other hand, then turns the bolt into the nut and places both in a hole in the board. Twenty practice motions are allowed, and 80 motions are timed. Disassembly reverses the process and involves timing 100 motions. Up to four persons can be tested at once provided each has a separate board. Testing time is 12 minutes. Assembly and disassembly times can be converted to percentage ranks and standard scores. A special supplement contains directions for administering test to blind persons. Examiner required and evaluated. Suitable for group use. Materials include the board, nuts and bolts, 50 record forms and a vinyl carrying case for $98.50. *Publisher:* American Guidance Service

PERSONALITY INVENTORY FOR CHILDREN (PIC)
Robert D. Wirt, David Lachar, James E. Klinedist, Philip D. Seat, and William E. Broen

Evaluates the personality attributes of children ages 3-16. Used by professionals for counseling and identification of learning and social disabilities.

The 600 item paper-pencil , true-false inventory is filled out by a parent. It provides comprehensive profiles based on the model of the Minnesota Multiphasic Personality Inventory (MMPI). A total of 33 scales are measured. The 16 primary scales are graphically presented on the Profile Form, they consist of three validity scales and the following clinical and screening scales: Adjustment, Development, Family Relations, Anxiety, Social Skills, Achievement, Somatic Concern, Delinquency, Psychosis, Intellectual Screening, Depression, Withdrawal, and Hyperactivity. An additional 17 experimental scales (not included on the Profile Form) are also provided: Adolescent Maladjustment, Ego Strength, Infrequency, K (defensiveness), Sex Role, Somatization, Aggression, Cerebral Dysfunction, Excitement, Internalization, Learning Disability Prediction, Asocial Behavior, Delinquency Prediction, Externalization, Introversion-Extroversion, Reality Distortion, and Social Desirablity. Norms and profiles are available for two age groups: 3-5 years and 6-16 years. Revised format allows administration of two short forms of inventory, providing information on shortened Clinical Scales and Factor Scales. Examiner-administered. Not for group use. Scoring is by hand key; computer scoring available. Complete kit costs $42.20. *Publisher:* Western Psychological Services

112, 191

PICTORIAL TEST OF INTELLIGENCE   *Joseph L. French*

Measures general ability of three to eight year old children. Used for curriculum planning and evaluation.

The test is a multiple item, oral, picture test in six sections. The subtests are: Picture Vocabulary, Information and Comprehension, Form Discrimination, Similarities, Size and Number, and Immediate Recall. The examiner presents picture cards on which are represented four possible answers and asks questions of the child. The cards are designed so that the examiner, by observing eye movement, can also determine the response of children who are physically handicapped. Testing time is approximately 45 minutes. Examiner required. Scoring is by hand key. Not for group use. Materials include cards, manual and record forms for $190.00. *Publisher:* Institute of Psychological Research, Inc.

153

PRG INTEREST INVENTORY

Measures vocational/occupational interests of visually handicapped individuals.

The 150 item paper-pencil questionnaire assesses interests in the following ten areas: mechanical, computational, scientific, persuasive, artistic, literary, musical, social service, clerical, and outdoor. Questionnaires and answer sheets presented in large print format. Examiner required and evaluated. Suitable for group use. Test kit (includes test booklet, 10 answer sheets, and instructions for administration and scoring) costs $10.00. *Publisher:* Associated Services for the Blind

| *Test Title*

PSYCHOEDUCATIONAL PROFILE (PEP)

Measures learning abilities and characteristics of autistic and related developmentally disordered children. Used to establish individualized special education curricula or home programs for developmentally disabled children who were previously regarded as untestable.

Test results comprise a learning profile reflecting the individual characteristics of the child. This profile is translated into an appropriately individualized special education curriculum or home program according to the teaching strategies described in Volume II of the manual. Examiner required and evaluated. Test kit includes the following standard materials required for uniform and accurate administration of the test: bubbles, tactile blocks, kaleidoscope, call bell, clay, cat and dog puppets, three-piece geometric formboard, four-piece formboard, three-piece mitten formboard, four-piece kitten puzzle, six-piece cow puzzle, matching item, clapper, whistle, writing booklet and lotto letters, pouch and objects, felt board and nine felt pieces, scissors, blocks and box, number cards, beads and string, function cards, hand bell, category cards I and II, and language for $200.00. Materials needed but not provided include: mirror, candy, large ball, styrofoam cups, and a wheeled walker. The manual *(Individualized Assessment for Autistic and Developmentally Disabled Children)* is published in two volumes by University Park Press. Volume I describes the psychoeducational profile, and Volume II discusses teaching strategies for parents and professionals. *Publisher:* Orange Industries

PURDUE PERCEPTUAL-MOTOR SURVEY (PPMS)
Eugene G. Roach and Newell C. Kephart

Identifies preschool to eight year old children with perceptual-motor disabilities, tracing a child's development to the point where developmental dysfunction occurs. Assists teachers in developing remedial programs.

The 22 item task assessment test measures laterality, directionality, and perceptual-motor matching skills. Walking board and jumping tests measure balance and posture. Body Image and Differentiation tests include naming ten parts of the body, imitation of movements, obstacle course, Krauss-Weber test, and angels in the snow. A chalkboard test for rhythmic writing, ocular control, and form perception measures Perceptual-Motor Matching Skills. Examiner required and evaluated. Not for group use. Twenty-five surveys cost $16.50. *Publisher:* Charles E. Merrill Publishing Company

QUICK NEUROLOGICAL SCREENING TEST
Harold M. Sterling, Margaret Mutti and Norma V. Spalding

Assesses neurological integration as it relates to the learning abilities of children, teen-agers, and adults.

The test is a multiple task, nonverbal test of 15 functions, each involving a motor task similar to those observed in neurological pediatric examinations. The areas measured include: maturity of motor development, skill in controlling large and small muscles, motor planning and sequencing, sense of rate and rhythm, spatial organization, visual and auditory perceptual skills, balance and cerebellar-vestibular function, and disorders of attention. Examiner required and evaluated. Testing time is approximately 20 minutes. Materials include geometric form reproduction sheets and flipcards printed with directions for administration and scoring for $20.50. Scoring occurs simultaneously and neurodevelopmental difficulties result in an increasingly larger numerical score. *Publisher:* Academic Therapy Publications

35, 191   QUICK TEST (QT)   *R.B. Ammons and C.H. Ammons*

Assesses individual intelligence in individuals ages 2 and older. May be used for evaluation of severely physically handicapped, those with short attention spans, or uncooperative subjects.

The 50 item test of general intelligence has subject look at plates with four line drawings and indicate which picture best illustrates the meaning of a given word. Answers are usually given by pointing. Requires no reading, writing or speaking. Usual administration involves presentation of 15 to 20 of the items and takes 3-10 minutes. Items are administered until there have been six consecutive passes and six consecutive failures. Examiner required and evaluated; scoring is by hand key. Materials include plates with stimulus pictures, and three alternate forms. Complete Kit (includes manual, 3 plates, 100 record sheets, instruction cardboard and item cardboard) costs $16.00. *Publisher:* Psychological Test Specialists

28, 30, 34   REITAN EVALUATION OF HEMISPHERIC ABILITIES AND BRAIN IMPROVEMENT TRAINING (REHABIT)
Ralph M. Reitan

Diagnoses neuropsychological functions that may be impaired or deficient in both adults and children who may be suffering from brain damage or neurological dysfunction, specific neurocortical training sequences are included.

The REHABIT is a task assessment and oral response test which measures three fundamental areas of brain function: verbal and language functions (left hemisphere); visual-spatial, manipulatory, and sequential abilities (right hemisphere); and abstraction, reasoning, logical analysis, and ability to understand the essential nature of problem-situations (cerebral cortical functioning). Based on the results of the testing, five tracks of remedial training have been developed. Track A contains equipment and procedures that are specifically designed for developing expressive and receptive language and verbal skills. Track B also specializes in language and verbal materials, but includes elements of abstraction, reasoning, logical analysis, and organization. Track C includes various tasks that do not depend upon particular content as much as they do on reasoning, organization, and abstracion. Track D also emphasizes abstraction but used material that requires the subject to deal with visual-spatial, sequential, and manipulatory skills. Track E specializes in tasks and materials that require the subject to exercise fundamental aspects of visual-spatial and manipulatory abilities. The training materials in each track are organized roughly from simple to complex; the subject is started at a level that is simple for him to perform satisfactorily. Examiner required and evaluated. Not for group use. For cost contact publisher. *Publisher:* Reitan Neuropsychology Laboratory

30, 42

REITAN-INDIANA NEUROPSYCHOLOGICAL TEST BATTERY FOR CHILDREN   *Ralph M. Reitan and others*

Assesses brain-behavior functioning in children ages 5-8 years. Used for clinical evaluation.

This battery of tests assesses the neurological functioning of young children, including: the Wechsler Intelligence Scale for Children, sensory perceptual tests, modifications of the Reitan-Indiana Aphasia Screening Test and the Halstead Neuropsychological Test Battery, and a number of additional tests (Color Form Test, Target Test, Matching Pictures Test, Progressive Figures Test, Marching Test, and Individual Performance Tests). This battery is related to the Halstead-Reitan Neuropsychological Test Batteries for adults and older children, but a number of adaptations have been made for use with this age group. The Category Test uses a different set of slides for stimuli and colored instead of numbered caps as the guide to lever choice on the answer panel. The Tactual Performance Test uses a 6-hole board in a horizontal instead of a vertical position. The Aphasia Screening Test deletes a number of items from the adult version, adds a number of simple procedures, and uses a different recording form. An electric finger tapping apparatus was devised because young children had trouble manipulating the manual apparatus. Examiner required and evaluated. Materials include: all necessary equipment, test stimuli, slide carousels, recording forms, and manual for administration, scoring, and evaluation of all tests for $1,115.00. Components may be purchased separately. *Publisher:* Reitan Neuropsychological Laboratory

60, 115, 193

RORSCHACH PSYCHODIAGNOSTIC TEST
Hermann Rorschach

Evaluates personality through projective technique in individuals ages 3 and older. Used in clinical evaluation.

The test is a ten card oral response projective personality test. The subject is asked to interpret what he sees in ten inkblots, based on the assumption that the individual's perceptions and associations are selected and organized in terms of his motivations, impulses, and other underlying aspects of personality. Extensive scoring systems have been developed. Although many variations are in use, this entry refers only to the Psychodiagnostic Plates first published in 1921. Materials include: inquiry charts, tabulation sheets, and set of 10 inkblots. Set of 10 Kodaslides of the inkblots may be imported on request. Trained examiner required. Examiner evaluates responses. Contact publisher for cost. *Publisher:* Hans Huber-distributed by Grune & Stratton (U.S.A.)

151

ROTTER INCOMPLETE SENTENCES BLANK
Julian B. Rotter

Assesses personality of adolescents and adults in a 40 item paper-pencil test. Items are stems of sentences to be completed by the subject. Responses may be classified into three categories: unhealthy responses, neutral responses, and positive or healthy responses. Self-administered. Examiner evaluated with scoring by hand key. Suitable for group use. Materials include a High School, College, and Adult Form. Twenty-five blanks (specify High School, College or Adult) costs $4.50; manual costs $7.00. *Publisher:* The Psychological Corporation

42

SEIZURE DISORDER SURVEY SCHEDULE
Barbara A. Balaschak and David I. Mostofsky

Assesses the nature, severity, and history of a child's seizure disorder and related treatment programs. Used for intake screening purposes with pediatric seizure disorder patients.

The 67 item paper-pencil structured interview guide assesses the frequency, onset, and nature of a child's seizures, as well as the child's neurological history, related medical and developmental history, present drug therapy and behavior treatment programs, and the interviewer's psycho-social impressions of the child. May be administered by trained paraprofessionals. Examiner required and evaluated. Not suitable for group use. *Source:* Mash, E.J., and Terdal, L.G. (Eds.). (1981). *Behavioral assessment of childhood disorders,* 618-625. New York: Guilford Press

152

SEQUENTIAL TESTS OF EDUCATIONAL PROGRESS: CIRCUS LEVELS A-D

Assesses achievement of preprimary-grade 3 students. Used to diagnose instructional needs of the child and evaluate curriculum.

This is a multiple item testing program (30 minutes per test) which includes subtests and teacher completed instruments. The test assesses children's interests, problem solving, prereading and reading skills, mathematics concepts and perceptual-motor coordination. Level A is for nursery school and beginning K; Level B, K.5-1.5; Level C, 1.5-2.5; Level D, 2.5-3.5. A slide presentation with accompanying script is available. "El Circo" is a Spanish version of Level A. Examiner required. Scoring is by hand key with

	Test Title

computer socring available. Suitable for group use. Contact publisher for cost. *Publisher:* CTB/McGraw-Hill

SEQUENTIAL TESTS OF EDUCATIONAL PROGRESS (STEP III: LEVELS E-J) *Educational Testing Service*

Measures achievement in language, mathematics, science, and social studies in grades 3.5-12.9. Used to assess individual and group academic mastery and to evaluate curriculum program.

This is a multiple item, comprehensive testing program (40 minutes per test) consisting of eight tests: Reading, Vocabulary, Writing Skills, Mathematic Computation, Mathematic and Basic Concepts, Study Skills/Listening, Social Studies, and Science. Designed for grades 3.5 to 12.9 with six levels available. To test across grade levels, multi-level tests are available and are selected on the basis of a short language and math "locator test" to determine the appropriate test level for each student. Examiner required. Scoring is by hand key with computer scoring available. Suitable for group use. Complete battery for 35 students (specify level) costs $34.65. *Publisher:* CTB/McGraw-Hill

SINGLE AND DOUBLE SIMULTANEOUS STIMULATION TEST (SDSS) *Carmen C. Centofanti and Aaron Smith*

Assesses children and adults suspected of having central nervous system diseases or injuries. May be used with patients with confirmed lesions.

This nonverbal, touch discriminations test measures the accuracy with which subjects can identify single and double simultaneous tactile stimulation applied to the cheek and/or hand. Tests specific somatosensory functions and takes only a few minutes to administer and score. Correctly identifies two of every three patients with diverse types of acute cerebral lesions, and one of every two with chronic lesions, plus other persisting functional deficits. Especially useful when used in combination with the Symbol Digit Modalities Test. Examiner required and evaluated. Not suitable for group use. Complete kit (includes 50 score sheets and manual) costs $7.50. *Publisher:* Western Psychological Services

SLOSSON INTELLIGENCE TEST (SIT)/SLOSSON ORAL READING TEST (SORT) *Richard L. Slosson*

Measures the mental age, IQ, and reading level of children and adults. Used by psychologists, guidance counselors, special educators, learning disabilities teachers, and remedial reading teachers to provide a quick assessment of a person's mental abilities.

The 195 item oral screening instrument (approximately 10-20 minutes in duration) consists of questions arranged on a scale of Chronological Age from one-half month to 27 years. A Basal Age is established at the point before which the subject gives an incorrect answer after giving at least ten correct answers in a row. Additional credit is then added for correct answers given above the Basal Age. The Basal Age plus added months credit are used to determine mental age and IQ. Norms provided include: percentiles, Normal Curve Equivalents, Stanine Categories, and T-Scores. The results can be used to predict reading achievement, to plan educational programs, to predict success and acceptance in college, to screen students for reading disabilities, and as an IQ test for the blind. Also includes the Slosson Oral Reading Test (SORT), which yields a reading grade level from primer into high school based on the ability to pronounce words at different levels of difficulty. Also used to identify reading handicaps. SIT item analysis available to identify strengths and weaknesses in eight learning areas. Examiner required and evaluated. Not for group use. Complete kit (includes Manual of Questions, directions, 1981 norms tables, 50 Slosson Oral Reading Tests, 50 score sheets for the SIT and vinyl binder) costs $35.00. *Publisher:* Slosson Educational Publications, Inc.

126

SMITH-JOHNSON NONVERBAL PERFORMANCE SCALE
Alathena J. Smith and Ruth E. Johnson

Provides a nonverbal assessment of the developmental level of children ages 2-4 years. Used especially to evaluate hearing impaired, language delayed, culturally deprived, and handicapped children.

This 14 category examination (30-45 minutes in duration) uses nonverbal tasks to measure the developmental level of a broad range of skills in young children. Each category consists of a series of subtasks presented in order of increasing difficulty. With the exception of two tasks, the examiner proceeds to the first task in the next category as soon as two consecutive tasks have been failed. All but one of the tasks are untimed. The test measures strengths and weaknesses across a broad range of skills without constricting the evaluation by labeling the child with a single quantitative score. Norms are provided for both hearing impaired and normals. Examiner required and evaluated. Scoring is by hand key. Not for group use. Complete kit (includes test materials, record sheets and manual) costs $52.70. *Publisher:* Western Psychological Services

128

THE STANDARD PROGRESSIVE MATRICES (SPM-1938)
J. C. Raven

Measures an individual's (ages 8-65) mental ability through assessment of nonverbal abstract reasoning tasks. Used for school and vocational counseling and placement.

The test is a 60 item paper-pencil nonverbal test in five sets of 12 problems each. In each problem, the subject is presented with a pattern or figure design which has a part missing. The subject then selects one of six possible parts as the correct one. The patterns are arrayed from simple to complex. Testing time is approximately 45 minutes. The test is often used with the Mill Hill Vocabulary Scale. Examiner required. Suitable for group use. Scoring is by hand key; the test may be machine scored. Standardized in Great Britain. Examination kits containing test booklet, answer document, and key (Manual: General Overview; section 2, 3, or 4 appropriate to matrices) cost $12.50. *Publisher:* H.K. Lewis & Co., Ltd./U.S. Distributor—The Psychological Corporation

5, 6, 17, 18, 42, 51,
94, 115, 149, 151

STANFORD-BINET INTELLIGENCE SCALE: FORM L-M
Lewis M. Terman and Maud A. Merrill

Measures an individual's (ages 2 and older) mental abilities. Used to substantiate questionable scores from group tests and when the subject has physical, language, or personality disorders which rule out group testing.

The 142 item verbal and nonverbal IQ test assesses the following factors: language, memory, conceptual thinking, reasoning, numerical reasoning, visual motor, and social reasoning. Measures IQ through individual assessment from ages two years through adulthood. In most cases, only 18-24 test items need be administered to a given subject. The basal age is established (year level at which all items are passed), and testing continues until the ceiling age is reached (year level at which all items are failed). Responses are then scored according to established procedures to yield mental age and IQ. Results identify children and adults who would benefit from specialized learning environments. Administered only by professionally trained, certified examiners. Test time ranges from 45-90 minutes. Examiner required and evaluated. Not for group use. Examiner's kit, form L-M (includes manual, large and small printed card material and miniaturized objects) costs $162.00. *Publisher:* The Riverside Publishing Company

130, 131

STANFORD MEASUREMENT SERIES-STANFORD ACHIEVEMENT TEST: 6TH EDITION
Richard Madden, Eric F. Gardner, Herbert C. Rudman, Bjorn Karlsen, and Jack C. Merwin

Assesses school achievement status of children in grades 1 through 9 with a six level battery of paper-pencil tests.

The six levels are Primary Level I, Primary Level II, Primary Level III, Intermediate Level I, Intermediate Level II, Advanced Level. Primary Level I measures the following areas: vocabulary, reading comprehension, word study skills, mathematics concepts, mathematics computation, spelling, and listening comprehension. Primary Level II tests these areas plus Mathematics applications, social science and science. Language is added at Primary Level III and Intermediate Levels I and II. The Advanced Level drops the word study skills and listening comprehension subtests. Superseded by Stanford Achievement Test: 7th Edition. Scoring is by hand key;

Refer to page(s):	*Test Title*

computer scoring service available. Examiner required. Suitable for group use. A specimen set (includes complete battery, teacher's directions, norms booklet; primary and intermediate levels include practice test and directions—specify level) costs $5.00.

152   STANFORD MEASUREMENT SERIES-STANFORD DIAG-
NOSTIC READING TEST (SDRT)
Bjorn Karlsen, Richard Madden and Eric F. Gardner

Measures major components of the reading process. For use in diagnosing specific pupil needs in grades 1.5-13.

Multiple item paper-pencil test of four aspects of reading including comprehension, decoding, vocabulary, and rate. Cutoff scores indicate need for remedial programming. SDRT is divided into four levels: red, Grades 1.5-3.5; green, Grades 2.5-5.5; brown, Grades 4.5-9.5; and blue, Grades 9-13. Materials include handbooks with instructional suggestions and instructional materials. Two alternate and equivalent forms, A and B. Linked statistically with the Stanford Achievement Test Series. Scoring is by hand key, with computer scoring service available. A specimen set (includes test, manual, instructional placement report, brown and blue levels also include answer document) costs $5.00. *Publisher:* The Psychological Corporation

151   STANFORD-OHWAKI-KOHS BLOCK DESIGN INTEL-
LIGENCE TEST FOR THE BLIND: AMERICAN
REVISION   *Richard M. Suinn and William L. Dauterman*

Measures intelligence of partially sighted and functionally blind individuals 16 years of age and older.

The multiple item task assessment test uses tactile sense to identify and duplicate the Kohs design block test. Testing time is 1-2 hours. This revision of the Ohwaki-Kohs Tactile Block Design Intelligence Test provides standardization on American subjects. Results yield percentile and IQ scores. Scoring is by hand key. Examiner required and evaluated. Not for group use. Complete kit (includes 1 set of test materials, 25 record forms and manual) is available for $94.80. *Publisher:* Western Psychological Services

43, 170, 171   STATE-TRAIT ANXIETY INVENTORY FOR CHILDREN
(STAIC)   *Charles D. Spielberger*

Assesses anxiety in children in grades 4-8. Used for research in screening and treatment evaluation.

The two untimed (10-20 minutes) 20-item scales measure two types of anxiety: state anxiety (A-State), and trait anxiety (A-Trait). The A-State scales ask how the child feels at a particular moment in time, while the A-Trait scales ask how he generally feels. Based on the same concept as the State-Trait Anxiety Inventory and is used in conjunction with the adult form manual. Evaluated by examiner after hand key scoring. Suitable for group use. Specimen set is available for $4.00. *Publisher:* Consulting Psychologists Press, Inc.

STRONG-CAMPBELL INTEREST INVENTORY (SCII)
E.K. Strong, Jr. and David P. Campbell

Measures occupational interests in a wide range of career areas requiring, for the most part, advanced technical or college training. Used to make long-range curricular and occupational choices, as well as for employee selection and placement, and vocational rehabilitation placement.

The 325 item paper-pencil multiple-choice test asks the examinee to respond either "like", "indifferent", or "dislike" to items covering a broad range of familiar occupational tasks and day-to-day activities. General topics include: occupations, school subjects, activites, amusements, types of people, preference between two activities, and "your characteristics". Testing time is approximately 30-40 minutes. Responses are then analyzed by computer to yield a profile that presents scores on a number of scales and offers interpretive advice. Specifically, the respondent is scored on: Six General Occupational Themes (based on Holland's RIASEC themes), 23 Basic Interest Scales (measuring strength and consistency of specific interest areas), and 162 Occupational Scales (reflecting degree of similarity between respondent and people employed in particular occupations). The scoring services also provide 11 additional non-occupational and administrative indexes as a further guide to interpreting the results. Computer scoring required and available from a number of sources (test results available immediately via ARION II Teleprocessing). Self-administered. Suitable for group use. Available in Spanish. Contact publisher for costs. *Publisher:* Stanford University Press

SYMBOL DIGIT MODALITIES TEST   *Aaron Smith*

Measures individual brain damage in persons 8 years old and up. Used to screen and predict learning disorders and to identify children with potential reading problems.

The test is a multiple item test in which the subject is given 90 seconds to convert as many meaningless geometric designs as possible into their appropriate numbers according to the key provided. Useful as a screening device when group-administered; may be individually administered with an oral presentation for those who cannot take written tests. Since numbers are nearly universal, the test is virtually culture-free. Standardized on more than 3,600 boys and girls ages 8-17 years and 431 adults ages 18-75 years with norms given for each year by sex. Examiner required. Scoring is by hand key. Complete kit (includes 50 tests, key and manual) is available for $10.85. *Publisher:* Western Psychological Services

Test Title

SYSTEM OF MULTICULTURAL PLURALISTIC ASSESS-
MENT (SOMPA)   *Jane R. Mercer and June F. Lewis*

Assesses cognitive abilities, sensorimotor abilities and adaptive behavior of children ages 5 to 11. Used for assessment of children from varied cultural backgrounds.

The multiple instrument measures of various aspects of functioning of children from diverse cultural backgrounds. SOMPA has two major components: The Parent Interview and Student Assessment Materials. The Parent Interview takes place in the home, and includes administration of the Adaptive Behavior Inventory for Children (ABIC), Sociocultural Scales, Health History Inventories. Student Assessment Materials data are collected in the school environment, and include the Physical Dexterity Tasks, Weight by Height, Visual Acuity, Auditory Acuity, Bender Visual Motor Gestalt Test (sold separately), and the WISC-R, or WPPSI (sold separately). Interpretation of SOMPA should be done by psychologist or a qualified team. The Parent Interview takes 60 minutes; the individual interview takes 20 minutes in addition to time required for the Wechsler and Bender-Gestalt. Examiner required. Not suitable for group use. Parent Interview available in Spanish. The basic kit (includes parent interview manual, 25 parent interview record forms, ABIC scoring keys, student assessment record forms, 25 profile folders and the technical manual) costs $82.50. *Publisher:* The Psychological Corporation

THE TACTILE TEST OF BASIC CONCEPTS

Assesses the visually impaired child's mastery of concepts that are commonly found in preschool and primary grade instructional materials and that are essential to understanding oral communications from teachers and fellow pupils in a 50 item tactile test of verbal comprehension and conceptual development format. Used with children from kindergarten to grade 2 who require braille and other tactile media.

Five practice cards are provided to familiarize the child with the test task and to determine if he is familiar with the raised outline forms used in the test (circle, square, triangle, rectangle). The 50 test items are identical to those of the Boehm Test of Basic Concepts, presented with raised outline forms. A few items consist of simple raised outline drawings. BTBC test manual included for use in interpreting the test results. Examiner required. Not for group use. The complete set which includes 5 practice cards, 50 test cards, 1 class record form, TTBC test manual and BTBC test manual costs $31.59. *Publisher:* American Printing House for the Blind

       Test Title

TEST FOR AUDITORY COMPREHENSION OF LANGUAGE (TACL) *Elizabeth Carrow-Woolfolk*

Analyzes a child's (ages 3.0-6.11) recepive language, including vocabulary, morphology, and syntax. Used for language therapy.

In the 101 item point-and-tell test, the child responds to pictorial stimuli, each containing three line drawings depicting the correct response, the incorrect response, and a decoy item, by pointing to one of the three items. The test is not appropriate for deaf subjects. Materials include the pictures, and instructions and scoring/analysis forms. Examiner required and evaluated. Not for group use. Available in Spanish. The cost is $50.00. *Publisher:* DLM Teaching Resources

TEST OF LANGUAGE DEVELOPMENT (TOLD-PRIMARY) *Phillis L. Newman and Donald D. Hammill*

Assesses the speaking abilities of children ages 4-8 years. Used as a language achievement test and to identify children with language problems, including mental retardation, learning disabilities, reading disabilities, speech delays, and articulation problems.

The 170 item oral response test consists of seven subtests measuring different components of spoken language. The Picture Vocabulary (25 items) and Oral Vocabulary (20 items) subtests assess the understanding and meaningful use of spoken words. The Grammatic Understanding (25 items), Sentence Imitation (30 items), and Grammatic Completion (30 items) subtests assess differing aspects of grammar. The Word Articulation (20 items) and Word Discrimination (20 items) subtests are supplemental tests measuring the ability to say words correctly and to distinguish between words that sound familiar. Test results are reported in terms of standard scores, percentiles, age-equivalents, and quotients. By combining various subtest scores, it is possible to diagnose a child's abilities in relation to specific language skills, including: overall spoken language, listening (receptive language), speaking (expressive language), semantics (the meaning of words), and syntax (grammar). The test takes approximately 40 minutes to complete. Examiner required. Not for group use. Scoring is by hand key. Complete kit which includes examiner's manual, picture plates and 50 answer sheets costs $59.00. *Publisher:* PRO-ED

TEST OF WRITTEN LANGUAGE (TOWL) *Donald D. Hammill and Stephen C. Larsen*

Identifies students grades 2-12 who have problems in written expression, pinpointing specific areas of deficit.

This is a paper-pencil, free-response test in which students are given a theme and asked to write a story about it. Yields information in six areas of writing competence: thematic maturity, spelling, vocabulary, word usage, style, and handwriting. Information derived is from an analysis of a sample of continuous writing, as well as from an analysis of a subtest performance. Materials include answer and profile sheets and a manual which includes a section dealing with informal methods for evaluating the quality of written products. Standardized on 3,418 students with the same characteristics as those reported in the 1980 census. Examiner required and evaluated. Available in Spanish. The complete kit (includes examiner manual, 50 student response sheets and 50 profile sheets) for $46.00. *Publisher:* PRO-ED

43, 60, 114   THEMATIC APPERCEPTION TEST (TAT)
Henry Alexander Murray

Assesses personality in individuals ages 14-40 through projective technique focusing on dominant drives, emotions, sentiments, complexes, attitudes, and conflicts.

Twenty item projective type test in which a subject is shown pictures one at a time and asked to make up a story about each picture. The examiner records the subject's stories for later analysis. The projective test seeks to measure, among other things, the subject's temperament, level of emotional maturity, observational ability, intellectuality, imagination, psychological insight, creativity, sense of reality and factors of family and psychic dynamics. Generally the subject is asked to make up stories based on ten cards in each of two sessions. A trained examiner is required. Testing time is one hour per series. Examiner required and evaluated. Not suitable for groups. Specimen set is available for $11.50; manual $1.50. *Publisher:* Harvard University Press

213   URBAN CHILDHOOD LEVEL OF LIVING SCALE (CLL)
Norman Polansky, Mary Ann Chalmers, Elizabeth Buttonwieser and David Williams

Measures the quality of child care being provided in the home for children ages 4-7 years. Used by social workers and home health care workers to identify cases of child neglect and to determine areas in which parents are in need of education in the care of their child.

The 99 item paper-pencil true-false checklist consists of two parts. Part A contains 47 items and measures five dimensions of the child's physical care: general positive child care, state of repair of house, negligence, quality of household maintenance, and quality of health care and grooming. Part B contains 52 items and measures four dimensions of the child's emotional/cognitive (psychological) care: encouraging competence, inconsistency of discipline and coldness, encouraging superego development, and material giving. Each test item contains a statement which describes a single aspect

Test Title

of the child's living condition which is rated true or false by a social worker or home health worker who knows the family. Interpretive guidelines are provided for classifying the quality of the child care provided in the home into one of the following five categories: severely neglectful, neglectful, marginal child care, acceptable child care, or good child care. Self-administered by observer. Examiner evaluated. Not suitable for group use. *Source:* (1978) *Child Welfare, 57* (7), 439-449: requests for reprints to Norman Polansky, Ph.D., Professor of Social Work, University of Georgia, Athens, Georgia 30601.

UTAH TEST OF LANGUAGE DEVELOPMENT
Merlin J. Mecham and J. Dean Jones

Identifies children ages 2-14 years with language-learning disabilities who may be in need of further evaluation and assistance.

The 51 item task assessment oral response test measures the following factors: receptive semantic language, expressive semantic language, receptive sequential language, and expressive sequential language. Test items are arranged in developmental order. Examiner begins testing at or just below a child's expected level of ability and works down until eight consecutive correct answers are obtained, and then upward from the starting point until eight consecutive incorrect answers are obtained, at which time the test is discontinued. Testing time ranges 20-30 minutes. Items are scored as correct (plus) or incorrect (minus). Total score is the total number of pluses. Test kit includes: manual, line-drawing plates, booklet, object kit, and 25 score sheets in a vinyl carrying case. Restricted to persons trained in psychological or educational testing. Examiner required and evaluated. Not for group use. The complete kit costs $37.50. *Publisher:* Communication Research Associates, Inc.

VINELAND ADAPTIVE BEHAVIOR SCALES
Sara S. Sparrow, David A. Balla and Dominic V. Cicchetti

Measures the personal and social sufficiency of individuals from birth to adulthood. Used with mentally retarded and handicapped individuals. This is the 1984 revision of The Vineland Social Maturity Scale.

The 244-577 item inventory (depending on which of the three forms is used) assesses adaptive behavior in the following four domains: Communication (receptive, expressive, and written), Daily Living Skills (personal, domestic, and community), Socialization (interpersonal relationships, play and leisure time, and coping skills), and Motor Skills (gross and fine). These four domains are combined to form the Adaptive Behavior Composite. An optional Maladaptive Behavior domain is included in the Survey Form and Expanded Form. The Interview Edition, Survey Form contains 297 items. A trained interviewer administers the inventory to a parent or care-giver in semi-structured interview. The record booklet is used to record item scores and informal observations and contains a score summary page for recording and profiling derived scores.

The Interview Edition, Expanded Form includes 577 items, offers a more comprehensive assessment of adaptive behavior and provides a basis for perparing individual educational, habilitative, or treatment programs. Administration is similar to the Survey Form. Scores are recorded in the item booklet. The score summary and profile booklet includes a page for summarizing derived scores and four program planning profiles, each of which identifies clusters of items which describe activities that should be included in the individual programs.

The Classroom Edition includes 244 items and assesses adaptive behavior in the classroom. This edition is administered in the form of a questionnaire which is independently completed by teachers. A qualified professional is required to determine and interpret derived scores.

All forms include their own manual with guidelines for administration, scoring, and interpreting results. Supplementary materials include: audiocassette presenting sample Survey and Expanded Form interviews; ASSIST microcomputer software programs for score conversion, profiling, and record management; the Technical and Interpretive Manual; and reports to parents explaining an individual's derived scores in relation to strengths and weaknesses. Examiner required and evaluated. Not suitable for group use. The Survey Form, record booklet and reports to parents for all three versions are available in Spanish. The Survey Form Starter Set costs $18.50, Expanded Form Starter Set costs $30.50 and The Classroom Edition Starter Set costs $13.50. *Publisher:* American Guidance Service

42, 52, 62, 114, 129, 193

VINELAND SOCIAL MATURITY SCALE   *Edgar A. Doll*

Measures successive stages of social competence or adaptive behavior in individuals aged 30 years and younger. Used to measure normal development or individual differences which may be significant in cases of handicaps such as mental deficiencies and emotional disturbances in order to plan therapy or individual education.

The 117 item interview covers eight categories: Self-help General, Self-help Eating, Self-help Dressing, Locomotion, Occupation, Communication, Self-direction, and Socialization. The examiner interviews a parent, close relative or other primary caregiver and enters the response against each item listed in the record form. Raw scores are converted to an age equivalent score (social age) which may be used to compute a social quotient. Examiner required and evaluated. Not for group use. Materials include record form and manual for $9.00.

81   VULPÉ ASSESSMENT BATTERY   *Shirley German Vulpé*

Assesses the development of atypically developing children from birth through age six years. Identifies program goals and techniques to meet the needs of individual children. May be administered by anyone who has experience working with handicapped children, including parents, volunteers, and caregivers from a wide variety of backgrounds, training and professions (the reflex part of the test, however, should be administered only by a qualified therapist).

One thousand one hundred twenty-seven item paper-pencil observational inventory measuring development in eight skill areas (domains) and one environmental domain. The nine domains include: basic senses and functions, gross motor behaviors, fine motor behaviors, language behaviors, cognitive processes and specific concepts, the organization of behavior, activities of daily living, and environment. Most test items are presented in developmental sequential order within each domain, with some overlapping of items between the domains. Test items are statements of developmental activities which the examiner scores on the basis of the child's ability to perform the activity and the degree of assisstance which the child requires for successful completion of the item. Items are rated on the basis of observation and/or interviews with parents or primary caregivers. Time required for administration varies greatly, depending on the age and handicap of the child, the experience of the examiner, and the environment in which the assessment is performed. No total score is derived. Results are expressed as a profile of the child's developmental abilities, with a depth of performance analysis that provides a total profile of the individual child and provides a basis for designing an individual program plan. This profile is useful in preparing educational programs, child/parent programs, language therapy programs, physical therapy programs, infant stimulation programs, occupational therapy programs, developmental stimulation programs, behavior management programs, descriptive ability assessments, child performance tracking, home training programs, and residential programs. Examiner required and evaluated. Not suitable for group use. The complete assessment battery and the manual are contained in a 397-page volume which is available in the United States for $20.00. *Publisher:* National Institute on Mental Retardation

44, 55   WALKER PROBLEM BEHAVIOR IDENTIFICATION
            CHECKLIST: Revised 1983   *Hill M. Walker*

Identifies preschool and elementary grade children who have behavior problems. Used to evaluate children for counseling and possible referral.

The fifty-item paper-pencil inventory consisting of behavior statements which are applied to the child being rated. The checklist can be completed by anyone familiar with the child in five minutes although it is especially valuable for teachers. Provides a Total

Test Title

Score, with a cut-off to indicate the need for further evaluation or referral. Also provides scores for the following five scales: Acting-Out, Withdrawal, Distractability, Disturbed Peer Relations, and Immaturity. Standardized on preschool, primary, and intermediate samples, and used for more than 1,250,000 administrations. Suitable for group use. Scoring is by hand key. Complete kit which includes pad of 100 checklists and the manual costs $12.30. *Publisher:* Western Psychological Services

WECHSLER SCALES: WECHSLER ADULT INTEL-
LIGENCE SCALE-REVISED (WAIS-R)   *David Wechsler*

Assess intelligence in adolescents and adults. The 11 subtests divided into two major divisions yield a verbal IQ, a performance IQ and a full scale IQ for persons age 16 and older. The Verbal section of the WAIS consists of the following subtests: Information, Comprehension, Arithmetic, Similarities, Digit Span and Vocabulary. The Performance or nonverbal section of the test consists of the following subtests: Digit Symbol, Picture Completion, Block Design, Picture Arrangement, and Object Assembly. Some units of the test require verbal responses from the subjects and others require the subject to manipulate test materials to demonstrate performance ability. Testing time is 75 minutes. Raw scores are converted into scale scores after the subject's performance has been recorded and scored on the provided answer form by the examiner. The WAIS-R is a revision of the 1955 WAIS edition. Examiner required and evaluated. Not suitable for group use. Available in Spanish. The complete set costs $98.00. *Publisher:* The Psychological Corporation

WECHSLER SCALES: WECHSLER INTELLIGENCE SCALE
FOR CHILDREN-REVISED (WISC-R)   *David Wechsler*

Assess mental ability in children. The 12 subtests divided into two major divisions yielding a verbal IQ, a performance IQ and a full scale IQ for children tested individually. The Verbal section of the test consists of the following subtests: General Information, General Comprehension, Arithmetic, Similarities, Vocabulary, and Digit Span. The Performance section consists of the following subtests: Picture Completion, Picture Arrangement, Block Design, Object Assembly, Coding and Mazes. Some units of the test require verbal responses from the subjects and others require the subject to manipulate test materials to demonstrate performance ability. Testing time is one hour. Raw scores are converted into scale scores after the subject's performance has been recorded and scored on the provided answer form by the examiner. The WISC-R is a more recently revised form of the 1949 WISC. Examiner required and evaluated. Not suitable for group use. Available in Spanish. The complete set costs $115.00. *Publisher:* The Psychological Corporation

Test Title

WECHSLER SCALES: WECHSLER PRESCHOOL AND PRI-
MARY SCALE OF INTELLIGENCE (WPPSI)   *David Wechsler*

Assesses intelligence in children ages 4-6½. The 10 subtests divided into two major divisions yield a verbal IQ, a performance IQ and a full scale IQ for children tested individually. The Verbal section of the test consists of the following subtests: Information, Vocabulary, Arithmetic, Similarities, and Comprehension. (A supplementary Sentences Test is available within the Verbal section of the test.) The Performance section consists of the following subtests: Animal House, Picture Completion, Mazes, Geometric Design, and Block Design. (An Animal House Retest unit is available within the Performance section.) Selected subtests require verbal responses while others require that the subject demonstrate abilities through manipulating test materials provided within the WPPSI test kit. Testing time is one hour. Raw scores are converted into scale scores after examiner has recorded and scored subject responses on an answer sheet. Examiner required and evaluated. Not suitable for group use. Available in Spanish. Complete set costs $100.00. *Publisher:* The Psychological Corporation

THE WERRY-QUAY CLASSROOM OBSERVATIONAL SYS-
TEM   *John S. Werry and Herbert C. Quay*

Assess the behavior of children with conduct or acting out disorders. Used to evaluate the effect of therapeutic intervention programs on the classroom behavior of the children.

The multiple item paper-pencil observational assessment procedure consists of a frequency counting technique in which one child is observed for a period of time during which certain types of behavior are noted as occuring or not occuring. Three categories of behavior are observed: deviant behaviors (out of seat, physical contact, noise, turns, vocalizations, "other," and times out), attending or work oriented behaviors, (attending, irrelevant activity, and daydreaming), and teacher-pupil interactions (total, teacher initiated positive, teacher initiated negative, pupil initiated positive, and pupil initiated negative). Observation periods of 15 minutes which are broken down into 20 second cells are recommended. Examiners are encouraged to sample as long a time period of the child's behavior on as many occasions as is practical in order to produce a combined or aggregate score which will contribute to the stability and validity of the assessment procedure. Subsequent readministrations during the school year will allow the examiner to plot the progress (or lack of progress) which students show to specific intervention procedures. Examiner required. Not suitable for group use. *Source:* (1969) *Exceptional Children, 35,* (6) 461-470: address reprint requests to the Council for Exceptional Children, 1920 Association Drive, Reston, Virginia 22091; (703)620-3660.

Refer to page(s):	*Test Title*

9, 19, 28, 30, 34, 35, 44, 61, 95, 117, 118, 131, 152, 193

WIDE RANGE ACHIEVEMENT TEST (WRAT)
Joseph F. Jastak and Sarch Jastak

Measures the basic educational skills of word recognition, spelling and arithmetic, and identifies individuals, ages 5 and older, with learning difficulties. Used for educational placement, measuring school achievement, vocational assessment, job placement and training.

The three paper-pencil subtests (50-100 items per subtest) assess the coding skills of: Reading (recognizing and naming letters and pronouncing printed words), Spelling (copying marks resembling letters, writing name and printing words), and Arithmetic (counting, reading number symbols, oral, and written computation). Time administration is 10 minutes per subtest. Test consists of two levels printed on the same form: Level I for ages 5-11 and Level II for ages 12-adult. Optional word lists for both levels of the reading and spelling test are offered on plastic cards, and a recorded pronunciation of the lists is provided on cassette tape. The tape itself can be used to administer the spelling section. A One Level edition is available for clinicians and teachers who are willing to spend more time in testing in order to be able to analyze error patterns. A Large Print edition is available for those who require magnification of reading material. Normed for age rather than grade for better accuracy. In conjunction with other tests, such as the Wechsler Scales, WRAT is useful for determining personality structure. Restricted to Educational and Psychological professionals. Examiner required and evaluated. Spelling and Arithmetic subtests are suitable for group use. Reading subtest must be individually administered. The cost of the manual is $13.65; 50 test forms cost $9.75.
Publisher: Jastak Assessment Systems

9, 61, 95, 100, 130

WOODCOCK-JOHNSON PSYCHO-EDUCATIONAL BATTERY (WJPEB) *Richard W. Woodcock and Mary Bonner Johnson*

Evaluates individual cognitive ability, scholastic achievement, and interest level in preschool to adult range. Used to diagnose learning disabilities, and for instructional planning, vocational rehabilitation counseling, and research.

The 27 test battery in three parts, some paper and pencil, can be administered in its entirety or as single tests or clusters to meet specific appraisal needs. Part one tests cognitive ability in areas such as picture vocabulary, sentence memory, visual-auditory learning, antonyms-synonyms, and concept formation. Part two covers letter-word identification, calculation, dictation, proofing, and science. Part three tests interest levels in reading, mathematics, language, and physical and social fields. Materials include the test books, response booklets, cassette tape, and a technical manual, which also may be ordered separately. Not for group use. Examiner required and evaluated; computer scored. Available in Spanish.

Test Title

Complete set is available for $125.00. *Publisher:* DLM Teaching
Resources

WOODCOCK READING MASTERY TESTS (WRMT)
Richard W. Woodcock

Measures individual reading achievement in grades K-12.
Used to detect reading problems. For classroom grouping, program
evaluation, clinical and research use.

The 400 item verbal test in A and B forms consists of: 45
identification items, 150 word items, 70 word comprehension
items, and 85 passage comprehension items in an individually
administered battery. The examiner shows a test plate to the student
and asks a question to which the student responds orally. Only those
items within the student's fuctioning level are administered. Materials include test plates bound into an easel and 25 response forms.
The test is norm and criterion referenced. Derived scores are grade
equivalents, grade percentile ranks, age equivalents, standard
scores and mastery scores. Normal curve equivalents for Chapter I
programs are available for grades 2-6. Examiner required and
evaluated. Not for group use. Computer scoring is available. Complete kit (form A or B) costs $39.50. *Publisher:* American Guidance
Service

Publisher Index

ACADEMIC THERAPY PUBLICATIONS, 20 Commercial Boulevard, Novato, California 94947; (415)883-3314

AMERICAN FOUNDATION FOR THE BLIND,15 West 16th Street, New York, New York 10011; (212)620-2000

AMERICAN GUIDANCE SERVICE, Publisher's Building, Circle Pines, Minnesota 55014; (800)328-2560, in Minnesota (612)786-4343

AMERICAN ORTHOPSYCHIATRIC ASSOCIATION, INC., (THE), 1775 Broadway, New York, New York 10019; (212)586-5690

AMERICAN PRINTING HOUSE FOR THE BLIND, 1839 Frankfort Avenue, P.O. Box 6085, Louisville, Kentucky 40206-0085; (502)895-2405

ASSOCIATED SERVICES FOR THE BLIND (ASB), 919 Walnut Street, Philadelphia, Pennsylvania 19107; (215)627-0600

AUSTRALIAN COUNCIL FOR EDUCATIONAL RESEARCH LIMITED (ACER), Radford House, Frederick Street, Hawthorn, Victoria 3122, Australia; (03)818-1271

BOBBS-MERRILL EDUCATIONAL PUBLISHING, 4300 West 62nd Street, P.O. Box 7080, Indianapolis, Indiana 46206; (317)298-5479

CALLIER CENTER FOR COMMUNICATION DISORDERS, THE UNIVERSITY OF TEXAS AT DALLAS, 1966 Inwood Road, Dallas, Texas 75235; (214)783-3000

CENTER FOR CHILD DEVELOPMENT AND EDUCATION, COLLEGE OF EDUCATION, UNIVERSITY OF ARKANSAS AT LITTLE ROCK, 33rd and University, Little Rock, Arkansas 72204; (501)569-3422

COLLEGE BOARD PUBLICATIONS, (THE), Box 2815, Princeton, New Jersey 08541; (609)771-7600

COMMUNICATION RESEARCH ASSOCIATES, INC., P.O. Box 11012, Salt Lake City, Utah 84147; (801)292-3880

CONSULTING PSYCHOLOGISTS PRESS, INC., 577 College Avenue, P.O. Box 60070, Palo Alto, California 94306; (415)857-1444

C.P.S. INC., Box 83, Larchmont, New York 10538; no business phone

CTB/McGRAW-HILL, PUBLISHERS TEST SERVICE, Del Monte Research Park, 2500 Garden Road, Monterey, California 93940; (800)538-9547, in California (800)682-9222, or (408)649-8400

CURRICULUM ASSOCIATES, INC., 5 Esquire Road, North Billerica, Massachusetts 01862-2589; (800)225-0248, in Massachusetts (617)667-8000

DEVEREAUX FOUNDATION PRESS, (THE), 19 South Waterloo Road, Box 400, Devon, Pennsylvania 19333; (215)964-3000

DLM TEACHING RESOURCES, P.O. Box 4000, One DLM Park, Allen, Texas 75002; (800)527-4747, in Texas (800)442-4711

EDUCATIONAL AND INDUSTRIAL TESTING SERVICE (EdITS), P.O. Box 7234, San Diego, California 92107; (619)222-1666

GRUNE & STRATTON, INC., 111 Fifth Avenue, New York, New York 10003; (212)741-6800

HARVARD UNIVERSITY PRESS, 79 Garden Street, Cambridge, Massachusetts 02138; (617)495-2600

HISKEY-NEBRASKA TEST, (THE), 5640 Baldwin, Lincoln, Nebraska 68507; (402)466-6145

INSTITUTE FOR PERSONALITY AND ABILITY TESTING, INC. (IPAT), P.O. Box 188, 1602 Coronado Drive, Champaign, Illinois 61820; (217)352-4739

INSTITUTE OF PSYCHOLOGICAL RESEARCH, INC., 34, Fleury Street West, Montreal, Quebec, Canada H3L 1S9; (514)382-3000

JASTAK ASSOCIATES, INC., 1526 Gilpin, Wilmington, Delaware 19806; (302)652-4990

LADOCA PUBLISHING FOUNDATION, Laradon Hall Training and Residential Center, East 51st Avenue & Lincoln Street, Denver, Colorado 80216; (303)629-6379

LIPPINCOTT/HARPER PUBLISHERS, INC., JOURNALS DIVISION, 2350 Virginia Avenue, Hagerstown, Maryland 21740; (800)638-3030

MERRILL, (CHARLES E.), PUBLISHING COMPANY, 1300 Alum Creek Drive, Box 508, Columbus, Ohio 43216; (614)258-8441

MODERN CURRICULUM PRESS, INC., 13900 Prospect Road, Cleveland, Ohio 44136; (216)238-2222

NATIONAL INSTITUTE ON MENTAL RETARDATION (NIMR), Kinsman NIMR Building, York University Campus, 4700 Keele Street, Downsview (Toronto), Ontario, Canada M3J 1P3; (416)661-9611

NCS PROFESSIONAL ASSESSMENT SERVICES, P.O. Box 1416, Minneapolis, Minnesota 55440; (800)328-6759, in Minnesota (612)933-2800

NFER-NELSON PUBLISHING COMPANY LTD., Darville House, 2 Oxford Road East, Windsor, Berkshire SL4 1DF, England; (07535)58961

NORTHWESTERN UNIVERSITY PRESS, Dept. SLD-82, 1735 Benson Avenue, Evanston, Illinois 60201; (312)492-5313

ORANGE INDUSTRIES, 229 West Tyron Street, Hillsborough, North Carolina 27278; (919)732-8124

PRO-ED, 5341 Industrial Oaks Boulevard, Austin, Texas 78735; (512)892-3142

PSYCHOLOGICAL CORPORATION, (THE), 7500 Old Oak Boulevard, Cleveland, Ohio 44130; (216)234-5300

PSYCHOLOGICAL TEST SPECIALISTS, Box 9229, Missoula, Montana 59805; no business phone

REITAN NEUROPSYCHOLOGY LABORATORY, 1338 East Edison Street, Tucson, Arizona 85719; (602)795-3717

RIVERSIDE PUBLISHING COMPANY, (THE), 8420 Bryn Mawr Avenue, Chicago, Illinois 60631; (800)323-9540, in Alaska, Hawaii, or Illinois call collect (312)693-0040

SCIENCE RESEARCH ASSOCIATES, INC. (SRA), 155 North Wacker Drive, Chicago, Illinois 60606; (800)621-0664, in Illinois (312)984-2000

SLOSSON EDUCATIONAL PUBLICATIONS, INC., P.O. Box 280, East Aurora, New York 14052; (800)828-4800, in New York (716)652-0930

STANFORD UNIVERSITY PRESS, Stanford, California 94305; (415)497-9434

STOELTING COMPANY, 1350 S. Kostner Avenue, Chicago, Illinois 60623; (312)522-4500

TEACHERS COLLEGE PRESS, TEACHERS COLLEGE, COLUMBIA UNIVERSITY, 1234 Amsterdam Avenue, New York, New York 10027; (212)678-3929

UNIVERSITY OF ILLINOIS PRESS, 54 E. Gregory Drive, Box 5081, Station A, Champaign, Illinois 61820; institutions (800)233-4175, individuals (800)638-3030, or (217)333-0950

UNIVERSITY OF VERMONT, COLLEGE OF MEDICINE, DEPARTMENT OF PSYCHIATRY, SECTION OF CHILD, ADOLESCENT & FAMILY PSYCHIATRY, 1 South Prospect Street, Burlington, Vermont 05401; (802)656-4563

UNIVERSITY PARK PRESS, INC., 300 North Charles Street, Baltimore, Maryland 21201; (800)638-7511, in Maryland (301)547-0700

WESTERN PSYCHOLOGICAL SERVICES, A DIVISION OF MANSON WESTERN CORPORATION, 12031 Wilshire Boulevard, Los Angeles, California 90025; (213)478-2061

General Index

About the Contributors

MARCIA S. COLLINS-MOORE, PH.D. is director of the Low Vision Clinic, Dean A. McGee Eye Institute, and Adjunct Assistant Professor of Ophthalmology, University of Oklahoma School of Medicine, Oklahoma Health Sciences Center in Oklahoma City, Oklahoma. She received her doctorate in counseling psychology and training in teaching visually impaired students from the University of Texas at Austin. Dr. Moore's experience with visually impaired and multihandicapped children includes individual, group, and family therapy, psychoeducational and psycho-social assessment, and low-vision evaluation and treatment. She has been active in training and consultation with teachers and parents of visually impaired children since 1973. Her research and publications with Dr. Natalie Barraga have focused on development of efficiency in visual functioning and parental reactions and adjustment to the visually handicapped child.

JAN L. CULBERTSON, PH.D. is Assistant Professor of Pediatrics, University of Oklahoma Health Sciences Center. Dr. Culbertson is director of neuropsychological services at the Child Study Center and a member of the Clinical Training Program, Department of Psychiatry and Behavioral Sciences. Dr. Culbertson is the author of numerous publications and chapters on children with communication disorders, learning disabilities, the gifted, and children with health-related disorders. Her research interests include neuropsychological sequelae of acute lymphocytic leukemia and Reyes Syndrome, as well as the effects of profound hypothermia and cardiopulmonary arrest on children.

JEAN ELBERT, PH.D. is Assistant Professor of Psychology in Pediatrics at the Child Study Center, University of Oklahoma Health Sciences Center. After receiving her doctoral training in learning disabilities at Northwestern University, Dr. Elbert served as assistant director of a therapeutic day school for emotionally disturbed children at Rush University Medical Center. She has been involved in assessment of learning and language-disordered children through the schools and in the Learning Disabilities Center at Northwestern University. Dr. Elbert is currently involved in the psychoeducational assessment of children with developmental and acquired learning problems, and teaches pediatric residents and clinical psychology interns. Dr. Elbert's research interests include the visual information processing and memory coding of dyslexic children, the study of genetically inherited learning disorders, and the psychoeducational follow-up of children surviving childhood leukemia and Reyes Syndrome.

ROBERT G. HARRINGTON, PH.D. is Assistant Professor of Educational Psychology and Research, University of Kansas at Lawrence. After receiving his Ph.D. from the University of Iowa, Dr. Harrington served as school psychologist at the Lakeland Area Education Agency in Cylinder, Iowa, and supervised practicum students in school psychology, learning disabilities, emotional disabilities, and special education at the University of Iowa. He currently teaches courses at the Ed.S and doctoral level in individual intelligence testing, personality assessment, and preschool assessment, as well as supervising students on their practica and internships in school psychology. Dr. Harrington has presented over fifteen papers at professional meetings and his recent publications include papers on the topic of assessing school-age children and a chapter in a book on the assessment of emotionally disturbed children.

J. RAY HAYS, PH.D., J.D. is head of the training division at the Texas Research Institute of Mental Sciences, where he has been employed since 1968. Dr. Hays holds a doctoral degree in clinical psychology from the University of Georgia and a degree in law from the South Texas College of Law in Houston, and is currently licensed both as a psychologist and an attorney. His work consists of evaluating clients for attorneys, advising on trial strategy, and the training of psychiatrists and psychologists on the legal aspects of mental-health work. Dr. Hays has served as chairman of the Texas State Board of Examiners of Psychologists and as president of the American Association of State Psychology Boards. He is the author of over eighty scientific articles, several book chapters, and two books.

MARC S. HERMAN, PH.D. is a staff psychologist in the department of child psychiatry at Mt. Carmel/Mercy Hospital in Detroit, Michigan. Dr. Herman received his Ph.D. in developmental psychology from Wayne University and took his postdoctoral training at the University of Kansas Medical Center (Children's Rehabilitation Unit). He is currently involved in evaluations and individual therapy on an in-patient and out-patient basis, and also maintains a small private practice in Detroit. Dr. Herman's recent publications include an article co-authored with Carolyn Shantz, Ph.D. (published in the *Journal of Applied Developmental Psychology*) dealing with social problem-solving and mother-child interactions with educable mentally retarded children. Dr. Herman's research interests lie in the use of imagery through story-telling, drawing, and metaphor in the clinical treatment of children and adults.

STANLEY H. KOHN, J.D. is presently the general counsel to the South Carolina Department of Social Services. Mr. Kohn, whose specialization was in family law following service as a Special Family Court judge in Columbia, South Carolina, founded a volunteer program that provided adults as intervenors in the lives of children in trouble in the court system, which was named in 1975 the Outstanding Volunteer Program in the nation. He also founded the Richland County Council on Child Abuse and Neglect, a multidisciplinary group providing volunteer services in programs on prevention. Mr. Kohn is the author of the handbook for guardians *ad litem* used in the state court system, and has written a handbook for child protective workers on avoiding liability.

ROBERT D. LYMAN, PH.D. is Assistant Professor of Psychology and executive director of the Brewer-Porch Children's Center at the University of Alabama. Dr. Lyman received his Ph.D. from the University of Alabama and completed clinical internships at the Tuscaloosa, Alabama, Veterans Administration Hospital and the University of Alabama Psychological Clinic. He has published a number of articles in professional journals on childhood emotional problems. Dr. Lyman is past-president of the Association of Psychiatric Outpatient Centers of America, and his primary research and clinical interests involve behavioral treatment of emotional disturbances in children.

LEE M. MARCUS, PH.D. is Associate Professor of Psychiatry and clinical director of the Piedmont TEACCH Center at the University of North Carolina at Chapel Hill. Dr. Marcus received his Ph.D in psychology from the University of Minnesota and completed his psychology internship at the Washburn Child Guidance Center and the Minnesota Medical Center. He later completed two years of postdoctoral training at the University of Rochester Medical Center. Dr. Marcus' interests include the assessment of children and youth with autism and the involvement of parents in the assessment and education of handicapped children.

RUTH ANN MERTENS, PH.D. is Clinical Assistant Professor of Pediatrics and Psychiatry at the University of Oklahoma Health Sciences Center and heads up forensic psychology experiences at the Child Study Center, Oklahoma Children's Memorial Hospital,

Oklahoma City, Oklahoma. She is a past coordinator of a regional guidance center in the State of Oklahoma. Dr. Mertens is involved in assessment of emotional disturbances in children, with a particular interest in the use of projective and diagnostic play techniques. She also is engaged in play therapy, individual psychotherapy, and family therapy with emotionally disturbed children and their families. Dr. Merten's clinical interests also include work with abused children and their families.

MARY MIRA, PH.D. is Associate Professor of Pediatrics (Psychology) at the University of Kansas Medical Center (Child Rehabilitation Unit), where she also received her Ph.D. in special education research and speech pathology. Dr. Mira previously served as a psychologist at the Children's Rehabilitation Unit, which is an interdisciplinary training and clinical facility servicing developmentally disabled children and families. She directed the training program for psychologists in a special project in the psychology of the deaf within the hearing and speech department. Dr. Mira has had experience in pediatric settings and public schools as well as with community facilities. Her areas of special interest include individual human operant analysis, infant development, psychology of the deaf and the deaf-blind, and neuropsychology. Dr. Mira's publications have focused on the evaluation and training of deaf and deaf-blind children, child behavior therapy via parent training, functional analysis of clinical behavior, and direct measurement of developing behavior.

J. GREGORY OLLEY, PH.D. is Clinical Associate Professor in the department of psychiatry and the division of special education, and director of training for Division TEACCH, at the University of North Carolina at Chapel Hill. Dr. Olley received his Ph.D. in psychology from George Peabody College of Vanderbilt University. His graduate training emphasized research and clinical training in mental retardation. Dr. Olley completed a child clinical psychology internship at the University of Kansas Medical Center and was Assistant Professor of Psychology at the University of Massachusetts at Amherst. His interests include the development of social skills in young handicapped children and the training of teachers of autistic children, which he pursues in his work at Division TEACCH.

KATHLEEN N. OSBORN, PH.D. is a psychologist with the Child Study Center, Oklahoma Children's Memorial Hospital, and Clinical Associate Professor of Pediatrics, University of Oklahoma, Oklahoma Health Sciences Center in Oklahoma City, Oklahoma. She received her doctorate in counseling psychology from the University of Oklahoma. Dr. Osborn was associated with the public schools for twenty years as an elementary teacher, a high school teacher and counselor, and school psychologist. Her experience with multihandicapped children includes psychoeducational and psycho-social assessment, and individual and family therapy. Currently Dr. Osborn is supervisor of master level practicum students in counseling psychology, and staff psychologist for team evaluation of visually impaired and multihandicapped children. She also conducts seminars for foster-care parents, and is involved in research studies with burn unit patients.

MICHAEL C. ROBERTS, PH.D. is Associate Professor of Psychology and coordinator of clinical child psychology training concentration at the University of Alabama. Dr. Roberts received his Ph.D. from Purdue University and completed his clinical internship at the Oklahoma University Health Sciences Center (Oklahoma Children's Memorial Hospital). In addition to over forty published articles, he co-edited with C.E. Walker the *Handbook of Clinical Child Psychology* (Wiley-Interscience) and with L. Peterson the *Prevention of Problems in Childhood* (Wiley-Interscience). Dr. Roberts is president-elect of the Society of Pediatric Psychology and associate editor of the *Journal of Pediatric Psychology*. His research and clinical interests involve the application of psychology to pediatric problems, including prevention of accidents and medical fears.

DONALD K. ROUTH, PH.D. is Professor of Psychology at the University of Iowa, where he also serves as coordinator of the clinical psychology program. Dr. Routh received his Ph.D. in clinical psychology from the University of Pittsburgh. He has served as editor of the *Journal of Pediatric Psychology* and is presently chairperson of the Behavioral Medicine Study Section of the U.S. National Institutes of Health. Dr. Routh has published well over 100 articles, chapters, and books, mainly in the area of clinical child psychology. In 1981 Dr. Routh was given the award for Distinguished Contribution to Pediatric Psychology by the Society of Pediatric Psychology.

DENNIS P. SWIERCINSKY, PH.D. is a nationally recognized clinical neuropsychologist who currently maintains a private clinical practice in neuropsychology in the Kansas City area. Dr. Swiercinsky received his Ph.D. from the University of Kansas and is a professional member of the International Neuropsychological Society and the National Academy of Neuropsychologists. His many published works in psychodiagnostics include *A Manual for the Adult Neuropsychological Evaluation*, which has been used extensively for training student neuropsychologists. Dr. Swiercinsky has also worked in computer adaptations of psychological testing and his System for the Administration and Interpretation of Neuropsychological Tests is familiar to many clinicians using computerized testing.

S. JOSEPH WEAVER, PH.D. is Associate Professor of Pediatrics (Psychology) at Kansas University Medical Center and director of psychology at the University of Kansas Medical Center (Child Rehabilitation Unit). Dr. Weaver received his Ph.D. in clinical psychology from George Peabody College (now Vanderbilt University). He has served as associate editor of *Professional Practice of Psychology* since 1980. Dr. Weaver has been a member of the executive board of the American Association of State Psychology Boards since 1979, and served as president of the association in 1982-83. He is currently serving on the national advisory committees for the Educational Test Service "Job Analysis of Licensed Psychologists" and the Kellog-Pennsylvania State University Project on continuing education in clinical psychology. Dr. Weaver has achieved over forty publications and presentations at national meetings.

KAREN WESTPHAL, PH.D. is project director in the psychological measurement division of The Psychological Corporation, where she is involved primarily with the Wechsler tests and microcomputer support products for interpretation of psychological testing. Dr. Westphal received her Ph.D. in psychology from the University of South Carolina. She then worked as a school psychologist in a suburban school district near Columbia, South Carolina, and performed independent evaluations as provided for by PL 94-142 for a University Affiliated Facility/Developmental Disabilities Council. Dr. Westphal became interested in the skills needed by expert witnesses as an outgrowth of exposure to the PL 94-142 due process procedures related to both evaluations and hearings, consulting with Mr. Kohn, her co-author, on child-abuse and neglect cases, and conducting parent groups on the psychological and legal issues of divorce and custody.

DIANE J. WILLIS, PH.D. is director of psychological services at the Child Study Center, and Professor of Medical Psychology, Department of Pediatrics, at the University of Oklahoma Health Sciences Center. Dr. Willis is past president of the Society of Pediatric Psychology and Clinical Child Psychology sections of the American Psychological Association; a past editor of two journals; and is now on the editorial board of the *Journal of Clinical Child Psychology, Journal of Pediatric Psychology,* and *Professional Psychology.* Dr. Willis is a recipient of the Distinguished Contribution Award from the Society of Pediatric Psychology. She is the author of numerous chapters and articles, and is co-author of a text on exceptional children. Her research interests include child abuse, seizure disorders, and other pediatric psychology related topics.